beverages from our regular
menu and receive the second
entree of equal or lesser value
FREE
(Up to a $7.00 value)

or dinner en
beverages fr
menu and rec
entree of equ

(Up to a   **F**

BAKING
CHEZ MOI

DORIE GREENSPAN

PHOTOGRAPHS BY ALAN RICHARDSON

A Rux Martin Book

HOUGHTON MIFFLIN HARCOURT

Boston | New York | 2014

BAKING
CHEZ MOI

Recipes from My Paris Home to Your Home Anywhere

Library of Congress Cataloging-in-Publication Data
Greenspan, Dorie, author.
Baking chez moi : recipes from my paris home
to your home anywhere / Dorie Greenspan ;
photographs by Alan Richardson.
    pages cm
  ISBN 978-0-547-72424-9 (hardback);
      978-0-547-70832-4 (ebook)
1. Desserts. 2. Cooking, French. 3. Baking.
I. Title.
  TX773.G698596 2014
  641.86—dc23   2014016312

Book design by Shubhani Sarkar
Food styling by Karen Tack and Ellie Ritt
Prop styling by Deb Donahue

Printed in the United States of America

DOW 10 9 8 7 6 5 4 3 2 1

FOR MICHAEL
AND JOSHUA,
COMME TOUJOURS
AND POUR TOUJOURS,
WITH LOVE.

ACKNOWLEDGMENTS

IF YOU'RE A VERY LUCKY AUTHOR—and I consider myself among the luckiest—publishing a book means having the chance to work with old friends and to make new ones. With each book, my circle of gratitude grows.

For the past three books, Rux Martin, my editor, and David Black, my agent, have been at the center of my writing world. For more than a decade, they have been the people who are there at the start when everything is joyous potential, and they're there all through the process, when, invariably, they can still see the potential and I'm not so sure it's still there (or ever was or ever will be). They're the ones who trust and believe in me more than I trust and believe in myself.

To edit well is an art. To be an editor and to have your authors love you après editing is a gift. Rux is extraordinarily gifted, and I love her for it and for so much more. She has made every page of this book better by magnitudes. From start to finish, she has been my partner and my friend, and for this I am more grateful than I can express.

David, as my husband always says, is "the real deal." He's fabulous at what he does and extra-fabulous at being smart and caring and encouraging and understanding. That David has become a treasured friend is the cherry on the cake. The whipped cream? That would be Antonella Iannarino, who works with me on special projects and whose intelligence and creativity would be scary if they weren't so welcomed.

No writer should ever go into print without having her manuscript pass through the hands of Judith Sutton. To call her a magician would not be to exaggerate her editing skills. Judith's talent is to "get you," to understand just what you really meant to say—even though you missed saying it clearly and well—and then to help you say it perfectly. Judith has copyedited every book I've written, and I hope it will always be so.

Then there is the team that made every picture in this book sighworthy. Alan Richardson did the photographs splendidly; Karen Tack and her assistant, Ellie Ritt, styled the food beautifully; and Deb Donahue propped each picture evocatively. They ushered Paris into the studio—*merci infiniment*.

My warmest thanks go to Shubhani Sarkar, who brought my recipes to life in the beautifully designed cover of *Baking Chez Moi* and in its pages. I'm grateful to Michaela Sullivan and Melissa Lotfy at Houghton Mifflin Harcourt, who oversaw the design as though it were their very own book; to Jackie Beach, who shepherded the book through production; to Jill Lazer, a baker in her own right, who worked with the printer to make sure the book was perfect; and to Laney Everson, Rux's assistant, who always makes it seem as though she's got nothing else to do but respond to my endless requests for help.

Many thanks for keeping me in line and making me look good to Jessica Sherman, to Jane Tunks Demel and Lilian Brady and to Jacinta Monniere, who, should she ever decide to give up typing manuscripts (heaven forbid), could become an ace cryptographer.

For supporting this book with verve, style and smarts, my thanks to Carrie Bachman (the mention of whose name seems always—and fittingly—to be preceded by the word *"awesome"*), Brittany Edwards, Rebecca Liss and Brad Parsons.

Thanks and more thanks to Mary Dodd, first for convincing me that I needed her to test these recipes and then for proving over and again that she was right. Mary has been at my side ever since I began working on this book, and both the book and I are better for her limitless energy, her intelligence, her enthusiasm and, of course, her talent.

Before being the assistant-I-never-want-to-be-without, Mary was sharpening her baking skills along with hundreds of other members of the virtual baking club, Tuesdays with Dorie. Started in 2008 by the remarkable Laurie Woodward, the group made every recipe in my book *Baking: From My Home to Yours* and then started another group, French Fridays with Dorie, to cook their way through my next book, *Around My French Table*. Laurie and the wonderful people who work on the sites with her, Mary Hirsch, Betsy Pollack-Benjamin, Julie Schaeffer and Stephanie Whitten have created a true international community, its members bound by their love for cooking and sharing. The world could learn a lot from these groups—I know that I have.

Merci mille fois and a thousand times more to my friends in France, who make my life there so delicious, among them: Martine and Bernard Collet, Hélène Samuel, Patricia and Walter Wells, Juan Sanchez, Drew Harré, Alec Lobrano, Bruno Midavainne, Meg Zimbeck, Christian Holthausen, Simon Maurel, Renee Vollen, Eugene Shapiro, Apollonia Poilâne, David Lebovitz, Nicola Mitchell, Marie-Hélène Brunet-Lhoste, Isabelle Desormeau, Michel and Twiggy Sanders, Yves Camdeborde, Bertrand Auboyneau, Laëtitia Ghipponi and my friend and mentor, Pierre Hermé.

This is my eleventh book and so the eleventh opportunity I've had to close with love to my husband, Michael, and our son, Joshua. They're my true luck.

CONTENTS

Parisian Macarons (page 288)

Odile's Fresh Orange Cake (page 28)

Bubble Eclairs (page 230)

Apple Tarte Flambée (page 118)

Strawberry Shortcakes Franco-American Style (page 338)

INTRODUCTION

DURING THE MORE THAN FIVE YEARS that I spent collecting recipes for this book, the following scene would play out with little variation: I'd ask French friends to give me a recipe, and they'd shake their heads, saying, "This one's not for you, it's too simple." Then, for emphasis, "*Extrêmement simple*." I'd persist, they'd relent and, in the end, they were only half right: The recipe was always extremely simple, but it was also perfect.

Very much later, I realized that the recipes I was gathering were something more: They were deeply personal, almost private, and I would never have known about them and could never have coaxed them from their makers if I didn't live in Paris and have friends who shared them with me.

These are the recipes the French bake at home for their families and their closest friends. They are generous, satisfying recipes tied to places, traditions, customs and culture. They're the opposite of the complex, fussy, time-consuming desserts most of us associate with French pastry. Some of the sweets are modern, some are riffs on classics; some are light, others are substantial; and some are sophisticated, but most are casual, easygoing and fun.

They have nothing to do with fancy techniques and even fancier frills. They have nothing to do with towering confections, spun sugar and pristinely elegant tarts. They're plain and homey—even when they come, as many of these recipes do, from renowned chefs. And they were a revelation to me, offering a glimpse into a parallel universe completely different from the world of pastry I'd studied and challenged myself to replicate at home for so many years.

FOR MUCH OF MY ADULT LIFE, I studied the classic canon of French pâtisserie with the fervor of a religious convert. And although I worked with great pastry chefs, I didn't pay attention to them when, after they'd described their latest, fabulously imaginative creations, they'd tell me about their mothers' sturdy chocolate cakes, the rustic tarts they themselves prepared with whatever fruit was in the market, the madeleines they craved or the crème caramel from the corner café that made them just as happy as their own beautifully layered puff pastry.

Because I was such an ambitious home baker—I delighted in spending an entire day preparing a dessert—I assumed that this passion stretched across the ocean. I was wrong. How wrong became evident one evening shortly after I'd begun my life as a part-time Parisian. I brought a tall chocolate cake to the table. It was layered with ganache and finished with chocolate glaze and berries. After the oohs and aahs, my French friends asked where I'd gotten it. When I said that I'd made it, there was just one response: Why?

Here's what I now know: Real French people don't bake! At least they don't bake anything complicated, finicky, tricky or unreliable. Not one of my friends, all good cooks, understood me when I explained that I had started baking intricate pastries at home as a hobby. According to them, what I was doing was best left to the pros. Pastry, the fancy stuff, is what pastry shops are for, and France has plenty of them.

When the French bake at home, they bake for love, for the people they care about most and for the joy of making them happy. They'll make a weekend cake (that's what many loaf cakes are called) for a picnic or a pick-me-up, or because friends are coming for *le week-end*. They'll make cookies for their children and pots de crème to cap a midweek dinner. My friend Martine bakes the same birthday cake for her husband that his mother made for him: a domino-like construction of store-bought cookies dipped in espresso and filled with mocha buttercream. It's the Gallic version of our classic icebox-cookie cake, and it's just as charming, if a little less sweet and a lot more grown-up. And all my friends know how to put together a snack-cum-dessert that's so good that I only serve it when I know there will be enough people around the table to finish the treats off or take them home, because I am powerless to resist them. Their name, Desert Roses, is poetic, but their ingredients are plain: dried fruit, nuts, chocolate and cornflakes for crunch. My stateside friends call this "comfort baking," and they're right.

"Real French people don't bake! At least they don't bake anything complicated, finicky, tricky or unreliable."

I HAVE ADAPTED MANY DESSERTS from sweets I discovered when I was traveling—the apple *tarte flambée* that won my heart in Alsace, the dipped-in-icing Palets de Dames cookies from Lille, the Tarte Tropézienne made famous by Brigitte Bardot, and other desserts from Normandy, Brittany and Provence. There are also recipes of pure invention that I created in my Paris kitchen. When cream cheese took the city by storm (Kraft Philadelphia Cream Cheese has a cult following there), I treated my friends to a no-bake cheesecake topped with blueberries. My little Apple Pielettes are completely American, even if my French friends claimed them as a play on their own covered pies, called *tourtes*. And Strawberry Shortcakes Franco-American Style—an almost all-American shortcake built on very French ladyfinger disks—prove that there are no frontiers when it comes to goodness.

Here and there you'll find recipes that are more elaborate than those my French friends bake, but they're favorites of mine, and I didn't want you to miss tasting what some of today's most creative chefs are doing. Take the time for Hugo & Victor's Pink Grapefruit Tart—it's a miracle (gorgeous, too). And stretch your imagination with the recipes for the fancy or simple Carrément Chocolat cakes, with chunks of salted chocolate (total genius), my adaptation of the specialties from my pastry hero, Pierre Hermé.

If a recipe is here, it means I love it. I was so delighted when I constructed my first *paille,* a type of jam sandwich cookie, using, as all French home bakers do, store-bought puff pastry, that I thought my upstairs neighbors might have heard my little yelp of triumph. The same was true of cannelés, the crenellated pastry that's dark and crispy—almost burnt—on the outside and custardy inside. A perfect stranger, a woman I met because we were sitting side by side in a bistro, gave me the recipe. And when I learned to glaze madeleines, you'd have thought I'd found the Rosetta stone.

Even after forty years, France—its people, its traditions, its food and its pastry—has the power to surprise me. These recipes are the record not only of discoveries but also of friendships and my love for the country and its remarkable cooks.

ABOUT THE RECIPES: All measurements are given in both traditional American volume and European metric weights. If you have a scale, I urge you to use the metric measures. It won't take long for you to get used to them, and you'll find that the task of preparing your ingredients before you start to bake will go faster. Also, because weight measurements are more accurate than volume, your results will be more consistent from one time to the next.

All recipes were tested with all-purpose flour, large eggs, unsalted butter and fine sea salt.

When measuring flour by volume, I use the scoop-and-sweep method. I stir the flour in the bin to aerate it, then dip in my measuring cup, scoop up a mounded cupful and lightly sweep the flour level with the edge of the cup using the back of a knife. My metric measure for 1 cup of flour is 136 grams. (For more about flour, see page 56.)

A WORD ON TIMING: Everyone's oven is different, and the best way to up your baking game is to make friends with your oven. Get to know its quirks, its hot spots (they all have them) and, especially, its temperature variations. Buy an oven thermometer and remember to use it. I've given you a range of baking times for each recipe and some visual cues to help as well, but things may not be the same chez you as they are chez me. To be safe, check whatever you're baking at the low end of the time range (maybe even a minute or two before). If the baking time in your oven is different from what it was in the several ovens that were used to test these recipes, write your time in the book—you'll be happy to have it when you return to the recipe.

SIMPLE CAKES

Brown-Butter-and-Vanilla-Bean Weekend Cake

Makes 10 servings

SERVING: If you have time, wrap the cooled cake in plastic film or foil and let it age for a day before slicing it and serving it with tea, coffee or even a small snifter of rum. If you have the cake long enough for it to go stale, rejoice—it's lovely toasted.

STORING: Wrapped in plastic film, the cake will keep at room temperature for at least 4 days. Wrapped airtight, it can be frozen for up to 2 months; leave the cake in its wrapping while it defrosts.

IF BROWN BUTTER WEREN'T CLASSIC in savory cuisine and traditional in some pastries, it would be easy to think of it as a trick to make us pay attention to an everyday ingredient. Brown butter, known in France as *beurre noisette*, or "hazelnut butter," is what you get when you boil butter and let the milk solids darken. It's a fine line between brown butter and burned butter, but stay on the right side of that line and you get the aroma of nuts and the flavor of caramel, perfect companions to vanilla. You can use a great vanilla extract in this recipe, but if you have a vanilla bean, give it preference. It not only tastes just right in the cake, the flecks of seed are enticing.

The French call this a weekend cake because it will last all weekend, and it's good with so many kinds of weekend meals and outings. It can be put together quickly. If you start a day ahead, though, you'll be rewarded with fuller flavor: The cake is best if you keep it under wraps overnight.

1 stick (8 tablespoons; 4 ounces; 113 grams) unsalted butter	1 moist, fragrant vanilla bean, split lengthwise and scraped (see page 372), or 4 teaspoons pure vanilla extract
1¾ cups (238 grams) all-purpose flour	4 large eggs, at room temperature
1½ teaspoons baking powder	⅓ cup (80 ml) heavy cream
¼ teaspoon fine sea salt	2 tablespoons dark rum or amaretto (optional)
1¼ cups (250 grams) sugar	

Center a rack in the oven and preheat the oven to 350 degrees F. Pull out an insulated baking sheet or stack two regular baking sheets one on top of the other. Line the (top) sheet with parchment paper or a silicone baking mat. Butter a 9-×-5-inch loaf pan, dust with flour and tap out the excess (or use baker's spray). I suggest preparing the pan this way even if it's nonstick. Set the loaf pan on the baking sheet(s).

Put the butter in a small saucepan and bring it to a boil over medium heat, swirling the pan occasionally. Allow the butter to bubble away until it turns a deep honey brown, 5 to 10 minutes. Don't turn your back on the pan—the difference between brown and black is measured in seconds. And don't worry about the little brown flecks in the bottom of the pan—they're a delicious part of the process. Remove the pan from the heat.

Whisk the flour, baking powder and salt together in a medium bowl.

Put the sugar and the vanilla-bean pulp in a large bowl and rub them together until the sugar is moist and fragrant. (If you're using vanilla extract, you'll add it later.) Whisk the eggs into the sugar, beating for about 1 minute, or until they're thoroughly incorporated. Still working with the whisk, beat in the extract, if you're using it, then the heavy cream, followed by the rum, if you're using it. Continuing to whisk or switching to a large flexible spatula, gently and gradually stir in the dry ingredients until you have a thick, smooth batter. Fold in the melted butter in 2 or 3 additions. Pour the batter into the prepared pan and smooth the top.

Bake the cake for 55 to 65 minutes, or until a knife inserted into the center comes out clean. Take a look at the cake after it's been in the oven for about 30 minutes; if it looks as if it's browning too quickly, cover it loosely with a foil tent. When the cake tests done, transfer it to a rack to cool for 5 minutes, then unmold it and let cool right side up.

WEEKEND CAKES AND GÂTEAUX VOYAGES

The French are very precise about how they break up the day. Morning goes from dawn until a little after noon, unless you are saying good-bye to someone at around 11:00 a.m.—then you'd wish them a "good end of the morning" (*bonne fin de matinée*). The afternoon is delineated in a similar way: after about 4:00 p.m., the parting words are "good end of the afternoon." There's an end to the evening and a time to say "good night" as well. With all this precision, it strikes me as funny that while you can wish someone a "*bonne fin de semaine*" ("*good end of the week*"), you can't wish them a good weekend in proper French. For that, the French borrow from us and say "*bon week-end.*"

What they didn't borrow from us is the concept of a weekend cake: a simple, sturdy cake that will last the weekend, that can be put out to be nibbled by family and houseguests, that will be as good for a dessert as it will be for an end-of-the-afternoon snack or an end-of-the-morning tide-me-over.

When the French say the word *cake*, they almost invariably mean a loaf cake. The word *gâteau* is usually saved for round cakes and for fancier cakes—except when the cake in question is a *gâteau voyage*, a "travel cake." The *gâteau week-end* (yes, it's what the French say) and the *gâteau voyage* are the same (I still can't figure out how you decide which name to use when). I like to think of a *gâteau voyage* as a cake that just might travel, even if it's only from one home to another, to a picnic (the French are great picnickers) or to the park to treat the team when they finish their game of pétanque.

Plain and Simple Almond Cake

Makes 8 servings

SERVING: If you're not serving the cake for an out-of-hand snack, it's nice to serve it with jam—in fact, sometimes I slice the cake in half and fill it with jam—or a drizzle of honey, maple syrup or even chocolate sauce (page 442).

STORING: Well covered, the cake will keep for about 4 days at room temperature. The texture may get a little denser, but the deliciousness will remain.

ONE SUNDAY MORNING, as my friend Hélène Samuel and I were shopping at the Boulevard Raspail organic market—it's one of our favorite weekend activities—she was pondering the mystery of a cake she'd made the day before. The question was this: How could this cake, which has just three basic ingredients, have so much flavor and be so good? Good enough to keep you cutting off slices and eating them out of hand. Good enough to make you want to whip up another one before the first cake's gone. Hélène went home and baked another cake that afternoon; I went home and made one too. And I came up with the answer to our question: I don't know.

If cakes could be plucked from almond trees, you'd think this one came straight from the orchard—the almond flavor is that intense. Yet all that's in the cake are equal weights of eggs, sugar, and almond flour. I added the salt and vanilla, and you could add a pinch of spice, maybe nutmeg, maybe an even smaller pinch of cloves. But really the cake needs nothing more than its magic trinity of ingredients—and a tender touch. Beat the egg whites until they form supple, rather than stiff, peaks, and fold the whites and almond flour gently into the egg yolk mixture. Lightness wins more points than thoroughness here.

Because this cake has no flour and no leavening, it's a good choice for Passover. It's also good for anyone on the prowl for a gluten-free treat.

5 large eggs, separated, at room temperature	2 cups (200 grams) almond flour
1 cup (200 grams) sugar	
1 teaspoon pure vanilla extract	Confectioners' sugar, for dusting (optional)
Pinch of fine sea salt	

Center a rack in the oven and preheat the oven to 350 degrees F. Butter a 9-inch round cake pan; the pan should be at least 1½ inches deep, but 2 inches would be better. You could also use a 9-inch springform pan. Butter the pan, line the bottom with parchment paper, butter the paper, dust the pan with flour and tap out the excess. (Use almond flour if you want the cake to be gluten-free or good for Passover.)

Whisk the egg yolks and all but 2 tablespoons of the sugar together in a large bowl until the mixture thickens and lightens in color. Whisk in the vanilla extract.

Working in the bowl of a stand mixer fitted with the whisk attachment, or in a large bowl with a hand mixer, beat the egg whites and salt at medium speed until they turn opaque, about 1 minute. Sprinkle in the remaining 2 tablespoons sugar and continue to whip until the whites are shiny and hold medium peaks. You don't want completely stiff, stand-up-at-attention whites.

Using a flexible spatula, stir about one quarter of the whites into the yolks to lighten them—no need to be gentle here. Scrape the rest of the whites onto the yolks, spoon over one third to one half of the almond flour and fold the mixtures together. Now's the time to be gentle, but not too thorough: They should be only partially blended. Spoon over the rest of the almond flour and continue folding until you have a light, homogeneous batter. Pour the batter into the pan and shimmy the pan gently to settle it and level the top.

Bake the cake for 33 to 38 minutes, turning the pan around after 20 minutes, or until the top is golden brown and springy to the touch; the sides will have pulled away from the pan just a bit. Transfer the pan to a cooling rack and let the cake rest for 5 minutes, then run a table knife around the edges of the pan and invert the cake onto the rack. Carefully peel away the parchment paper and turn the cake over to cool to room temperature right side up. When the cake is cool, dust the top with confectioners' sugar, if you're using it.

Martine's Gâteau de Savoie

Makes 10 servings

MARTINE EHRINGER is a woman with great style, the kind of Frenchwoman who would never go unnoticed, even in a roomful of other stylish Frenchwomen. She can talk about art as easily as she can talk about politics, and she can really talk about food—she cooks at home and loves to bake. "But," she says, "I make only the simplest sweets. In part it's because these are what I grew up with, but mostly it's because these are the kinds of desserts I love."

When Martine offered to give me a recipe, I was delighted; when it arrived, I was surprised. I don't know why I didn't take her at her word: She said she loved "simple," but I was waiting for something as elaborate as the knot of her scarf. Instead, as she promised, this classic sponge cake, one from her childhood, is, in her words, *extrêmement simple* and *vraiment basique*. It's also light, satisfying and beautiful in its plainness.

The Savoy cake is one of the oldest in the French repertoire, and in the Italian repertoire too. Whether it originated in France or Italy is disputed, but it seems likely that it was first made in 1358 by a Savoyard pastry chef whose count had ordered him to create a cake that would astonish him. The cake, which we consider simple today, was a marvel then. The surprise was its lightness, achieved by beating yolks and sugar until thick and pale, and then beating in whipped egg whites to create a cake that rose prodigiously and startled with its golden, springy interior.

The *gâteau de Savoie* is usually made in a ring pan—the kind used to make a savarin or a Jell-O mold—but it's lovely baked in a Bundt pan, which is how I make it.

SERVING: In Martine's family the cake is served with a bowl of currant, cherry or red fruit jam. You certainly can't go wrong following her lead. Nor would it be a mistake to serve wedges of the cake with lemon curd (page 433) or lemon cream (page 182). You might even want to cut the cake in half and sandwich the layers with the curd or cream. Or think about serving the cake with cherries cooked in red wine (page 376).

STORING: Sponge cakes are fragile and stale quickly. But a stale sponge cake is not a lost cake: It makes the best dunker or toasted sweet. Keep the cake well wrapped, though, and you should be able to stave off dunkerhood for about 2 days.

1½ cups (300 grams) sugar, plus extra for dusting	1¼ cups (170 grams) all-purpose flour
6 large eggs, separated, at room temperature	Confectioners' sugar, for dusting
2 teaspoons pure vanilla extract	
½ teaspoon fine sea salt	

Center a rack in the oven and preheat the oven to 350 degrees F. Butter a Bundt or other tube pan with a capacity of at least 12 cups. Dust with sugar and tap out the excess.

Put the egg whites in the bowl of a stand mixer fitted with the whisk attachment or in a large bowl that you can use with a hand mixer. Put the yolks in a large bowl.

Add the sugar to the yolks and immediately start beating with a whisk or a hand mixer (you don't want the yolks and sugar to stand, because the sugar will "burn" the yolks and cause them to form a skin). Beat until the mixture is pale and so thick that when you lift the whisk (or beaters), it falls back on itself in a slowly dissolving ribbon. Beat in the vanilla.

Add the salt to the egg whites and whip until they hold firm, glossy peaks. Scoop out about 2 tablespoons of the whites, put them on top of the yolks and, using a flexible spatula, stir them in to thin the yolks a little. Pour the flour over the yolks and fold it in. The mixture, which will be thick, should be well blended. Add another 2 tablespoons or so of whites and, once again, stir them in to lighten the mixture. Finally, scrape all the remaining whites into the bowl and gently fold them in with the spatula. It's better to have a few streaks of whites in the batter than to work the mixture so long that the whites deflate. Turn the batter out into the prepared pan.

Bake the cake for 45 to 50 minutes, or until a bamboo skewer inserted deep into the center of it comes out dry. Transfer the pan to a rack and let the cake sit for 5 minutes, then use a table knife to pry the cake away from the sides of the pan if necessary. Turn the cake over onto a cutting board and let it rest there for about 3 minutes, just to create some steam, then remove the pan. Transfer the cake to the rack to cool right side up.

Just before serving, dust the cake with confectioners' sugar.

TESTING AND TESTERS

The more you bake, the more your senses become an early-warning system alerting you that doneness might be just minutes away. My desk is in my kitchen and there have been hundreds of times when I've been deep at work and then suddenly been brought bolt upright by the smell of whatever is in the oven. No matter how many times this has happened, I'm still surprised and always oddly proud that I've caught the sweet at the right moment. Depending on what you're baking, you might be able to confirm what your nose has told you by checking that the color is golden brown (if it's a cookie, you can flip it over and check the color there too); that if it's in a pan, it's just starting to pull away from the sides; if it's a pudding, that it's stopped jiggling everywhere but in the center; and that if it's a sponge cake, it feels set to the touch and springs back when poked gently.

And then there are the deceivers: the big cakes that brown quickly but need more time; the tart fillings with puffed edges that make you think the moment of perfection is nigh (warning: If the edges puff, you usually have to wait for the center to puff as well); and those supermoist sweets, hovering between pudding and cake, that look done but might be overbaked or not baked enough.

The only way to handle deceivers is to probe. When I first started baking, I'd stick a toothpick into the center of a cake and if it came out dry or had only little crumbs on it (or it met whatever criteria the recipe specified), I called it done. Years later, when I worked with Pierre Hermé, he suggested that the tester needed a larger area and told me to probe with a knife. And I did and I still do for some things, usually sturdy loaf cakes. But knives leave slashes in a cake's inner crumb, so these days I'm more likely to use a long bamboo skewer (my grandmother used a broom straw) or a metal cake tester.

Each recipe includes details of how you'll know that something is done, but keep at it, and you'll just know. Catch the scent, and you'll probably be seconds ahead of your timer.

Apple Weekend Cake

Makes 10 servings

SERVING: This is a substantial cake with a compact crumb, so it's best served in medium-thin slices. Of course it can be served as a dessert, but I think it's better as a morning or snack cake or, best of all, as a picnic loaf.

STORING: Once the cake is cool, it should be wrapped well (I wrap it in wax paper), and if you've got the time, set aside to ripen for a day. The cake will keep for about 4 days at room temperature or, if it's not glazed, for up to 2 months in the freezer. Defrost it in its wrapper.

THIS IS A RECIPE FROM NORMANDY, the region of France known for butter, cream and apples of many varieties, but it's a cake that you find all over the country, one that might turn up with coffee in the morning or with tea in the afternoon at a bed-and-breakfast. It's a tight-crumbed loaf with enough moisture to keep it fresh over a long weekend. And, like so many cakes with fruit, it's even tastier the day after it's made.

Cakes like these don't often include flavoring, but I think the addition of dark rum, vanilla and cinnamon is great with the apples. If you wanted to tinker just a bit more, you might consider grating in some lemon or orange zest, and maybe stirring in some plump raisins or chopped nuts too.

A WORD ON THE APPLES: The cake itself doesn't have much sugar—the real sweetness comes from the apples. For the best flavor, use juicy apples that are sweeter than they are tangy. Think Mutsu, Fuji or Gala, for example.

1⅓ cups (181 grams) all-purpose flour	3 large eggs, at room temperature
1 teaspoon baking powder	1 tablespoon dark rum, or an additional 1 teaspoon vanilla extract
½ teaspoon ground cinnamon	
¼ teaspoon fine sea salt	1 teaspoon pure vanilla extract
1 stick (8 tablespoons; 4 ounces; 113 grams) unsalted butter, at room temperature	2 medium apples, peeled, cored and cut into small chunks
½ cup (100 grams) sugar	About ⅓ cup (106 grams) apple jelly or strained apricot jam (optional)
½ cup (60 grams) confectioners' sugar	

Center a rack in the oven and preheat the oven to 325 degrees F. Butter an 8½-×-4½-inch loaf pan, dust with flour, tap out the excess and put the pan on a baking sheet lined with parchment paper or a silicone baking mat.

Whisk the flour, baking powder, cinnamon and salt together in a small bowl.

Working in the bowl of a stand mixer fitted with the paddle attachment, or in a large bowl with a hand mixer, beat the butter on medium speed until smooth. Add both sugars and beat until creamy. Add the eggs one at a time, beating for a minute after each one goes in. The mixture will be thin and look curdled. Beat in the rum and vanilla—it will curdle even more, but that's fine. Reduce the mixer speed to low and add the dry ingredients, mixing only until they disappear into the batter, which will now be thick and shiny. With a flexible spatula, fold in the apple pieces, then scrape the batter into the prepared pan. Use the spatula to cajole the batter into the corners of the pan and level the top.

Bake the cake for 60 to 65 minutes, or until golden, crowned and cracked in the middle; a knife inserted into the center should emerge clean. Transfer the pan to a cooling rack and wait for 5 minutes, then turn the cake out of the pan and let it cool right side up on the rack.

If you'd like to glaze the cake, bring the jelly or jam and a splash of water to a boil (you can do this on the stove or in a microwave oven) and brush the hot glaze over the top of the cooled cake.

Apple Kuchen:
A Tall Apple-Custard Tourte

Makes 10 servings

SERVING: The kuchen is meant to be served at room temperature, when the custard filling is at its creamiest, but it's awfully good chilled, when the custard has firmed and the apples have too. Dust the tourte with confectioners' sugar just before serving.

STORING: This is a sweet to be eaten within a day or so of being made. If you don't serve it a few hours after it comes from the oven, cover it, refrigerate and serve cold.

I FOUND THIS RECIPE in one of my notebooks from the 1980s, and I'm not exactly sure where it came from. With the name *kuchen*—German for "cake"—it might have come to me by way of Alsace or Lorraine, the French regions bordering Germany, but you hear the word *kuchen* in Paris too. Wherever you hear it, it's confusing, since it might turn out to be a plain cake, a crumb cake, a fruit tart or a tourte, a tall, creamy concoction like this one, which is hardly a cake or, even with its crust, hardly a tart.

This particular kuchen is both regal and homey. The regal part is the elegant crust, a sweet, soft, lemon-scented dough that climbs to the top of the springform pan. But what's inside the crust is almost spoonable and certainly comforting: a heap of apples suspended in custard. At the last minute, the kuchen is run under the broiler so that the tips of the apple chunks char seductively. I'm not certain if that part counts as regal or homey, but I know it's good.

FOR THE FRUIT

- ⅓ cup (53 grams) plump, moist raisins or finely chopped dried apricots
- 3 tablespoons dark rum, Calvados, applejack, apple cider or apple juice

FOR THE CRUST

- 1¾ cups (238 grams) all-purpose flour
- ¼ cup (50 grams) sugar
- ½ teaspoon fine sea salt
  Finely grated zest of ½ lemon (optional)
- 1¼ sticks (10 tablespoons; 5 ounces; 142 grams) cold unsalted butter, cut into 20 pieces
- 3 large egg yolks, lightly beaten

FOR THE FILLING

- 6 tablespoons graham cracker or store-bought Petit Beurre cookie (homemade, page 270) crumbs
- 2 tablespoons (1 ounce; 28 grams) unsalted butter, melted
- 3 pounds (1361 grams) apples (Golden Delicious, Fuji or Gala), peeled, cored and cut into 1-inch chunks

FOR THE TOPPING

- 2 large eggs
- 1 large egg yolk
- ½ cup (100 grams) plus 2 tablespoons sugar
- 1¼ cups (300 ml) heavy cream (or crème fraîche, if you've got it)
- ½ stick (4 tablespoons; 2 ounces; 57 grams) unsalted butter, melted

Confectioners' sugar, for dusting

TO SOAK THE RAISINS OR APRICOTS: Put the fruit in a small jar, pour in the rum, cover with the lid and shake. Allow the mixture to sit, shaking it now and then, while you work on the other elements (or let the fruit soak overnight, if it's more convenient for you).

TO MAKE THE CRUST: Put the flour, sugar, salt and lemon zest, if you're using it, in a food processor and pulse just to mix. Drop in the cold butter and pulse until the butter is broken up and the mixture looks like coarse meal. Pour in some of the yolks and pulse to incorporate: Repeat until all the yolks have been added. Then use longer pulses to mix the dough until it is corn yellow and has formed small, moist curds that hold together when pressed.

Turn the dough out and knead it gently to incorporate any dry bits. Press the dough into a disk and place it between two pieces of parchment or wax paper. Roll the dough into the largest circle you can—a 15-inch circle is ideal. The dough will be thin, and that's fine. Slide the dough, still sandwiched between the papers, onto a cutting board or the back of a large baking sheet and refrigerate for about 15 to 20 minutes, until the dough is firm but is still pliable enough to be folded.

Butter a 9- to 9½-inch springform pan, dust with flour and tap out the excess (or coat the pan with baker's spray).

Remove the top piece of paper from the chilled dough, flip the dough over, and center the paperless side of the dough over the springform pan. Remove the paper and very gently press the dough down into the bottom of the pan and up the sides. The dough may crack and tear; just keep going. Once the dough is in the pan, trim the excess dough flush with the top of the pan and use the little scraps to patch any cracks: Moisten them lightly with water and just smooth them over the breaks. Cover the dough and refrigerate for at least 2 hours. (*The dough can be refrigerated for as long as overnight.*)

WHEN YOU'RE READY TO BAKE: Center a rack in the oven and preheat the oven to 400 degrees F. Line a baking sheet with parchment paper or a silicone baking mat.

TO MAKE THE FILLING: Mix the graham cracker or cookie crumbs and melted butter together in a small bowl just until the crumbs are moist. Sprinkle the crumbs over the bottom of the crust and top with the apples. Drain the raisins, reserving the rum, and sprinkle them over the apples.

Place the springform on the lined baking sheet and bake for 15 minutes (this short prebake roasts the fruit lightly, a nice touch).

MEANWHILE, MAKE THE TOPPING: Whisk the eggs, yolk and ½ cup of the sugar together in a small bowl. Add the heavy cream (or crème fraîche) and the reserved rum and whisk until you have a smooth, homogeneous batter.

When the kuchen is prebaked, pour the topping over the apples. Lower the oven temperature to 375 degrees F and bake for another 60 to 70 minutes, or until the filling is puffed and browned and a knife inserted deep into the tourte comes out clean. Remove the baking sheet from the oven and turn on the broiler.

Sprinkle the remaining 2 tablespoons sugar over the kuchen and pour over the melted butter. Run the kuchen under the broiler until the sugar bubbles and burns just a bit. Transfer the kuchen, still on its baking sheet, to a cooling rack and allow it to cool to room temperature. When the tourte is cool, remove the sides of the springform pan. Just before serving, dust the tourte with confectioners' sugar.

Custardy Apple Squares

Makes 8 servings

SERVING: Most often I serve the squares plain, but whipped cream, crème fraîche or ice cream makes a great partner.

STORING: The cake, which is good a few minutes out of the oven or at room temperature the day it is made, can also be refrigerated, covered, for up to 2 days and served chilled.

I THINK OF THIS AS A "BACK-POCKET RECIPE," one I can pull out when I need something quick and wonderful, something I can make on the spur of the moment without trekking to the market. The cake is primarily apples (or pears or mangoes, see Bonne Idées) and the batter, which resembles one you'd use for crêpes, has more flavor than you'd imagine the short list of ingredients could deliver and turns thick and custard-like in the oven. Through some magic of chemistry, the apples, which go into the pan in a mishmash, seem to line themselves up and they come out baked through but retaining just enough structure to give you something to bite into. That it can be served minutes out of the oven makes this the perfect last-minute sweet.

I've made this with several kinds of apples and the cake has always been good. In general, I go for juicy apples that are not too soft (Gala and Fujis work well), and if I've got a few different kinds on hand, I use them all. I slice the apples on a mandoline or Benriner, tools that make fast work of the job, give you thin slices and allow you to use almost all the fruit. When you're finished slicing an apple on one of these, all you've got left is a neat rectangle of core.

3 medium juicy, sweet apples, such as Gala or Fuji, peeled	2 teaspoons pure vanilla extract
½ cup (68 grams) all-purpose flour	6 tablespoons whole milk, at room temperature
1 teaspoon baking powder	2 tablespoons (1 ounce; 28 grams) unsalted butter, melted and cooled
2 large eggs, at room temperature	
⅓ cup (67 grams) sugar Pinch of fine sea salt	Confectioners' sugar, for dusting (optional)

Center a rack in the oven and preheat the oven to 400 degrees F. Butter an 8-inch square baking pan and line the bottom with parchment paper.

Slice the apples using a mandoline, Benriner or a sharp knife, turning the fruit as you reach the core. The slices should be about ¹⁄₁₆th inch thick—elegantly thin, but not so thin that they're transparent and fragile. Discard the cores.

Whisk the flour and baking powder together in a small bowl.

Working in a large bowl with a whisk, beat the eggs, sugar and salt together for about 2 minutes, until the sugar just about dissolves and, more important, the eggs are pale. Whisk in the vanilla, followed by the milk and melted butter. Turn the flour into the bowl and stir with the whisk until the batter is smooth. Add the apples, switch to a flexible spatula and gently fold

the apples into the batter, turning everything around until each thin slice is coated in batter. Scrape the batter into the pan and smooth the top as evenly as you can—it will be bumpy; that's its nature.

Bake for 40 to 50 minutes, or until golden brown, uniformly puffed—make sure the middle of the cake has risen—and a knife inserted into the center comes out clean. Transfer the pan to a cooling rack and allow to cool for at least 15 minutes.

Using a long knife, cut the cake into 8 squares (or as many rectangles as you'd like) in the pan (being careful not to damage the pan), or unmold the cake onto a rack, flip it onto a plate and cut into squares. Either way, give the squares a dusting of confectioners' sugar before serving, if you'd like.

Bonne Idées

You can add a couple of tablespoons of dark rum, Calvados, applejack or Armagnac or a drop (really just a drop) of pure almond extract to the batter. If you have an orange or a lemon handy, you can grate the zest over the sugar and rub the ingredients together until they're fragrant. You can also change the fruit. Pears are perfect and a combination of apples and pears even better. Or make the cake with 2 firm mangoes—the texture will be different, but still good—or very thinly sliced quinces. Finally, if you want to make this look a little dressier, you can warm some apple jelly in a microwave and spread a thin layer of it over the top with a pastry brush.

Fluted Carrot-Tangerine Cake

SERVING: Because this cake has a light, open crumb, it seems to beg to be dunked, and it makes a good dunker for both coffee and tea. It also makes a great breakfast or brunch cake; serve it with your favorite marmalade.

STORING: Loosely covered, the cake will keep at room temperature for up to 3 days. It can be wrapped airtight and frozen for up to 2 months; defrost in its wrapper. If you've got some leftover cake that seems a little stale, you're in for a treat: Cut a wedge, slice it crosswise in half, toast it and spread it with butter or jam—or both—while it's still hot.

BANISH ALL THOUGHTS OF the tall, rich, substantial, cream cheese–frosted American carrot cake and meet its slim, chic French cousin. Where the American cake is grand, this is an inch high. Where the American cake is dense, moist and chewy, this is light and spongy. And where the American version is boldly flavored, this cake whispers carrot, ginger and citrus.

My cake is a riff on a recipe from the Parisian author, critic and restaurateur Bruno Verjus, who created it in homage to the founder of the Slow Food movement, Carlo Petrini. The original called for carrots and oranges, but since I always have tangerines or clementines in the house, and I like their brightness, that's what I grabbed. I also love fresh ginger in the mix.

As with many cakes made with ginger, citrus zest and juice, this one is good as soon as it cools but better a few hours or even a day later, after the flavors have had time to get to know one another better.

If you have a fluted quiche pan, use it for this cake. It doesn't change anything about the cake, which is fine baked in a pie plate or regular cake pan, except its looks: The little ruffles around the edges give the simple cake a touch of the flirt.

1	cup (136 grams) all-purpose flour	1	tangerine, 2 clementines or 1 orange
¾	teaspoon baking powder Pinch of fine sea salt	9	tablespoons (4½ ounces; 128 grams) unsalted butter, at room temperature
1	medium carrot, peeled	1	cup (200 grams) sugar
1	teaspoon grated fresh ginger	2	large eggs, at room temperature

Center a rack in the oven and preheat the oven to 350 degrees. Butter a 9- to 9½-inch quiche pan (a ceramic or metal pan with fluted edges and a non-removable bottom), pie plate or cake pan. Fit the bottom with a round of parchment paper, butter the paper and dust the pan with flour; tap out the excess.

Whisk the flour, baking powder and salt together in a small bowl.

Using a fine grater, grate the carrot into a bowl—you want short, thin, stubby pieces—and pour whatever juice is produced into a glass measuring cup. Add the ginger to the carrot, then grate the tangerine (or clementine or orange) zest into the bowl. Squeeze the juice from the tangerine into the measuring cup until you reach ¼ cup; if the juice has some pulp in it, so much the better.

Working in the bowl of a stand mixer fitted with the paddle attachment, or in a large bowl with a hand mixer, beat the butter at medium speed for about 2 minutes, until smooth and creamy. Add the sugar and beat for 2 minutes more. Add the eggs one at a time, beating for 1 minute after each one goes in, or until you have a light, fluffy, homogeneous mixture. Reduce the mixer speed to low and scrape in the grated carrot mixture, followed by the juice. Your batter might curdle and look quite ugly at this point, but that's okay. Still on low speed, add the dry ingredients and give them just a spin or two: You want to keep the batter light, so it's best to finish mixing by folding the dry ingredients in with a flexible spatula. When the flour has disappeared into the batter and the batter is back to looking pretty, scrape it into the pan.

Bake the cake for 25 to 30 minutes, or until the top is golden and springy to the touch and a skewer inserted into the center comes out clean. Transfer the pan to a cooling rack and cool for 5 minutes. If the cake is stuck around the edges, gently pry it away from the pan with a table knife. Turn the cake over onto a rack, remove the parchment and turn the cake again to cool to room temperature right side up on the rack.

Bonne Idée

TANGERINE GLAZE: The cake is perfectly nice plain, but it's also nice with a drizzle of glaze. Mix 1 cup confectioners' sugar with 2 to 3 tablespoons tangerine, clementine or orange juice in a small bowl until the mixture is thick enough to drip slowly from the tip of a spoon. Either brush the glaze over the surface of the cake, making a thin layer— I like it when there are some bare spots and you can see the brush marks—or go all Jackson Pollock and just let the glaze fall off the spoon this way and that.

Rhubarb Upside-Down Brown Sugar Cake

Makes 8 servings

SERVING: Depending on your whim and whether you're snacking or making the cake the gala finish to a meal, you can serve it in thick wedges with nothing but a fork and a cup of tea or coffee, or you can top it generously with crème fraîche or whipped cream and lots of sliced strawberries.

STORING: Kept covered at room temperature (please don't chill it), the cake will stay moist and delectable for up to 3 days.

WHETHER OR NOT it feels like spring in Paris (where spring has the iffiest weather), you can always tell when you go to the market. The sure signs are asparagus, strawberries and rhubarb. But while asparagus are piled high in pyramids and the berries are so plentiful that vendors often scoop them up by the bucketful, the rhubarb pickings are still slim at the start of the season. Sometimes a farmer will have a bundle of stalks, sometimes a bit more, but no matter the quantity, only the early birds will get them.

One Saturday during the first week of April, I got to the market at Maubert-Mutualité at 11-ish and saw a vendor with lots of strawberries and greens, fava beans and asparagus—and one lone stalk of rhubarb. Who'd want just one? It seemed so odd. When I asked if the stalk had siblings hidden under the table, the vendor said, "No, and you should know better. If you wanted rhubarb, you should have come sooner." Had his hands not been full, I'm sure he would have shaken a finger at me.

His limited supply created desperate desire, and I set off in search of a bundle. Once I found it, I baked this cake and, as soon as it came out of the oven, I was sorry I hadn't bought strawberries to go with it. I'm sure that Mr. Vendor would have told me I ought to have planned better.

In the end, no one missed the berries. And while it's true that the brown sugar cake topped with bracingly tart caramelized rhubarb is fine unadorned, I think it's even finer served with crème fraîche and sweetened strawberries. Plan ahead.

FOR THE RHUBARB TOPPING

1¼ pounds (567 grams) rhubarb (4–6 stalks), trimmed and rinsed

¾ cup (150 grams) sugar

1½ tablespoons (¾ ounce; 21 grams) unsalted butter

FOR THE CAKE

1 cup (136 grams) all-purpose flour

1 teaspoon baking powder
Pinch of fine sea salt

3 large eggs, at room temperature

¾ cup (150 grams) packed light brown sugar

Finely grated zest of 1 orange (optional)

1½ teaspoons pure vanilla extract (or 1¼ teaspoons vanilla extract plus ⅛ teaspoon pure almond extract)

1 stick (8 tablespoons; 4 ounces; 113 grams) unsalted butter, melted and cooled

TO MAKE THE RHUBARB TOPPING: Peel—string is more like it—the rhubarb, using a vegetable peeler or a small knife. Don't worry about being too thorough, especially if your rhubarb is young and thin. Cut the rhubarb into chunks about 1 inch long and toss them into a medium bowl. Stir in ½ cup of the sugar, then set aside, stirring occasionally, for about 30 minutes, at which point the sugar will have created a syrup.

Drain the rhubarb over a bowl, and reserve the syrup—you won't need it for the cake, but it's nice in club soda, iced tea or white wine spritzers.

Butter a 9-inch round cake pan with sides that are at least 1½ inches high.

Melt the butter in a large skillet over medium-high heat, then stir in the remaining ¼ cup sugar. When the sugar is melted and just starting to color, add the drained rhubarb (work in batches if your skillet can't handle so much fruit) and cook, stirring sparingly, for about 3 minutes, or until the sugar is lightly caramelized and the rhubarb is brown here and there. Rhubarb can be a little tricky—heat it too much, and you'll get mush—so keep an eye on the pan and be gentle when you toss and turn the fruit. Scrape the fruit and liquid into the buttered cake pan and set aside to cool while you make the cake.

TO MAKE THE CAKE: Center a rack in the oven and preheat the oven to 350 degrees F. Line a baking sheet with parchment paper or a silicone baking mat and have a serving plate at hand.

Whisk the flour, baking powder and salt together in a small bowl.

Working in a large bowl with a whisk, beat the eggs and brown sugar together until thick and smooth. Whisk in the zest, if you're using it, and the vanilla extract. Pour in the melted butter—I usually do this in 3 additions—and work it in gently and completely with the whisk, making sure to get to the bottom of the bowl, as the butter has a tendency to sink and remain there. Finally, add the dry ingredients, again in 3 additions, whisking gently until they disappear into the batter. Scrape the batter into the pan over the rhubarb, level the top and put the pan on the lined baking sheet.

Bake the cake for about 25 minutes, rotating it after 12 minutes, or until it is golden brown, springy to the touch and just beginning to pull away from the sides of the pan; a skewer inserted into the center should come out clean. Transfer the pan to a cooling rack and let it rest for about 2 minutes, then run a table knife around the sides of the cake, place the serving plate over the cake and carefully turn the cake over onto the platter. Wait for 1 minute (time enough for gravity and steam to loosen the cake), then lift off the pan. If a

few pieces of rhubarb have stuck to the pan, use the knife to scrape them off and return them to the top of the cake.

TO GLAZE THE CAKE (IF USING): If you'd like to give the cake some shine—and fill in the spaces that inevitably form between the pieces of rhubarb—bring the jelly and water to a boil in a small saucepan or a microwave oven. When the bubbling subsides, brush or spoon the jelly over the warm cake. Set the cake aside to cool. Serve with strawberries and crème fraîche.

Odile's Fresh Orange Cake

Makes 8 servings

SERVING: There's nothing to stop you from eating the cake the minute you've finished soaking it, but it benefits from a couple of hours' rest. I think it's even better the next day.

STORING: Well covered, the cake will keep for up to 4 days at room temperature. Wrapped airtight, it can be frozen for up to 2 months. Defrost it in the wrapping.

WHEN ODILE DE LANNOY came to our house for the first time—she had only met me once, years before, and then only for minutes—but she came bearing the perfect present: a family recipe, handwritten in neat, straight-as-an-arrow script on a long sheet of paper. Had she brought me kilos of chocolate, I couldn't have been happier.

Odile prefaced her gift by saying, "I hope you won't think the recipe is too simple," then added, "but these are the kinds of cakes that I make for my family." Odile was right that the cake was simple, but it is simple in ways that I love. It's simple to make—the batter comes together in less than 10 minutes. It has a simple look—you can dress it up if you'd like (see Bonne Idée), but I think it has great appeal left plain. Its texture is simple: soft and moist. And it tastes of simple ingredients: butter, sugar, flour and eggs—the baker's quartet—and fresh oranges.

Odile told me that she likes to really soak the cake with orange syrup when it comes out of the oven. My preference is to use only half the amount of syrup, but I leave it to you to decide. If you make it the way Odile does, it will be just what she said it should be: "*humide, même mouillé*" ("moist, even wet").

A WORD ON TIMING: You should make the syrup as soon as the cake goes into the oven, so that the sugar has time to dissolve.

AND A WORD ON ORANGES: If you can find blood oranges, use them—they're wonderful in this cake.

FOR THE CAKE

¾ cup plus 2 tablespoons (119 grams) all-purpose flour

1½ teaspoons baking powder

½ teaspoon salt

½ cup (100 grams) sugar

1 large orange

1 stick (8 tablespoons; 4 ounces; 113 grams) unsalted butter, at room temperature

2 large eggs, at room temperature

FOR THE SYRUP

½ cup (100 grams) sugar

Juice of 1 orange

TO MAKE THE CAKE: Center a rack in the oven and preheat the oven to 350 degrees F. Butter an 8-inch round cake pan, dust with flour and tap out the excess.

Whisk the flour, baking powder and salt together in a small bowl.

Put the sugar in the bowl of a stand mixer or in a large bowl in which you can use a hand mixer. Grate the zest of the orange over the sugar. Squeeze the juice into a measuring cup—you should have about ⅓ cup, but a little more or a tad less won't throw things off.

Poached Orange-Topped Cake

Rub the sugar and zest together with your fingertips until the sugar is moist and fragrant. If you're using a stand mixer, fit it with the paddle attachment and attach the bowl. Add the butter to the bowl and beat on medium speed working with the stand mixer or hand mixer for about 2 minutes, until the mixture is smooth and creamy. Add the eggs one at a time, beating for 1 minute after each one goes in, then pour in the juice and beat to blend. Reduce the mixer speed to low and add the dry ingredients, mixing only until they disappear into the batter. The batter may look a little lumpy and grainy, but that's fine. Turn the batter out into the cake pan and smooth the top.

Bake the cake for 20 to 25 minutes, or until a knife inserted into the center comes out clean. The top of the cake will be pale, the bottom even paler. As soon as you take the cake out of the oven, unmold it onto a cooling rack, invert it onto another rack and then put the rack over a baking sheet lined with plastic film or foil.

MEANWHILE, MAKE THE SYRUP: As soon as the cake goes into the oven, stir the sugar and orange juice together in a small bowl, and then stir a couple of times while the cake is baking. Don't worry if the mixture is a little grainy—it will still soak into the cake nicely.

Spoon or brush the syrup over the hot cake, working slowly so that it soaks into the cake. I usually use only half of the syrup—I like the cake moist, but not wet—but you can use more if you want a thoroughly-soaked-through cake.

Bonne Idée

POACHED ORANGE–TOPPED CAKE:

The cake is the same, but it's topped with poached oranges and the poaching liquid becomes the soaking syrup. To make the decorative (and delicious) topping, you'll need 3 additional oranges. Cut the tops and bottoms off each orange, stand the orange up and remove the remaining peel by cutting straight down the sides of the orange 5 times, to shape it into a pentagon. Then turn the oranges on their sides and slice them about 3/8 inch thick. Bring 1 cup water, 1 cup sugar, 1 short cinnamon stick (optional) and 1 quarter-size piece fresh ginger (also optional) to a boil in a medium saucepan, then reduce the heat and simmer for 2 minutes. Gently drop the orange slices into the syrup and cook over low heat for 3 minutes. Carefully remove the slices with a slotted spoon; strain and reserve the syrup.

Arrange the oranges on the top of the cake so that they fit together like a jigsaw puzzle, trimming the pieces around the edges of the cake with a knife if necessary. Pour about half of the warm poaching syrup over the cake. (Refrigerate the remaining syrup— it's great in tea.) Then finish with a glaze: Melt some orange marmalade and brush it over the fruit. Cool the cake completely.

For a pretty multicolored top, finish the cake with poached slices of blood oranges, navel oranges and ruby grapefruits.

Cheesecake, Alsace Style

Makes 10 servings

SERVING: The cake should be served cold, in hefty slices. Maybe that's what this sweet has in common with our all-American cheesecake: Neither is meant to be served in dainty slivers.

STORING: Well covered, the cheesecake will keep in the refrigerator for up to 2 days; wrapped airtight, it will hold in the freezer for up to 2 months. Defrost it, still wrapped, in the refrigerator overnight.

MORE ETHEREAL THAN our American cheesecake but somewhat heartier than most French pastries, this tall cake, with its yogurt-cream filling and sturdy crust, is typical of Alsace, France's easternmost region. There, dough-encircled cakes like this one (and its cousin, the similarly creamy Apple Kuchen, page 16) are sometimes called *tourtes*.

The cake's crust is beautiful and its filling, dotted with rum-soaked raisins, is remarkably light, just a little rich and just a little sweet. When I'm in France, I do as the Alsatians do and make the filling with fromage blanc, adding a splash of eau-de-vie. But in America, I use thick Greek yogurt, heavy cream and rum. (To make this with fromage blanc, replace the yogurt and cream with 1¼ cups fromage blanc.)

1 recipe Galette Dough (page 420)	4 large eggs, separated, at room temperature
⅓ cup (53 grams) moist, plump raisins, preferably golden	¾ cup (150 grams) sugar
1 tablespoon dark rum or Cognac	3 tablespoons cornstarch, sifted
1 cup (225 grams) plain whole-milk Greek yogurt (the thickest you can find)	2 teaspoons pure vanilla extract
	¼ teaspoon fine sea salt
¼ cup (60 ml) heavy cream	Confectioners' sugar, for dusting

Lightly butter a 9-inch springform pan.

Place the galette dough between two large sheets of parchment or wax paper and roll it into a circle about 15 inches in diameter; don't worry about raggedy edges. If the dough is very soft, slide it onto a baking sheet and pop it into the refrigerator for about 20 minutes. You want the dough to be firm enough that you can work it into the springform, but not so firm or cold that it will crack.

Remove the top sheet of paper from the dough. Flip it over and lay the dough, paper side up, over the springform pan, remove the paper and gently ease it down into the base of the pan and up against the sides. The sides will fold over on themselves and pleat, and that's just fine—and pretty. Put the pan in the freezer while you preheat the oven. (*The crust can be wrapped tight and frozen for up to 2 months; it can be refrigerated overnight.*)

Center a rack in the oven and preheat the oven to 400 degrees F.

Put the springform on a baking sheet lined with parchment paper or a silicone baking mat. Line the crust with parchment paper or aluminum foil and weight the bottom of the crust with rice, beans or light pie weights.

Bake the crust for 20 minutes. Remove the paper and weights and bake for 5 to 8 minutes more, or until the crust is lightly browned. (The crust will bake again with the filling, but it's good to get some color on the base now.) Put the springform on a cooling rack to cool. Set the lined baking sheet aside.

When you're ready to make the cheesecake, preheat the oven to 350 degrees F. Put the springform pan back on the baking sheet.

Put the raisins in a small bowl, add the rum or Cognac, and stir. Set aside while you prepare the batter.

Working in a large bowl, whisk the yogurt and cream together until blended. Then whisk in the egg yolks one at a time. Whisk in ½ cup of the sugar, the cornstarch and vanilla extract. Stir in the raisins and rum.

Working in the bowl of a stand mixer fitted with the whisk attachment, or in a large bowl with a hand mixer, beat the egg whites and salt at medium speed until foamy and opaque. Gradually add the remaining ¼ cup sugar and beat on medium-high speed until the whites hold glossy peaks that tip over gracefully.

Scoop a spoonful of the whites over the batter and whisk it in, then turn all of the whites onto the batter. Switch to a flexible spatula and gently fold in the whites. You'll have a light, fluffy batter that won't be anything like the thick batter for American cheesecake. Scrape the batter into the crust— it might mound over the edges of the crust, and that's okay.

Bake the cheesecake for 40 to 50 minutes, or until it is uniformly puffed and golden (or even deep) brown. The top will crack, but that's fine and even appealing. The cake should feel firm and set to the touch. If you're not certain that it's done, stick a bamboo skewer or a thin knife into the center— it should come out clean. Transfer the cake to a cooling rack and allow it to cool to room temperature in the pan. Remove the sides of the pan and chill for at least 2 hours, or for as long as overnight.

Sprinkle the cake with confectioners' sugar just before serving.

Double-Chocolate Marble Cake

Makes 8 servings

SERVING: Because of the cake's lovely texture, you can cut it thin or thick and it will be good either way. It's meant to be served plain, but every plain cake is good with ice cream and this one's good with ice cream and chocolate sauce too.

STORING: Wrapped well, the cake will keep at room temperature for up to 4 days. It can be wrapped airtight and frozen for up to 2 months; defrost it in its wrapper.

As ALL-AMERICAN AS MARBLE CAKES SEEM, that's how all-French they seem as well. No matter where you go in France, no matter if the pastry shop is ritzy or rustic, you're bound to find a marble cake. Aside from their obvious tastiness, marble cakes are beloved because they are hearty, long lasting and good from breakfast through late-night snacking. And when you bake them at home, they're good for another reason: They're fun to make. Running a knife through the dark and light batters, producing arcs, curves and swirls, can make anyone feel like Picasso. In fact, the temptation to keep swirling is so strong that the risk of ending up with a cake that goes from marbled to monochromatic is high. Resist!

I've given you a recipe for marbling a cake with white and dark chocolate. Because you're adding chocolate to the entire cake, it's a little more substantial than a traditional marble cake, which is part white cake and part chocolate cake. If you'd like to keep to tradition, see Bonne Idée.

2 cups (272 grams) all-purpose flour	½ cup (120 ml) whole milk, at room temperature
1¼ teaspoons baking powder	4 ounces (113 grams) best-quality white chocolate, melted and cooled
¾ teaspoon fine sea salt	
1½ sticks (12 tablespoons; 6 ounces; 170 grams) unsalted butter, at room temperature	¼ teaspoon orange or peppermint oil (optional)
1 cup (200 grams) sugar	4 ounces (113 grams) semisweet or bittersweet chocolate, melted and cooled
4 large eggs, at room temperature	
1½ teaspoons pure vanilla extract	

Center a rack in the oven and preheat the oven to 325 degrees F. Pull out an insulated baking sheet or stack two regular baking sheets one on top of the other. Line the (top) baking sheet with parchment paper or a silicone baking mat. Butter a 9-×-5-inch loaf pan, dust with flour and tap out the excess; set it on the baking sheet(s).

Whisk the flour, baking powder and salt together in a small bowl.

Working in the bowl of a stand mixer fitted with the paddle attachment, or in a large bowl with a hand mixer, beat the butter on medium speed for 3 minutes, or until smooth. Add the sugar and beat for another 2 to 3 minutes, then add the eggs one at a time and beat for a minute after each one goes in. The batter may curdle, but you needn't worry. Reduce the mixer speed to low and mix in the vanilla. Still on low speed, add the flour mixture in

Bonne Idée

TRADITIONAL MARBLE
CAKE: Omit the white
chocolate. Stir the melted
and cooled bittersweet
chocolate into half of the
batter and leave the other
half plain. If you do this,
you might want to add
another ½ teaspoon vanilla
extract to the plain batter.

Another Bonne Idée

CARDAMOM AND MOCHA
MARBLE CAKE: Make the
batter and stir 1 teaspoon
ground cardamom into the
white-chocolate portion.
Dissolve 2½ teaspoons
instant coffee or espresso
in 1 tablespoon boiling
water and stir into the dark-
chocolate portion.

3 additions and the milk in 2, beginning and ending with the dry ingredients and mixing only until each addition is incorporated.

Scrape half of the batter into another bowl. Using a flexible spatula, gently stir the white chocolate into half of the batter. If you're using the orange or peppermint oil, stir it in as well. Stir the dark chocolate into the other half of the batter.

Using a spoon or scoop, drop dollops of the light and dark batters randomly into the prepared pan—don't think too much about the pattern—and then plunge a table knife deep into the batter and zigzag it across the pan. It's best to move forward and not to backtrack. Don't overdo it—6 to 8 zigzags should suffice.

Bake the cake for 80 to 90 minutes, or until a tester inserted deep into the center comes out clean. Check the cake at the halfway mark, turn it around and, if it's getting too brown, cover it loosely with a foil tent. Transfer the cake to a cooling rack and let it rest for 10 minutes, then unmold it, turn right side up on the rack and let come to room temperature.

Cornmeal and Berry Cakes

*Makes 4 mini
loaf cakes*

SERVING: I usually do
nothing more than slice
these cakes and serve as
is with tea or coffee, as an
afternoon treat or dessert
after a substantial meal,
whether brunch or dinner.
But you can dress them
up by serving them with a
raspberry coulis (page 449)
or a dollop of something
rich, like whipped cream,
ice cream or crème fraîche.

STORING: Wrapped
well, the cakes will keep at
room temperature for up
to 2 days; wrapped airtight,
they can be frozen for up
to 2 months (defrost in
the wrappers). If the cakes
seem stale, cut them into
thick slices and toast them
or, better yet, skillet-brown
them in butter.

TWENTY YEARS AGO, when I first met Pierre Hermé, he made a plain round cake with raspberries and mild Ligurian olive oil. For years after, I'd see olive oil cakes here and there, mostly in trendy Parisian restaurants and traditional Riviera pastry shops. Back then, the cakes were a rarity; today they're hip. And if they use cornmeal and berries, as this cake does, they're so much hipper.

French recipes for cakes like these usually call for polenta, and most people use the instant kind that's easily found in supermarkets. (Don't try it with beautiful yellow coarse polenta, or you'll end up with a cake too gritty to enjoy.) But I think these little cakes are best made with fine cornmeal, the kind you'd use for corn bread. They're prettiest with yellow meal, and the flavor is most balanced when made with a fruity oil.

Instead of the 4 mini cakes, you can make cupcakes if you like (use paper liners and bake them for 20 to 25 minutes). Any way you make them, the cakes can be glazed (see Bonne Idée) or served simply with something creamy or jammy on the side. Leave them plain, and you'll be able to stow them in the freezer, always a good thing.

1¼ cups (165 grams) fine cornmeal or fine polenta	1 teaspoon pure vanilla extract
⅔ cup (90 grams) all-purpose flour	7 tablespoons (3½ ounces; 99 grams) unsalted butter, melted and cooled
¼ cup (32 grams) cornstarch	⅓ cup (80 ml) fruity olive oil
1½ teaspoons baking powder	
Pinch of fine sea salt	
1 cup (200 grams) sugar	½ pint (123 grams) fresh raspberries
Finely grated zest and juice of 1 lemon	
4 large eggs, at room temperature	Confectioners' sugar (optional)

Center a rack in the oven and preheat the oven to 350 degrees F. Butter four 5-×-3-inch mini loaf pans (you can use foil pans), dust with flour and tap out the excess (or use baker's spray). Place the pans on a baking sheet.

Whisk the cornmeal or polenta, flour, cornstarch, baking powder and salt together in a small bowl.

Put the sugar and lemon zest in the bowl of a stand mixer or, if you'll be working with a hand mixer, a large bowl. Use your fingertips to rub the ingredients together until the sugar is fragrant and moist. If using a stand mixer, fit it with the paddle attachment and attach the bowl. Drop the eggs into the

bowl and, working with the stand mixer or hand mixer on medium speed, beat until pale and slightly thickened, about 4 minutes. Lower the speed and add the vanilla and lemon juice. With the machine on low, add the cornmeal mixture and mix until it disappears into the batter. Add the melted butter in a slow, steady stream, mixing until combined, then do the same with the olive oil.

Divide half of the batter evenly among the prepared pans. Sprinkle the berries into the pans and then pour over the rest of the batter; the pans will be about three-quarters full.

Bake the cakes for 30 to 35 minutes, until they are golden brown and a skewer inserted into the center comes out clean; the cakes will have started to pull away from the sides of the pans. Transfer the pans to a rack and cool for 5 minutes, then unmold, running a table knife around the sides of the cakes if needed. Allow the cakes to cool completely on the rack.

Dust the tops of the cakes with confectioners' sugar, if you'd like.

Bonne Idée

LEMON DRIZZLE GLAZE: Stir together 1 cup confectioners' sugar (it's a good idea to sift it), 2 tablespoons freshly squeezed lemon juice and 2 tablespoons melted unsalted butter in a small bowl until the glaze is smooth and falls off the tip of a spoon. If you need to thin the glaze, stir in a tiny splash of water. Drizzle (or brush) the glaze over the cooled cakes and let stand at room temperature until set.

Double-Corn Tea Cake

Makes 8 servings

SERVING: I like this best plain, but it's the kind of cake that's happy to share a plate with a spoonful of jam, marmalade or fruit. It's also nice with a drizzle of maple syrup.

STORING: Wrapped in plastic film, the cake will keep for about 4 days at room temperature; wrapped airtight, it can be frozen for up to 2 months (defrost in its wrapper). If the cake dries out a bit, cut it into thick slices, then toast and butter them. Jam is optional but not discouraged.

I CAME TO THIS CAKE BY ACCIDENT—it was a case of mistaken identity. I was in the natural foods shop near our Paris apartment looking for cornmeal, and it wasn't until I got home that I realized I'd bought corn flour instead. It was a beautiful yellow, as fine as cake flour and not at all a substitute for the rough stone-ground meal I'd set out for. I'd never made anything with corn flour before, and I might just have taken it back to the shop if there hadn't been a recipe for a cake printed on the sack. Nothing about the recipe looked right, but I couldn't get the idea of it out of my head. So I tinkered and tweaked, tasted and tinkered, until I finally got a recipe that I love. Is it like the one on the sack? I don't have a clue. But what it is, is lovely: The color of the plain-looking loaf cake is sunshine yellow; the crumb tight and fine; the texture almost melt-in-your-mouth, with a surprisingly pleasant roughness on the tongue; and the taste bursting with the true flavor of sweet corn. A breakfast, brunch or teatime treat, for sure.

I add corn kernels to the cake—they can be fresh (and if they are, it's best to lightly steam them before mixing them in), frozen or even canned—and a touch of ground coriander. If you're a tinkerer too, I think you'll discover that the cake can be varied in so many ways (see Bonne Idée).

A WORD ON CORN FLOUR: The flour for this cake is not masa harina, nor is it cornstarch or cornmeal. It is a finely ground flour that, because it is made with only corn, is naturally gluten-free. In the United States, I use Bob's Red Mill corn flour, which is widely available in supermarkets.

1¾ cups (203 grams) yellow corn flour

1½ teaspoons baking powder

½ teaspoon fine sea salt

½ teaspoon ground coriander

1 stick (8 tablespoons; 4 ounces; 113 grams) unsalted butter, at room temperature

1 cup (200 grams) sugar

3 large eggs, at room temperature

3 tablespoons whole milk

1 cup (125 grams) corn kernels, steamed fresh; thawed frozen; or canned, patted dry

Center a rack in the oven and preheat the oven to 350 degrees F. Butter an 8½-×-4½-inch loaf pan, dust with flour and tap out the excess or use baker's spray (even if you're using a nonstick pan, it's best to butter and flour or spray it). Set the pan on a baking sheet.

Whisk the corn flour, baking powder, salt and coriander together in a small bowl.

Working in the bowl of a stand mixer fitted with the paddle attachment, or in a medium bowl with a hand mixer, beat the butter at medium speed until smooth. Add the sugar and beat for 2 minutes or so, until blended. The mixture will be grainy, but that's fine. One by one, add the eggs, beating for 1 minute after each addition. Reduce the mixer speed to low and add the dry ingredients. Because the corn flour is gluten-free, you don't have to worry about overbeating, but there's really no need to do more than just mix until you have a thick golden-yellow batter. On low speed, add the milk and, once it's incorporated, the corn kernels. Give the batter a good turn with a flexible spatula, just to make certain that there are no dry ingredients left lurking at the bottom of the bowl. Scrape the batter into the prepared pan and smooth the top.

Bake the cake for 55 to 65 minutes, rotating the pan at the halfway point, until it is deeply golden and a knife inserted in the center comes out clean. If after 30 or 40 minutes it looks as though the cake is browning too much, cover it loosely with a foil tent. Transfer the cake to a cooling rack and let it rest for 5 minutes, then run a table knife between the cake and the sides of the pan and unmold it. Turn it right side up and allow to cool completely on the rack.

Bonne Idée

If you'd like to add a little crunch to the cake, you can either sprinkle chopped nuts over the top—just keep an eye on the cake so that they don't burn—or stir chopped toasted nuts (about ½ cup) into the batter with the corn. For a little color, try adding moist, plump dried cranberries or chopped dried cherries with the corn. Or for crunch, color and surprise, make a mix of chopped toasted nuts and dried fruit tossed with sugar or brown sugar, or, if you'd like, sugar and spice. Scrape half of the batter into the pan and smooth it, sprinkle over the fruit and nut mix and top with the remaining batter.

Saint-Pierre Poppy Seed Cake

Makes 10 servings

SERVING: The cake is ready to serve as soon as it cools, but, like so many loaf cakes, it is even better if you let it rest for a day; wrap it in plastic film and tuck it away. Essentially a tea cake, it is meant to be served plain.

STORING: Well wrapped, the cake will keep for up to 4 days at room temperature; wrapped airtight, it keeps for up to 2 months in the freezer. Defrost in the wrapper.

WHEN MY HUSBAND, MICHAEL, and our friend Bernard Collet set off for an afternoon together, they remind me of two kids looking for adventure. Part of it is the helmets and scooter and part of it is their sense of anticipation: No matter where they go (and sometimes it's just to a neighborhood café), they know that they're going to have "*un bon moment,*" as Bernard says. Since their good moments rarely include more than an espresso, I was surprised one afternoon when they returned from seeing an art exhibit with a hastily wrapped packet containing a sliver of poppy seed cake. The cake came from the café in the Halle Saint-Pierre, the museum they'd just visited, and it was notable in several ways: Its texture was dense and springy (a combination I love); the poppy seeds were front and center, strongly flavoring the cake; and it was just sweet enough.

"Can you make this?" Bernard asked with a twinkle. When he and some other friends came for dinner the following night, my version of the Saint-Pierre cake was part of dessert (I served it with Laurent's Slow-Roasted Spiced Pineapple, page 333).

The café's cake was heavily flavored with orange—perhaps orange oil. My version has citrus zest and a little juice, which is subtler. If you'd like to pump up the flavor, add just a drop or two of orange oil, but don't overdo it—citrus oils are powerful.

A WORD ON POPPY SEEDS: Like nuts, they are rich in oils, which can go rancid. Try to buy them from a source that has a high turnover, and no matter where you get them, taste them before you use them. If you're not going to use all the seeds you bought, pack them airtight and store them in the freezer.

1½ cups (204 grams) all-purpose flour	¾ teaspoon pure vanilla extract
1 teaspoon baking powder	½ cup (120 ml) heavy cream, at room temperature
¼ teaspoon fine sea salt	5½ tablespoons (2¾ ounces; 78 grams) unsalted butter, melted and cooled
3 clementines, 2 tangerines or 1 orange	
1¼ cups (250 grams) sugar	⅓ cup (47 grams) poppy seeds
4 large eggs, at room temperature	

Center a rack in the oven and preheat the oven to 350 degrees F. Pull out an insulated baking sheet or stack two regular baking sheets one on top of the other. Line the (top) sheet with parchment paper or a silicone baking mat.

Butter an 8½-×-4½-inch loaf pan, dust with flour and tap out the excess. Set the pan on the baking sheet(s).

Whisk the flour, baking powder and salt together in a small bowl.

Grate the zest of the clementines, tangerines or orange into a large bowl. Squeeze 2 tablespoons of juice from the fruit and set aside.

Add the sugar to the bowl with the zest and, using your fingertips, work the ingredients together until the sugar is moist and aromatic; if the sugar turns pale orange, so much the better. One by one, add the eggs, whisking vigorously after each one goes in. Whisk in the reserved juice and the vanilla, followed by the heavy cream. Switch to a flexible spatula and add the dry ingredients in 2 or 3 additions, stirring only until they disappear into the batter, which will be thick and smooth. Stir in the butter, again in 2 or 3 additions—the batter will be beautifully shiny—and finish by stirring in the poppy seeds. Scrape the batter into the prepared pan and smooth the top.

Bake the cake for 60 to 70 minutes, rotating the pan at the 30-minute mark and loosely covering the cake with a foil tent if you think it's browning too quickly. When baked through, the cake will have an attractive split down the middle and a knife or skewer inserted deep into the center will come out clean. Transfer the cake to a cooling rack and let it rest for 5 minutes, then run a table knife between the sides of the cake and the pan. Turn the cake out onto the rack, turn it right side up and cool to room temperature.

Hazelnut, Ginger and Olive Oil Cake

Makes 10 to 12 servings

SERVING: The cake needs to cool completely before you cut it. In fact, I think it's even better the day after it's baked. Cut the cake into thickish slices and serve with sugared berries (pour a little of the berries' syrup over the cake), roasted rhubarb (page 335; omit the bitters) or ice cream—Betty suggests ginger or vanilla. The cake is good served with tea.

STORING: Because it is so moist, the cake keeps really well. Wrapped in plastic film or wax paper, it can be stored at room temperature for about 4 days; wrapped airtight, it can be frozen for up to 2 months.

IT SEEMS RIGHT THAT this isn't a typical French combination for a tea cake, because Betty Edry, who gave me the recipe, isn't a typical French pastry chef. Her training is French, but her experience includes working in North Africa and Israel, as well as catering to London hostesses, and with each experience in new territory, she's learned new flavors and ideas.

The bones of the cake are French—it's a loaf cake and a member of the weekend-cake clan—but the addition of polenta, ginger and olive oil push it beyond France's borders. It's best made with a fruity olive oil and a fine-grained polenta, but if cornmeal's what you've got in the cupboard, go with it. Similarly, if you'd prefer almond flour to hazelnut flour, make the swap. But please keep the ginger: It's the high-note ingredient, the one that gives the cake zip.

Of course you can eat this cake as soon as it cools, but its moist texture, fragrance and lovely blend of flavors are even better after a day's rest.

2 cups (200 grams) hazelnut flour	7 tablespoons (3½ ounces; 99 grams) unsalted butter, melted and cooled
⅓ cup plus 1 tablespoon (54 grams) all-purpose flour	3 large eggs, at room temperature
⅓ cup plus 1 tablespoon (52 grams) fine polenta or fine cornmeal	1 cup (200 grams) sugar
1 teaspoon baking powder	1 tablespoon finely grated peeled fresh ginger (grated so that it is like a puree; I use a Microplane)
½ teaspoon fine sea salt	
½ cup (120 ml) fruity olive oil	

Center a rack in the oven and preheat the oven to 325 degrees F. Butter a 9-×-5-inch loaf pan and line the bottom with parchment or wax paper. Butter the paper, then dust the pan with flour and tap out the excess. Put the pan on a baking sheet.

Whisk the hazelnut flour, all-purpose flour, polenta or cornmeal, baking powder and salt together in a small bowl. Stir the olive oil and butter together in another small bowl.

Working in a large bowl with a whisk, beat the eggs and sugar until they are thick and their color lightens, about 2 minutes. Add the ginger and whisk to incorporate. Gradually add the dry ingredients, whisking only until they disappear into the thick batter. Gently whisk in the oil-butter mixture. The batter will be thickish and pleasantly bumpy from the hazelnut flour, polenta and ginger. Scrape it into the prepared pan.

Bake the cake for 55 to 60 minutes, rotating it front to back at the halfway point, or until the top springs back to the touch and a tester inserted into the center comes out clean. Transfer the cake to a cooling rack and let it rest for 10 minutes, then, if it looks as though it has stuck, run a table knife around the edges of the pan. Turn the cake out of the pan onto a rack, peel away the paper and invert the cake onto the rack to cool to room temperature.

Caramel-Topped Rice Pudding Cake

Makes 8 servings

SERVING: This is good at almost any temperature. You can serve it warm—just let it rest until it is firm enough to slice. Or you can serve it at room temperature—the choice of the French—or chilled. As for the caramel sauce, it, too, can be served warm (heat it gently in a saucepan or in a microwave oven) or at room temperature. Whether the cake is warm or cool, I'm apt to serve the sauce at room temperature.

STORING: The cake can be covered and left at room temperature overnight or wrapped and stored in the fridge for up to 3 days. Ditto the caramel sauce, which can be warmed in a saucepan or microwave oven, if you want to take the chill off it.

WE DON'T USUALLY THINK OF FRANCE as a rice culture, yet the French affinity for rice desserts runs deep. Just consider the attachment so many of them have to *riz au lait* ("rice pudding"; page 380), a bond that starts in toddlerhood. While pudding is the most beloved rice dessert, this cake comes in a close second. It's so popular that you can buy do-it-yourself box mixes for caramel-topped rice pudding cakes in every French supermarket.

The cake is an easy one to make sans mix: It is rice pudding enriched with eggs and baked in a caramel-lined pan. Nothing about it is difficult, but you do have to pay attention at a few important moments—a small price to pay for a cake that is so satisfying. And so pretty: The simple, low cake with its caramel topping that runs around each grain of rice is an invitation to pleasure. And I love that the caramel plays a double role: Half of it is used to line the cake pan and the other half is served as a sauce.

A WORD ON RICE: Just about any white rice will do, but the best cakes are made with short-grain rice, preferably Arborio.

FOR THE RICE
Salt
½ cup (100 grams) short-grain rice, such as Arborio
4 cups (960 ml) whole milk
⅓ cup (67 grams) sugar
1 tangerine or orange (optional)
2 large eggs
1 tablespoon pure vanilla extract

FOR THE CARAMEL
1 cup (200 grams) sugar
1 tablespoon freshly squeezed lemon juice
¼ cup (60 ml) water

TO MAKE THE RICE: Bring 3 cups lightly salted water to a boil in a 4-quart saucepan. Add the rice and boil for 10 minutes, then drain.

Rinse out the saucepan, pour in the milk and sugar and bring to a boil, stirring to dissolve the sugar. Don't step away from the stove while the milk is coming to a boil—if you move, the milk is just about guaranteed to bubble over the pan and make a colossal mess. As the milk bubbles up, stir it until it goes down, then lower the heat to a simmer and stir in the rice. Another word of warning: Until some of the milk has cooked away and the ingredients have settled into a simmering rhythm, there's still the threat of bubble-overs, so stay close. (I stand by the stove for the first 10 minutes and then set a must-stir alarm to go off every 5 minutes.) Cook, stirring regularly, especially at the beginning and toward the finish, for 40 to 50 minutes, until almost all the milk has been absorbed and the pudding is creamy. Scrape the pudding into a medium bowl.

MEANWHILE, WHEN THE RICE HAS COOKED FOR ABOUT 30 MINUTES, PREPARE THE CARAMEL: Center a rack in the oven and preheat the oven to 400 degrees F. Put an 8-inch round cake pan in the oven as soon as the oven heats up; it's much easier to line a pan with caramel when the pan is warm. Line a baking pan with paper towels to use later for a water bath (I use a 9-×-13-inch Pyrex baking dish) and have a kettle of hot water ready. You'll also need a heatproof measuring cup.

Stir the sugar, lemon juice and water together in a medium skillet, preferably nonstick, and bring to a boil over medium-high heat. As soon as the sugar starts to take on color around the edges, start stirring with a wooden spoon in small circular motions, working your way around the edges of the pan and steadily into the center, until all the sugar is a pale amber color. Remove from the heat; the caramel will continue to darken and be just the right color, a medium amber, in the time it will take you to line the pan and measure out the sauce.

Carefully remove the cake pan from the oven. Pour half of the caramel into the cake pan and the other half into the measuring cup. Working quickly and carefully—the pan is hot, the caramel a lot hotter—swirl the caramel until it covers the bottom. If you can get some of the caramel to go up the sides of the pan, do it.

The caramel that's in the measuring cup is going to become the sauce for the cake. Add warm water until you get the color and consistency that you want.

BACK TO THE RICE: If you want the flavor of citrus (I think it's a real plus), finely grate the zest of the tangerine or orange over the warm rice and then stir it in. Lightly stir the eggs and vanilla extract together in a small bowl. Add a heaping spoonful of the rice to the eggs and stir to blend—this keeps the eggs from being scrambled in the next step. Add the egg mixture to the bowl of rice, stirring with a wooden spoon or a heatproof spatula until everything is nicely blended. Turn the rice into the caramel-lined cake pan and smooth the top. Place the cake pan in the baking dish, slide the setup into the oven and pour enough hot water from the kettle into the baking dish to come halfway up the sides of the cake pan. Tent the cake with a piece of foil.

Bake the cake for about 1 hour, or until it is firm; if you stick a skewer into the center, it should come out clean. Carefully remove the cake pan from the water bath and dry the bottom and sides. To unmold the cake, grab a large platter with a rim. Run a table knife between the sides of the cake and the cake pan, place the platter over the top of the cake and very, very carefully— we're in hot-caramel land again—turn the cake and platter over. Wait for a few seconds to let the cake and the caramel settle, then lift off the cake pan. Allow the cake to cool until it's only slightly warm or it reaches room temperature. Serve with the caramel sauce in the measuring cup.

Spiced Honey Cake

Makes 12 servings

SERVING: This is the perfect tea cake, but it's not all that sweet, so it's particularly nice with red wine, cider—hot or cold, sweet or hard—or even mulled wine. My preference is to serve thin slices, but if you want to dunk, you'd do better to cut the cake thicker and perhaps to even cut the slices into strips.

STORING: *Pain d'épices* is the quintessential good keeper. It should ripen for a couple of days; after that it can be kept, well wrapped, for at least a week at room temperature.

EVERYTHING ABOUT THIS CAKE turned out to be a surprise. My intention had been to make a *pain d'épices*, a traditional honey-and-spice cake. While the cake comes in as many varieties as snowflakes, its texture ranging from dense and quick-bready to very firm and almost like a cookie (never light and airy), its batter, plain or studded with dried fruits and nuts, it is invariably made with a mix of spices not always thought of as typically French. As with just about everything having to do with *pain d'épices*, there's no hard-and-fast rule for which spices are requisite, so blends may include anise and star anise, cinnamon, ginger, cardamom, black or white pepper, nutmeg, cloves and/or coriander in varying proportions. I've even seen *pain d'épices* mixes with mustard or hot peppers. The blend is always lively and, in France, it's never farther than your local supermarket.

My version of the classic cake is made with honey and a spiced infusion, but it doesn't have rye flour as the traditional recipes often do, and it doesn't have the usual mix of spices. When I decided to make it, I went with what I had in the cupboard and fridge: ginger, lavender, orange, Sichuan peppercorns and chopped dried cherries, and ended up happy.

The texture falls close to the bread end of the spectrum (oddly, it's reminiscent of my Russian grandmother's honey cake), and the flavor is fascinating: You taste the honey first and then the spice, but since the mix is so out of the ordinary, it's unplaceable and almost haunting. Your cake may be even more fascinating than mine; much depends on the honey. The traditional *pain d'épices* is made with a strong-flavored honey, very often pine, but if you use a pale flower honey, you'll get a cake that I think of as a summery *pain d'épices*. Darker honey will make a cake that's just right for fireside nights.

But whichever honey you use, the cake will need a rest after it cools: *Pain d'épices* only begins to come into its own a day or two (or three or four) later.

1	orange	⅓ cup (113 grams) honey	
¾	cup (180 ml) water	⅓ cup (67 grams) sugar	
2	teaspoons edible dried lavender flowers	2½ cups (340 grams) all-purpose flour	
1	teaspoon Sichuan peppercorns or white or black peppercorns	1 tablespoon baking powder	
1	1-inch chunk peeled fresh ginger, cut into 4 pieces	1 cup (142 grams) plump, moist, dried cherries, coarsely chopped or snipped	
¾	stick (6 tablespoons; 3 ounces; 85 grams) unsalted butter, melted	About ½ cup (50 grams) sliced almonds, for topping (optional but very nice)	

Using a paring knife or a vegetable peeler, cut off a fat strip of orange zest and toss it into a small saucepan; hold on to the rest of the orange. Add the water, lavender, peppercorns and ginger to the pan and bring to a boil. Remove from the heat, cover and allow the mix to infuse for at least 1 hour (or for up to 3 hours, if it's more convenient).

Center a rack in the oven and preheat the oven to 300 degrees F. Pull out an insulated baking sheet or stack two regular baking sheets one on top of the other. Line the (top) sheet with parchment paper or a silicone baking mat. Butter or spray an 8½-×-4½-inch loaf pan and line it with a piece of parchment paper or foil, leaving an overhang on the two long sides of the pan to serve as handles when you unmold the cake.

Strain the spiced water (you'll have about ½ cup) into a small bowl and discard the solids. Stir the melted butter and honey into the water.

Put the sugar in a large bowl and grate the remaining orange zest over it. Using your fingers, rub the zest into the sugar until it is moist and fragrant. Add the flour and baking powder and whisk to thoroughly blend the ingredients.

Give the liquid ingredients a stir to make sure they're blended, then pour them over the dry ingredients. Working with a sturdy flexible spatula, mix everything together gently and quickly—the batter will be thick and spongy, much like a muffin batter. Stir in the dried cherries. Scrape the batter into the lined loaf pan, using the tip of your spatula to get the batter into the corners of the pan. If you're finishing the cake with sliced almonds, scatter them over the top of the cake, patting them down lightly to glue them to the batter. Place the pan on the baking sheet(s).

Bake the cake for 75 to 85 minutes, or until a tester plunged deep into the cake comes out with dry crumbs. Transfer the loaf pan to a rack and allow the cake to cool for 20 minutes.

Lift the cake out of the pan. I leave it in its paper or foil to cool, but you can carefully peel it away now, if you'd like. Allow the cake to cool completely on the rack, then wrap it well in a double layer of plastic film. Set it aside for a day or two to ripen before serving.

Bonne Idée

You can easily vary the cake by changing the kind of honey or the types of dried fruit you use. Chopped dried apricots or prunes, raisins, pieces of figs or even chopped dates are all good, singly or together. You could also add toasted chopped nuts. Another alternative is to play around with the spices you use for the infusion; or you might even forgo the spices and go with strong tea instead. This is a cake to have fun with and make your own.

Touch-of-Crunch Chocolate Cake

Makes 12 servings

SERVING: Cakes like this are usually best served at room temperature, but this one shines brightly straight from the fridge—a boon if you're having a party and want to get dessert done early. Of course it can be dressed up, but it's also lovely with nothing more than a dusting of cocoa or confectioners' sugar. If you're finishing the cake with whipped cream or ice cream, you might sprinkle a few black sesame seeds over the cream, but I wouldn't—I like surprises too much to spoil them for others. It is also good with poached cherries (page 376) or with the syrup from Laurent's Slow-Roasted Spiced Pineapple (page 333). It's a most companionable cake.

STORING: The cake will keep, covered, at room temperature for up to 2 days and refrigerated for up to 3 days. If you'd like to freeze it, wrap it airtight; it will keep for up to 2 months (defrost still wrapped).

ACROSS BETWEEN a flourless chocolate cake and a dense mousse, this cake is fudgy at the edges and almost pudding-like in the center. It's got crunch on top, crackle inside and voluptuousness everywhere. It's the kind of sweet you can make at the last minute and serve with a flourish. Because it is baked in a pie plate, it looks rather plain Jane, but as the old adage says, looks can be deceiving. For starters, there's the chocolate—dark and rich and blended with butter, eggs and caramelish brown sugar. And then there's a surprise: a touch of crunch. The cake could have had, as American brownies do, coarsely chopped nuts or even chocolate chips, but I wanted something unexpected and tiny, something that pops with flavor, which is why I decided on black sesame seeds. Their color hides them in the cake, and their flavor is very good with chocolate. If you have a problem finding black sesame seeds, you can use poppy seeds or cocoa nibs, also dark and delicious with chocolate.

1¾ sticks (14 tablespoons; 7 ounces; 198 grams) unsalted butter, cut into 10 chunks	5 large eggs, at room temperature
7 ounces (198 grams) bittersweet chocolate, coarsely chopped	1¼ cups (250 grams) packed light brown sugar
	1 tablespoon all-purpose flour or 2 teaspoons cornstarch
	3 tablespoons black sesame seeds, poppy seeds or cocoa nibs

Center a rack in the oven and preheat the oven to 400 degrees F. Generously butter a 9-inch ceramic or glass pie plate and put it on a baking sheet for easy in-and-out-of-the-oven transport.

Toss the chunks of butter into a heatproof bowl set over a saucepan of simmering water. Add the chopped chocolate and heat, stirring frequently, just until melted. You don't want the butter and chocolate to get so hot that they separate; you should have a thick, shiny mixture. Transfer the bowl to the counter and let it cool while you work on the rest of the batter.

Working in a large bowl with a whisk, beat the eggs for a minute, until broken up and blended. Add the brown sugar, sprinkle the flour or cornstarch over the sugar and whisk until everything is smooth, about 2 minutes. Pour the chocolate mixture into the batter and whisk gently to blend it evenly. Stir in the sesame seeds, poppy seeds or cocoa nibs. Rap the bowl against the counter a couple of times to debubble the batter, then pour the batter into the pie plate.

Bake for 28 to 32 minutes. The top will rise and crack—it will sink as it cools—and a bamboo skewer inserted into the center of the cake will come out almost clean. The center of the cake is mousse-like, so it will seem under-baked, and that's fine. Transfer the pie plate to a rack and let the cake cool to room temperature.

Carrément Chocolat, The Simple Loaf

Makes 8 servings

SERVING: I think the cake is best cut into thick slices. It can be served straight-up plain for an afternoon or brunch treat, but it's very nice served with crème fraîche or lightly sweetened whipped cream sprinkled with cocoa nibs.

STORING: The cake will keep at room temperature for up to 4 days—make sure it's well wrapped—or it can be wrapped airtight and frozen for up to 2 months; let it defrost overnight in the refrigerator, still in its wrapper.

IF SOMETHING IS completely, absolutely, incontrovertibly itself, whether it's wholly good or bad, the French describe it as *carrément*, or straight-out whatever it is. In this case, what's *carrément* is chocolate and the Carrément Chocolat is a cake created by Pierre Hermé. The root of *carrément* is *carré*, or "square," so Pierre's cake was made in that shape and it was intensely chocolaty. His first *carrément chocolat* was an elegant gâteau that kept its pleasures hidden under a cloak of glossy glaze. After that, there were bonbons and loaf cakes and sweets playing variations on the theme.

Since Pierre has published this recipe in one form or another from fancy to plain, I decided to play topsy-turvy with his idea and start with this plain cake, then jump to a fancy one (page 175).

This cake is a simple loaf. It's got a tender texture enhanced by a sugar-syrup soak, and it's speckled with salted chocolate chunks: dark chocolate that you melt, salt, freeze and then chop. Since the day I learned this technique, I haven't stopped using it. For anyone who loves the combination of chocolate and salt, it's a gift.

FOR THE SALTED CHOCOLATE
- 6 ounces (170 grams) bittersweet chocolate, coarsely chopped
- ½ teaspoon fleur de sel (or ¼ teaspoon fine sea salt)

FOR THE CAKE
- 1 cup (136 grams) all-purpose flour
- ⅓ cup (28 grams) unsweetened cocoa powder
- 1½ teaspoons baking powder
- Pinch of fine sea salt
- 13 tablespoons (6½ ounces; 184 grams) unsalted butter, at room temperature
- 1 cup (200 grams) sugar
- 4 large eggs, at room temperature

FOR THE SYRUP
- ½ cup (120 ml) water
- 2½ tablespoons sugar

TO MAKE THE SALTED CHOCOLATE: Line a mini loaf pan or two or three custard cups or muffin tin cups with plastic film. Melt the chocolate (you can do this in a double boiler or a microwave oven), and when it is perfectly smooth, stir in the fleur de sel. Pour the chocolate into the loaf pan or divide it among the other containers—you want a layer of chocolate that's between ¼ and ½ inch thick. Freeze for at least 1 hour (*when the chocolate is solid, you can wrap it airtight and freeze for up to 1 month*). For this recipe to succeed, the chocolate must be very cold and very firm.

TO MAKE THE CAKE: Center a rack in the oven and preheat the oven to 350 degrees F. Pull out an insulated baking sheet or stack two regular baking sheets one on top of the other. Line the (top) baking sheet with parchment paper or a silicone baking mat. Butter an 8½-×-4½-inch loaf pan, dust with flour and tap out the excess. Set the pan on the baking sheet(s).

Put the flour, cocoa, baking powder and salt in a food processor and pulse several times to blend thoroughly. Turn the dry ingredients out onto a sheet of parchment or wax paper. (Don't bother cleaning the food processor bowl now.)

Cut the butter into pieces and toss it into the food processor, along with the sugar and eggs. Pulse a few times to get things going, then process for 6—count 'em, 6—minutes, scraping down the bowl a couple of times, until the mixture is light, liquefied and full of bubbles. Gently scrape the mixture into a large bowl.

Meanwhile, remove the salted chocolate from the freezer, peel away the plastic, and using a heavy chef's knife, cut it into cubes that are ¼ to ½ inch on a side. The chocolate melts quickly, so work with alacrity and immediately return the cubes to the freezer.

Add the dry ingredients to the butter mixture and, using a large flexible spatula, fold them in gently but thoroughly. Drop the chocolate cubes into the bowl, stir to distribute them as evenly as you can and then scrape the batter into the loaf pan.

Bake the cake for about 50 minutes, or until a bamboo skewer inserted deep into the center comes out dry. Transfer the cake to a rack and let it rest for 5 minutes, then unmold it onto the rack and turn it right side up. Set the baking sheet aside.

TO MAKE THE SYRUP: Bring the water and sugar to a boil in a small saucepan, stirring to dissolve the sugar. Remove from the heat.

TO FINISH THE CAKE: Put the hot cake, still on the rack, on the parchment- or silicone-lined baking sheet. Brush the syrup over the top and sides of the cake, working slowly and allowing it to soak into the cake. Cool the cake completely on the rack.

Granola Cake

Makes 16 servings

SERVING: I think of this as a snack cake and nibble it out of hand, but that's so not French. When I serve it in Paris, I cut it into 2-inch squares, put them on plates, top with ice cream and serve with forks and spoons.

STORING: The cake is very moist and will keep, wrapped in plastic film, at room temperature for about 4 days. You can also wrap it airtight and freeze it for up to 2 months; defrost it still wrapped.

I CREATED THIS CAKE to do something fun and unusual with the granola I was making for friends (page 408), and now I just keep making it, whether I have homemade granola or not. Naturally, the cake's best when the granola is great, but, having made it with granola *ordinaire* on both sides of the ocean, I can promise you that as long as you don't choose a granola with a lot of spices (or one with hard pieces of dried fruit), you'll have a cake you'll love. You'll also have one that will be surprising. The chocolate provides an unexpected spot of flavor, as does the coconut, but the real puzzler is the granola. Once baked into the soft, chewy cake, it's hard to identify, because it loses its crunch, though it keeps its wholesome whole-grain flavor. As all-American as this treat is, I can't quite get my French friends to give us Yankees full credit—they think it's related to the *moelleux*, a soft cake with a large extended family. If the *moelleux* family wants to adopt my cake, I'm happy to cede both maternity and national pride.

1 cup (136 grams) all-purpose flour	½ cup shredded coconut, sweetened (60 grams) or unsweetened (40 grams)
¼ teaspoon baking powder	1 stick (8 tablespoons; 4 ounces; 113 grams) unsalted butter, at room temperature
¼ teaspoon baking soda	
¼ teaspoon ground cinnamon (if granola is not spiced) Pinch of freshly grated nutmeg (if granola is not spiced)	½ cup (100 grams) packed light brown sugar
	¼ cup (50 grams) sugar
1 cup (120 grams) granola, preferably homemade (page 408)	1 large egg, at room temperature
4 ounces (113 grams) bittersweet, milk or white chocolate, finely chopped	1½ teaspoons pure vanilla extract
	¼ teaspoon fine sea salt

Center a rack in the oven and preheat the oven to 325 degrees F. Butter an 8-inch square baking pan and line the bottom with parchment or wax paper.

Whisk the flour, baking powder, baking soda and cinnamon and nutmeg, if you're using them, together in a small bowl. Toss the granola, chocolate and coconut together in another bowl.

Working in the bowl of a stand mixer fitted with the paddle attachment, or in a large bowl with a hand mixer, beat the butter at low-medium speed for 2 to 3 minutes, or until soft and creamy. Add both sugars and beat for 2 minutes. Add the egg and beat until the mixture is smooth, about 2 minutes more. Beat in the vanilla and salt. Reduce the speed to low and add the flour mixture, mixing only until it disappears into the batter. Add the granola mixture, again mixing just until incorporated. Scrape the batter into the prepared pan, smooth the top and jiggle the pan a little to make sure that the batter gets into the corners.

Bake the cake for 35 to 40 minutes, until the top is honey brown and sugar-crackly; a skewer inserted into the center should come out clean. Transfer the pan to a rack and let rest for 10 minutes, then run a table knife around the edges of the cake and unmold it onto the rack; invert and cool to room temperature on the rack.

MEASURING FLOUR
French and American: Cups vs. Scales

You can't get much more basic than flour, and yet it's the ingredient that has caused me the most problems as I travel back and forth between America and France and bake. I have fiddled with my American recipes to get them to work in my Paris kitchen and I've fiddled with my French recipes to get them to work in the United States.

In general, French flour has less protein than American flour. And sometimes French flour seems to be milled finer than ours. These two factors mean that even when you weigh the flour rather than measure it in cups, you won't get a perfect one to one ratio. I've never had a failure when I've used one flour or the other, but what I bake is never exactly the same from coury to country.

Finally I decided to carry American flour with me when I go to France. It adds five pounds to my carry-on and ten minutes to my security search at the airport, but it means that when I see something delicious in a French pastry shop, I can go home and figure out how to make it, knowing that it will work when I test it again across the Atlantic.

If I measure flour by volume (with cups and spoons), I always do it the same way—the way Julia Child insisted on. With a table fork or knife, I reach into the flour bin and stir the flour around to aerate it; if it is compacted (as it usually is in a bag), you'll get a too-heavy measure if you don't stir things up. Dip the measuring cup into the bin and scoop up a heaping cupful—don't shake it or press on it. To level it, sweep the back of a table knife across the cup, sliding the knife against the rim.

I tested all the recipes in this book with both bleached and unbleached all-purpose flour, so choose whichever you prefer.

Finally, I use 136 grams as the metric weight for 1 cup of all-purpose flour, which I arrived at by measuring 10 cups of flour, weighing each one and taking the average. It seemed the most sensible way to account for the inevitability of individual differences.

Alsatian Christmas Bread

For all the pastry shops I've visited in Alsace—and for all the Alsatian pastry shops I've gone into in Paris—I'd never tasted the specialty that is showcased in each one, *baerewecke*. It wasn't until I had it at a dinner in Paris that I realized that I'd been missing something wonderful.

I'm fearful of saying that *baerewecke* springs from the same source as fruit-cake, because I don't want to send you scurrying, there's no denying that the two share a family resemblance. But where fruitcake is big and heavy and loaded with rum or whiskey, *baerewecke* (or at least my version), while still appropriately dense, is slender and nonalcoholic, chock-full of dried fruits, nuts and spices—it's a cake with no butter, wheat flour, sugar or eggs! While I probably couldn't get a full-blooded Alsatian to agree with me, I think that this very old-fashioned *baerewecke* is less like a fruitcake and more like the best energy bar imaginable.

I make my *baerewecke* with dried pears—the only must-have in the recipe (the translation of *baerewecke* from the Alsatian dialect is "pear bread")—dried apricots, apples, figs (I love the seeds here), prunes and raisins (you can use dried cherries or cranberries), chopped walnuts and, to hold it all together, almond flour. (If you want to add other fruits or use different fruits, of course you can; see Bonne Idée.) The fruits and walnuts are soaked in a mix of orange or apple juice and spices, drained, blended with the almond flour and then shaped into two slim logs. It's very important that the logs be as compact as possible (see page 61), so that you'll be able to cut them neatly after they're baked. I'm told that in Alsace, they are wrapped and tucked away to ripen for a couple of months. I've never done this, in part because I don't have that kind of patience, and in large measure because I never plan that far in advance. Happily, they're delicious a day after they're made.

Baerewecke is traditionally served at Christmas and New Year's, but it's so beloved and so much a part of the culture that I've seen pâtisseries in Alsace display it right next to their strawberry tarts in June. And I understand: chez moi, it's a year-round treat.

A WORD ON PLANNING AHEAD: The fruit needs to macerate for 1 hour but can soak another hour or so, if that's more convenient for you. Also, after the logs are baked, you want to let them age for at least a day (preferably a week or more before slicing and serving).

Makes 2 logs; about 20 servings

SERVING: The *baerewecke* should be cut with a serrated knife into thick or thin slices. It is good eaten out of hand as a snack (slice it thick), with cheese (I like to serve it with cheese as a combination cheese platter/dessert) or with fruit curd, marmalade or jam at breakfast or brunch. If the bread has been refrigerated, cut it while it's cold (it's easier to cut then) and let it come to room temperature to serve.

STORING: Well wrapped, in wax or parchment paper and then in foil, the *baerewecke* can be refrigerated for up to 1 month.

1 cup (240 ml) orange or apple juice or apple cider

3 points from 1 star anise pod

1 short piece cinnamon stick

1 clove or a pinch of ground cloves

¾ teaspoon ground cinnamon

½ teaspoon ground ginger

¼ teaspoon ground cardamom

Pinch of freshly ground black pepper

6 (100 grams) large plump, moist dried pears

15 (75 grams) plump, moist dried apricots

7 (75 grams) plump, moist dried figs

7 (50 grams) plump, moist pitted prunes

½ cup packed (50 grams) moist dried apple rings

½ cup packed (about 53 grams) plump, moist raisins, dried cherries or dried cranberries

½ cup (60 grams) chopped walnuts

1½ cups (150 grams) almond flour

Pour the juice or cider into a small saucepan and stir in all the spices, including the pepper. Bring the mixture to a boil and let it simmer for 1 minute, then turn off the heat, cover the pan and set aside.

The dried fruit needs to be cut into slivers (not the raisins or cranberries, but if you're using cherries and they're large, you should cut them). I prefer to cut thin pieces of fruit about ⅛ inch across, but while you want slender slivers, it makes no difference if some are skinnier and some fatter. As you cut the fruit, toss it into a medium heatproof bowl. Add the chopped walnuts and mix everything together—a good job to do with your hands.

If the spiced juice has cooled down, rewarm it. Strain the juice over the fruit; discard the whole spices. Stir the juice into the fruit, cover the bowl and let the fruit macerate for 1 hour, giving it a stir once or twice. (If it's more convenient for you, you can leave the fruit and juice to macerate for another hour or two.)

When you're ready to continue, center a rack in the oven and preheat the oven to 300 degrees F. Pull out an insulated baking sheet or stack two regular baking sheets one on top of the other. Line the (top) baking sheet with parchment paper or a silicone baking mat.

Set a strainer over a bowl, spoon the fruit into the strainer and cover the fruit with a piece of plastic film. Press your palm against the plastic to squeeze out as much of the juice as you can; there won't be much, because the fruit will have sopped up most all of it, so press hard (discard the liquid). Wipe out the first bowl, scrape the fruit back into it and add the almond flour. Using a sturdy spatula, stir the heavy, sticky mixture until the flour is evenly incorporated.

Because the dough is sticky, I shape it on a piece of parchment or wax paper. Divide it in half and roll one half into a log that's 7 inches long. Don't worry about the diameter; get the length and the diameter will follow. Repeat

Bonne Idée

You can play around with the fruits as long as they're plump and moist and you cut them into slivers. To change things up no matter what fruits you're using, add a small amount of candied orange peel (page 459), cut very thin, or even some slivered crystallized ginger or ginger in syrup. Finally, you can do as many Alsatians do and add 1 to 2 tablespoons of kirsch (cherry eau-de-vie) to the fruit mix after you've added the warm juice.

with the remaining dough. When the logs are formed, tighten them using the paper-and-ruler technique (see page 61). The tightened logs will be about 8 inches long (maybe a bit longer); discard the paper. Place the logs on the baking sheet(s), leaving some room between them.

Bake for 90 minutes, or until the logs are deep golden brown, a little crusty and slightly firm. Transfer the baking sheet(s) to a cooling rack and let the logs cool completely. These are slow to bake and slow to cool. When they are entirely cool, wrap each log in parchment or wax paper and then in aluminum foil. Leave them out at room temperature for at least 1 day before slicing.

MOIST DRIED FRUIT

Every time I write the words "moist dried fruit," I shake my head at the oxymoron. But unless your dried fruit is moist, what you bake won't be nearly as good as it would had you taken the time for an extra step called plumping. Hard, wizened fruit will never become softer in the oven, and it just might ruin your sweet.

"Plump" is a baker's term for adding moisture to dried fruit.

If your fruit is hard and dry, you can plump it by putting it in a bowl of very hot tap water, by giving it a quick dunk in boiling water or by steaming it. (Depending on the recipe, you can also plump fruit in wine or juice.) Any way you do it, remember to pat the fruit dry before mixing it into your soon-to-be delectable dessert.

LOGGING:
How to Get Compact, Even Rolls of Dough and Cake

When you're making logs of cookie dough or rolling up a bûche de Noël, you want to get logs that are as tight as possible and, particularly in the case of cookies, free of air pockets. (It's the pockets that give you holes in your cookies.)

To tighten your logs, you'll need a large sheet of parchment (my choice) or wax paper and a ruler. With a short edge of the paper toward you on the counter, place the cookie or cake log horizontally on the paper about one third up from the edge closest to you. Fold the top portion of the paper over the log.

Grab the ruler with one hand and grab the part of the parchment that's closest to you (the bottom part) with the other. Wedge the ruler against the bottom of the log. Push the ruler under the log at the same time that you pull the bottom paper toward you. Don't be afraid to put a little muscle into the pulling and pushing; it will help you get a firm log. If your log is longer than your ruler, move the ruler along the log so that you can make it more compact.

Lift the paper off the dough and admire your work—for all the years that I've been doing this, I still think of it as a party trick.

FANCY CAKES

Moka Dupont

Makes 8 servings

SERVING: Bernard would tell you that the cake needs nothing but birthday candles; I suggest some coffee ice cream.

STORING: The cake can be kept covered in the refrigerator for up to 3 days or wrapped airtight and frozen for up to 2 months; defrost, still wrapped, in the refrigerator.

SOON AFTER I MET MY FRIEND BERNARD COLLET, about thirty years ago, he began to tell me about Moka Dupont, the cake he always requested for his birthday when he was a child. He'd say it was simple; his wife, Martine, would shrug and mumble something about it being too simple to even talk about; and the subject of Moka Dupont would get dropped for a while. But only for a while.

Finally, I stamped my whisks and insisted on being given the recipe and, a week later, Martine arrived at our apartment with a Moka Dupont on a platter. The moka part was obvious: The cake was flavored with chocolate and coffee. The Dupont part less so: In Bernard's family, the cake carried the name of their neighbor Madame Dupont, because she was the one who gave them the recipe.

Was it simple? Yes! It was an icebox cake constructed of store-bought cookies, dunked in sweetened espresso and layered with a quickly made buttercream. Was it delicious? Yes!

Since Martine gave me the recipe, I've made a little discovery that I'm sure she knows and has kept a secret from Bernard: Mme Dupont did not invent this cake—it's as common in France as chocolate-cookie-and-whipped-cream icebox cakes are in America. But please, mum's the word.

A WORD ON THE COOKIES: The cake was created for Thé Brun cookies, and Bernard insisted that it should never, ever be made with anything but. However, I can't find Thé Brun in American supermarkets, so I use store-bought Petit Beurre.

1	very fresh large egg, preferably organic (it will not be cooked)	½	cup (120 ml) hot espresso (made fresh or with instant espresso powder)
1	stick (8 tablespoons; 4 ounces; 113 grams) unsalted butter, at room temperature	24	Petit Beurre (or Thé Brun) cookies (one 7-ounce/ 198-gram package)
½	cup (100 grams) plus 1 tablespoon sugar		Grated chocolate, for decoration
3	ounces (85 grams) bittersweet chocolate, melted and cooled		

Before you start assembling the cake, decide on the size you want. I make a slender cake that's 2 cookies wide (I place the cookies end to end) and 4 cookies long. This is how Mme Dupont did it, but you can make a tall tower or small individual cakes. Choose a plate on which to both build and serve the cake. Cut four strips of parchment or wax paper and arrange them in a rectangle, leaving the center of the plate bare. The paper, which will be removed before serving, will protect the plate from errant frosting.

To make the buttercream frosting, separate the egg, putting the yolk in a cup and the white in a small bowl. Whip the white with a whisk until it holds soft peaks—a short but strenuous exercise (you can use a mixer if you prefer). Give the yolk a quick whisking, just to break it up. Set the egg aside for the moment.

Put the butter in a medium bowl and beat it with a flexible spatula until smooth. Add ½ cup of the sugar and beat until it's thoroughly incorporated. Whisk the egg white again, pour the yolk over the white and give them both another quick whipping with the whisk, then add them to the butter bowl, stirring to blend. Pour in the melted chocolate and, stirring and folding, mix until the frosting is homogeneous. This buttercream is not meant to be perfectly smooth. Taste it, and you'll feel sugar grains on your tongue— that's the way it's meant to be.

Dissolve the remaining 1 tablespoon sugar in the hot espresso and pour the espresso into a wide, shallow bowl.

One by one, dip the cookies into the espresso: Drop a cookie into the espresso, count 3 seconds, flip it over, count 3 seconds more and place it on the serving plate so that there is a small strip of parchment or wax paper underneath the edge of the cookie on all four sides—then, when you remove the strips, the plate will be clean and ready to serve. Continue until you have your first layer of cookies in place.

Using a small offset spatula or a table knife, spread one third of the buttercream over the cookies, working the cream to the edges. Build two more layers of dunked cookies and smoothed buttercream; if you'd like, you can reserve a little of the buttercream and use it to cover the sides of the cake, but I leave them bare and ruffly because I think they're pretty that way.

Top the last layer of buttercream with grated chocolate. Refrigerate the cake for at least 3 hours before serving; when the frosting is set, carefully pull away the paper strips.

Betty's Chocoholic Cake

T HE WORD "CHOCOHOLIC" is a giveaway that Betty Edry, the cake's creator, has spent time away from her home in Paris. Chocoholic is not a usual name for a dessert in France—it hovers too close to feelings of guilt for the French, who associate food with nothing but pleasure. But this cake was Betty's bestseller when she was a caterer in London, and every French person who's ever had it has polished it off, guilt-free. It is totally a chocolate cake and so it must be made with very fine chocolate. Most important, it must be chocolate you love—since the flavor is barely muted by the cake's other ingredients. While Betty recommends making the cake with a chocolate that has at least 70 percent cacao, and the ganache filling and frosting with a chocolate with a slightly lower percentage of cocoa solids, I use Valrhona Manjari, a chocolate with 64 percent cacao with flavors of spice and fruit, kind of like wine, for both the cake and the ganache.

This is a big cake, the kind you make for a crowd when there's something wonderful to celebrate. And it deserves to be fussed over. Betty finishes it with white chocolate curls, but it's also lovely with a thick topcoat of whipped cream.

The cake is composed of three layers of chocolate *biscuit*, which has a texture not unlike that of a cakey brownie. In fact, you can use a single layer of it as a stand-in for brownies or as a base for a strawberry shortcake, an ice cream cake or a hot fudge sundae. Two or three layers are also luscious filled and finished with a whipped cream or marshmallow frosting. Since the layers can be frozen, you might want to keep some handy.

Makes about 16 servings

SERVING: Not surprisingly, something with this much chocolate cries out for contrast. I like the cake best with lightly sweetened whipped cream, a spoonful of crème fraîche or a scoop of vanilla ice cream, but it's also good with fresh berries, a berry coulis (page 449) or both.

STORING: You can make the layers ahead and keep them well wrapped at room temperature overnight or freeze them for up to 2 months. Once the cake is filled and frosted, it can be kept lightly covered at room temperature for about 3 days or frozen for up to 2 months. To freeze the cake, put it on a cutting board and freeze it until solid, wrapping it well. Allow the cake, still wrapped, to defrost overnight in the refrigerator.

FOR THE LAYERS

3½ sticks (14 ounces; 397 grams) unsalted butter, cut into chunks

14 ounces (397 grams) bittersweet chocolate, finely chopped

6 large eggs, at room temperature

1½ cups (300 grams) sugar

1¼ cups (170 grams) all-purpose flour

FOR THE GANACHE

9 ounces (255 grams) bittersweet chocolate, finely chopped

1¼ cups (300 ml) heavy cream

FOR THE DECORATION (OPTIONAL)

A block or bar of premium-quality white chocolate, at warm room temperature

TO MAKE THE LAYERS: If your oven can comfortably hold three 9-inch round cake pans on one rack, center a rack in your oven; if it can't, position two racks to divide the oven in thirds. Preheat the oven to 350 degrees F.

Generously butter three 9-inch round cake pans, dust with flour, tap out the excess and line the bottom of the pans with parchment paper.

Put the butter in a heatproof bowl set over a saucepan of simmering water. Scatter the chopped chocolate over the butter and let the ingredients melt slowly, stirring from time to time, then remove the bowl from the saucepan.

Working in the bowl of a stand mixer fitted with the paddle attachment, or in a large bowl with a hand mixer, beat the eggs and sugar together at medium speed for about 3 minutes, or until the mixture lightens in color. Reduce the mixer speed to low and gradually mix in the flour. Scrape the bowl and, still on low speed, mix in the chocolate-butter mixture. The batter will have the tempting look of a perfect chocolate mousse. Divide it evenly among the cake pans.

Bake the cakes for 16 to 19 minutes. After about 10 minutes, rotate the pans top to bottom and front to back if you're baking on two racks, or front to back if you're baking on one. When the cakes are done, their tops will be dry and crinkly and a thin skewer or toothpick inserted in their centers will come out slightly moist or with just a few crumbs. Transfer the cakes to a rack and let rest for 3 minutes, then run a table knife around the edges and unmold them onto racks. Gentyl peel away the paper and allow the cakes to cool to room temperature. (*The cakes can be wrapped airtight and kept at room temperature overnight or frozen for up to 2 months.*)

TO MAKE THE GANACHE: Place the chopped chocolate in a heatproof bowl. Bring the heavy cream to a boil in a small saucepan. Pour half of the cream into the center of the chocolate, wait 30 seconds and then, using a small flexible spatula or whisk and starting in the center of the bowl, stir the cream into the chocolate in small concentric circles. When the cream and chocolate form an emulsion—you'll know, because the chocolate at the center of the bowl will become dark and glossy—pour in the remainder of the cream. Once again, starting at the center and moving in ever-widening concentric circles, stir the cream into the chocolate. Be patient. By the time your last circle reaches the edges of the bowl, you should have a thick, smooth, glossy ganache.

Leave the ganache at room temperature, stirring it frequently, until it is thick enough to spread on the cake, about 40 minutes. If your kitchen is warm it might take longer; don't rush it.

TO ASSEMBLE THE CAKE: Set one layer right side up on a cake plate. Cut four strips of wax or parchment paper and slip the strips under the cake to protect the plate. Spoon about one quarter of the ganache onto the center of the cake and, using an offset icing spatula or a knife, smooth the ganache over the top of the cake. Top with a second layer, again right side up, and cover it with the same amount of ganache. Place the last layer flat side up on top of the cake and use the remaining ganache to cover the sides and top of the cake. The cake is officially finished and ready to serve, but you might want to decorate it.

TO DECORATE THE CAKE: If you'd like to finish the cake the way Betty does, use a vegetable peeler to shave curls of white chocolate off the block or bar onto a plate or a piece of parchment or wax paper. You'll get the prettiest and longest curls if your chocolate is warm; cold chocolate is brittle and will crack before it curls. (If your chocolate is cold and your nerves are steady, you can hold the chocolate about a foot above a burner and pass the chocolate quickly over the heat until it's just slightly warm but not melted.) Then, if the shavings seem soft to you, refrigerate them for a couple of minutes, or until they're firm enough for you to lift them easily. Arrange the curls on top of the cake.

CHOCOLATE

··

The chocolate of choice among the French is bittersweet, and I admit to being as partial to it as they are: My house chocolate is bittersweet and it's what I use in my daily baking.

But not all bittersweets are truly bitter, and some are even sweet—and I believe the only thing that's a must when you're baking with chocolate is to choose one you love. If you prefer a semisweet chocolate, you can use it in any of my recipes that call for bittersweet.

What you shouldn't do is substitute milk chocolate—America's favorite—for bittersweet, or vice versa. Nor, when a recipe calls for white chocolate, should you swap it for anything else. Both milk and white chocolate contain a high percentage of milk solids, a low (or in the case of white chocolate, zero) percentage of cocoa solids and a fair amount of sugar, so they behave differently from semisweet or bittersweet chocolate. However, if you're using the chocolate as a chip or a chunky add-in, follow your fancy—nothing in the recipe's chemistry will be affected.

Whatever the chocolate, I hope you'll use one made with cocoa butter (not any other kind of fat). Also, I hope you'll base your choice more on flavor than on the percentage of cacao (chocolate liquor). All French chocolates and more and more American chocolates list the percentage of cacao on their labels, but since chocolate varies widely from manufacturer to manufacturer and so much depends on how the cacao bean was grown, harvested, dried, fermented and roasted, percentages are of secondary importance to flavor. Once you've found a chocolate maker you like, you can find the cocoa percentages you prefer within the company's offerings.

Chocolate and cocoa percentages can be a little complicated, but basically, what's not chocolate liquor in a bar is milk solids and sugar. (Unsweetened chocolate is pure cacao and so bitter that it will make you grimace—it's not meant to be eaten out of hand.) In general, the higher the cocoa percentage, the stronger (and perhaps more bitter) the chocolate flavor.

When you're shopping for white and milk chocolate, however, it is worth looking at percentages. White chocolate gets its flavor from cocoa butter and it should have at least 30 percent cocoa butter. As for milk chocolate, it can have as little as 10 percent cacao, making it more sweet than chocolaty. Look for milk chocolate with at least 30 percent cocoa solids—it will be revelatory.

Sunday in Paris Chocolate Cake

Makes 12 servings

SERVING: If you'd like, you can certainly serve whipped cream or ice cream alongside this treat, but you don't have to—there's enough flavor and texture to make it a standout on its own.

STORING: Wrapped well, the cake(s) will keep for up to 2 days at room temperature or up to 2 months in the freezer; defrost, still wrapped, in the refrigerator overnight.

UN DIMANCHE À PARIS—"A Sunday in Paris"—is the name of a coolly crafted pastry shop on an old cobblestone street off the Boulevard Saint-Germain. Like the store, the pastries are modern and chic, and even the simplest cakes, like this chocolate loaf, are given fillips and flourishes that make them whimsical and even more winning.

At the pâtisserie, this cake is made in a special long, very slender loaf pan; it emerges looking more supermodel than *grand-mère*. It comes packed in a snug box, and it's topped with whole roasted peanuts and squares of caramel candy (which are delicious but difficult to negotiate).

Thanks to a combination of cocoa and a micro portion of bittersweet ganache, the cake itself is dark brown, and it's lightly flavored with an ingredient rarely found in French pastry: creamy peanut butter! In fact, peanut butter is used so infrequently in France, a crazy-for-Nutella country, that it took me days to turn up a jar so that I could try the recipe for the first time in my Paris kitchen.

This is my adaptation of the shop's specialty. My favorite way to make it is to spoon the batter into small rectangular molds, each holding a quarter cup, and then, when the cakes are baked and cooled, to dip their tops in ganache and speckle them with chopped toasted peanuts and chocolate. Done this way, they teeter between adorable and sophisticated. If you don't have rectangular molds, you can use a muffin tin or make a single loaf cake.

FOR THE CAKE(S)

- ¾ cup (102 grams) all-purpose flour
- 3 tablespoons unsweetened cocoa powder
- 1½ teaspoons baking powder
- ¼ teaspoon fine sea salt
- 1 ounce (28 grams) bittersweet or semisweet chocolate, finely chopped
- ¼ cup (60 ml) whole milk
- ¾ stick (6 tablespoons; 3 ounces; 85 grams) unsalted butter, at room temperature
- 2½ tablespoons creamy peanut butter (not natural)
- ⅓ cup (67 grams) sugar
- 2 large eggs, at room temperature, lightly beaten
- 3 tablespoons roasted salted peanuts, toasted and very finely chopped (optional)

FOR THE TOPPING

- 3 ounces (85 grams) semisweet or bittersweet chocolate
- 3 tablespoons heavy cream
- 3 tablespoons roasted salted peanuts, toasted and coarsely chopped

TO MAKE THE CAKE(S): Center a rack in the oven and preheat the oven to 325 degrees F. You can bake the batter in a dozen 2-ounce rectangular financier or mini loaf molds (mine measure 3 × 1¼ × 1¼ inches), a muffin tin or an 8½-×-4-inch loaf pan. No matter what you use, butter the pan(s) and dust with flour, tapping out the excess. (This isn't necessary if you're using silicone molds.) Set the pan(s) on a baking sheet lined with parchment paper or a silicone baking mat.

Sift the flour, cocoa, baking powder and salt together into a small bowl and whisk to blend.

Put the chopped chocolate in a heatproof bowl. Bring the milk to a boil, pour it over the chocolate and wait for 30 seconds, then gently stir the mixture until the chocolate is melted and the ganache is smooth.

Working in the bowl of a stand mixer fitted with the paddle attachment, or in a large bowl with a hand mixer, beat the butter, peanut butter and sugar together on medium speed until smooth, about 2 minutes. Add the eggs in a slow, steady stream and beat for 2 minutes more. Reduce the mixer speed to low and add the dry ingredients, mixing only until they disappear into the batter. Scrape down the bowl. Give the ganache a last stir to make certain that it's homogeneous and then, with the mixer on low speed, add it to the batter, mixing until blended. Finally, mix in the peanuts, if you're using them. Spoon, scoop or scrape the batter into the pan(s).

Bake mini loaves or mini muffins for 15 to 18 minutes, the loaf for 30 to 35 minutes, or until the cake(s) is set and a skewer inserted into the center comes out clean. Transfer the cake(s) to a rack and let rest for 2 to 3 minutes, then unmold and turn right side up on the rack to cool to room temperature.

TO MAKE THE TOPPING: Finely chop 2 ounces of the chocolate. Toss it into a small bowl set over a pan of simmering water; heat just long enough to soften the chocolate.

Bring the cream to a boil. Pour it over the warm chocolate and wait for about 30 seconds, then stir gently until the ganache is smooth and shiny.

Coarsely chop the remaining 1 ounce chocolate and set aside.

TO FINISH THE CAKE(S): If you've made a single cake, put it on a sheet of parchment or wax paper and pour the ganache over the top of the cake, smoothing it with a metal spatula if necessary. (Some of the chocolate may drip down the sides—let it.) If you've made small cakes, dip the top of each cake into the ganache, let the excess chocolate drip back into the bowl and then turn the cake right side up. Sprinkle the cake(s) with the chopped chocolate and toasted peanuts and refrigerate for about 15 minutes, just until the glaze is set. Bring to room temperature before serving.

Carrément Chocolat, The Fancy Cake

THIS IS THE SIMPLE CARRÉMENT CHOCOLAT (page 52) all dressed up and ready for its star turn. It's inspired by Pierre Hermé's original—a shiny square of soft chocolate cake layered with chocolate mousse, chocolate cream, chocolate crunch and whisper-thin sheets of snap-at-a-touch chocolate, finished with a glossy chocolate glaze. My variation, which is doable by ordinary mortals, consists of a single layer of chocolate cake, cut in half, brushed with sugar syrup and filled with a chocolate pastry cream that could double as pudding. The cake is glazed with a dark chocolate ganache and topped with one of my favorite Pierre Hermé touches: salted-chocolate shards or cubes made of dark chocolate that is melted and salted, frozen and chopped.

As its name declares, the *gâteau* is straight-out chocolate. It's also a show-stopper. But for all its bravura, it's not difficult to make. The recipe is long and it looks like a lot of work, but it's really just a series of simple steps that can be spread out over a couple of days. If you're like me, you'll love having a mini project that you can pick up again and complete when you're free. And I know you'll love the reward from time well spent.

A WORD ON PLANNING: Each element in the recipe can be made ahead, and it's good to put the cake together at least a few hours before serving so that the syrup can permeate the layers, and the filling and glaze can firm in the refrigerator.

A WORD ON HEIGHT: In traditional French fashion, this cake is low. The recipe for the chocolate cake makes one very slim layer that you carefully slice in half before filling with pastry cream. If you'd like a taller gâteau, just double the recipe for the cake layer and bake it in two pans. Leave the layers intact, soaking each with the syrup and then filling them with cream. There's no need to change anything else in the recipe.

Makes 10 servings

SERVING: The cake can be served cold, straight from the refrigerator, or at cool room temperature. And it can be served on its own, as a study in chocolate intensity, or served with its opposite: something white and creamy. My favorite finish for the cake is a spoonful of unsweetened crème fraîche or sour cream.

STORING: The cake and all its components can be made ahead. The cake can be made up to 1 day ahead and kept at room temperature or frozen for up to 2 months; the chocolate shards or cubes can be frozen for up to 1 month; the filling can be refrigerated for up to 2 days; the syrup can be refrigerated for up to 1 month; and the glaze can be refrigerated for up to 5 days (then warmed before using). Once the cake is put together, it can be refrigerated for up to 1 day or frozen for up to 2 months: Freeze it until it is firm and then wrap it airtight; thaw, still wrapped, in the refrigerator overnight.

FOR THE CAKE

½ cup (68 grams) all-purpose flour

3 tablespoons unsweetened cocoa powder

¾ teaspoon baking powder
Pinch of fine sea salt

6½ tablespoons (3¼ ounces; 92 grams) unsalted butter, at room temperature

½ cup (100 grams) sugar

2 large eggs, at room temperature

FOR THE CHOCOLATE SHARDS OR CUBES

8 ounces (227 grams) bittersweet chocolate, coarsely chopped

¾ teaspoon fleur de sel or ½ teaspoon fine sea salt

1 cup (240 ml) whole milk

3 tablespoons sugar

3 large egg yolks

2½ tablespoons cornstarch

Pinch of fine sea salt

3½ ounces (99 grams)
bittersweet chocolate,
melted

1 teaspoon pure vanilla extract

½ cup (120 ml) water

2½ tablespoons sugar

4 ounces (113 grams)
bittersweet chocolate, finely
chopped

½ cup (120 ml) heavy cream

2 tablespoons sugar

2 tablespoons water

TO MAKE THE CAKE: Center a rack in the oven and preheat the oven to 350 degrees F. Butter an 8-inch round cake pan, one with sides that are at least 1½ inches high, dust with flour and tap out the excess. Put the pan on a baking sheet lined with parchment paper or a silicone baking mat.

Put the flour, cocoa, baking powder and salt in a food processor and pulse several times to blend thoroughly. Turn the dry ingredients out onto a sheet of parchment or wax paper.

Cut the butter into pieces and toss it into the processor, along with the sugar and eggs. Pulse the machine a few times to get things going, then process for 6—yes, 6—minutes, scraping down the bowl a couple of times, until the mixture is light, liquidy and full of bubbles. Gently scrape the mixture into a large bowl.

Add the dry ingredients to the bowl and, using a large flexible spatula, fold the two mixtures together gently and thoroughly. Scrape the batter into the prepared pan.

Bake the cake for about 25 minutes, or until a tester inserted into the center comes out dry. Transfer the cake to a rack and let it rest for 5 minutes, then unmold it onto the rack; turn the cake right side up to cool to room temperature on the rack. (*You can cool the cake, wrap it in plastic film and keep it at room temperature for 1 day or freeze it for up to 2 months.*)

TO MAKE THE CHOCOLATE SHARDS OR CUBES: Line a loaf pan (a mini loaf pan is good here) with plastic film. Melt the chocolate (you can do this in a heatproof bowl set over a saucepan of simmering water or in a microwave). When it is perfectly smooth, stir in the salt. Pour the salted chocolate into the loaf pan; you want to have a layer of chocolate that's a minimum of ½ inch thick. Freeze for at least 1 hour. The chocolate has to be very cold and very hard before you cut it. (*When the chocolate is solid, you can wrap it airtight and freeze it for up to 1 month.*)

TO MAKE THE FILLING: Bring the milk and 1½ tablespoons of the sugar to a boil in a medium saucepan. Remove from the heat.

Whisk the remaining 1½ tablespoons sugar, the yolks, cornstarch and salt together in a medium bowl until thick and well blended. Whisking nonstop, drizzle in about ¼ cup of the hot milk—this will temper, or warm, the yolks—and then, still whisking, add the remainder of the milk in a steady stream. Pour the mixture into the pan, put the pan over medium heat and, whisking vigorously, constantly and thoroughly (make sure to get into the edges of the pan), bring to a boil. Keep at a boil—don't stop stirring—for 1 to 2 minutes, then take the pan off the heat.

With a whisk or spatula, stir the melted chocolate into the filling, making certain that it's completely blended in. Stir in the vanilla. Scrape the filling into a bowl and press a piece of plastic film against the surface to create an airtight seal and refrigerate the filling until chilled. Or, if you want to cool it quickly, put the bowl with the filling into a larger bowl filled with ice cubes and cold water and stir occasionally until it is thoroughly chilled, about 20 minutes, then refrigerate until ready to use. (*The filling can be covered and refrigerated for up to 2 days.*)

TO MAKE THE SYRUP: Bring the water and sugar to a boil in a small saucepan, stirring to dissolve the sugar. You can use the syrup as soon as it's made or allow it to cool. (*The syrup can be kept covered in the refrigerator for up to 1 month.*)

TO SOAK AND FILL THE CAKE: Put a cooling rack on top of a rimmed baking sheet lined with foil or parchment—your drip catcher. If your cake has crowned or domed on top, use a long knife and a gentle sawing motion to even it. Cut the cake in half horizontally.

Put the top layer of the cake upside down on the rack and, using a pastry brush, brush it with half of the syrup (or use a spoon). Allow the syrup to soak in for a couple of minutes.

Remove the filling from the refrigerator and whisk it gently to loosen it. Spread the filling over the cake with a long offset icing spatula, covering the cake to the edges and smoothing the top. Top with the other layer, cut side down. Jiggle it gently so that it settles evenly on the filling, then use your spatula to smooth whatever filling has escaped—and some is sure to have. Brush the top of the cake with the remaining syrup. Refrigerate the cake for at least 1 hour. If you leave the cake on the rack-and-baking-sheet setup, it will be ready for the glazing step. (*You can cover the cake and chill it for up to 8 hours before glazing and finishing.*)

TO FINISH THE CHOCOLATE SHARDS OR CUBES: Remove the salted chocolate from the freezer, peel away the plastic film and put the chocolate block on a cutting board. Working quickly, either cut the chocolate into slivers and shards of varying lengths and thicknesses, or chop it into cubes that are about ¼ inch on a side. Don't worry about evenness: The cake is prettiest when the chocolate is cut into different sizes and shapes. Return the chocolate to the freezer.

TO MAKE THE GLAZE: Put the chocolate in a heatproof liquid measuring cup. Bring the cream, sugar and water to a boil in a small saucepan, stirring to dissolve the sugar. Pour the hot liquid over the chocolate and wait for 30 seconds, then, using a small whisk or heatproof spatula and starting in the center, stir the mixture in tiny circles. When the center of the glaze is dark, smooth and shiny, work in widening circles to bring the glaze together. (*You can make the glaze up to 5 days ahead, cover and chill it; bring it back to the proper consistency by heating it in a double boiler or in a microwave on low power.*)

TO FINISH THE CAKE: Set the chilled cake on a cooling rack over a lined baking sheet (just as when you soaked and filled it) and have a long offset icing spatula at hand.

Working quickly, pour the glaze over the top of the chilled cake, allowing it to run down the sides. If the glaze needs a little help moving to the sides, use the spatula to send the glaze over the top. Then smooth the glaze around the sides of the cake. Don't worry about how the top looks (although it's probably gorgeous); most of it is going to be hidden.

Remove the chocolate pieces from the freezer. If you've made slivers and shards, you can pile them on top of the cake or poke them into the cake so that they stand up. If you've made cubes, scatter them over the top of the cake and press them into the glaze with your fingertips. Small pieces of chocolate will no doubt fall off the cake and you may not use all the slivers, shards or cubes you've cut. If that's the case, collect the tumblers and leftovers, wrap them in plastic film and freeze them. You'll be happy to have them to sprinkle over ice cream or nibble as a snack.

Return the cake to the refrigerator for at least 1 hour (or up to overnight) to set and chill.

Tarte Tropézienne

THE TARTE TROPÉZIENNE IS EASY TO DESCRIBE, the cult surrounding it less so. Pierre Hermé introduced me to it more than twenty years ago, and he told me it was *mythique*. I'm sure I nodded, but I know that I hadn't a clue what he meant or really how mythic the cake truly was. I didn't get an inkling until I went to Saint-Tropez, where the streets are lined with pastry shops, and each one has a Trop.

The story goes that a bread baker, Alexandre Mika, had a shop in Saint-Tropez and that he made this cake using a recipe that he brought with him from his native Poland. But it wasn't until 1955, when a film crew set up across from the shop, that the dessert became the "it" cake. The crew included a bunch of then-unknowns: the actors Jean-Louis Trintignant and Curd Jürgens; first-time director Roger Vadim; and starlet Brigitte Bardot. When Mika started making meals for them, the cake became the most requested item on the menu. It was so beloved that Bardot is said to have advised Mika that he should have a special name for it and that's when it was christened "La Tarte Tropézienne."

The cake itself is an egg and butter-rich brioche dough, rolled into a free-form round, washed with egg and speckled with pearl sugar—the original was probably made with crushed sugar cubes (still an option)—and baked. Once cooled, it's split like a layer cake and filled with a combination of creams: in some cases, buttercream, pastry cream and heavy cream. Here, I opt for thick vanilla pastry cream lightened with a little whipped cream. I've seen Tropéziennes flavored with rum (my favorite), kirsch (regionally incorrect, but delicious) and, most commonly and most authentically, orange-flower water. These days, the Trop can be found studded with berries or filled with chocolate, and every shop in the beautiful Riviera town has a picture of Bardot.

A WORD ON SIZE: This recipe makes a big cake, just right for parties. If you'd like, you can divide the dough and make two smaller cakes; freeze one to cut and fill at a later time.

A WORD ON PEARL SUGAR: Sometimes called Swedish Sugar, pearl sugar is nugget-like, crunchy and as white as a perfect pearl. You can find it in specialty stores, Ikea or online from King Arthur Flour.

AND A WORD ON MIXING: You need a stand mixer to make this dough— I've never found a hand mixer strong enough for the prolonged beating that the heavy, sticky dough demands.

Makes 12 servings

SERVING: In Saint-Tropez, the cake is sometimes a dessert, sometimes a pick-me-up and, if it's bought as a miniature from a pâtisserie in town, sometimes a snack. Since it comes from a town once known for its wild and crazy ways, it's not surprising that there are no real rules.

STORING: You can make the pastry cream up to 3 days ahead and refrigerate it, and you can keep the brioche dough in the refrigerator for 1 day before you bake it. Once cut and filled, the cake can be kept in the refrigerator, away from foods with strong odors, for about 8 hours, or you can wrap it airtight and freeze it for up to 2 months. Defrost, still wrapped, in the refrigerator overnight.

FOR THE CAKE

- 2½ teaspoons active dry yeast
- ⅓ cup (80 ml) warm whole milk (see yeast package for exact temperature)
- 2 cups (272 grams) all-purpose flour
- 3 tablespoons sugar
- 2 large eggs, at room temperature, lightly beaten
- ½ teaspoon fine sea salt
- 2 teaspoons dark rum or kirsch (optional)
- 1 teaspoon pure vanilla extract
- 7 tablespoons (3½ ounces; 99 grams) unsalted butter, at room temperature

FOR THE FILLING

- 1½ cups (360 ml) whole milk
- 4 large egg yolks
- ⅓ cup (67 grams) sugar
- ¼ cup (32 grams) cornstarch
  Pinch of fine sea salt
- 1 tablespoon pure vanilla extract or 1 tablespoon orange-flower water plus 1 teaspoon pure vanilla extract
- ¾ stick (6 tablespoons; 3 ounces; 85 grams) unsalted butter, cut into bits, at room temperature
- ¼ cup (60 ml) very cold heavy cream

- 1 large egg, for glazing
  Pearl sugar or crushed sugar cubes, for finishing

TO MAKE THE CAKE: Put the yeast in a small bowl and pour over the warm milk. Allow the yeast to stand for a couple of minutes, until it's fully dissolved; it might or might not bubble.

Put the flour and sugar in the bowl of a stand mixer fitted with the paddle attachment. Mix at low speed to blend the dry ingredients, then scrape in the yeast mixture and beat just to distribute it; you'll have a shaggy mix. Keep the mixer spinning on low and add the eggs in a slow stream, then beat in the salt, rum or kirsch, if you're using it, and vanilla. Increase the mixer speed to medium and beat, scraping down the bowl occasionally, for 5 to 8 minutes. The dough will start off rough and pockmarked, then it will pull into strands as the mixer spins and, finally, it will be smooth and form a ball.

Check the butter—you want it to be soft but not oily. If it's not soft, smear it across a work surface with the heel of your hand. Up the mixer speed to medium-high and toss in the pieces of butter a couple at a time. Keep mixing after the last bit of butter goes in until you've got a dough that forms a ball around the paddle, another 8 to 10 minutes.

Turn the dough out into a large bowl, then cup your fingers under the dough, lifting it and letting it slap down into the bowl again as you work your way around the bowl; when you've come full circle, you should have a nice, smooth, somewhat flattened ball of dough. Cover the bowl tightly with plastic film and put it in a warm place (70 to 75 degrees F) until it rises to approximately double its original volume, 2 to 3 hours.

When the dough has risen, deflate it, using that same lift-and-drop method, cover the bowl tightly again and put it in the freezer for 30 minutes to arrest the dough's development. Then transfer it to the refrigerator and chill for another 2 hours. (*The dough can be refrigerated for up to 2 days.*)

About an hour before you're ready to bake, line a baking sheet with parchment paper or a silicone baking mat. Remove the bowl from the refrigerator and turn the dough out onto a lightly floured work surface. Gently pat the dough down, lightly flour the top and roll it into a 10-inch circle. Don't worry about it being exactly 10 inches; concentrate on getting it round and almost that diameter, or smaller. Slide the dough onto the baking sheet, cover with a piece of plastic film—don't press down on it—and let the dough rest in a warm place for 1 hour.

MEANWHILE, MAKE THE FILLING: Bring the milk to a boil in a medium saucepan.

Whisk the yolks, sugar, cornstarch and salt together in a medium bowl. Whisking constantly, drizzle in one quarter of the hot milk. When the yolks are warm, add the rest of the milk in a steadier stream. Pour the mixture into the pan, return the pan to medium heat and, whisking vigorously, bring back to a boil. Keep at a boil, still whisking, for 1 to 2 minutes, making sure to get your whisk into the corners of the pan. Scrape the pastry cream into a bowl, add the vanilla and allow it to sit for 10 minutes at room temperature.

Add the bits of butter to the pastry cream a couple pieces at a time, whisking to incorporate. Press a piece of plastic film against the surface of the cream and chill for at least 2 hours, or, to speed up the chilling, put the bowl in a larger bowl filled with ice cubes and cold water and whisk until cold, then refrigerate until ready to fill the cake. (*You can make the pastry cream up to 3 days ahead and keep it well covered in the refrigerator.*)

TO BAKE THE CAKE: About 20 minutes before you're ready to bake, center a rack in the oven and preheat the oven to 400 degrees F.

Lightly beat the egg and add a splash of cold water to it. Brush the top of the dough with the egg wash and sprinkle over the pearl or crushed sugar, patting it down lightly so that it sticks. Be generous with the sugar—you want to pretty much cover the top.

Slide the baking sheet into the oven and immediately turn the oven temperature down to 350 degrees F. Bake the cake for 20 to 25 minutes, rotating the sheet after 10 minutes, or until it is golden brown on both the top and bottom. Transfer the cake to a cooling rack and let it come to room temperature.

When you're ready to fill the cake, whip the heavy cream until it holds firm peaks.

Remove the pastry cream from the refrigerator and whisk to loosen it. Stir a little of the whipped cream into the pastry cream, then fold in the rest of the whipped cream with a flexible spatula.

TO FINISH THE CAKE: Using a long serrated knife and a very gentle sawing motion, cut the cake horizontally in half(ish)—it's good to have the bottom layer a little thicker than the top. Put the bottom layer on a cake plate. Spread the filling over it, leaving a slim border bare, and replace the top of the cake, jiggling it slightly to settle it into the cream. Chill the cake for at least 1 hour, or for up to 8 hours. The filling needs to set in the refrigerator and the cake should be served cold.

Whoever invented the silicone spatula should be given the Nobel Kitchen Prize. Sure, people were able to make sticky caramel and thick pastry cream before silicone, but now we can make them with less care and easier cleanup. While the initial excitement with silicone was that it was heatproof up to about 500 degrees F, the fact that it's so steadfastly nonstick is a bonus worth applauding.

I'm persnickety about spatulas. I don't like them too stiff—I want them to bend with the curve of a bowl or the angle of a pan. But I don't like them too flexible either—it's annoying to have the end of a spatula waggle when you're using it to stir a heavy batter or to fold one batter into another—they've got to be firm enough to support batters and doughs. And I'm fussy about the handle—I want to be able to hold on to it, but I don't want it to be so thick or have such defined edges that I can't turn the spatula around in my hand when I'm folding. These days, all my spatulas are silicone and my favorite is actually a spoonula: a spatula with a shallow spoon shape. Whenever I find a spatula I like, I buy several, a safeguard against the manufacturers deciding they don't like their product as much as I do.

Gingerbread Bûche de Noël

SERVING: Bringing the cake to the table is its own dramatic event, but there's no reason not to add to the drama by making it the sole event. Instead of waiting to serve the log *après* dinner, have an afternoon holiday party and serve just the cake and Champagne. It's a very chic way to say Merry Christmas!

STORING: Covered lightly and kept away from foods with strong odors, the cake will keep in the refrigerator for up to 2 days. Serve it chilled.

YULE LOGS ARE SUCH A PART OF the French Christmas tradition that a month or two before the holiday, pâtissiers start previewing their new creations, rather like fashion designers with their collections. And weeks before, every newspaper and food magazine runs a photo-filled story on what the top pastry houses will offer. It's a dream book and shopping list rolled into one.

Since we spend the holidays in Paris, I get a chance to sample a few cakes each season. My bûche strategy for dinners at home is simple: One time I'll buy one, the next time I'll bake one. With so many fanciful cakes in the shops, making my own is unnecessary, but I'll never give it up, mostly because it's so much fun to make a rolled up cake and even more fun to serve it. It's a project, yes, but a completely satisfying and delicious one.

This bûche has the flavor of gingerbread—it's spiced with cinnamon, ginger and black pepper, sweetened with brown sugar and rolled up around a cream cheese and praline filling that's lick-the-spoon wonderful. (The filling, packed in a jar, is a great gift on its own, to be spread over toast or on cookies.) The pecan praline is quick and easy to make and it adds terrific flavor and crunch. I chop some of it very finely—you can crush it, if you prefer—and stir it into the filling. I chop the remainder a little more coarsely and sprinkle it over the billowing, snow-white marshmallow frosting.

Everything but the frosting can be made ahead, so you can get a jump on things. You need to spread the frosting as soon as it's made, but the cake needs to be refrigerated after it's frosted and it can stay in the fridge for up to 2 days, so there are no last-minute to-dos with this beauty.

And just because it's called a bûche de Noël doesn't mean you can't stud it with candles and call it a birthday cake.

A WORD ON TOOLS: You'll need a candy thermometer for the frosting and a stand mixer.

FOR THE PRALINE
- 1 cup (120 grams) pecan halves or pieces
- ⅓ cup (67 grams) sugar
- ¼ cup (60 ml) water

FOR THE CAKE
- ¾ cup (102 grams) all-purpose flour
- ¼ cup (32 grams) cornstarch, sifted
- ¾ teaspoon ground cinnamon
- ¾ teaspoon ground ginger
- ¼ teaspoon fine sea salt
- ¼ teaspoon freshly ground black pepper
- 6 large eggs
- ¾ cup (150 grams) packed light brown sugar
- ½ stick (4 tablespoons; 2 ounces; 57 grams) unsalted butter, melted and cooled

Confectioners' sugar, for
dusting and rolling

½ teaspoon ground cinnamon
2 teaspoons pure vanilla extract

FOR THE FILLING

8 ounces (227 grams)
cream cheese, at room
temperature
1 stick (8 tablespoons;
4 ounces; 113 grams)
unsalted butter,
at room temperature
Pinch of fine sea salt

FOR THE FROSTING

½ cup (120 ml) egg whites
(about 4 large)
1 cup (200 grams) sugar
¾ teaspoon cream of tartar
1 cup (240 ml) water
1 tablespoon pure vanilla
extract

TO MAKE THE PRALINE: Center a rack in the oven and preheat the oven to 350 degrees F.

Line a baking sheet with parchment or a silicone baking mat and spread the pecans out on the baking sheet. Bake the nuts for 3 minutes (you want to heat, not toast, them), stir them around and then put them in a warm spot while you cook the sugar.

Put the sugar in a small saucepan and pour over the water. Swirl to moisten the sugar, then put the pan over medium-high heat. Cook the sugar, washing down the sides of the pan if needed with a pastry brush dipped in cold water, until the sugar turns a medium amber color. (Stay close; sugar changes color quickly.) Turn off the heat, add the nuts to the saucepan (set the lined baking sheet aside) and stir a few times with a heatproof spatula or a wooden spoon, just to coat the nuts with syrup. Pour the caramelized nuts out onto the baking sheet and use the spatula, spoon or an offset metal spatula to spread them out. If they won't spread out, no matter—you're going to chop them anyway. Let cool completely. (*The praline can be made up to a day ahead, packed in a container and kept in a cool, dry place—moisture is praline's nemesis.*) Finely chop ½ cup of the praline; coarsely chop the remainder.

TO MAKE THE CAKE: Center a rack in the oven and preheat the oven to 350 degrees F. Line a 12-×-17-inch rimmed baking sheet with a piece of parchment paper. Butter the paper, dust with flour and tap out the excess.

Whisk the flour, cornstarch, cinnamon, ginger, salt and pepper together in a small bowl.

Have a wide skillet about one-third full of simmering water on the stove. Working in the bowl of a stand mixer, or in a heatproof bowl in which you can use a hand mixer, whisk together the eggs and brown sugar. Set the bowl in the pan of simmering water (pour off some water if you're concerned that it will slosh over the sides) and whisk nonstop until the mixture is very warm to the touch, about 2 minutes. Remove from the heat.

If you're using a stand mixer, attach the bowl to the stand and fit it with the whisk attachment, or use a hand mixer. Working on high speed, beat the

sugared eggs until they are thick and pale, have more than doubled in volume and have reached room temperature, 7 to 10 minutes. Switch to a flexible spatula and fold in the flour mixture in 2 additions. Be as delicate as you can and don't be overly thorough now—you're going to continue to fold when the butter goes in. Put the melted butter in a small bowl, scoop a big spoonful of the batter over it and stir. Turn this mixture out onto the batter in the bowl and fold it in: Cut deep into the center of the bowl and search the bottom for unincorporated flour—find it and fold it. Scrape the batter out onto the prepared baking sheet and spread it evenly with an offset spatula.

Bake for 13 to 15 minutes, or until the cake is golden brown, lightly springy to the touch and starting to pull away from the sides of the baking sheet. Transfer the baking sheet to a cooling rack, but keep it on the rack for no more than 5 minutes; you want to roll the cake while it's hot.

Lay a cotton or linen kitchen towel (not terrycloth or microfiber) on the counter and dust it generously with confectioners' sugar. Run a table knife around the sides of the cake and invert the cake onto the towel. Carefully peel away the parchment. Lightly dust the cake with confectioners' sugar and replace the parchment, putting the clean side against the cake (or use a new piece). Starting at a short end, roll the cake into a log; this is a preroll, so it doesn't have to be tight or perfect. If the cake cracks, keep rolling—the filling and frosting will patch everything. Return the rolled-up cake (still in its towel) to the rack and let it cool, seam side down, to room temperature.

MEANWHILE, MAKE THE FILLING: Put the softened cream cheese, butter and salt in the bowl of a stand mixer fitted with the paddle attachment, or work in a large bowl with a hand mixer. With the mixer on medium speed, beat until the cream cheese and butter are homogeneous and smooth. Beat in the cinnamon and vanilla. If you're going to use the filling now, stir in the ½ cup finely chopped praline; if not, wait until you're ready to fill the Yule log. Transfer to a bowl, cover and refrigerate. (*You can make the filling—without the praline—up to 2 days ahead and keep it well covered in the refrigerator.*)

TO FILL THE LOG: If the filling has been chilled, give it a good whisking to return it to a spreadable consistency; add the praline if you haven't already done so.

Unroll the log and carefully remove the parchment; leave the cake on the kitchen towel. Beginning with a short end, gently roll up the cake, peeling away the towel as you go. Unroll the cake onto the towel or a clean piece of parchment.

Spread the filling across the surface of the cake, leaving a scant 1-inch border uncovered on the long sides. Again starting from a short side, roll up the cake, leaving the towel or parchment behind and trying to get as tight a roll as you can. If you'd like, tighten the log using the paper-and-ruler technique (see page 61). Place the cake on a parchment-lined cutting board, cover it and chill it for 30 minutes.

MEANWHILE, MAKE THE FROSTING: Put the egg whites in the clean, dry bowl of a stand mixer fitted with the whisk attachment or in a large bowl that you can use with a hand mixer.

Stir the sugar, cream of tartar and water together in a small saucepan. Bring to a boil over medium-high heat, then cover and boil for about 3 minutes. Uncover, attach a candy thermometer to the pan and cook until the thermometer reads 242 degrees F (this can take almost 10 minutes).

When the sugar reaches 235 degrees F, begin beating the whites on medium speed. If you get to the point where the whites look like they're about to form stiff peaks and the syrup isn't at 242 degrees F yet, lower the mixer speed and keep mixing until the sugar is ready.

At 242 degrees F, with the mixer on medium speed, stand back and carefully and steadily pour the hot syrup into the bowl. Try to get the syrup between the side of the bowl and the whisk. Perfection is impossible, so ignore any spatters; don't try to stir them into the frosting. Add the vanilla and keep beating until the frosting cools to room temperature, about 5 minutes. You'll have a shiny, marshmallow frosting, which you should spread now.

TO FROST AND FINISH THE LOG: Remove the cake from the refrigerator. You can frost it on the cutting board and then transfer it to a serving platter or put it on the platter now. To keep the platter clean during frosting, tuck strips of parchment under the log, putting just a sliver of the parchment under the cake and leaving the lion's share to protect your platter.

If the ends of the log look ragged, trim them. Using an offset spatula, table knife or the back of a spoon, swirl the frosting all over the cake in a thick layer. Refrigerate for at least 1 hour to set the frosting and firm up the filling.

Sprinkle the cake with the remaining coarsely chopped praline before serving.

Black-and-White Baked Alaska

SERVING: Baked Alaska is spectacle enough—no further embellishments needed.

STORING: You can make the cake up to 3 days ahead and keep it well covered on the counter (where it will be a daily temptation), or you can wrap it airtight and freeze it for up to 2 months. (If storing it at room temperature, chill it before assembling the Alaska.) There's no need to defrost the frozen cake before topping it with ice cream and meringue. In fact, if you'd like to just offer the cake plain, you can cut it straight from the freezer and serve it—it never freezes rock hard. Once you've put the meringue on it, you can freeze it for up to 1 week and then brown it whenever you're ready.

CALLED AN *OMELETTE NORVÉGIENNE* IN FRANCE, Baked Alaska is a dessert that must have astounded people when it was first served in the 1800s; it still amazes me. It's a three-part affair: a layer of cake, a filling of ice cream and a thick topping of meringue. The dessert is assembled, frozen and then baked at super-high heat so that the meringue browns quickly. While I understand how the cake and marshmallow meringue keep the ice cream from melting, I prefer to think of it as a miracle.

This Baked Alaska is especially delicious because it's built on a cake that holds its flavor when frozen (true of very few cakes). A recipe from my friend Hélène Samuel, it's a dark, thick, flourless chocolate cake, really a fallen soufflé, with a brownie-like texture. That it's delectably dense and chewy at any temperature makes it the perfect base for the Alaska.

FOR THE CAKE

- 4 large eggs
- 8 ounces (227 grams) bittersweet chocolate, coarsely chopped
- 15 tablespoons (7½ ounces; 213 grams) unsalted butter, at malleable room temperature
- 2 tablespoons unsweetened cocoa powder, sifted
- ⅓ cup (67 grams) plus ¼ cup (50 grams) sugar

Pinch of fine sea salt

FOR THE FILLING

- 1–2 pints (473–946 grams) premium ice cream (your favorite flavor)

FOR THE MERINGUE

- 3 large egg whites
  Pinch of fine sea salt
- ¾ cup (150 grams) sugar

TO MAKE THE CAKE: Center a rack in the oven and preheat the oven to 325 degrees F. Butter a 9-inch springform pan, line the bottom with a piece of parchment paper and butter the parchment. Dust the pan with flour and tap out the excess. Set the pan on a baking sheet lined with parchment or a silicone baking mat.

Separate 3 of the eggs. Put the 3 yolks and the whole egg in a medium bowl. Put the 3 whites in the bowl of a stand mixer or a large bowl.

The heatproof bowl that you use to melt the chocolate will be the bowl that all the ingredients (including the whipped whites) will eventually go into, so choose a large one. Put the chocolate in it and set the bowl over a saucepan of simmering water. Warm the chocolate, stirring occasionally, only until it is just melted; you don't want to overheat it. Transfer the bowl to the counter and let the chocolate cool for about 5 minutes.

Meanwhile, put the butter in a medium bowl and work it with a flexible

spatula until it is as soft and smooth as mayonnaise. Add the cocoa and mix until thoroughly blended.

Whisk the egg and yolks together with ⅓ cup of the sugar until the mixture pales and thickens slightly, about 1 minute.

Whip the egg whites and salt, using the whisk attachment or a hand mixer, until opaque. Add the remaining ¼ cup sugar and continue to whip at high speed until the whites form shiny peaks.

Turn the cocoa-butter mixture into the bowl of still-warm chocolate and, with the spatula, gently stir and blend until you have a thick, shiny, smooth mixture that reminds you of ganache. Blend in the egg and yolks, stirring and folding until they are completely incorporated and the mixture looks like brownie batter. Finally, stir a little of the whipped egg whites into the batter, just to lighten it, then gently fold in the remaining whites. Scrape the batter into the prepared pan and smooth the top.

Bake the cake for 35 to 40 minutes, or until a bamboo skewer or toothpick inserted into the center comes out with just a few moist crumbs sticking to it. The cake will have risen and the top will have cracked. That's the nature of this sweet, and it's only temporary: Within minutes, the center will sink and you'll have a bowl—perfect for ice cream! Transfer the cake to a rack and let it cool to room temperature.

When you're ready to unmold it, run a table knife between the edges of the cake and the pan and then, because the butter will have congealed, making it hard to release the bottom of the cake, turn on a burner, hold the cake pan about a foot above the heat and keep it there for 5 seconds or so. Remove the sides of the springform, turn the cake over onto a cooling rack, lift off the pan's base and peel away the parchment. Invert the cake onto a cutting board or a plate. Refrigerate for at least 4 hours, or wrap it in plastic film and freeze it for at least 2 hours. (*The cake can be frozen for up to 2 months. There's no need to defrost it before filling and finishing it.*)

TO MAKE THE FILLING: Make the filling at least 2 hours before you plan to serve the cake. Cakes rise and fall differently, but in general, 1 pint of ice cream should fill your cake's hollow and come just about even with the rim; 2 pints will give you a little dome. However much ice cream you decide on, cajole it out of its container into a large bowl and leave it on the counter for 5 to 10 minutes, or until it's mushable. Using a big spoon (or even a potato masher), work the ice cream until you can spoon it into the hollow, then smooth the top. Freeze the cake, uncovered, for at least 2 hours. (*The cake can be frozen for up to 1 week; wrap it airtight once the ice cream has set.*)

TO MAKE THE MERINGUE AND FINISH THE CAKE: Center a rack in the oven and preheat the oven to 500 degrees F. Line a baking sheet with parchment paper or foil.

Set the bowl of your stand mixer or a large heatproof bowl that you can use with a hand mixer over a large pot of simmering water. (If the bottom of the bowl touches the water, that's fine.) Pour the egg whites and salt into the bowl, whisk to blend and then add the sugar. Whisk constantly, until the whites thicken a little, turn ivory and are hot to the touch, about 5 minutes. Remove the bowl from the heat and, using the whisk attachment or a hand mixer, whip the whites on medium-high speed until they are cool and marshmallowy, about 10 minutes. This meringue is extremely stable, but it's best used quickly.

Remove the cake from the freezer and put it on the lined baking sheet. Spread the meringue in a thick layer all over the cake and down the sides, all the way to the baking sheet. Meringue shrinks and shimmies upward in baking, so you want to layer on a little extra around the base. (*The cake can go back into the freezer now. If it's just going to stay a couple of hours, leave it uncovered; if you want to store it for up to a week, wait for the meringue to freeze and then wrap the cake airtight.*)

Bake the cake for 3 to 5 minutes, or until the meringue is a color you like. All you're doing here is drying the very outside of it, so color is your only judge. Remove the cake from the oven and carefully transfer it to a serving platter. Serve immediately.

Bonne Idée

CHUNKY CHOCOLATE-CAKE SUNDAE: You can make this sundae in any kind of bowls or coupes, and you can also make it in jars (don't fill them to the top; you need to leave freeze-and-expand space) and have your sundaes waiting for you and your fellow indulgers. For each sundae, layer small cubes of cake; some syrup, which is optional but nice (plain, page 52; chestnut-vanilla, page 172; or store-bought, in whatever flavor you like); your favorite ice cream; and chocolate sauce (page 442). You can top the sundaes with meringue, if you'd like—left unbrowned, it's like marshmallow sauce—or finish it with whipped cream. Cherries are optional.

Le Cheesecake Round Trip

Makes 16 servings

SERVING: There are two good ways to slice the cake: you can use a long piece of dental floss—hold it taut by both ends and wiggle it down the cake. Or use a long, slim knife—run it under hot water, wipe it dry and cut. Repeat the water-wipe ritual with each slice. Serve the slices of cake plain or with a drizzle of caramel sauce.

STORING: Well wrapped and kept away from foods with strong odors, the cheesecake can be refrigerated for about 3 days. The whole cake—or leftovers—can be wrapped airtight and frozen for up to 2 months; defrost, still wrapped, in the refrigerator overnight.

FOR MOST OF THE YEARS that I've been living in France, cream cheese has been a hard-to-find cult ingredient. In fact, it was so rare and so coveted that I once flew from New York to Paris with ten pounds of it in my suitcase. I kept four pounds and gave the rest away to friends who'd requested it.

I froze half of my own stash and used the rest—along with the graham crackers that I'd also hauled across the ocean—to make a New York cheesecake. A few months later, planning to repeat my little feat of international diplomacy, I had the frozen cream cheese but no graham crackers. That's when I Paris-ized my cake, using crushed spice cookies and almond flour for the crust, then tossing more cookie crumbs into the cake and serving it with a pitcher of salted caramel sauce. It was a hit in Paris and just as big a hit back in New York, where it became known as the Paris Cheesecake.

A WORD ON THE COOKIE CRUMBS: I like to use LU Cinnamon Sugar Spice cookies for the crust and filling, but Biscoff speculoos are delicious too (no surprise). If you'd like, make your own Speculoos (page 320) or, for a nonspice version, use the crumbs you get after the first bake of the Double-Butter Double-Baked Petit Beurre Cookies (page 270). All in all, you need about 9 ounces of cookies or 2½ cups crumbs, so plan accordingly.

FOR THE CRUST

1 9.17-ounce (260-gram) box LU Cinnamon Sugar Spice cookies or the equivalent weight of other cookies (see above; to make 2½ cups [260 grams] crumbs)

¼ cup (25 grams) almond flour (or ¼ cup, 25 grams, cookie crumbs)

2 tablespoons sugar

¼ teaspoon fine sea salt

½ stick (4 tablespoons; 2 ounces; 57 grams) unsalted butter, melted

FOR THE FILLING

2 pounds (907 grams) full-fat cream cheese, preferably Philadelphia Original, at room temperature

1¼ cups (250 grams) sugar

½ teaspoon fine sea salt

1 tablespoon pure vanilla extract

¼ teaspoon pure almond extract (optional)

4 large eggs, at room temperature

1 cup (240 ml) heavy cream, at room temperature

⅓ cup (75 grams) plain Greek yogurt (or ⅓ cup more heavy cream)

1 cup (100 grams) cookie crumbs reserved from the crust

Cold Salted Caramel Sauce (page 447), for serving (optional)

TO MAKE THE CRUST: Butter a 9- to 10-inch springform pan. The pan should be 2¾ inches high; if it's lower, you'll have extra filling. Wrap the bottom of the pan in a double thickness of aluminum foil: Make a cross with two pieces of foil, put the pan in the center and wrap. You want the foil to go up as high and to be as tight as possible—it's your defense against water seeping into the pan. Line a baking sheet with parchment or foil (your drip-catcher).

Break up the cookies, toss them (in batches) into a food processor or blender and whir until they're crumbed and crushed. (Alternatively, put the cookies in a plastic bag and crush them with a rolling pin.) You need 2½ cups (260 grams) crumbs—1½ cups (158 grams) crumbs for the crust; save the remaining crumbs for the cake.

Put the crumbs, almond flour (or more crumbs), sugar and salt in a medium bowl, pour over the melted butter and, using a fork or your finger-tips, toss everything together until uniformly moist. Turn the mixture into the pan and press it as evenly as you can onto the bottom and up the sides. Ideally, the crumbs should go halfway up the sides or even a little higher, but the crust needn't be perfect. Freeze the crust for at least 15 minutes.

Center a rack in the oven and preheat the oven to 350 degrees F.

Put the springform pan on the lined baking sheet. Bake the crust for 10 minutes, then put it on a rack to cool while you make the filling. Lower the oven temperature to 325 degrees F.

TO MAKE THE FILLING: Put a kettle of water on to boil and have a roasting pan large enough to hold the springform pan at the ready.

Working in the bowl of a stand mixer fitted with the paddle attachment, or in a large bowl with a hand mixer, beat the cream cheese at medium speed for about 4 minutes, or until it is completely smooth. Add the sugar and salt and mix for another 4 minutes. Beat in the vanilla extract and almond extract, if you're using it, then add the eggs one by one, beating for a minute after each one goes in. As you're working, stop frequently to scrape down the sides of the bowl and to make certain that whatever's on the bottom of the bowl is getting mixed in. Reduce the mixer speed to low and mix in the cream and yogurt (or additional cream). When the batter is silky smooth, stir in the cookie crumbs and give the batter a few last turns with a flexible spatula.

Put the springform pan in the roasting pan and fill it with the batter. The batter will probably come up to the top of the pan; if you have any left over, you can bake it in a small buttered soufflé mold or custard cup, either along-side the cake or in another baking pan that you'll fill with water. Slide the roasting pan into the oven and pour enough hot water into the roasting pan to come halfway up the sides of the springform.

Set a timer for 90 minutes; resist the temptation to open the oven, and don't worry about rotating the pan unless your oven's heat is very uneven. The cheesecake will rise above the rim of the pan—that's fine. The top will brown and it might crack—also fine. When the timer goes off, turn off the oven, prop the oven door open with a wooden spoon and leave the cake to rest in its water bath for 1 hour more. (This is not a dessert for the impatient!)

Carefully lift the springform out of the roasting pan—no matter how tightly you've wrapped the cake, there's bound to be hot water in the foil. Remove the foil, transfer the cheesecake to a cooling rack and let come to room temperature.

Cover the cooled cake loosely and refrigerate it for at least 4 hours. Cheesecake should always be served very cold—it tastes much better that way and it's impossible to cut otherwise. (*The cheesecake can be wrapped and refrigerated for up to 3 days.*)

When you're ready to serve the cake, run a table knife between the crust and the sides of the pan, then use a hair dryer to warm the sides of the spring-form and make it easier to remove. Gingerly remove the sides of the pan. It's pretty much a hopeless task to remove the cake from the bottom of the pan, so it's best to make peace with serving it on the base. If you'd like, serve the cheesecake with caramel sauce.

Pithiviers

THE PITHIVIERS IS ONE OF the great forgotten pastries of France, nudged out of the spotlight by its next of kin, the Galette des Rois (see page 102). Named after a city in the north of the country, it's composed of two rounds of puff pastry sandwiching a thick cushion of almond cream. I've had a soft spot for the Pithiviers ever since I first tasted it. And I have the softest spot for it when it's made as that first one was: with prunes, actually a prune marmalade, very much like the old-fashioned Eastern European specialty *lekvar*. I make the almond cream then top it with the prune jam. If you'd like to add another textural element to the filling, try soaking a few pitted prunes in strong black tea, Armagnac or dark rum. If you decide on Armagnac (so good with prunes), you might want to use it in the almond cream instead of the rum or vanilla.

There's nothing about this dessert that isn't wonderful: It's easy to construct, it's thoroughly delicious and it's unfailingly beautiful. Unfailing beauty is the magic of puff pastry.

Makes 8 servings

SERVING: The Pithiviers is good as a tea treat and great after dinner. I've never seen it accompanied by anything, but that doesn't mean it can't go with a little whipped cream or even ice cream.

STORING: You can make the prune jam up to 1 week ahead and keep it covered in the refrigerator. The almond cream will hold for up to 3 days. You can roll and cut the puff pastry and cover and freeze the circles for up to 1 month. You can even construct the Pithiviers and keep it covered in the freezer overnight (no need to defrost before egg-washing and baking). However, once baked, the Pithiviers is an eat-it-now-and-enjoy-it sweet.

FOR THE PRUNE JAM
- ⅓ cup (80 ml) water
- 2 tablespoons sugar
- 4½ ounces (128 grams) pitted prunes (about 20)
- 1 large egg yolk, lightly beaten
  Pinch of freshly ground black pepper

FOR THE ALMOND CREAM
- 3 tablespoons (1½ ounces; 43 grams) unsalted butter, at room temperature
- ⅓ cup (67 grams) sugar
  Freshly grated lemon or orange zest, to taste (optional)

- 6 tablespoons (38 grams) almond flour
- 1 teaspoon all-purpose flour
- ½ teaspoon cornstarch
- 1 large egg white
- 1 teaspoon dark rum or ½ teaspoon pure vanilla extract

- 2 sheets thawed puff pastry, each about 8 ounces (227 grams), ready to roll
- 1 large egg
  Sugar, for dusting

TO MAKE THE PRUNE JAM: Combine the water and sugar in a small saucepan and stir over medium heat until the sugar dissolves. Stir in the prunes and bring the mixture to a boil, then lower the heat and cook, stirring occasionally, until most of the liquid has evaporated and the prunes are so soft that you can mash them easily with the back of a spoon, about 10 minutes. If necessary, add more water so the prunes cook to the right consistency.

Scrape the mixture into a bowl and mash the prunes into a thick, not completely smooth jam. Vigorously stir in the egg yolk, followed by the pepper. Press a piece of plastic film against the surface of the jam and chill for at least 2 hours. (*The jam can be packed airtight and refrigerated for up to 1 week.*)

TO MAKE THE ALMOND CREAM: You can use a hand mixer or a stand mixer (fitted with the whisk attachment) to make the cream, or you can blend the cream with a flexible spatula. Mix together the butter, sugar and zest, if you're using it, in a medium bowl or in a mixer bowl until smooth. Add the almond flour, incorporating it completely. Blend in the all-purpose flour and cornstarch, then add the egg white, mixing until the cream is homogeneous. Stir in the rum or vanilla.

Turn the almond cream out onto a piece of plastic film and mold it into a disk that's 6 to 7 inches in diameter. Refrigerate it for at least 2 hours, or freeze it for 1 hour. (*The almond cream can be refrigerated for up to 3 days.*)

TO ASSEMBLE THE PITHIVIERS: Working on a floured surface, roll out each sheet of puff pastry until it's a scant ⅛ inch thick. Using the top of a pot, a plate or your best judgment, cut an 8-inch circle from one piece of dough and an 8½-inch circle from the other. (Save the scraps for another purpose.) If the dough is still cold, proceed; if it's soft, place the rounds on sheets of parchment paper, cover with plastic film and refrigerate until firm.

Line a baking sheet with parchment paper or a silicone baking mat. Beat the egg with a splash of cold water in a small bowl.

Place the 8-inch circle of dough on the baking sheet and center the disk of almond cream on it. Spoon the prune jam over the almond cream, spreading it to the edges of the cream; don't worry if some spills over. Brush the border of the dough circle with egg wash—it's the glue that will hold the top in place, so be generous, and make the border about 1 inch wide. Top with the larger piece of dough and press the edges together with your fingertips or the side of your hand. (I always press the top piece gently around the mound of filling.)

You have to double-seal the edges and you have a choice of how you want to do this: The easiest way is to press the tines of a fork around the border. The more traditional way is to cut the outer edge in a scallop pattern. My favorite way is to use a paring knife to cut out small triangles of dough, so that the Pithiviers is encircled by points. If you're making scallops or points, don't cut in more than about ½ inch. Brush the entire surface of the Pithiviers with some of the the remaining egg wash, taking care that it doesn't drip down the sides, which would keep them from rising. Using the tip of a paring knife, score the top of the dough. The most usual pattern is a series of backward Cs that start at the top and end at the border, but don't feel the need to be bound by tradition.

Chill the Pithiviers for at least 30 minutes. Cover the egg wash and chill it; you'll use it again.

WHEN YOU'RE READY TO BAKE: Center a rack in the oven and preheat the oven to 450 degrees F.

Remove the Pithiviers from the refrigerator and give it another coat of egg wash. Sprinkle the top lightly with sugar and slide the baking sheet into the oven. Immediately turn the oven temperature down to 375 degrees F. Bake for 35 to 40 minutes, or until the Pithiviers is deeply golden brown and gloriously puffed. Transfer the baking sheet to a cooling rack and allow the Pithiviers to cool for at least 30 minutes, or until it reaches room temperature.

GALETTE DES ROIS

The Pithiviers and the Galette des Rois, or "Kings' Cake," are almost identical: Both are made by encasing a mound of almond cream between two circles of puff pastry. But while the Pithiviers is a year-round indulgence, the galette was originally meant to appear only once annually, on January 6—the day that celebrates the Three Kings bringing gifts to the Baby Jesus.

What really separates a Galette des Rois from a Pithiviers is a small prize buried in the almond cream and the game that's played to nab it. Traditionally, the galette is placed on a table and the youngest person in the room is told to crawl under it and hide his eyes, so that he can't peek at what's happening above. Then, as each portion of galette is cut, the child declares who should be served. The lucky person who gets the slice with the prize, which was originally a *fève*, or "bean," wins a paper crown to offer to his or her favorite. The child is usually given the bean.

But things have changed, particularly in Paris, where pastry chefs have made the Galette des Rois almost as popular as the bûche de Noël.

Nowadays galettes go on sale the day after Christmas and don't leave shop windows until the end of January, and they might be filled with almond cream flavored with anything from chocolate and lemon to clementine, pear or rose. While the prizes are still called *fèves*, the only time a bean appears is if the galette is made at home or if a pastry chef has whimsically reimagined it in porcelain. *Fèves* have become collectibles (and so coveted that even adults have been known to cheat to get them) and the crowns have gotten fancy too: Some of them, created by famous artists and fashion designers, would look handsome on the heads of true royals.

To make your own Galette des Rois, follow the directions for the Pithiviers but omit the prune jam. Make a double recipe of the almond cream, doubling all the ingredients but using ¾ cup (75 grams) almond flour and 1 whole large egg. Before you lay on the top piece of puff pastry, press a dried bean or small charm of some kind into the almond cream. And don't forget to tell your guests that it's there! A Galette des Rois can be dangerous for the unsuspecting.

Rose Fraisier

FRAISE MEANS "STRAWBERRY," and Le Fraisier is the French cake that celebrates the fruit. It's a classic in pâtisseries all over the country, and as close to a strawberry shortcake as the French get, even though there's nothing short about it. It's a grand cake that heralds spring and the arrival of the first berries from Provence. The base of the traditional cake is a genoise (sponge cake), which is often baked in a thin sheet and then cut into two squares and moistened with syrup. This sweet is all about the berries and cream—the skinny cake is just there to frame them. For the classic Fraisier look, some berries are halved from top to bottom and stood up all around the outside of the cake, their cut sides facing out, and then whole berries are lined up snugly to cover the bottom layer of the cake. This strawberry forest is enveloped in buttercream before the top layer of cake is settled over the filling and decorated with a layer of rolled-out almond paste, often colored green.

For the base of my springtime Fraisier-in-the-round, I chose France's most popular home-baked cake, the yogurt cake, which I flavored with ginger, lime and rose extract and syrup (if you use a rose syrup from the Middle East, your cake may end up pink). I split the cake in two, stood a battalion of berries straight up on the bottom layer and filled in the crannies with a mixture of vanilla pastry cream and whipped cream (lighter than buttercream, but made stand-up strong with the addition of a little gelatin). I skipped the almond paste for the top layer and finished the cake with a swirl of lightly sweetened whipped cream and a cluster of cut and sugared berries. You can decorate it in as many ways as an Easter bonnet, so have fun with it.

A WORD ON ROSE SYRUP AND EXTRACT: My favorite syrup is made by Monin. Because you won't be using it daily (even if it does make good cocktails), I suggest buying a small bottle and keeping it refrigerated after you've opened it. You can also find rose syrups, usually less expensive (also sweeter and considerably redder), in stores specializing in Middle Eastern ingredients. If you use a deep-colored sweet syrup, use just 2 tablespoons. Look for pure rose extract—my brand of choice is Star Kay White. Rose is a tricky flavor, and to get the right fragrance and a taste that is subtle but clearly rose, you need the best-quality syrup and extract you can find. Unfortunately, rose water, which is fairly easy to find, doesn't have the full flavor you want for this cake.

Makes 10 to 12 servings

SERVING: Once the cake gets its berries-and-cream crown, it should be served soon. Slice it with a serrated knife and serve it with something as special as it is: Champagne or sparkling wine (a rosé would be lovely), sweet wine or a strawberry-rose spritzer (add a tiny bit of rose syrup to sparkling water and finish with sliced berries).

STORING: You can bake the cake ahead and keep it covered at room temperature overnight or frozen for up to 2 months. And the pastry cream can be made and stored in the refrigerator for up to 2 days. But once the cream and berries join the party, you've got to finish assembling the cake, chill it and serve it on the same day.

FOR THE CAKE

- 1½ cups (204 grams) all-purpose flour
- 2 teaspoons baking powder
- ½ teaspoon ground ginger
- ¼ teaspoon fine sea salt
- 1 cup (200 grams) sugar
  Finely grated zest of 1 lime
- ½ cup (113 grams) plain yogurt (it can be Greek), at room temperature
- 3 large eggs, at room temperature
- 3 tablespoons rose syrup, preferably Monin (see previous page)
- ½ teaspoon pure vanilla extract
- ¼ teaspoon pure rose extract, preferably Star Kay White (see previous page)
- ½ cup (120 ml) canola or other flavorless oil

FOR THE FILLING

- 1½ cups (360 ml) whole milk
- 4 large egg yolks
- 6 tablespoons (75 grams) sugar
- ¼ cup (32 grams) cornstarch, sifted
- 2 teaspoons pure vanilla extract
- 1½ teaspoons unflavored gelatin
- 2 tablespoons cold water
- 1¾ cups (420 ml) very cold heavy cream
- ⅓ cup (40 grams) confectioners' sugar, sifted

About 36 large strawberries, hulled

FOR THE TOPPING

- 1 teaspoon water
- ⅓ cup (106 grams) red currant jelly
- ½ cup (120 ml) very cold heavy cream
- 1 tablespoon confectioners' sugar
- ¼ teaspoon pure vanilla extract or 1 drop pure rose extract
  Strawberries, sliced or whole, tossed with a little sugar and then drained

TO MAKE THE CAKE: Center a rack in the oven and preheat the oven to 350 degrees F. Butter a 9- to 9½-inch springform pan and line the bottom with a circle of parchment paper. Set the pan on a baking sheet.

Whisk the flour, baking powder, ginger and salt together in a small bowl.

Put the sugar and lime zest in a large bowl and, using your fingertips, rub them together until the sugar is fragrant. One by one, add the yogurt, eggs, syrup and vanilla and rose extracts, whisking vigorously after each ingredient goes in. Gently whisk in the dry ingredients until thoroughly incorporated, then gradually fold in the oil with a flexible spatula—you'll have a thick, smooth batter. Scrape it into the pan.

Bake the cake for 35 to 40 minutes, or until the sides start to come away from the pan, the top is springy to the touch and a skewer inserted deep into the center of the cake comes out clean. Transfer the cake to a rack and let it rest for 10 minutes, then remove the sides of the pan, turn the cake over onto the rack, remove the pan bottom and peel away the paper. Allow the cake to cool to room temperature upside down. (*The cake can be baked ahead and kept, covered, at room temperature overnight or frozen, well wrapped, for up to 2 months.*)

Turn the cake right side up. If you'd like the interior of the cake to show around the edges—pretty and traditional—use a serrated knife and a gentle sawing motion to slice away the crust around the sides of the cake. Cut the cake evenly into two layers and place the bottom layer cut side up on a serving plate.

TO MAKE THE FILLING: Bring the milk to a boil (I do this in a microwave oven).

Meanwhile, whisk the yolks, sugar and cornstarch together in a medium heavy-bottomed saucepan until thick. Still whisking, drizzle in about ¼ cup of the hot milk and then, continuing to whisk, gradually add the remainder. Put the pan over medium heat and cook—whisking nonstop and making sure that you get into the corners of the pan—until a bubble pops at the surface. Lower the heat to low and whisk the pastry cream for another minute to ensure that the cornstarch is fully cooked.

Scrape the pastry cream into a medium bowl and whisk in the vanilla. To cool the cream down quickly, put the bowl into a large bowl filled with ice cubes and cold water and let it sit, stirring frequently, until it is cold. Refrigerate until needed. (*The pastry cream can be covered tightly—press a piece of plastic film against the surface—and refrigerated for up to 2 days.*)

Put the gelatin in a small microwave-safe bowl and pour over the cold water. Let stand until the water is absorbed and the gelatin is soft, about 3 minutes, then microwave for 15 seconds, or until the gelatin is melted.

Working in the bowl of a stand mixer fitted with the whisk attachment, or in a large bowl with a hand mixer, beat the cream on high speed until it starts to thicken. Add the confectioners' sugar and continue to beat until the cream holds peaks. Reduce the mixer speed to medium and beat in the still-warm gelatin. The cream will thicken almost instantly, and that's fine.

Whisk the cold pastry cream to loosen it, then add a big spoonful of the whipped cream and whisk energetically. When the mixture seems supple enough to be beaten easily, whisk in the remaining whipped cream until blended and smooth.

TO FILL THE CAKE: Spread a thin layer of filling over the bottom layer of the cake. Cut some of the berries in half vertically and trim them at the base so that they're all the same height. Stand them up, cut side out, around the sides of the cake, leaving some space between the berries. Continue to cut and arrange the berries until you've circled the outer edge of the cake. Trim the rest of the whole berries so they are all the same height and place them, base end down, over the bottom cake layer, fitting them snugly over the cake.

You want to fill in all the spaces between the berries with cream and then smooth a generous layer of filling over the tops of the berries, so either spoon the filling into a piping bag (no need to fit it with a tip) or into a zipper-lock plastic bag (snip off one corner of the bag). Pipe cream between the berries.

When all the spaces are filled, pipe a generous layer of cream over the tops of the berries, taking care to leave the cut side of the outer berries cream-free, and smooth it with an offset spatula or a table knife. Settle the top cake layer, cut side down, onto the cake, rocking it gently from side to side so that the filling "glues" it into place. (*If you'd like, you can refrigerate the cake for up to 6 hours. Press pieces of wax paper against the sides of the cake and keep the cake away from foods with strong odors.*)

TO MAKE THE TOPPING AND FINISH THE CAKE: Stir the water into the red currant jelly in a small bowl and heat in the microwave until it bubbles. Brush the top of the cake with the jelly, coating it evenly, to give it a shine; save a little jelly for the berry garnish.

Whip the cream in a small bowl until it just starts to mound, add the confectioners' sugar and continue to whip until the cream holds peaks. Whisk in the vanilla or rose extract.

Spoon and swirl or pipe the cream into a circle in the center of the cake. Scatter the strawberries over the cream and drizzle the reserved jelly over the fruit. If the cake has not been refrigerated, chill it for at least 1 hour.

Bonne Idée

ROSE-SCENTED LOAF CAKE: To make a pale loaf cake with the light and lovely fragrance of rose, omit the rose syrup and increase the rose extract to 1¼ teaspoons and the vanilla extract to 1 teaspoon. Pour the batter into a generously buttered 8½-x-4½-inch loaf pan. Pull out an insulated baking sheet or stack two baking sheets one on top of the other; line the (top) sheet with parchment paper or a silicone baking mat. Put the loaf pan on the baking sheet(s). Bake in a preheated 350-degree-F oven for 50 to 55 minutes, or until the cake begins to come away from the sides of the pan and is golden brown and a knife inserted into the center comes out clean. Cool in the pan for 5 minutes, then unmold the cake and cool it right side up on a rack. I love this cake with Roasted Rhubarb with Bitters (page 335).

TARTS AND GALETTES

Gâteau Basque Fantasie

Makes 8 servings

SERVING: In the Pays Basque, the gâteau is served as a snack or as the finish to a fine dinner, and I'd suggest you treat this tourte the same way. I'd also suggest that, as long as we're living in fantasy-land, you serve it in the most American fashion: a la mode.

STORING: You can make the filling up to 3 days ahead and keep it covered in the fridge. You can also make the dough as much as 2 months ahead and freeze it. Once the tourte is baked, you can keep it at room temperature for up to 2 days, although it really is best the day it is made.

WHEN SOMETHING ISN'T MADE according to the strict laws of the French culinary canon, it might be given a new name: It might be considered *revisité* ("revisited") or, my favorite, *relooké* (literally, "relooked"); or it might be called a *fantasie*. It was this custom that came to mind when I created my fantasy of a gâteau Basque.

A proper gâteau Basque consists of a sweet crust fitted into a cake pan, a filling of either pastry cream or cherry jam (from the region, to be sure) and another layer of crust that seals in the filling during baking. Although I still find it hard to think of this double-crusted wonder as something other than pie or tourte, in its homeland, the Pays Basque, it's called a gâteau, and it's everywhere. To be fair, once it's out of the pan, it looks like a cake and, because of the inclusion of baking powder in the crust, it has a texture that resembles a crumbly butter cake.

My gâteau began with leftover fruit in a basket at home; lots of apples, a couple of oranges and some clusters of red grapes. I cooked the fruits together with some ginger, added some dried cherries and nuts and chopped in some of the candied orange peel that was in the fridge. And I loved it! The filling was chunky and not very juicy—not right for an American pie, but perfect for a gâteau Basque.

A WORD ON THE FILLING: There's no reason for you to go out and buy these particular fruits. The apples could be pears. It's nice to have the orange segments, but if all you've got is juice, you can carry on. Similarly, you can use whatever dried fruits and nuts you have. If you don't have fresh ginger, skip it. And if you don't have grapes, you can skip those too. Look around, see what you've got and bake your own version.

FOR THE CRUST

- 2 cups (272 grams) all-purpose flour
- ¾ teaspoon baking powder
- ½ teaspoon fine sea salt
- 1¼ sticks (10 tablespoons; 5 ounces; 142 grams) unsalted butter, at room temperature
- ¼ cup (50 grams) packed light brown sugar
- ¼ cup (50 grams) sugar
- 1 large egg, at room temperature

FOR THE FILLING

- 2 oranges or about ½ cup (120 ml) orange juice
- 3 medium apples, such as Fuji or Gala, peeled, cored and cut into ½-inch cubes
- ¼ pound (113 grams) seedless red grapes, stemmed and halved (optional)
- 3 tablespoons plump, moist dried cherries (chopped), raisins or dried cranberries
- 2 tablespoons chopped toasted nuts (any kind)

¼ cup (50 grams) sugar

1 quarter-sized slice peeled fresh ginger, finely chopped (optional)

¼ cup (60 ml) water

1–2 tablespoons chopped Candied Orange Peel (page 459; optional)

1 large egg, beaten with a splash of water, for glaze

Sugar, granulated or sanding, for sprinkling

TO MAKE THE CRUST: Whisk the flour, baking powder and salt together in a medium bowl.

Working in the bowl of a stand mixer fitted with the paddle attachment, or in a medium bowl with a hand mixer, beat the butter, brown sugar and granulated sugar together on medium speed until smooth, about 3 minutes. Add the egg and beat for 2 minutes more. Don't worry if the mixture looks curdled at this point. Turn off the mixer, add the dry ingredients and then pulse the machine a few times to start blending them in. Turn the mixer to low and mix only until the flour is fully incorporated and you have a soft, sticky dough.

Place a large sheet of parchment or wax paper on your work surface and put half of the dough in the center of the sheet. Cover with another piece of paper, then roll the dough into a circle just a little larger than 8 inches in diameter. As you're rolling, turn the dough over and lift the paper frequently so that you don't roll it into the dough and form creases. Transfer the dough, still between the papers, to a cutting board or baking sheet. Repeat with the other half of the dough and slide it on top of the first round.

Refrigerate the dough for at least 3 hours, or freeze for 1 hour. (*The dough can be refrigerated, well wrapped, for up to 3 days or frozen for up to 2 months.*)

TO MAKE THE FILLING: If using oranges, use a vegetable peeler to shave off a couple of strips of zest from 1 orange, then cut the orange in half. Toss the strips into a 4-quart saucepan and squeeze that orange's juice into the pan. Use a paring knife to cut off the peel from the second orange, cutting down to the fruit, then remove the orange segments, cutting along the membranes on both sides of each segment to release it. Cut the segments crosswise in half, toss them into the pan and squeeze in the juice from the membranes. Or, if you're using orange juice, not fruit, just pour it into the pan.

Put all of the remaining fruit and nuts, as well as the sugar and ginger, if you're using it, into the pan along with the water. Put the pan over high heat and cook, stirring, to get the juices bubbling. Lower the heat after about 3 minutes and cook, stirring pretty much constantly, until the fruit is soft and the liquid is just about gone, about 15 minutes. Remove the strips of zest and stir in the candied orange peel, if you're using it. Scrape the mixture into a heatproof bowl and cool to room temperature. (*If it's more convenient, you can cover the mixture and refrigerate it for up to 3 days.*)

TO ASSEMBLE AND BAKE THE GÂTEAU: Center a rack in the oven and preheat the oven to 350 degrees F. Generously butter an 8-inch round cake pan with 2-inch-high sides.

Remove the dough from the refrigerator (or freezer) and let the rounds rest on the counter for a couple of minutes before peeling away the paper. It's best to work with the dough when it's cold, but pliable, so let it sit a few more minutes, if necessary. Fit one piece of dough into the pan; if it breaks, just press the pieces together. If there's a little extra dough running up the sides of the pan, just leave it or, if you're very neat, trim it away. Spoon most of the filling onto the dough, leaving about an inch of bare dough around the edges. Add more filling if you think your top piece of dough will be able to fit over it—it's hard to be precise here, but it's equally hard to fail, so just make your best call.

Moisten the bare border of dough with a little water, top with the second piece of dough and press it around the edges to seal. If you can, work your fingers between the top piece of dough and the edges of the pan, and tuck the dough under a little. Because the dough is soft and leavened, what might look a little messy now will look beautiful *après* baking. Cut a small circle of dough out of the center of the pie for a steam vent (I use a piping tip for this job).

Brush the top of the dough with the egg glaze. Use the tines of a fork to etch a crosshatch pattern across the top. Sprinkle the top with sugar.

Bake the tourte for 55 to 65 minutes, or until the top is golden brown; if the fruit bubbles up through the opening, that's great. Transfer the tourte to a cooling rack and let it rest for 10 minutes.

Carefully run a table knife around the edges of the pan. Turn the tourte out onto a cooling rack covered with a piece of parchment or wax paper, then quickly and carefully invert it onto another rack and remove the paper. Cool the tourte right side up until it is only just warm or until it reaches room temperature before serving.

Bonne Idée
TRADITIONAL GÂTEAU BASQUE: Instead of the fruit filling, sandwich the rounds of dough with about ¾ cup Vanilla Pastry Cream (page 430) or thick black cherry jam. If you can find jam from Itxassou in the Pays Basque, you'll be enjoying the gâteau at its most authentic.

Jammer Galette

Makes 8 servings

SERVING: I dust the Jammer with confectioners' sugar when I'm ready to serve it—I like the way the sugar accentuates the streusel's bumps and dips—and often top it with ice cream.

STORING: Like most tarts, the galette is best the day it is made, but it can also be frozen. When it is completely cool, wrap it airtight and freeze for up to 2 months. Defrost it in its wrapper. If you'd like, you can warm it for a few minutes in a 350-degree-F oven before serving.

'VE OFTEN SAID THAT PARIS IS the city that most inspires me and that I go there to dream. I was being metaphorical, of course, until I wasn't. One cold Paris morning, I awoke from a dream—literally—and baked a cookie that became a family favorite. It was the Jammer, a vanilla sablé topped with a spoonful of jam and circled with streusel. And after Paris's pastry god, Pierre Hermé, pronounced it perfect, I went on to bake smaller and larger versions, including this thick, chunky galette.

This is a recipe to play with, so use whatever jam you love—just make sure it's not too runny. And, if you'd like, you can vary the streusel, adding a pinch or two of spice or maybe some chopped nuts. You can even add spice or nuts to the crust. Dream on!

FOR THE CRUST

- 1 stick (8 tablespoons; 4 ounces; 113 grams) unsalted butter, at room temperature
- ¼ cup (50 grams) sugar
- 2 tablespoons confectioners' sugar
- ¼ teaspoon fine sea salt
- 1 large egg yolk, at room temperature
- 1¼ teaspoons pure vanilla extract
- 1 cup (136 grams) all-purpose flour

FOR THE STREUSEL

- ¾ cup (102 grams) all-purpose flour
- ⅓ cup (67 grams) sugar
- ¼ teaspoon fine sea salt
- ¾ stick (6 tablespoons; 3 ounces; 85 grams) cold unsalted butter, cut into small cubes
- ¼ teaspoon pure vanilla extract

- 1 jar (about 13 ounces; 369 grams) thick fruit jam or marmalade

Confectioners' sugar, for dusting

TO MAKE THE CRUST: Working in the bowl of a stand mixer fitted with the paddle attachment, or in a medium bowl with a hand mixer, beat the butter, sugar, confectioners' sugar and salt together on low speed until smooth and creamy, about 3 minutes. You want to blend, not aerate, the mixture. Drop in the yolk and beat until incorporated, then beat in the vanilla extract. Turn off the mixer and add the flour, then pulse the mixer a few times just to start working it in. Turn the mixer to low and beat only until the flour is incorporated and the dough has come together.

Turn the dough out, gather it together and flatten it into a disk. Put the disk between two pieces of parchment or wax paper and roll it into a circle that's about ¼ inch thick (slightly thinner is fine). Don't worry about ragged edges or exact size; you're going to cut the dough to fit into a tart pan, so neatness doesn't count now. Slide the dough onto a cutting board or baking sheet and freeze for at least 1 hour or refrigerate for at least 3 hours. (*The dough can be frozen for up to 2 months or refrigerated for as long as overnight.*)

TO MAKE THE STREUSEL: While the dough is chilling (or even a few days or so ahead), put the flour, sugar and salt in a medium bowl and mix everything together by running the ingredients through your fingers. Drop in the butter and squeeze and rub the cubes into the mixture until you have a sandy mix. If you press a little streusel together, you'll get lumps, which is just what you want. Drizzle the vanilla over the streusel and toss, squeeze and rub to distribute it. Cover the bowl and chill the streusel until needed. (*You can make the streusel up to 1 week ahead; pack it in an airtight container and keep it refrigerated.*)

TO ASSEMBLE AND BAKE THE TART: Center a rack in the oven and preheat the oven to 350 degrees F. Generously butter a 9- to 9½-inch tart pan with a removable bottom. Line a baking sheet with parchment or a silicone baking mat.

Remove the dough from the freezer or fridge and peel off the top sheet of paper. Using the bottom of the tart pan as a guide, cut out a circle of dough. Turn it over, peel away the paper and fit the dough into the pan. Put the pan on the baking sheet.

Spoon the jam onto the dough: You can dollop it or spread it into an even layer, but in either case you want to leave a jamless border of about ½ inch. Give the streusel mixture a few squeezes to clump it. Cover the top of the galette with streusel, going all the way to the edges of the crust and not worrying if some streusel falls against the pan's rim.

Bake the galette for 45 to 50 minutes, or until the streusel is golden brown and the jam is bubbling. Transfer the baking sheet to a rack and cool the galette for 15 minutes.

Remove the sides of the pan and cool the galette to room temperature. Just before serving, dust it with confectioners' sugar.

Martine's Lemon and Apple Tart

Makes 8 servings

SERVING: Martine served this tart plain and it's the way I serve it most often. But because it's very tart, you can serve a little whipped cream with it to tone down the tang. If you do, add only a little or no sugar to the cream. Other possibilities are crème fraîche, sour cream or a spoonful of Greek yogurt (which might need a sprinkle of sugar).

STORING: Best served the day it is made, the tart can be kept overnight in the refrigerator and eaten cold. It will taste different, but it will still be good.

I F YOU HAVE SOMETHING YOU LOVE at Martine Collet's house, the only way to enjoy it again is to ask for the recipe and make it yourself: She never repeats a dish! In addition to being a great friend, a wonderful hostess and a terrific cook, Martine is the most organized person I've ever met. She keeps a set of notebooks in which she records every meal she makes for friends, her insurance that she'll never serve anyone the same thing twice. Heaven forbid you're hoping for something she made thirty years ago (her notebooks go back even further). So knowing I'd never see this tart again chez Martine, I asked for the recipe immediately.

The unmistakable and assertive flavor of this tart is sharp lemon. Grated apple helps to round out the blend, but it's there mostly for texture: The lemon clings to it, and the tang lingers because of it.

1 partially baked 9- to 9½-inch tart crust made with Sweet Tart Dough (page 414), cooled	2 large eggs, at room temperature
	3 medium apples, such as Fuji or Golden Delicious
2–3 lemons	½ stick (4 tablespoons; 2 ounces; 57 grams) unsalted butter, melted and cooled
⅔ cup (132 grams) sugar	

Center a rack in the oven and preheat the oven to 400 degrees F. Place the tart pan with the partially baked crust on a baking sheet lined with parchment paper or a silicone baking mat.

Grate the zest of 2 of the lemons into a large bowl. I like the zest to be a little coarse for this recipe, but fine works too. Squeeze the juice of the 2 lemons into a measuring cup. If you don't have ¼ cup, squeeze enough juice from the third lemon until you do.

Pour the sugar over the zest and, using your fingers, rub the sugar and zest together until the mixture is fragrant. Add the eggs to the bowl and immediately whisk them in (so that the yolks don't "cook"), then whisk in the lemon juice.

Peel the apples and then grate them: You can grate the apples with the grating blade of a food processor or use the big holes on a box grater, which is what I do. To avoid having the apples turn dark, I peel and grate each one in turn, holding the box grater over the bowl, and stirring them in to the sugar mixture as I go. If you use the processor, stir all the apples into the bowl. Whisk in the butter. (At this point, the filling will not look pretty, but don't lose faith—heat will fix everything.) Immediately pour the filling into the crust and use the tip of your whisk (or a spoon) to move the apple strands around so that they come close to being evenly distributed.

Bake the tart for 40 to 45 minutes, or until it is set to the center—tap the pan to see if the filling is firm. Check after about 25 minutes and if the crust is getting too dark, cover the edges with a ring of aluminum foil. Place the baking sheet on a cooling rack and let the tart cool to room temperature before you serve it.

Apple Tarte Flambée

Makes 4 servings

SERVING: Just like pizza, *tarte flambée* is meant to be eaten seconds out of the oven. At Flamme & Co, the dessert is served with a fork and knife (the way just about everything is served in France), but chez you, it's fine to pick it up and eat it out of hand—it's what we do chez moi.

STORING: Once made, the tart has to be eaten immediately. You can make the dough a day ahead, let it rise, flatten it and put it in the refrigerator. Keep flattening it as it rises and then, when it's worn itself out (usually in an hour or two), wrap it tightly in plastic film and keep it cold. When you're ready to make the tart, take the dough out of the refrigerator, put it in a covered bowl in a warm place and allow it to rise to double its size again.

IT'S OKAY IF YOU THINK *tarte flambée* is pizza—everyone in France does, except the Alsatians, who created and treasure it. The classic *tarte flambée* — sometimes called *flammkuchen*—is savory and, like pizza, it's built on a thin base of bread dough that's baked in a ferociously hot oven until it bubbles and blisters. It's topped with fresh cheese—usually fromage blanc and crème fraîche—and scattered with bacon and onions. Like pizza, it's ubiquitous, at least in eastern France. And also like pizza, it can be very, very good or very, very bad. It is wonderful at Flamme & Co restaurant, where the chef, Olivier Nasti, who trained with the greats and earned the Meilleur Ouvrier de France, the highest award a chef can attain, decided to turn his talents to making the best—and most modern—*tarte flambée* in the region.

At Flamme & Co, the *tarte flambée* is paper-thin, bursting with flavor and either sweet or savory. Their tarts are rolled out in rectangles, baked in a flash and served on wooden cutting boards. My husband and I each had a savory one and then we shared a version of this apple tart. By the time dessert came around, I had asked the server so many questions that he suggested I go into the open kitchen and make my own tart with the chef—an invitation I didn't refuse.

The instant we got back to Paris, I went on a *tarte-flambée-*baking binge, and I amazed my Alsatian friends, not because I'd made the tarts, but because I'd made my own yeast-risen dough instead of using store-bought bread dough or puff pastry. If you'd like, you've got my permission to go Parisian and use store-bought dough. Do that, and you'll be able to whip up a *tarte flambée* on the spur of the moment.

A WORD ON BAKING AND GEAR: The best tartes are baked in wood-burning ovens, but you can get a great crust by cranking your oven up to its max and using a baking stone. Put the baking stone into the cold oven, turn up the heat and let the oven preheat for another 20 minutes after it's reached temperature. If you don't have a baking stone, use a heavy cookie sheet. If you've got a pizza peel, pull it out; if not, use a rimless cookie sheet as a peel. The *tarte flambée* is going to be big, so if your baking stone isn't large, make two smaller tarts.

FOR THE CRUST

¾ teaspoon active dry yeast

2 teaspoons sugar

About ½ cup (120 ml) warm water, plus a bit more if needed

1 cup (136 grams) all-purpose flour

2 tablespoons whole wheat flour

2 tablespoons rye flour

¾ teaspoon fine sea salt

4 teaspoons olive oil

FOR THE TOPPING

1½ ounces (43 grams) cream cheese, at room temperature

¼ cup (56 grams) plain Greek yogurt (nonfat is fine) or use ⅓ cup (95 grams) fromage blanc in place of the cream cheese and yogurt

2 tablespoons heavy cream or crème fraîche

2 tablespoons sugar

1 tablespoon all-purpose flour

2 large apples, such as Golden Delicious or Fuji

Sugar or cinnamon sugar, for dusting

TO MAKE THE CRUST: Put the yeast, 1 teaspoon of the sugar and ¼ cup of the warm water (check the yeast package for the correct temperature) in a small bowl. Stir and let stand for about 5 minutes, or until the yeast dissolves and becomes creamy. The mixture may or may not bubble.

Put the all-purpose, whole wheat and rye flours, along with the remaining 1 teaspoon sugar and the salt, in the bowl of a stand mixer fitted with the paddle attachment. (Alternatively, you can make this dough in a bowl with a wooden spoon.) Turn the mixer to low and beat just to blend the dry ingredients. Pour in the yeast mixture and continue to mix for a minute or two; the dough will be dry and shaggy, but that's fine. Mix the olive oil with the remaining ¼ cup warm water, pour it into the bowl and mix at medium speed. The dough will quickly absorb the liquid and, in a minute or so, start to ball up around the paddle and slap the sides of the bowl. If the dough looks dry and doesn't come together, add some more water a teaspoonful at a time. Depending on your flour (and the day), the dough might need just a splash or a couple of teaspoons water. Keep the mixer at medium speed and beat the dough for 5 minutes. (If you're working by hand, turn the dough out onto a lightly floured work surface and knead the dough until it is smooth.) You'll have a springy, slightly sticky dough.

Shape the dough into a ball, place it in a clean bowl and cover the bowl tightly with plastic film. Put the bowl in a warm spot (between 70 and 75 degrees F) and allow the dough to rise until doubled in volume, 2 to 2½ hours.

Position a rack in the lower third of the oven and remove any higher racks; you'll need room to get the *tarte flambée* in and out quickly. If you've got a pizza or bread stone, put it on the rack; if not, put a heavy cookie sheet on the rack (or, in a pinch, flip over a rimmed baking sheet). Preheat the

Because the dough and
cream topping are so
accommodating, you can
play around endlessly with
the fruit topping, as long as
you keep the slices thin. In
summer, think about sliced
peaches, apricots, plums or
whole berries and perhaps
a few sprigs of herbs. In
winter, think sliced pears,
pineapple, mango or even
bananas.

oven to its highest setting, as close to 600 degrees F as you can get. After the temperature indicator goes off, keep preheating for another 20 minutes—remember, you've got to heat the stone as well as the oven. If you've got a pizza peel, have it at the ready; a rimless cookie sheet makes a good stand-in. (Take a look at the note on baking and gear on page 118.)

MEANWHILE, MAKE THE TOPPING: Whisk all of the ingredients together in a medium bowl until smooth. Cover until needed.

Turn the dough out onto a floured work surface and press it down with your palms. Lightly flour the top of the dough and start rolling it out. You can roll the dough into a rectangle, a circle or something more free-form. Rolling a springy yeast dough like this isn't easy and so I'm content to go with whatever shape I end up with; the shape is less important than the thinness. You want to roll the dough as thin as you possibly can and, to get it to behave and thin out, you might have to roll, let it rest for a few minutes, roll and rest again. Relax, and the dough will too. Each time you let the dough rest, cover it with plastic film or a kitchen towel.

Lightly flour the preheated peel or rimless cookie sheet and transfer the dough to it. (I roll the dough up around my floured rolling pin and then unroll it onto the peel.) Brush off any excess flour and use a fork to prick the dough all over—really, all over. You want to make sure you prick the dough all the way through, so listen for the rat-a-tat of the fork against the peel.

Slide the baking stone into the oven, shut the oven door and set a timer for 1 minute. When the timer rings, pull out the tart. Depending on what kind of work surface you have, you can either put the hot tart on the counter or slide it onto a cooling rack.

Using a flexible spatula or a large spoon, spread the topping over the crust, going very close to the edges.

Cut a small slice off two opposite sides of each apple to expose the flesh and then slice each apple, from top to bottom, paper-thin on a mandolin or Benriner until you've almost reached the core on the first side of the apple. (If you don't have a mandoline, cut the apples in half from top to bottom and slice them with a thin blade on a food processor, or do this by hand.) Turn the apple to the opposite side and slice almost to the core. (The leftover piece encasing the core is the baker's nibble.) Arrange the apple slices in a single layer over the cream topping. Sprinkle generously with sugar or cinnamon sugar.

Slide the tart back onto the baking stone and bake for about 5 minutes more. You want the crust to be dark and well baked on the bottom, and if you've got a burnt edge here or there and the occasional curled and browned apple slice, so much the better.

Transfer the tart to a cutting board, immediately cut it with a pizza wheel or chef's knife and serve.

Apple Pielettes

I CREATED THESE LITTLE PIES as a bring-along dessert for a potluck dinner in Connecticut, and then I made them again and again on both sides of the Atlantic. The dough is pure French and the filling pretty much American, but they're appreciated no matter where I serve them. In the United States, they're enjoyed as a charming play on our nationally beloved apple pie; in France, they're greeted as a nationally beloved tourte (think double-crusted tart). With their golden tops speckled with bubbled-over juices and dotted with caramelized sugar, they're more homey than polished, and most likely to be the first thing grabbed from any dessert spread.

If you have little pie pans, you can use them for this recipe (you might get fewer than a dozen), but my pan of choice here is a muffin tin. It's a little fussier to work with—it takes a bit more fiddling to get the dough molded into the cups—but I love the shape you get (so very like a French mini tourte) and it gives you the perfect size for a pielette. Similarly, you can make the pielettes with your favorite pie dough (in fact, I used pie dough the first time), but Galette Dough (page 420) is now my go-to for this: It's a pleasure to work with, holds its shape and tastes great.

Just as you can play with the pan and the dough, you can play with the filling. Feel free to change the dried fruits or omit them; add nuts if you'd like; or grate in some zest. When I've got applesauce in the house, I add a spoonful to the mix. And there's nothing sacred about the jelly or marmalade. Think of the muffin tins lined with dough as cups waiting to be filled with what you love.

Makes 12 servings

SERVING: The pielettes are good warm or at room temperature, plain (perhaps eaten out of hand), dolled up with whipped cream or given the à-la-mode treatment.

STORING: They may be pielettes, but they behave just like their bigger brethren: They're best the day they're made. However, you can make the dough, cut it out and keep the rounds in the freezer for up to 2 months; defrost and soften them, still wrapped, in the refrigerator. You can also construct the pielettes and freeze them, unbaked, for up to 2 months. The best way to do this is to line the muffin cups with plastic film, assemble the pielettes, chill them until firm (they'll be easier to handle) and then remove them from the cups and pack them airtight. Bake them straight from the freezer in a buttered tin, knowing that they'll need a little more time in the oven.

FOR THE CRUST
Double recipe Galette Dough
(page 420), just made

FOR THE FILLING
3 medium apples, such as Fuji, Gala or Golden Delicious, peeled, cored and cut into small chunks
¼ cup (40 grams) plump, moist dark or golden raisins
3 plump, moist dried apricots, cut into small cubes
1 tablespoon sugar (or perhaps a little more)
1 tablespoon apple jelly or orange marmalade
¼ teaspoon pure vanilla extract (optional)
Tiny pinch of freshly grated nutmeg
Tiny pinch of ground cinnamon

Sugar, for sprinkling

TO MAKE THE CRUST: Cut the dough in half and pat each half into a disk. Working with one disk at a time, sandwich the dough between two pieces of parchment or wax paper and roll it out (don't worry about the shape) to a thickness of between ⅛ and ¼ inch. Stack the rolled-out pieces of dough one on top of the other on a cutting board or baking sheet and put them in the freezer for 30 minutes (or the fridge for 1 hour) to firm.

Lightly butter a 12-cup muffin tin.

To make the bottom crusts, use a biscuit or cookie cutter to cut out rounds of dough that are about 3 inches in diameter. Wait for the rounds to soften enough to be pliable, then carefully fit them into the cups. (If the dough cracks or tears, moisten the edges of the crack and press them together.) Put the muffin tin in the fridge.

To cut out the tops, use the next smallest biscuit or cookie cutter, one that's about 2¾ inches in diameter. Put the rounds on a lined baking sheet, cover and pop into the refrigerator. Gather the scraps together, reroll them, chill and cut out more rounds as needed.

Center a rack in the oven and preheat the oven to 400 degrees F. Line a baking sheet with parchment paper or a silicone baking mat.

TO MAKE THE FILLING: Mix all the ingredients together in a medium bowl. Taste to see if you'd like a bit more sugar or a touch more spice.

Remove the muffin tin from the refrigerator and divide the filling among the cups. Moisten your finger with water and run it around the rim of each crust, then top each with a round of dough, pressing against the sides of the pielettes to "glue" the top and bottom crusts together. Brush the tops lightly with water and sprinkle with sugar, then cut 3 short slits for steam vents in each one. Put the muffin tin on the lined baking sheet.

Bake for about 45 minutes, rotating the pan from back to front at the midway mark, until the top crusts are deeply golden brown and the syrupy apple juices are bubbling up through the vents. Often some of the juice will bubble over and dribble down the sides of the pielettes, an accident to be wished for, since the drips turn into a nice caramel coating. Transfer the muffin tin to a cooling rack and let rest for 3 minutes, then carefully run a table knife around the sides of the pielettes to loosen them. Turn the muffin tin over onto the rack to unmold the pielettes, then turn the pielettes right side up and let them cool until just warm or at room temperature before serving.

THE "FRENCH BAKE"

A few years ago, when my son and I were doing a cookie pop-up shop, Sarabeth Levine, a New York baker, was very generous and let us work with her in her kitchen. The first time I pulled sheets of cookies out of her oven, she said, "I see you like the French bake."

I didn't have a clue what she meant.

For Sarabeth, when something is French-baked, it has turned a deep golden brown. She was right: That's the way I like things.

When you're baking, color equals flavor. If you don't brown your butter crusts and cookies—as well as some pastries, cakes and breads (and this is most true for buttery sweets)—then you're not bringing out all the full flavor of your ingredients. So that's why I'm known as Miss One-More-Minute— I'm always putting the baking sheets back in the oven for a little more time and a bit more color.

As I looked around French pastry shops, I saw that Sarabeth was right: The pastries are always fully golden—French-baked. If you don't share my obsession, start testing your crusts and cookies a little earlier than I tell you to. But while the choice is yours, I hope you'll give the French bake a try— for starters, with the Vanilla-Bean Sablés (page 261).

Pear Tart with Crunchy Almond Topping

THE TOPPING OF THIS TART has crunch, color and flavor and it could be a show-stealer, but it's not: The pears, caramelized in butter and sugar and flamed with brandy, more than hold their own. And because the components are so full flavored, you can play mix and match with them. The topping, which is made of sliced almonds, confectioners' sugar and egg whites baked to a crisp, is perfect over apples, quinces, rhubarb or even berries. And the pears are terrific under streusel, whipped cream, or ice cream and Salted Caramel Sauce (page 447).

Makes 8 servings

SERVING: The tart would be nice with whipped cream or ice cream, but I never serve it any way but the plain way.

STORING: This is a tart to make and savor on the same day, although it can be made up to 8 hours ahead and kept at room temperature. Should you find yourself with leftovers, or if the day turns humid and the topping goes from snappy to sticky, pop the tart into a 400-degree-F oven for 5 minutes.

FOR THE TOPPING

- 1 cup (120 grams) confectioners' sugar
- 3 large egg whites
- 1½ cups (150 grams) sliced almonds (blanched or unblanched)
- 1 fully baked 9- to 9½-inch tart crust made from Sweet Tart Dough (page 414), cooled

FOR THE FILLING

- 3 tablespoons (1½ ounces; 43 grams) unsalted butter
- 5 ripe but firm pears, peeled, cored and cut into ½-inch chunks
- 2½ tablespoons sugar
- 2 tablespoons brandy, rum or bourbon (optional)

Confectioners' sugar, for dusting

TO MAKE THE TOPPING: Put the confectioners' sugar in a wide bowl and pour the egg whites over it. Using your fingers (you can use a fork, but your hands really work best here), mix the sugar and whites together gently—don't worry about lumps, just moisten the sugar with the whites. Add the almonds and toss until they are thoroughly coated with the sweet mixture. Leave the bowl on the counter while you get the filling ready.

Center a rack in the oven and preheat the oven to 400 degrees F. Place the tart pan with the fully baked crust on a baking sheet lined with parchment paper or a silicone baking mat.

TO MAKE THE FILLING: Toss the butter into a medium skillet—I use a 9-inch nonstick pan—and put the pan over medium-high heat. When the butter is melted and bubbling, add the pears. Let the pears cook, turning them only a couple of times, until they are browned here and there and just starting to soften, about 5 minutes. Sprinkle over the sugar and continue to cook and stir (again, not a lot) until the fruit is lightly caramelized, about 2 minutes more. If you're using the liquor, pour it over the fruit and allow it to warm, then turn off the heat, stand back, set a match to the pan and flame the alcohol. (If it looks as if the alcohol has almost evaporated—something that can happen if your pan is really hot—skip the flaming.) Scrape the pears and whatever bit of liquid remains in the pan into the crust and jostle the pears to make a roughly even layer.

Turn the topping around a few more times in the bowl—the mixture will be thick and sticky—and then spoon it over the pears, patting it down gently into an even layer all the way to the edges of the crust.

Bake the tart until the topping is golden brown all over and the nuts are shiny, 20 to 25 minutes. Transfer the tart to a rack and let cool until it is just warm or until it reaches room temperature.

Generously dust the tart with confectioners' sugar before serving.

Fall-Market Galette

I CAME HOME FROM THE FRIDAY MARKET on the Boulevard Raspail in Paris, emptied my basket, looked at the purple fruit piled on the counter and smiled with pleasure: I'd bought them separately, but seeing them bumping up against one another, I realized that they were meant to be together. There were Italian plums, the small, dusky, purple plums known in France as *quetsches*; soft-to-the-squeeze figs from Provence; and aromatic dark purple, almost black Muscat grapes. Knowing that the fruits would become almost honeyed in the oven, I mounded them on a circle of dough and turned them into this galette.

While I'm giving you a recipe, I'd like to think that you'll use it as a template, changing it to match whatever fruit you find in the market when fall comes. When I made my first purple galette, I broke up some walnuts and tossed them over the fruit, and I also stirred the grated zest of a clementine into the mix. Pears, apples and some plumped dried fruit made guest appearances in later versions. And when I'm in America, I add fresh cranberries.

Makes 6 servings

SERVING: Transfer the galette to a serving platter using a cake lifter or a small cookie sheet. If you'd like, dust the crust with confectioners' sugar. If you haven't glazed the fruit, you can give it a light dusting of sugar too.

STORING: The galette should be eaten the day it is made; the closer to the time it's made, the better, since the little seeds in the figs have a tricky way of getting hard faster than you'd think possible.

1 recipe Galette Dough (page 420), rolled out and chilled

20 black grapes, such as Muscat (preferably seedless)

10 Italian plums, halved and pitted

3 fresh figs, quartered

2 tablespoons packed light brown sugar
   Grated zest of 1 clementine, tangerine or lemon

3 plain butter cookies, such as Petit Beurre, homemade (page 270) or store-bought
   Broken walnuts (optional)

1 tablespoon cold unsalted butter, cut into bits

   Sanding, raw or granulated sugar, for sprinkling

¼ cup (80 grams) apple, quince or currant jelly, for glazing (optional)

   Confectioners' sugar, for dusting (optional)

Center a rack in the oven and preheat the oven to 400 degrees F.

Take the rolled-out dough from the refrigerator, remove the top piece of parchment paper and, if the dough isn't already on a rimmed baking sheet, move it to one. Leave it on the counter while you mix the fruit.

Put the grapes, plums, figs, brown sugar and zest in a medium bowl and stir to coat the fruit with sugar. Set aside for 5 minutes, stirring a couple of times, so that the sugar dissolves and you have a little liquid in the bowl.

Break the cookies into small pieces and crumbs (you can do this with your fingers or, if you'd like, you can "dice" the cookies with a knife—it's what I do)

and sprinkle them over the galette dough, leaving a bare border of about 2 inches all around.

Give the fruit a last stir and spoon it and whatever liquid has accumulated onto the galette, again leaving the border bare. If you're using walnuts, strew them over the galette, then scatter over the bits of cold butter. Gently lift the border of dough up and around the filling; as you lift the dough and place it against the filling, it will pleat—it's meant to. Brush it very lightly with a little water, then sprinkle it with (sanding, raw or granulated) sugar.

Bake the galette for about 45 minutes, or until the crust is deeply golden brown, the juices are bubbling and a knife poked into any piece of fruit meets no resistance; the fruit is meant to be truly cooked through.

Meanwhile, if you want to glaze the galette—a nice touch, since the fruit will lose its sheen as it cools—bring the jelly and a splash of water to a boil in a microwave oven (cover the bowl) or in a saucepan on the stove. Brush the hot jelly over the fruit as soon as the galette comes out of the oven.

Glazed or not, the galette should rest on the baking sheet until it is just warm or reaches room temperature. Dust the crust with confectioners' sugar before serving, if you'd like.

Pear-Cranberry Roll-Up Tart

Makes 6 servings

SERVING: The roll-up is good warm, at room temperature or even cold, plain or with whipped cream or—best, best, best—ice cream.

STORING: You can make the dough up to 2 months ahead and keep it rolled out, well covered, in the freezer, or roll it out and refrigerate it overnight, but once the tart is made, it's best enjoyed that day.

THE IDEA FOR THIS ALMOST-BUT-NOT-QUITE-A-TART came after a wonderful evening with friends. We'd met for drinks at a new wine bar near our apartment in Paris, and later everyone came back to our place for what I thought of as an indoor picnic and yes, more wine. Then, as the evening was winding down and we were sipping espresso and nibbling on the last of the cookies, Clotilde Bouchet asked if she'd ever mentioned how her mother, an Alsatian, and therefore almost by definition a baker, made her apple tart. I grabbed a pencil and paper and was all ears as Clotilde explained that her mother would make a sweet tart dough and roll it out into a large rectangle—thin and irregular. She'd top the dough with apples and nuts and then roll the dough up around the filling, jelly-roll style.

The following day, I tried my hand at the roll-up, using galette dough, and the recipe worked as promised—no surprises. Except the one when I brought it to the table: My friends exclaimed that they were delighted to have a sweet they hadn't had in a while: strudel! Hmmm. It wasn't my idea of strudel (a pastry I've never tackled), but if it made my friends happy, I wasn't about to argue over nomenclature.

Since then, I've made this roll-up with apples, in the style of Mme Bouchet (see Bonne Idée); with peaches, plums and berries (page 134), in homage to summer; and with pears and cranberries, as here, in a twist on Thanksgiving. Like an American pie, the French "strudel" can be filled with whatever is in season.

A WORD ON CONSTRUCTION: Even with easy-to-work galette dough, you're bound to have tears and cracks. To patch them before the tart goes into the oven, smooth them over and blend them together with a little water and your fingers. Once the tart goes into the oven, the dough might crack, but you won't be able to fix these fissures—just admire them.

FOR THE DOUGH

1 recipe Galette Dough (page 420), ready to roll

FOR THE FILLING

2 firm but ripe medium pears, peeled, cored and cut into ½-inch chunks

½ cup (50 grams) fresh or frozen (not thawed) cranberries

2 tablespoons orange marmalade or raspberry jam

1 tablespoon sugar

½ teaspoon finely grated peeled fresh ginger

¼ teaspoon ground ginger

1 large egg, for glazing
Sanding sugar (my choice) or granulated sugar, for dusting

TO ROLL OUT THE DOUGH: Place the dough between two sheets of parchment or wax paper and roll it until you have a rectangle (more or less) that's 11 × 14 inches (more or less). Slide the dough, still between the papers, onto a cutting board or baking sheet and refrigerate while you prepare the filling.

TO MAKE THE FILLING: Stir all the ingredients together in a medium bowl. Allow them to sit for about 20 minutes.

TO ASSEMBLE THE TART: Remove the dough from the fridge, peel off the top sheet of paper and allow the dough to sit at room temperature just until it's pliable enough to roll—a matter of a few minutes. If the dough is on wax paper, move it, when it's still cold, to a sheet of parchment or a silicone baking mat.

Meanwhile, beat the egg with a splash of cold water.

When the dough is workable, turn it so that a long side is toward you and spoon the filling—minus the juices that will have accumulated—over it, leaving 2 to 3 inches of dough bare at the top and bottom and about 2 inches of dough bare on either side. Lift the top of the dough over the filling and start rolling the dough toward you, doing the best you can to keep the filling within the roll. Finish with the seam on the bottom. Fold the ends in and under like a package and seal the exposed seams with the egg wash, smoothing them with your fingers. If the dough has cracked in any place, as

Center a rack in the oven and preheat the oven to 400 degrees F.

Line the crust with a piece of parchment or a buttered piece of aluminum foil and weight it down with rice, dried beans or light pie weights. Bake the crust for 20 minutes, then carefully remove the paper and weights and bake for 8 to 12 minutes more, or until the crust is golden. The crust will have shrunk, but that's fine. Set the crust on a rack to cool to room temperature.

WHEN YOU'RE READY TO FILL AND BAKE THE TART: Preheat the oven to 300 degrees F.

Spoon the jam into the crust and spread it evenly over the bottom.

Working in the bowl of a stand mixer fitted with the whisk attachment, or in a large bowl with a hand mixer, beat the egg whites with the salt at medium speed just until they turn opaque. With the mixer going, add the sugar in a very slow, steady stream, then keep beating until the whites are shiny and form peaks with pretty, droopy tips; they will look like marshmallow.

Pour the cranberries into the bowl and, using a flexible spatula, fold them into the meringue. Try to distribute the fruit evenly, but don't try too hard—you want to keep the meringue fluffy. Turn the meringue over the jam and spread it to the edges, making it swirly if you'd like. The jam will sneak up around the sides of the meringue, and that's fine.

Bake the tart for 1 hour, at which point the top will be light beige and most probably cracked here and there. (If you'd like more color, you can bake it longer or put it under the broiler.) Transfer the tart to a cooling rack and cool to room temperature. If you'd like, dust the tart with confectioners' sugar before serving.

Pink Grapefruit Tart

Makes 8 servings

SERVING: I always serve this tart bare, but because it's not overly sweet, it's also lovely with cream, lightly whipped and lightly sweetened.

STORING: The tart will hold nicely in the refrigerator for 8 hours. I've kept it longer and it's been fine, but it's really at its best the day it is made. However, you can make all the tart's elements ahead and assemble them a few hours before serving.

THIS IS ONE OF MY FAVORITE PASTRIES from Hugo & Victor, one of my favorite—and one of the most beautiful—pastry shops in Paris. The pâtisserie is so striking that the first time I entered, my intention was to whisper—it felt a touch museum-like—but instead I ended up exclaiming a not-at-all-genteel-nor-hushed all-American "wow!" It's the reaction most people seem to have. It's not because of the polished displays that spotlight each season's star ingredients. Nor is it because of the exquisite boxes with their stretch-ribbon closings that make them look like Moleskine journals. It's the stunning pastries themselves, which are made by the master pastry chef Hugues Pouget. Each is a little marvel of craftsmanship, art and imagination. I love the way the puckish chef combines flavors and textures, how he riffs on classics and how he takes what might be everyday and, as with this grapefruit tart, makes you reconsider it—not for more than a nanosecond, of course, since the urge to dig in always takes over.

The selection at Hugo & Victor changes with the seasons and for every holiday, but there are some pastries that never change; if they did, there'd be a customer revolt. This tart is one of those always-in-the-shop creations. It has four parts: a sweet crust; a thin, thin layer of baked almond cream flavored with lemon; a pink-hued grapefruit and Campari filling (which I would be happy to eat by the spoonful every day); and fresh grapefruit sections. It's a tour de force dessert. And while the filling may seem like the tart's raison d'être, the genius is in the interplay of textures and the way each of the elements reinforces the flavors of the others.

The filling is very much like the one used in the lime tart (page 184), a butter-enriched crème anglaise made with fruit juice instead of the classic milk and cream. But here it's technically a *crémeux* since it's stabilized with gelatin, which allows you to use fewer eggs. By design, this filling is not very sweet and the Campari, which gives the crémeux its gorgeous color, adds a touch of bitterness and a good deal of excitement to the flavor.

Yes, there are many parts to this tart, but they can all be made ahead. In fact, the *crémeux* must be made ahead and the lemon-almond cream is better made in advance, so you can prepare the elements over the course of a couple of days and assemble the tart the day you want to serve it. You could even omit the lemon-almond cream and treat this as you would a more traditional citrus tart.

3½ tablespoons (1¾ ounces;
50 grams) unsalted butter,
at room temperature
2 tablespoons packed light
brown sugar
½ cup (50 grams) almond flour
Finely grated zest of 1 lemon
1 large egg, at room
temperature

FOR THE GRAPEFRUIT
CRÉMEUX
2 teaspoons unflavored gelatin
1½ tablespoons cold water

¾ cup (150 grams) sugar
2 large pink grapefruits
3 large eggs
1¾ sticks (14 tablespoons;
7 ounces; 198 grams)
unsalted butter, cut into
14 pieces, at room
temperature
2½ tablespoons Campari

FOR THE TOPPING
2 large pink grapefruits

1 fully baked 9- to 9½-inch tart
crust made from Sweet Tart
Dough (page 414), cooled

TO MAKE THE LEMON-ALMOND CREAM: Using a food processor or working in the bowl of a stand mixer fitted with the paddle attachment, or a medium bowl with a hand mixer, beat the butter until smooth and creamy, about 3 minutes. Add the brown sugar and beat for a minute or two more. Add the almond flour and zest and beat until the mixture is smooth once again. Drop in the egg and beat for a minute or so, until it is thoroughly incorporated. If you're pressed for time, you can use the cream now, but it's better if you cover and refrigerate it for at least 1 hour (or for up to 3 days). Whisk before using.

TO MAKE THE GRAPEFRUIT CRÉMEUX: You'll need a blender—my first choice—or a food processor for this, so have it and a strainer nearby.

Put the gelatin in a small microwave-safe bowl and pour over the cold water. Set aside for about 3 minutes, until the gelatin absorbs the water and "blooms," or expands. When you're ready to use it, heat it in a microwave oven for about 15 seconds to liquefy.

Pour the sugar into a 2- to 3-quart heavy-bottomed saucepan and grate the zest from the 2 grapefruits over it. Using your fingertips, rub and work the sugar and zest together until the sugar is moist. Squeeze the juice from the 2 grapefruits into a measuring cup, stopping when you've got ¾ cup. Add the eggs to the saucepan and immediately start to whisk energetically. Just as energetically, whisk in the juice.

Place the saucepan over medium heat (medium-low if you've got a powerful burner) and continue whisking. You don't have to whisk vigorously, but you do have to whisk nonstop—let up for even a minute, and the crémeux may burn. For the first few minutes, you won't see much change in the custard, but keep at it and you'll notice that soon it will take a second for the custard to fill the space your whisk leaves at the bottom of the pan.

Keep whisking, making sure to get into the corners of the pan, and after 7 to 9 minutes, the custard will thicken. If you stick a wooden spoon into it and then run your finger down the back of the spoon, the custard won't fill the track you created. Here's the important sign: One bubble will pop at the surface. If you measure the temperature of the custard with an instant-read thermometer, it should be about 180 degrees F (don't go higher). When that bubble pops, immediately remove the pan from the heat and strain the crémeux into the blender; discard the zest and any bits of eggs that scrambled.

Allow the custard to sit in the blender for about 5 minutes—pulse a few times during this period—and then blend in the liquefied gelatin. With the blender on high, start adding the butter 2 chunks at a time. Keep whirring and tossing in the butter and then, when all the butter is in, whir for another minute. Add the Campari and whir it in. Scrape the beautiful pale pink crémeux into a bowl, press a piece of plastic film against the surface to keep a skin from forming and refrigerate for at least 6 hours (or for up to 2 days).

TO MAKE THE TOPPING: About 3 hours (or up to 8 hours) before you want to serve the tart, cut off the top and bottom of the grapefruits. One at a time, stand each grapefruit on a cutting board and, cutting from top to bottom, cut the peel and pith away from the grapefruit in strips, cutting all the way down to the flesh. Then, using a small paring knife, cut between the membranes to release the segments of fruit. Place the grapefruit segments on a triple thickness of paper towels, cover with three more paper towels and let sit at room temperature until ready to use. It's a good idea to change the paper towels once; you want to dry the fruit as much as possible.

TO BAKE THE TART: This is also best done a few hours before serving. Center a rack in the oven and preheat the oven to 375 degrees F.

Place the tart pan with the fully baked crust on a baking sheet lined with parchment or a silicone baking mat.

Spread the chilled lemon-almond cream over the bottom of the crust; you'll have a thin layer. Bake the tart for 6 to 7 minutes, or until the cream is set. Remove the tart from the oven and cool completely on a rack.

TO FINISH THE TART: About 2 hours before you're ready to serve the tart, remove the grapefruit crémeux from the refrigerator, whisk it to soften and smooth it (it will have become quite firm) and spread it evenly over the lemon-almond cream in the tart shell. Arrange the grapefruit segments attractively on the top of the grapefruit crémeux and return the tart to the refrigerator for another 2 hours (or up to 8 hours) before serving.

Brown Butter–Peach Tourte

SERVING: Whatever you serve with the tourte—vanilla ice cream or frozen yogurt (I like the tang of yogurt with the sweet peaches), softly whipped cream or even more softly whipped crème fraîche—don't let it cover the top of the tourte. The top crust is much too pretty to hide.

STORING: You can partially bake the bottom crust up to 8 hours ahead and you can have the top crust rolled out and ready to go ahead of time, but the filling shouldn't be prepared ahead. The baked tourte is really best served that day. If you've got leftovers, refrigerate them. The crust will lose its delicateness, but the tourte will still be satisfying.

BROWN BUTTER. PEACH. TOURTE. Each of these words makes me happy; together they describe one of my favorite desserts: a covered tart made with sweet dough and filled with peaches glistening in butter that's been simmered until it turns fragrant, golden brown and almost caramel flavored. The fact that the top crust melts just a little, following the contours of the filling and creating an undulating sugar-sparkled crown for the fruit, only adds to the tourte's temptations.

HEADS UP: You need good peaches for this tourte. There's only a little sugar, a little flour, some vanilla and a squirt of lemon juice, so all you get are the essentials: peaches, butter and crust.

FOR THE FILLING

- 2 pounds (907 grams) ripe but firm peaches
- 3 tablespoons (1½ ounces; 43 grams) unsalted butter
- 3 tablespoons sugar
- 1 tablespoon all-purpose flour
  Tiny pinch of fine sea salt
- ¼ teaspoon pure vanilla extract (or a drop of pure almond extract)
  Juice of ¼ lemon, or to taste

FOR THE CRUST

- 1 partially baked 9- to 9½-inch tart crust made with Sweet Tart Dough (page 414), cooled
- 1 recipe Sweet Tart Dough (page 414), rolled into a 12-inch circle and refrigerated

  Sugar, for dusting (or sanding sugar, if you prefer)

Center a rack in the oven and preheat the oven to 400 degrees F. Line a baking sheet with parchment paper or a silicone baking mat.

TO MAKE THE FILLING: Bring a large pot of water to a boil. Have a large bowl of ice cubes and cold water nearby.

Cut a small X in the base of each peach. Drop a few peaches at a time into the boiling water, leave them there for 30 seconds and then lift them out with a slotted spoon and drop them into the ice water. When they are cool enough to handle, slip off the skins. If you've got some hard-to-peel peaches, you can boil them for a few seconds more or just remove the remaining skin with a paring knife.

Dry the peaches, cut them in half, remove the pits and cut each peach into about a dozen chunks. If the peaches are small, cut fewer chunks; the tourte is best when the pieces are about an inch on a side. Put the peach chunks in a bowl.

Put the butter in a small saucepan over medium heat and allow it to melt and then bubble. Stay close to the butter as it boils, and when it reaches a

light caramel color, pull the pan from the heat. You may see some small dark brown spots on the bottom of the pan, and that's fine; for sure you'll catch the whiff of warm nuts. Wait a minute or two, then pour the butter over the peaches. Add the sugar, flour, salt and vanilla and gently stir everything together. Finish with the lemon juice, tasting as you go. I prefer the juice to be a background flavor, but you might want it to be more prominent, and, of course, the amount will depend on the sweetness of your fruit.

TO ASSEMBLE THE TOURTE: Put the tart pan with the partially baked crust on the lined baking sheet. Give the filling another stir and scrape it into the tart shell, smoothing the top. You should have just enough filling to come level with the edges of the crust.

Remove the circle of dough from the refrigerator and let it rest for a couple of minutes, just until it's soft enough to maneuver without cracking. Brush the edges of the partially baked tart shell with water, then position the circle of dough over the crust. Press the rim of the tourte with your fingers to glue the two pieces together and then, pressing on the rim as you go, cut the top circle so that it is even with the edges of the pan.

Use a knife, the wide end of a piping tip or a small cookie cutter to remove a circle of dough from the center of the tourte—this is your steam vent. Brush the surface of the tourte lightly with cold water and sprinkle it generously with sugar.

Bake the tourte for 40 to 50 minutes, or until the crust is deeply golden brown and, most important, the butter is bubbling. If you think the crust is browning too quickly—the thick rim has a tendency to get dark—cover the tourte lightly with a foil tent. Transfer the tourte, still on its baking sheet, to a rack and allow it to cool until it's only just warm or at room temperature before serving. As it cools, the buttery syrup will be reabsorbed by the peaches, which is just what you want—so don't be impatient.

Apricot-Raspberry Tart

THIS BASIC TART, with a good sweet crust, lots of apricots, a few raspberries, slivers of butter and as much sugar as you think you need, has
the knack of making even apricots that are not impeccably ripe and lushly
juicy taste great. When they are very ripe and full of juice (or when I use
peaches or plums, which are juicier), I cushion the fruit with crumbs of
stale cake or Brioche (page 421) or spokes of Ladyfingers (page 217). The
cake or crumbs absorb the fruit juice and protect the crust and they also
become another element in the dessert, a soft, sweet layer soaked through
with flavor.

Makes 8 servings

SERVING: Everything this
tart needs is tucked inside
the crust.

STORING: The tart is
meant to be eaten the day it
is made. You can make the
crust ahead (bake it up to
8 hours ahead and keep it
at room temperature) and
you can make the ladyfinger
disk or cookies days ahead,
but the baked tart is an eat-
it-now treat.

- 1 partially baked 9- to 9½-inch tart crust made with Sweet Tart Dough (page 414), cooled

- 1 About 8 homemade Ladyfingers (page 217) or about 1 cup stale cake or Brioche (page 421) crumbs
- 12–14 ripe apricots, halved and pitted

- 2 tablespoons sugar
- 1 tablespoon cold unsalted butter, cut into slivers
  About ¼ cup (about 30 grams, or more to taste) fresh raspberries

  About ¼ cup (about 30 grams) chopped pistachios, for decoration (optional)

Center a rack in the oven and preheat the oven to 350 degrees F. Put the tart
pan with the partially baked crust on a baking sheet lined with parchment
paper or a silicone baking mat.

If you've got ladyfingers, arrange them like spokes in the bottom of the
crust. If you've got crumbs, just scatter them.

Working from the outside in, arrange the apricots in concentric circles
in the crust keeping them almost upright, with the hollow sides facing the
center of the pan. Overlap the fruit slightly and get the circles as snug as you
can, using as many apricots as you need to fill the crust completely. Sprinkle
2 teaspoons of the sugar evenly over the fruit.

Bake the tart for 30 minutes. Sprinkle the remaining 4 teaspoons sugar
over the apricots, scatter the slivers of cold butter over the tart and strew the
raspberries over the apricots. Bake for 15 more minutes.

Sprinkle the pistachios over the top, if you're using them. Then bake for
another 15 minutes or so, whether you're using the pistachios or not. The
total time in the oven is about 1 hour; the apricots should be soft enough to
be pierced with the tip of a knife. Transfer to a rack and let the tart cool until
it is just warm or at room temperature before serving.

Bonne Idée

APRICOT–ALMOND
CREAM TART: Apricots and
almonds have a natural
affinity for one another.
In fact, the kernel within
an apricot pit is used
to make bitter almond
extracts and elixirs, so it's
only reasonable to pair the
two. To make a wonderful
tart, partially bake the
crust and, when it's cool,
spread 1 recipe (chilled)
Almond Cream (page 432)
over the bottom of the tart
shell. Arrange the apricots,
cut side down, over the
cream—you'll need fewer
(maybe half to two thirds
of the number in the recipe
on page 145), because you
have to allow space for the
almond cream to puff up
around the fruit. Bake the
tart at 350 degrees F for
about 1 hour, or until the
fruit is soft and the almond
cream is golden brown and
puffed from the edges to
the middle of the tart.

FRENCH WOMEN NEVER SAY "NON"

I have never, not once, heard a Frenchwoman say no to dessert. Not a plump woman. Not a thin woman. Not a very thin woman. A French woman always accepts dessert, always finishes it and never, ever says that she feels guilty.

Granted, she doesn't eat rich, sweet desserts every day. Often a school-night family meal will end with a piece of cheese or some yogurt and fruit. But when there's a real dessert—a pastry or tart, a few macarons or some ice cream—as there always is when friends are around the table, everyone becomes a member of the clean plate club.

As a French friend once said, "Nothing is sexier than a woman with an appetite."

···

Walk through any French market in the early spring and you're bound to hear someone comment on the color of the butter. All winter long, when the cows are eating hay, the butter is pale, almost white. But as the weather gets warmer and the cows have grass to eat, you see the butter begin to turn yellow. By the end of the summer, the butter is golden. Seeing these changes is one of the great pleasures of shopping in farmers' markets.

Of course, France has banal butter, just as we do, but it also has butters that have earned an Appellation d'Origine Contrôlée (AOC), like fine wines. This designation guarantees that the cream used to produce a certain butter comes from cows that have grazed on land within a certain (constrained) radius from the creamery. The butters are churned in small batches, and they're among the ones that change noticeably with the seasons.

There are more and more artisanal butters available in America, and they're worth searching out. But they may not melt, blend or bake as French butters do, because, in general, French butter has a higher butterfat content than American butter (and it's the fat that makes butter rich). By law, American butter must have a minimum of 80 percent butterfat, while France's minimum is set at 82 percent. And everything changes when you get AOC butters, because they're likely to have as much as 86 percent butterfat!

In addition, the best butters in France are cultured, meaning they're allowed to ferment, often for up to eighteen hours, before they're churned. Imagine crème fraîche, and you'll have an idea of how the butters are treated. The culturing process produces complex flavors—warm, grassy, slightly sweet, slightly acidic and memorable.

In America, butters from Vermont Creamery and Straus Family Creamery are cultured in the French way and contain higher percentages of butterfat. Yet as much as I love baking with these butters, I tested all the recipes in this book with Land O'Lakes or Cabot unsalted butter, good butters that you can find in the supermarket.

Cherry Crumb Tart

Makes 8 servings

SERVING: In true Alsatian fashion, the tart should be showered with confectioners' sugar before it is served. The tart is good with a little crème fraîche or a scoop of ice cream, but it's got so much flavor and texture that it really doesn't need further embellishment.

STORING: I think this tart is best served at room temperature on the day it is made, but my husband disagrees. As much as he likes it just made, he really likes it after it's spent a night in the refrigerator. He's not wrong about the chill—the tart is very good cold. So, if you'd like, you can keep it covered in the fridge for up to 1 day.

THE FRENCH TAKE THEIR CHERRIES SERIOUSLY. When it's *Le Temps des Cerises*, or "cherry time"—the name is the title of an 1866 Paris Commune song—the declaration shows up everywhere, even in fashion. If you love cherries, there's no time like *Le Temps des Cerises* to find cherry-dotted scarves, skirts, shirts, ties, dresses and even cherry pom-poms for your hair. And, of course, there are cherries in the market—but the season is short.

One June my husband, Michael, and I were in Alsace, where cherries—red and white, sweet and sour—are abundant. The day we arrived, we stopped at a roadside stand and bought big, fat red cherries and lovely pink and cream Rainiers (like Queen Anne cherries). They were the best we had ever tasted. The next day we drove around trying to find the stand again, and when we did, the Rainiers were gone. Not sold out. Gone. And it seemed to be the end of their run everywhere in Alsace.

When we got back to Paris, there were no Rainiers, but there were plenty of chubby red cherries that I turned into this tart, which has an almond-cream base flavored with Alsace's favorite eau-de-vie, kirsch. And, since Alsace is the land of streusel, I finished the tart with a crumb topping. The tart was so good—and Michael loved it so much—that I made it again and again, until the market was out of cherries and it was *le temps* for peaches.

A WORD ON THE CHERRIES: I like to make the tart with whole pitted cherries. I love the look of the full rounds. Instead of using a cherry pitter, you can pit the cherries with a chopstick—just push it straight through the fruit. Or use halved cherries, pitting them after you halve them.

AND A WORD ON SHAPE: If you'd like to make a square tart, use a 9- to 9½-inch square pan with a removable bottom. The proportions of filling and topping are the same for both square and round tarts.

FOR THE STREUSEL

⅓ cup (67 grams) sugar
  Grated zest of 1 orange (optional)
¾ cup (102 grams) all-purpose flour
¼ teaspoon fine sea salt
  Up to ¼ teaspoon ground cardamom (optional)
¾ stick (6 tablespoons; 3 ounces; 85 grams) cold unsalted butter, cut into small cubes

¼ teaspoon pure vanilla extract

FOR THE FILLING

¾ stick (6 tablespoons; 3 ounces; 85 grams) unsalted butter, at room temperature
⅔ cup (132 grams) sugar
¾ cup (75 grams) almond or hazelnut flour
1 teaspoon cornstarch
1 large egg, at room temperature

1 tablespoon kirsch or
  1½ teaspoons pure vanilla
  extract

1 partially baked 9- to 9½-inch
  tart crust made with Sweet

Tart Dough (page 414),
  cooled

1 pound (454 grams) cherries,
  pitted

Confectioners' sugar, for
  dusting (optional)

TO MAKE THE STREUSEL: Put the sugar in a medium bowl. If you're using the orange zest, sprinkle it over the sugar and work the two ingredients together with your fingers until the sugar is moist and fragrant. Add the flour, salt and cardamom, if you're using it, and mix everything together by running the ingredients through your fingers. Drop in the butter and squeeze and rub the butter into the mixture until it's sandy. If you press a little streusel together, you'll get lumps, which is just what you want. Drizzle the vanilla over the streusel and toss, squeeze and rub to distribute it. Cover the bowl and chill the streusel until needed; the crumbs are best used cold. (*You can make the streusel up to 1 week ahead; pack it in an airtight container and keep it refrigerated.*)

TO MAKE THE FILLING: You can make the filling in a food processor, or in the bowl of a stand mixer fitted with the paddle attachment or in a large bowl with a hand mixer. Beat the butter until it is smooth and creamy, about 3 minutes. Add the sugar and beat for a minute or two more. Add the nut flour and cornstarch and beat until the mixture is smooth once again. Drop in the egg and beat for a minute or so, until it is thoroughly incorporated. Finally, beat in the kirsch or vanilla. You can use the filling now, but it's best if you can give it at least 1 hour in the refrigerator. (*The filling can be refrigerated, tightly covered, for up to 3 days.*)

Center a rack in the oven and preheat the oven to 350 degrees F. Place the tart pan with the partially baked crust on a baking sheet lined with parchment paper or a silicone baking mat.

Using a short offset spatula or the back of a spoon, spread the filling evenly over the crust. Top with the cherries. You should have enough cherries to just about completely cover the filling.

Bake the tart for about 45 minutes, or until the filling is lightly colored—it won't be firm—and puckered up around the cherries. If you've used whole cherries, the tart will look tufted. Pull the baking pan out of the oven and sprinkle the top of the tart with the streusel. It's nice to have a bumpy topping, so pinch the streusel into nubbins as you take it out of the bowl. Gently pat the streusel down.

Bake the tart for another 30 to 35 minutes, or until the crumbs are a beautiful golden brown. You don't have to worry about overbaking the filling, so keep the tart in the oven until the top is just the color you want. Transfer the tart to a rack and cool to room temperature.

Before serving, dust the tart with confectioners' sugar if you're using it.

Classic Fruit Tart

THE PASTRY THAT CHANGED MY LIFE, that made me long to live in Paris and that later became my house special—in part because I was greedy to have it often and in part because it was a crowd-pleaser—was a strawberry tartlet about the size of my thumb. The boat-shaped sweet crust was filled with pastry cream, topped with three tiny wild strawberries and glazed with jam. It was the first pastry I ever had on French soil, and it might as well have been a magic potion for the effect it had on me. Happily for me, there were berry tarts in every Parisian pâtisserie, and there were pâtisseries on every other street.

For the most part, a pastry cream tart is a fruit tart, a dessert made to show off fresh berries, poached fruit or, less traditionally, a chunky jam. (Baked fruit tarts are usually made with a base of almond cream.) It doesn't really come with rules; and, depending on your artistic bent, the tart can be simple and symmetrical—say, with berries in concentric circles—or wildly fanciful—like the tarts in many pâtissiers' windows that have a dozen cut fruits arranged in a glossy still life.

When there are only three elements, as there are here, each one must be very good. The crust should be beautifully brown—if it's pale, you'll be cheating yourself of the full flavors of the ingredients. The pastry cream should be silky and cold and well flavored too. And, of course, the fruit should be ripe. If you assemble the tart no more than a few hours before you serve it, you'll achieve perfection.

As I said, this is not so much a recipe as a construction plan and a timetable with a few notes. Make one tart at home, and you won't have to return to this page ever again.

A WORD ON THE PASTRY CREAM: It's best to make the pastry cream a day ahead so that the flavors have time to fully blend and the cream has enough time to get very cold. Depending on the fruit that you've chosen, you might want to give the cream another flavor, maybe a little bit of pure almond extract, a droplet of pure orange or lemon oil or a splash of dark rum or kirsch (so good with berries).

A WORD ON THE TART CRUST: The dough can be made ahead and frozen until you are ready to bake it, but it should be baked as close to serving time as you can manage. Bake the crust fully and allow it to get golden brown.

A WORD ON THE BERRIES: As long as the berries are fresh and ripe and not bruised, the choice is all yours. If the berries don't have to be washed—if they can be cleaned with a damp paper towel or just a small brush—so much the better; the last thing you want is drops of water on the pastry cream. If they must be washed, of course you should wash them; just be assiduous in drying them. The berries can be left whole or, if using strawberries, sliced.

SERVING: Tarts like this are best cut with a serrated knife. Carefully unmold the tart and slide it onto a serving platter. Gently slice through the berries and pastry cream and then give the knife more pressure to crisply cut the crust.

STORING: The pastry cream can be made up to 3 days ahead and kept well covered in the refrigerator. Ideally, the tart should be served as soon as possible after it's assembled, but it can be kept in the refrigerator—away from foods with strong odors—for up to 4 hours.

1 recipe Vanilla Pastry Cream
  (page 430) or the flavor of
  your choice

1 fully baked 9- to 9½-inch tart
  crust made with Sweet Tart
  Dough (page 414) or Sweet
  Tart Dough with Nuts
  (page 415), cooled

1 quart (600–700 grams)
  berries

⅓ cup (107 grams) apple or red
  currant jelly, for glaze,
  or confectioners' sugar,
  for dusting

TO ASSEMBLE THE TART: Whisk the pastry cream vigorously to bring back its lovely texture—it will have firmed considerably in the refrigerator and become sliceable but unspreadable. Using an offset spatula or a knife, spread the cream evenly over the bottom of the fully baked tart crust. Jiggle the pastry cream to get it into the corners of the crust and smooth the top. Now, while the cream is still soft, arrange the berries on it, giving each berry a gentle poke so that it settles into the cream.

If you want to glaze the berries, bring the jelly and a teaspoon of water to a boil (I do this in the microwave). Using a feather pastry brush or the tip of a small spoon, put a dot of glaze on top of each berry. There are pastry chefs who fully glaze the berries, and you can too, but if your berries are beautiful, it seems a shame to hide them. (*The tart can be made ahead and refrigerated for up to 4 hours.*)

If you haven't glazed the berries, you can dust them with confectioners' sugar just before serving.

Simplest Plum Tart

EVERY ONCE IN A WHILE I come across a dessert that's barely a recipe, nothing more than a few ingredients put together in the most straightforward way to produce something thoroughly delicious. This tart is one of those sweets. It has a well-baked crust covered with a layer of crumbs—such as from spiced Biscoff cookies or homemade Speculoos (page 320), graham cracker crumbs, such as from butter cookies such as Petit Beurre (homemade, page 217, or store-bought) or leftover cake (Ladyfingers are perfect, page 217) or Brioche (page 421). Then there are snug circles of plums and a few spoonfuls of sugar; cinnamon is optional. I make the tart in the late summer and fall, when Italian purple plums are plentiful. Baked slowly, the plums soften and sweeten and the yellowish fruit becomes almost golden.

A WORD ON PLUMS: While Italian plums are my preference for this tart, you can use whatever plums you find in your market. Since most plums are larger than the Italian plums, you'll probably need only about a dozen to fill the crust.

Makes 8 servings

SERVING: As you'd expect, the tart is good with any kind of cream, but my favorite go-along is cold crème anglaise. The custard, as easy as it is to make, manages to turn this somewhat rustic tart into a city slicker. I cut wedges of the tart and pass the cold custard in a pitcher.

STORING: The tart is not a keeper: Enjoy it soon after you make it.

1 partially baked 9- to 9½-inch tart crust made with Sweet Tart Dough (page 414), cooled

½ cup crumbs (see above)
About 20 Italian plums, halved and pitted

Pinch of ground cinnamon (optional)

2 tablespoons sugar

Crème Anglaise (page 44), for serving (optional but very nice)

Center a rack in the oven and preheat the oven to 350 degrees F. Put the tart pan with the partially baked crust on a baking sheet lined with parchment paper or a silicone baking mat.

Sprinkle the bottom of the crust evenly with the crumbs.

Arrange the plum halves in the crust in tightly fitted concentric circles, placing them cut side up, side by side and slightly overlapping. It's okay if you have a few bare-ish spots, but it's best to keep things cozy.

Bake the tart for 30 minutes. If you'd like to use the cinnamon, add it to the sugar. Sprinkle the sugar evenly over the plums and then bake for another 30 minutes, or until the plums are easily pierced with the point of a knife and you see droplets of juice here and there. Transfer the tart to a rack and cool until it is just warm or reaches room temperature.

Serve the tart with crème anglaise, if you'd like.

Summer-Market Galette

SUMMER FRUIT IS SO SWEET, fragrant and abundant that eating it out of hand is almost irresistible. And the French market vendors know this. When stone fruits and berries are in season and the scents from their stalls rival those of any perfume counter, they hawk their wares in the most effective way possible: They hand out samples. Walk just a few feet down a market *allée* and you'll have cherry pits in your palm, the mark of peach juice down your chin and a smile on your face, put there perhaps by the honeyed goodness of the apricot you also tasted. It's a wonderful time to shop and to bake because, as good as these fruits are straight up, they become a different kind of special when the juices thicken and their sweetness magnifies under heat. It's when summer fruits are at their best and most plentiful that the urge to make this galette strikes.

An open-faced tart with a crust that bends and puckers around the fruit, this galette is less a recipe than a note of encouragement to send you into the kitchen to make your own version. Whether I use peaches or nectarines, black plums or red, apricots or pluots, I like to have some berries in the mix, although I never use strawberries—they become watery in the oven. In Paris I usually choose blackberries, and I might toss some raspberries in as well, while in America I almost always reach for sweet blueberries. To help ensure that the bottom of the galette stands up to so much juiciness, I scatter over some cookie or cake crumbs, and to brighten up the lot, I add lime zest, fresh ginger and chopped fresh mint.

Summer's fruit is fleeting, so make this tart as early in the season as you can and then keep making it until the vendors start giving you samples of grapes. When that happens, tuck this recipe away and turn to the Fall-Market Galette (page 129).

A WORD ON AMOUNTS: Because you need to fold the edges of the galette over and make a chubby package, you want enough fruit for each serving to be generous, but not so much that the dough can't contain it. If you choose about 1¼ pounds of fruit (not including the berries), you should be right on the mark.

1 recipe Galette Dough (page 420), rolled out and chilled	1 teaspoon minced peeled fresh ginger
	Grated zest of ½ lime
2 ripe black plums	3 plain butter cookies, such as
2 small ripe apricots	Petit Beurre, homemade
2 small ripe nectarines	(page 270) or store-bought;
1–2 tablespoons sugar	⅓ cup plain cake crumbs, or
1 tablespoon chopped fresh mint	Ladyfinger (page 217) crumbs

or Brioche (page 421)
crumbs

½ cup (75 grams) blueberries

1 tablespoon cold unsalted
butter, cut into bits

Sanding or granulated sugar,
for sprinkling

¼ cup (80 grams) apple, quince
or currant jelly, for glazing
(optional)

Center a rack in the oven and preheat the oven to 400 degrees F.

Take the rolled-out dough out of the refrigerator, remove the top piece of parchment paper and, if the dough isn't already on a rimmed baking sheet, move it to one. Leave the dough on the counter while you mix the fruit.

Cut the plums, apricots and nectarines in half, remove the pits and cut each half into quarters. (If your fruit is large, cut the halves into sixths.) Put the cut fruit into a medium bowl, add the sugar (1 tablespoon if your fruit is very sweet and ripe, 2 if not), mint, ginger and zest and stir to coat the fruit. Set aside for 5 minutes, stirring a couple of times, so that the sugar dissolves and you have a little liquid in the bowl.

Meanwhile, if using cookies, break them into small pieces and crumbs (you can do this with your fingers or, if you'd like, you can "dice" the cookies with a knife). Sprinkle the cookie, cake or brioche crumbs over the galette dough, leaving a bare border of about 2 inches all around.

Stir the berries into the fruit and then spoon the fruit and whatever juices have accumulated onto the dough, mounding the fruit high in the center and leaving the 2-inch border bare. Gently lift the border of dough up and around the filling. As you lift the dough and place it against the filling, it will pleat and fold—it's meant to. Dot the fruit with the cold butter bits, then brush the dough very lightly with a little water and sprinkle it with sanding (or granulated) sugar.

Bake the galette for 45 to 55 minutes, until the crust is deeply golden brown, the juices are bubbling and a knife poked into any piece of fruit meets no resistance; the fruit is meant to be truly cooked through.

Meanwhile, if you want to glaze the galette—a really nice touch, since the fruit will lose its sheen as it cools—bring the jelly and a splash of water to a boil in a microwave oven (cover the bowl) or in a saucepan on the stove. Brush the hot jelly over the fruit as soon as the galette comes out of the oven.

Glazed or not, the galette should rest on the baking sheet until it is just warm or reaches room temperature before serving.

Philadelphia Blueberry-Corn Tart

Makes 8 servings

SERVING: The tart is best served chilled. No need for any accompaniment, it's a self-sufficient sweet.

STORING: You can make the topping up to 1 day ahead and you can keep the assembled tart in the refrigerator, lightly covered, overnight.

WITH ALL THE AMAZING CHEESES that are made in France—and there are more than three hundred of them—you wouldn't think that the introduction of an American cheese, and a processed one at that, would be cause for celebration. But when cream cheese, known as "Philadelphia" in France, recently began turning up in supermarkets, with billboards and advertisements on buses announcing its arrival, there was cheering among the locals.

And everyone was delighted with this tart, which combines two very American ingredients, blueberries and corn, with Philadelphia. The crust is a classic French sweet tart shell and its texture is perfect with the filling, a light swirly mix of cream cheese, whipped cream and honey. As good as the filling is, it's even better with the topping, a quickly made blueberry jam, bolstered with lemon zest and scented with rosemary. Once the jam thickens, you stir in lemon juice, whole blueberries and corn kernels, so that you get a wonderful mix of cooked and fresh, smooth and chunky, soft and snappy.

FOR THE TOPPING
- 1½ pints (about 450 grams) fresh blueberries
- ¼ cup (50 grams) sugar
- 2 tablespoons water
- Finely grated zest of ½ lemon
- Sprig of rosemary
- Squirt of lemon juice
- Kernels from 1 ear fresh corn (or ¾ cup/113 grams frozen corn, thawed, or canned corn, drained)

FOR THE FILLING
- ½ cup (120 ml) very cold heavy cream
- ½ pound (227 grams) cream cheese, at room temperature
- ⅓ cup (67 grams) sugar
- 2 tablespoons honey
- Pinch of fine sea salt
- 1 teaspoon pure vanilla extract
- 2 tablespoons plain Greek yogurt (optional)

- 1 fully baked 9- to 9½-inch tart crust made with Sweet Tart Dough (page 414), cooled

TO MAKE THE TOPPING: Put 1 pint of the berries into a medium saucepan with high sides (berries spatter and can be messy), stir in the sugar, water and lemon zest and toss in the rosemary sprig. Put the pan over medium heat and cook, stirring, until the mixture comes to a boil and the berries begin to pop, about 5 minutes. Continue to cook and stir for another 3 minutes or so, until the jam thickens slightly—your spoon will leave tracks.

Remove the pan from the heat and scrape the jam into a bowl; discard the rosemary sprig. Stir in the lemon juice and corn kernels. Put the bowl into a larger bowl filled with ice cubes and cold water and let sit, stirring occasionally, until the topping is cool.

Stir in the remaining ½ pint blueberries. (*The topping can be made up to 1 day ahead and kept tightly covered in the refrigerator.*)

TO MAKE THE FILLING: Working in the bowl of a stand mixer fitted with the whisk attachment, or in a small bowl with a hand mixer, whip the heavy cream until it holds soft peaks. If you're using a stand mixer, scrape the cream into another bowl and fit the mixer with the paddle attachment (there's no need to wash the bowl); if you're using a hand mixer, work in a medium bowl.

Beat the cream cheese until it's soft. Add the sugar, honey and salt and beat until fully incorporated; the cream cheese will be smooth and satiny. Mix in the vanilla and then the yogurt, if you're using it.

With a flexible spatula, gently fold the whipped cream into the filling.

TO FINISH THE TART: Scrape the filling into the crust and smooth the top—it's okay if it domes. Spoon the topping over the filling, either spreading it to cover the filling or allowing it to go free-form. Chill for at least 1 hour before serving.

Tropical Tartlets

ONCE UPON A TIME, and not all that long ago, France had colonies in warm climates, among them the Antilles, islands in the Caribbean. It's because of this connection, no longer relevant in the political realm but still strong in the kitchen, that recipes with ingredients like mango, banana or rum are often called tropical, exotic, Creole or Antillean. It's a holdover from another time, but it's shorthand that the French understand.

In these small tarts, the mango is pureed and accented with coconut, lime, dark rum and pepper flakes, ingredients from the same tropical area. The filling is as bright as sunshine, the flavors as warm.

If you'd like to make this as one large tart, use a 9- to 9½-inch crust and double all the ingredients except the eggs; use 3 whole eggs, with no separate yolks.

Makes 4 tartlets

SERVING: Good at room temperature or chilled, these tartlets need no garnish.

STORING: You can keep the tartlets lightly covered in the refrigerator for up to 1 day.

4 fully baked 4-inch tartlet crusts made with Sweet Tart Dough (page 414) or, if you'd like, with Chocolate Tart Dough (page 418), cooled

1 large ripe mango, peeled, pitted and cut into chunks
1 large egg
1 large egg yolk
¼ cup (50 grams) sugar

¼ cup (30 grams) sweetened shredded coconut
Finely grated zest and juice of ½ lime, or more to taste
2 teaspoons dark rum (optional)
1 teaspoon honey
Pinch of red pepper flakes

Sweetened shredded coconut, for sprinkling

Center a rack in the oven and preheat the oven to 350 degrees F. Place the tartlet pans with their crusts on a baking sheet lined with parchment paper or a silicone baking mat.

Put all the remaining ingredients (except the coconut for sprinkling) in a food processor or blender. Process, scraping down the sides of the bowl as needed, until you have a puree. Taste (if you're not concerned about raw eggs) and add more lime juice, if you'd like. Divide the filling among the crusts. Sprinkle the tops of the tartlets with shredded coconut—be generous.

Bake the tartlets for about 25 minutes, or until their tops are puffed all the way to the middle and a bamboo skewer inserted into their centers comes out clean. The tops won't really brown, although the coconut will. And they might crack, but that's okay; when the cooled filling comes down to crust level, the tartlets will look fine. Transfer the baking sheet to a cooling rack and let the tartlets cool to room temperature. Chill, if you'd like, before serving.

Streusel-Topped Rhubarb Lime Tart

Makes 8 servings

SERVING: Most often I serve the tart on its own, but it's awfully good with a big spoonful of sugared strawberries or a drizzle of raspberry coulis (page 449).

STORING: You can make the streusel ahead—it will keep in the fridge for 1 week or in the freezer for up to 2 months—and the crust can be made ahead too. But the fully loaded tart is a dessert best enjoyed within a couple of hours.

I WAS READING THE MENU at a restaurant and considering the strawberry-rhubarb crumble, but when I ordered it, the server crinkled her nose, saying, "It's good, but I think it's a little too sweet—you don't get the sharpness of the rhubarb." I ordered it anyway and discovered that she was right: It was nice, but it didn't shout bright, fresh, just-this-side-of-shivery-sour rhubarb.

Rhubarb's tricky: Mix it with too much sugar, and you mask its character; mix it with too little, and you risk letting its acidity run roughshod over your dessert. I've had the best rhubarb pastries in Alsace. There, every pâtisserie shows off its rhubarb tart, every tart has pucker and almost every tart is topped with meringue, a great mate. Although I love the rhubarb-meringue combination and I've suggested a version (see Bonne Idée), this tart is the one that has my heart. It's topped with streusel (another Alsatian favorite), and it double downs on acidity: It brims with fresh rhubarb and covered with just enough tangy lime custard to fill in the spaces. I ratcheted up the rhubarb's pop by giving it a swish in lime juice and flavoring the custard with zest. The streusel is flavored with vanilla, but if you're bold, you can add lime zest to it too.

A WORD ON HOARDING RHUBARB: Rhubarb's season can be short, but its freezer life can be long. Wash and peel the rhubarb, dry it well and cut it into chunks. Put the fruit on a baking sheet lined with parchment or wax paper and freeze it until solid before packing it airtight in plastic bags.

FOR THE STREUSEL
Finely grated zest of ½ lime (optional)
⅓ cup (67 grams) sugar
¾ cup (102 grams) all-purpose flour
¼ teaspoon fine sea salt
5½ tablespoons (2¾ ounces; 78 grams) cold unsalted butter, cut into small pieces
¼ teaspoon pure vanilla extract

FOR THE FILLING
1 lime
1–1¼ pounds (trimmed weight; 454–567 grams) fresh rhubarb (about 5 stalks)

¼ cup (50 grams) plus 3 tablespoons sugar
3 large eggs
⅓ cup (80 ml) heavy cream
¼ cup (60 ml) whole milk
½ teaspoon pure vanilla extract

1 fully baked 9- to 9½-inch tart crust made with Sweet Tart Dough (page 414), cooled

Confectioners' sugar, for dusting (optional)

TO MAKE THE STREUSEL: If you'd like to include lime zest in your streusel, put the zest in a medium bowl, add the sugar and, using your fingertips, rub them together until the sugar is moist and fragrant. If you're not using the zest, just put the sugar in the bowl. Add the flour and salt and mix everything together by running the ingredients through your fingers. Drop in the butter and squeeze and rub it into the mixture until it's sandy. If you press pieces of streusel together, you'll get lumps, which is just what you want. Drizzle the vanilla over the streusel and toss, squeeze and rub to distribute it. Cover the bowl and chill the streusel until needed. (*You can make the streusel up to 1 week ahead; pack it in an airtight container and keep it refrigerated.*)

TO MAKE THE FILLING: Finely grate the zest of the lime into a medium bowl. Squeeze 2 teaspoons juice into another medium bowl.

If your rhubarb stalks are very thick, cut them in half lengthwise. You might also want to peel them, which I do if the outer layer is thick and it starts to come away as I'm cutting it. Cut the stalks into slices about ½ inch wide. As you cut the rhubarb, add it to the bowl with the lime juice. Sprinkle over the 3 tablespoons sugar, stir and let the rhubarb sit while you preheat the oven and finish the filling; stir occasionally.

Center a rack in the oven and preheat the oven to 350 degrees F. Put the crust on a baking sheet lined with parchment paper or a silicone baking mat.

Add the remaining ¼ cup sugar to the bowl with the lime zest and, using your fingers, rub the zest and sugar together until the sugar is moist and aromatic and perhaps even pale green. Add the eggs one by one, starting to whisk as soon as the first egg goes in. (Never allow eggs to sit on sugar—the sugar will "burn" them, causing a skin to form on the yolks.) When the mixture is smooth, whisk in the cream, milk and vanilla extract.

Drain the rhubarb, shaking off as much of the syrup as you can and reserving it. (Taste the syrup and, if it's not too astringent, save it for stirring into sparkling water or iced tea.) Pile the rhubarb into the tart crust; it might mound in the center, and it's fine if it does. Give the custard a last whisk and pour a little of it over the rhubarb. Gently shimmy the pan from side to side to settle the custard between the pieces of fruit and then pour in the remainder, or as much as you need to come to the rim of the crust (you might have some custard left over).

Carefully slide the baking sheet into the oven and bake the tart for 30 minutes, then remove it from the oven so you can top it with the streusel. Grab some streusel and pinch it before putting it on the tart. You want a bumpy coating; some of the streusel will look like fine crumbs and some will look like nuggets. Be generous with the streusel—you've got plenty and might even have some left over. Pat the streusel down gently.

Return the tart to the oven and bake for another 30 minutes, or until both the custard and the streusel are firm. The streusel will brown lightly. If you'd like more color, you can run the tart under the broiler. Stay close: The color changes quickly. Transfer the tart to a rack to cool to room temperature.

To serve, lightly dust the top with confectioners' sugar, if you'd like.

Bonne Idée

RHUBARB MERINGUE TART: I use the meringue from the Lemon Meringue Tart a New Way (page 182). Bake the rhubarb tart until the custard is set—start testing at 40 minutes—and then cover with the meringue and brown it under the broiler or with a kitchen torch. If you'd like, you can make the tart a few hours ahead and finish it with the meringue just before serving.

Caramelized Cinnamon–Milk Chocolate Tart

Makes 8 servings

SERVING: The tart can certainly go out into the world unadorned, but I think a drizzle of Salted Caramel Sauce (page 447) or a spoonful of softly whipped cream magically heightens the chocolate, caramel and cinnamon flavors. With or without sauce or cream, the tart is best served after it's been at room temperature for about 10 minutes.

STORING: The tart can be made up to 2 days ahead and kept tightly covered in the refrigerator. Wrapped airtight, it can be frozen for up to 2 months; defrost overnight in the refrigerator, still wrapped.

FRANCE IS A DARK-CHOCOLATE COUNTRY. America melts for milk. And this tart is the great and delicious compromiser: The filling is a mostly milk chocolate ganache with just enough bittersweet chocolate to give it a French edge.

It's also a ganache with outstanding texture—smooth and creamy and just slightly stretchy, like a good caramel candy—and wonderful sweet flavor that's a bit bitter from caramelized sugar and a bit spicy from caramelized cinnamon.

The technique of caramelizing the sugar with a spice so that it can flavor the ganache is a good one to have in your bag of tricks; see Bonne Idée. The cream is added after the spice is cooked, and the mixture is left to infuse before it's strained and used to make the ganache. The extra step of caramelizing gives you a deep, full, complex flavor that you couldn't get any other way. It's a little more effort for a big reward.

1½ cups (360 ml) heavy cream (or perhaps a little more)

¼ cup (50 grams) sugar

2 cinnamon sticks, each about 3 inches long

7 ounces (198 grams) best-quality milk chocolate, finely chopped

3 ounces (85 grams) bittersweet chocolate, finely chopped

1 fully baked 9- to 9½-inch tart crust made with Sweet Tart Dough (page 414), cooled

Salted Caramel Sauce (page 447) or whipped cream, for serving (optional)

Bring the cream to a boil in a saucepan or a microwave oven. Keep it close to the stove.

Sprinkle the sugar in an even layer over the bottom of a heavy-bottomed skillet—I use a 10-inch high-sided nonstick pan for this—and toss in the cinnamon sticks. Have a heatproof spatula or spoon and a small white plate at hand. Turn the heat to medium-high and, when the sugar starts to melt around the edges of the pan, stir it in little circles. Work your way around the pan and, as more sugar melts, move in toward the center of the pan. You want the sugar to caramelize to a burnished rust color—put a drop on the white plate to check. Don't be alarmed if you see a few wisps of smoke rise from the skillet. When you've got the color you're looking for, remove the skillet from the heat, stand back and slowly pour in the hot cream; it will bubble

Bonne Idée

CARAMELIZING OTHER
SPICES: The technique of
caramelizing the sugar
with cinnamon and then
infusing it into the cream
can be used with other
whole spices. Try it with
a mix of white and black
peppercorns and, if you
dare, just a few Sichuan
peppercorns, star anise,
allspice. I love allspice and
chocolate together; and
cardamom is best with a
milk chocolate ganache. Or
use coffee beans, which is
not a spice, but a classic
with chocolate.

furiously. When the seething has subsided, stir to make certain that the caramel and cream are blended. Let the mixture steep for 45 minutes.

Strain the caramel cream into a 2-cup measuring cup; discard the cinnamon sticks (or wash and dry them and bury them in a jar of sugar to make cinnamon sugar). If the cream measures less than 1¼ cups, add additional cream to bring it up to the measure.

Put the chopped milk and bittersweet chocolate in a large heatproof bowl. Transfer the caramel cream back to a nonstick skillet and bring to a boil over medium heat. Bring the cream back to a boil. Pour half of the hot caramel cream over the chocolate (because you have a lot of caramel cream, it's best to add it in 2 additions). Wait 30 seconds and then, using a small spatula or whisk and starting in the center of the bowl, stir the cream into the chocolate in small concentric circles. When the caramel cream and chocolate form an emulsion—you'll know, because the chocolate at the center of the bowl will become dark and glossy—pour in the remainder of the caramel cream. Once again, starting at the center and moving in ever-widening concentric circles, stir the cream into the chocolate. Be patient. By the time your last circle reaches the edges of the bowl, you should have a thick, smooth, glossy ganache.

Pour the ganache into the baked tart crust. Refrigerate until the ganache is set, about 2 hours. (*The tart can be refrigerated for up to 2 days.*)

Serve the tart garnished with the caramel sauce or whipped cream, if you'd like.

Caramel Tart

Makes 8 servings

CARAMEL IS AN ACROSS-THE-BOARD FAVORITE in France, beloved in all its many forms: hard or soft, sticky or creamy, salty or plain, hot or cold. It can be a candy or a sauce or an ice cream, a pudding, a frosting or a flavoring. And it can be the star of a tart like this one, whose name is perfectly straightforward though its taste and texture are less so. The flavor is definitely caramel, but it's a light caramel with just a hint of burnt sugar's characteristic bittersweetness, and the texture, also light, is soft and smooth, velvety like crème brûlée and just a little jiggly, like a soft gelée.

The caramel itself is easy to make perfectly—just exercise restraint: It shouldn't color too much. No smoke, no rusty hues. When the sugar turns the color of pale ale, it's ready.

SERVING: Because the caramel flavor is light, you can go two ways with this tart: Serve it unadorned, so the caramel is most present; or take advantage of its mild flavor to pair it with whipped cream, Bittersweet Chocolate Sauce (page 442) or a berry coulis (page 449). In any case, the tart is best served chilled.

STORING: The tart will keep in the refrigerator, covered and away from foods with strong odors, overnight, but it's at its peak the day it is made.

1 fully baked 9- to 9½-inch tart crust made with Sweet Tart Dough (page 414), cooled

1¼ cups (300 ml) heavy cream

6 tablespoons (75 grams) plus ⅓ cup (67 grams) sugar

¼ cup (60 ml) water
A few drops of freshly squeezed lemon juice

½ stick (4 tablespoons; 2 ounces; 57 grams) unsalted butter, cut into 4 pieces, at room temperature

½ teaspoon fleur de sel or ¼ teaspoon fine sea salt

4 large egg yolks, at room temperature

Center a rack in the oven and preheat the oven to 325 degrees F. Place the tart pan with the fully baked crust on a baking sheet lined with parchment paper or a silicone baking mat.

Pour the heavy cream into a microwave-safe cup with a spout and bring it to a boil in the microwave, or boil it in a saucepan on the stove and then pour it into a small pitcher.

Put the 6 tablespoons sugar, the water and lemon juice in a wide skillet, preferably nonstick. (It's much easier to make caramel in a nonstick pan.) Have a heatproof spatula or spoon, a white plate and a little bowl of water with a pastry brush (silicone's good here) nearby. Turn the heat to medium-high and let the mixture come to a boil without stirring. If you get spatters around the sides of the pan, dip the brush into the water and wash them down. As the bubbles grow big, be on the lookout for the sugar to start changing color around the edges. At the first sign of color, using the spatula, start stirring in circles around the outside of the pan until the color—which should be light blond—is uniform; check the color by putting a spot of caramel on the white plate. Standing back, add the chunks of butter one at a

time, stirring them in with the spatula and working quickly. Stir in the salt and immediately remove the pan from the burner. Stirring and still standing away—the caramel is very hot and has a tendency to spatter—slowly pour in the warm cream. Once it's all in, you should have a smooth caramel sauce.

Working in a heatproof bowl, whisk the egg yolks and the remaining ⅓ cup sugar together until pale and slightly thickened. Whisking gently all the while, stir in a little hot caramel to temper, or acclimatize, the eggs. Continuing to whisk without stopping, add the rest of the caramel in a slow, steady stream until it's completely incorporated and the mixture is smooth. If you have lots of foam, you can skim it off, but you don't have to. Pour the filling into the crust.

Bake the tart for 22 to 24 minutes, or until the filling is just set or wiggles only the slightest bit at the very center. Transfer the tart to a rack to cool to room temperature and then refrigerate it for at least 2 hours before serving.

Chocolate-Coconut Tart

Makes 8 servings

SERVING: You can spoon a dollop of whipped cream over each slice of the tart or put a scoop of ice cream next to it, but my druthers are to serve it just the way it is. It's got so much flavor that all it really needs is an espresso following your last bite.

STORING: The coconut filling can be made up to 2 days ahead and the assembled tart needs a good 4 hours in the refrigerator to chill. The crust is best, as most crusts are, the day it is baked, but this tart holds up surprisingly well and is still very enjoyable after a night in the refrigerator—just cover it and keep it away from foods with strong odors.

NECESSITY MAY BE THE MOTHER OF INVENTION, but craving can also do a pretty good job of pushing creation. If I hadn't had a rare and pretty much unsatisfiable craving for a Mounds bar, a candy you don't find on every Paris street corner, I might never have created this tart, inspired by the all-American treat but leaning almost totally Frenchward.

A Mounds bar has two elements: a sweet coconut filling and a dark chocolate coating. And so does this tart. The filling is a coconut pastry cream, one I fiddled with to make it lighter than the usual *crème pâtissière*—it's made with coconut milk and water, whole eggs instead of yolks and lots of sweetened coconut, both toasted for texture and untoasted for chew. The topping is a thick, velvety dark chocolate ganache. The tart has one element that the Mounds bar doesn't: crunch. It comes from the crust, and once you add it to the mix, you'll never want the original combo without it.

FOR THE COCONUT FILLING

- 1 cup (120 grams) sweetened shredded coconut
- ¾ cup (180 ml) unsweetened coconut milk (not light)
- ¼ cup (60 ml) water
- 2 large eggs
- 2 tablespoons sugar
- 2 tablespoons cornstarch, sifted
- 1 teaspoon pure vanilla extract or 2 teaspoons dark rum

- 1 fully baked 9-to 9½-inch tart crust made with Sweet Tart Dough (page 414), cooled

FOR THE GANACHE

- 4 ounces (113 grams) bittersweet chocolate, finely chopped
- ½ cup (120 ml) heavy cream
- 2 tablespoons (1 ounce; 28 grams) unsalted butter, cut into bits, at room temperature

Large-flake coconut, toasted or not, for decoration (optional)

TO MAKE THE FILLING: Set ½ cup of the shredded coconut aside and toast the other ½ cup. With a small amount like this, I find it easiest to use a microwave. Spread the coconut out on a microwave-safe plate or on a paper towel and heat at full power for 30 seconds. Stir the coconut and keep heating in short spurts until the shreds are golden, about 4 minutes.

Fill a large bowl with ice cubes and cold water and keep it at hand—it's what you'll use to rapidly cool the filling.

Pour the coconut milk and water into a heavy-bottomed saucepan (choose a pan that doesn't hold more than 2 quarts; you're making a small amount of filling and it will cook too fast in a large pan) and heat until it's almost at a boil.

Meanwhile, whisk the eggs, sugar and cornstarch together in a medium bowl until thick and smooth. Still whisking, slowly pour in the hot coconut milk. When all the milk is in, pour the mixture back into the saucepan, put the pan over medium heat and, whisking vigorously and without stopping, cook the pastry cream until it thickens and a bubble pops at the surface. Lower the heat and cook and stir for another minute or two, just to make sure that the cornstarch won't taste raw.

Remove the pan from the heat and scrape the filling into a bowl. Stir in the coconut, toasted and untoasted, and the vanilla or rum, then set the bowl into the ice bath. Stir the filling occasionally until it reaches room temperature or cooler. (*The filling can be packed airtight and refrigerated for up to 2 days before using.*)

Spoon the filling into the crust and smooth the top. Set aside while you make the ganache.

TO MAKE THE GANACHE: Put the chopped chocolate in a heatproof bowl. Bring the cream to a boil (there's such a small amount that I do this in the microwave) and pour it over the chocolate. Let the mixture sit for 15 seconds and then, using a whisk or a small flexible spatula and starting in the center of the bowl, stir the chocolate and cream together. Begin by stirring in small concentric circles and then expanding the circles until you almost reach the edges of the bowl. Add the butter bit by bit, stirring until each piece is incorporated before you add the next. You should have a thick, glossy, smooth ganache.

Pour the ganache over the coconut filling and tilt the pan as needed until you have an even layer of chocolate. If necessary, smooth the chocolate with an offset spatula. If you're using coconut as a topping (I rarely do—I like the sleek look of the shiny ganache), sprinkle it on now.

Chill the tart in the refrigerator for at least 4 hours (or for up to 8 hours) before serving.

Crème Brûlée Tart

Makes 8 servings

SERVING: Just like crème brûlée, a tarte crème brûlée needs no accompaniment. However, if you wanted to top it with fresh berries and perhaps a drizzle of raspberry coulis (page 449), I can't imagine that anyone would pass it up.

STORING: While you can make the filling up to 2 days ahead and keep it covered in the refrigerator, and while you need to chill the baked tart for at least 3 hours (or for up to 8), once you've caramelized the top, you need to dig into the tart soon.

CRÈME BRÛLÉE IS AN INTERNATIONAL CITIZEN of the dessert world. While it might be French or might just as truly be Spanish—many claim that *crema Catalana* came before the "burnt cream" of France—these days it turns up everywhere, in almost every flavor and in almost every kind of place, from serious restaurants to corner coffee shops. I loved it the first time I tasted it sometime in the 1980s at Le Cirque in New York City—the restaurant that was almost as famous for its crème brûlée as it was for its *Bonfire of the Vanities* clientele—and I love it just as much now. I especially like it in this tart, where the crust and the burnt sugar topping join to sandwich the rich filling.

My favorite way to make this tart is to line the crust with fresh raspberries or a mixture of raspberries and blueberries before pouring in the custard. But the berries, luscious as they are, are not necessary: The crème can just as well go solo.

1 partially baked 9- to 9½-inch tart crust made with Sweet Tart Dough (page 414), cooled	or 1 teaspoon vanilla extract plus 2 teaspoons kirsch
	½–1 cup (about 125 grams) fresh raspberries or blueberries, or a combination (optional)
1¼ cups (300 ml) heavy cream	
½ cup (120 ml) whole milk	
3 large egg yolks	About ¼ cup (50 grams) packed light brown sugar, for topping
⅓ cup (67 grams) sugar	
2 teaspoons pure vanilla extract	

Center a rack in the oven and preheat the oven to 325 degrees F. Put the tart pan with the partially baked crust on a baking sheet lined with parchment paper or a silicone baking mat.

Bring the cream and milk just to a boil in a small saucepan. Meanwhile, whisk the eggs and sugar together in a medium bowl for about 1 minute, until they thicken and lighten in color just a bit. Still whisking, little by little add about one quarter of the hot liquid—you don't want to shock (or cook) the yolks—and then whisk in the remainder of the hot liquid in a slow, steady stream. Stir in the vanilla (or vanilla and kirsch). Skim off as many of the surface bubbles as you can with a spoon—a nicety, not a necessity. (*The filling can be made up to this point, packed airtight and refrigerated for up to 2 days before using.*)

Scatter the berries over the bottom of the tart crust, if you're using them, and then strain the cream mixture over them. Depending on how high your crust is and how many berries you've put in, you might have some filling left over. Pour in enough to come almost to the edge of the crust; there might be some spillover when you move it—that's why you've got the lined baking sheet.

Bake the tart for 45 to 50 minutes, or until the tip of a small knife inserted into the center of the custard comes out clean. Don't panic when you see the custard bubble and heave—it looks scary and you might worry about the cream curdling, but it won't. Transfer the tart to a rack and let it cool to room temperature and then put it in the refrigerator to chill thoroughly, about 3 hours (or leave it for up to 8 hours).

When you're ready to serve, position a rack about 5 inches from your broiler and turn on the broiler. Or, if you've got a kitchen torch, have it at the ready.

Push the brown sugar through a strainer onto the tart, straining the sugar lightly but evenly over the custard. Slide the tart under the broiler or fire up the torch. In either case, give the sugar just enough heat to bubble, melt and then lightly burn. Remove the tart from the broiler or click off the torch and let the sugar settle down for a few minutes before serving.

Bonne Idée

CLASSIC CRÈME BRÛLÉE: If you'd like to make crème brûlée sans crust, pour the cream mixture into six shallow ramekins, about 1 inch high, 4 inches in diameter and holding about ¾ cup. Put the ramekins on a lined baking sheet and bake them in a 200-degree-F oven for 50 to 60 minutes, or until the centers are set. Let cool, then chill. When you're ready to cover them with brown sugar and burn the sugar, figure on about 1 tablespoon sugar for each ramekin.

Chocolate-Chestnut Tart
with Chestnut-Vanilla Syrup

Makes 8 servings

SERVING: You can cut and serve the tart when it's slightly warm or you can wait for it to reach room temperature. Top each serving with a scoop of ice cream and a drizzle of chestnut syrup; pass the remaining syrup in a small pitcher.

STORING: The tart is perfection the day it is made, but it can be kept overnight at room temperature or in the refrigerator, and it will be fine—though not perfect.

HERE'S A DESSERT that gives up its secrets slowly. At first glance it looks like many other luscious chocolate tarts with a rich filling. But because the filling is baked, it is even more luxurious than you might expect: It's soft, creamy and just shy of custard-ish. The little bumps here and there at the surface are candied chestnuts. And the sauce that's poured over the ice cream topping is a vanilla syrup, the one in which the chestnuts were cooked—a syrup so good you might just cook chestnuts so that you can have a jar of it in reserve. See Bonne Idée for what you might do with extra nuts and syrup.

For this tart, I've candied peeled and cooked chestnuts (buy them bottled or vacuum-packed) in a simple sugar syrup flavored with a vanilla bean. After 45 minutes of bobbing around in the syrup, the chestnuts are sweet to their centers and the syrup is the perfect blend of vanilla and nut. You can, if you want, add other flavors to the syrup—such as a small piece of cinnamon stick or even a few crushed coffee beans—but I urge you to go pure the first time around. I also urge you to go all out and serve the tart with ice cream as well as the chestnut syrup.

FOR THE CHESTNUTS
AND SYRUP

- 1½ cups (360 ml) water
- ¾ cup (150 grams) sugar
- 1 moist, fragrant vanilla bean
- 7 ounces; about 1 cup (198 grams) peeled cooked chestnuts (bottled or vacuum-packed)

- 1 fully baked 9- to 9½-inch tart crust made with Sweet Tart Dough (page 414), cooled

FOR THE FILLING

- 5 ounces (142 grams) bittersweet chocolate, finely chopped
- ½ cup (120 ml) heavy cream
- ½ stick (4 tablespoons; 2 ounces; 57 grams) unsalted butter, cut into 8 pieces
- 3 tablespoons sugar
  Pinch of fine sea salt
- 2 large eggs, cold
- 1 large egg yolk, cold

  Ice cream (try coffee or vanilla), for serving

TO MAKE THE CHESTNUTS AND SYRUP: Put the water and sugar in a medium saucepan and bring to a boil over medium heat, swirling the pan to dissolve the sugar. Slice the vanilla bean in half lengthwise, scrape the soft pulp from the pod and toss the pulp and pod into the pan. Rinse the chestnuts and toss them into the pan too. Return the liquid to a boil, then lower the heat and simmer for about 45 minutes, until the liquid has thickened and reduced by about half, the syrup's bubbles are big and slow to pop and the syrup is the color of strong tea with little flecks of vanilla bean running through it; the chestnuts will be dark and glistening. Remove from the heat.

Using a slotted spoon, spoon the chestnuts into a strainer set over a bowl and allow them to drain for a couple of minutes. You can leave them whole or cut them in half. Either way, scatter them over the bottom of the tart shell.

Strain the chestnut syrup into a heatproof jar; you're going to serve it with the tart. Discard the vanilla pod.

TO MAKE THE FILLING AND BAKE THE TART: Center a rack in the oven and preheat the oven to 300 degrees F. Put the tart pan with the fully baked crust on a baking sheet lined with parchment paper or a silicone baking mat.

Put the chopped chocolate in a medium heatproof bowl. Put the cream and butter in a small saucepan and bring just to a boil, stirring to make certain that the butter has melted. Pour the hot liquid over the chocolate, swirl the bowl so that all of the chocolate is covered and let everything sit for 30 seconds.

Working with a flexible spatula or a whisk, gently stir the cream and butter into the chocolate: Start by making small circles in the center of the bowl and then, when the ingredients at the center are blended, stir in widening concentric circles until you have a smooth, glossy ganache. Blend in the sugar and salt and then, one by one, add the eggs and yolk, stirring more vigorously so that the ganache remains smooth and shiny. Pour the ganache over the chestnuts in the crust.

Bake the tart for 27 to 30 minutes, or until the filling has set and no longer jiggles. Tap the tart pan—the filling should stay put. If you poke a skewer or a toothpick into the center, it should come out clean or just the least bit streaky. Transfer the baking sheet to a cooling rack and let the tart cool until warm or at room temperature.

Serve the tart with ice cream and the chestnut syrup.

Bonne Idée

CHESTNUT-FUDGE SUNDAE: Think of this as a more sophisticated version of the "wet walnuts" sundae. From the bottom up, each sundae should have a scoop of coffee ice cream, a spoonful of candied chestnuts and a drizzle of their syrup, a scoop of chocolate ice cream, a spoonful of chocolate or hot fudge sauce (page 442 or 444), a fluff of whipped cream and, to top it off, chocolate shavings.

Brown Sugar Tart

SERVING: My favorite topping for the tart is coffee ice cream—coffee ice cream with chicory would make it even more reminiscent of northern France. However, a scoop of vanilla ice cream or a dollop of whipped cream does the trick as well.

STORING: The tart can be kept in the refrigerator for up to 2 days.

Y OU FIND TWO KINDS OF BROWN SUGAR IN FRANCE: *sucre roux*, which can be as dry and coarse as sanding sugar; and *cassonade*, moist, soft, pale brown and very much like the brown sugar we know. This is the brown sugar of northern France and the sugar that gives its name to this dessert, simply called *tarte à la cassonade*. The traditional crust can be a crisp pastry, as it is here, or it can be made with a yeast dough and be soft. In either case, the filling is a basic custard of eggs, cream and a lot of brown sugar. It's sweet—sweeter than most French desserts—and very delicious too.

When my husband tasted the tart, the first thing he said was, "It's like pecan pie without the pecans." He was right, and now the northern French tart will forever be paired in my brain with the American Southern specialty.

Since I love knowing about tradition but have no qualms about flouting it, I'm behind you if you'd like to add pecans. What I like to add is crisp-cooked bacon and espresso powder.

1 fully baked 9- to 9½-inch tart crust made with Sweet Tart Dough (page 414), cooled	Pinch of instant espresso powder, or more to taste (optional)
	Pinch of fleur de sel or fine sea salt
1 cup (240 ml) heavy cream, at room temperature	
3 large eggs, at room temperature	4 strips bacon, crisp-cooked, patted dry and crumbled (optional)
1½ cups (300 grams) packed light brown sugar	Confectioners' sugar, for glazing (optional)

Center a rack in the oven and preheat the oven to 400 degrees F. Put the tart pan with the fully baked crust on a baking sheet lined with parchment paper or a silicone baking mat.

Using a whisk, beat the cream and eggs together in a medium bowl until well blended. Add the brown sugar—if it's lumpy, run it through your fingers before tossing it into the bowl—the espresso, if you're using it, and salt and whisk until you have a thick, smooth mixture. Rap the bowl against the counter a couple of times to pop the bubbles that will have formed or use a spoon to skim them off. (There's no need to be too thorough.) If you're using the bacon, scatter it over the bottom of the crust. Pour in as much of the filling as you need to fill the crust; depending on how thick you made your crust, you might have a few spoonfuls of filling left over.

Bake the tart for 30 to 35 minutes, or until the filling, which will bubble as it bakes, puffs all the way to the center and sets; a skewer poked into the center of the tart should come out clean. If you want to top the tart with a light glaze, sprinkle on some confectioners' sugar and run the tart under the broiler. Transfer the tart to a rack and let it cool to room temperature. The center of the puffed tart will depuff, but that's just what's meant to happen.

The tart is nice at room temperature, when the filling is soft and custardy, and if you've glazed it, it's also very good cold, when the sugar crystallizes slightly and the tart borders on candy-ish. If you'd like to serve it cold, refrigerate the tart for at least 4 hours (or for as long as 2 days).

Cream Cheese and Toast Tartlets

Makes 4 tartlets

SERVING: I serve the tartlets with forks and knives and an air of mystery. It's almost impossible for anyone to guess that the crunch is made of bread, so it's fun to keep it a secret until the last bite.

STORING: Like anything with gelatin, this is best served the day it is made. It will keep overnight, but the filling will become slightly spongy. You can make the crunch topping up to 1 week ahead and keep it tightly sealed, away from heat and humidity.

ABOUT A MINUTE AFTER GONTRAN CHERRIER opened his first Paris bakery, my friend Hélène Samuel and I were there. The shop, on one end of Montmartre's rue Caulaincourt, a street that seems to have more than its fair share of pâtisseries (even for Paris!), is modern, bright and spare, so that all eyes turn to what's really important: the long marble counter covered with tarts and cookies, loaf cakes as long as baguettes, small pastries and breads of infinite variety and almost as many shapes and colors. Cherrier's sweets looked so good that we bought a half dozen to share on the spot. And that's when we came across the fromage blanc tartlet with a surprise in the center: minuscule cubes of bread.

The tartlet stayed with me, so much so that when I got back to New York, I made these. They're not a re-creation of Cherrier's, but they were certainly inspired by his. My version uses cream cheese and heavy cream. And instead of soft bread in the center of the filling, I've put crisped bread on top. I was so excited when I created this crunch—tiny cubes of bread sautéed in butter, caramelized in sugar, flavored with cocoa and cinnamon and then chopped superfine—that I started sprinkling it over everything from yogurt to chocolate mousse, to ice cream and pots de crème. It's even good on thickly buttered soft toast.

The sweet tart dough is my choice for the crust—I keep it thick so that there's really something to bite into and to play against the very light filling—but if you need a shortcut, use a crumb or graham cracker crust.

As for the bread cubes, I've used baguette and country loaf and both have been good. There's no need to remove the crust, but there is a need to cut the bread cubes as small as you can. Aim for ⅛ inch on a side.

1 recipe Sweet Tart Dough (page 414), rolled out to a scant ¼ inch thick and chilled

FOR THE CRUNCH

1 teaspoon unsweetened cocoa powder
¼ teaspoon ground cinnamon
1 tablespoon unsalted butter
⅓ cup (20 grams) packed tiny fresh bread cubes (see above)
1 tablespoon sugar

FOR THE FILLING

1¼ teaspoons unflavored gelatin
1½ tablespoons cold water
3 tablespoons sugar
¼ teaspoon ground cinnamon
Small pinch of fine sea salt
6 ounces (170 grams) cream cheese, at room temperature
¼ cup (60 ml) heavy cream, at room temperature
1 teaspoon pure vanilla extract

TO MAKE THE CRUST: Generously butter four 4-inch tartlet pans. If they have removable bottoms, great. Line a baking sheet with parchment paper or a silicone baking mat.

Cut 4 circles from the tart dough—use the rim of a tartlet pan as a guide and cut a circle that's about ½ inch larger all around. Fit the circles into the pans, trim the tops and prick the bottoms with a fork. Place the pans on the baking sheet and chill for 1 hour, or freeze for 30 minutes.

Center a rack in the oven and preheat the oven to 400 degrees F. Line the dough in each tartlet pan with parchment or aluminum foil and fill with rice or dried beans.

Bake the crusts for 20 minutes. Remove the parchment and weights and bake, uncovered, for about 5 minutes more, or until the crusts are golden. Cool on a rack. If the crusts were made in pans with removable bottoms, you can leave them in the pans; if the tins are one piece, unmold the crusts.

TO MAKE THE CRUNCH: Stir the cocoa and cinnamon together in a small bowl. Melt the butter in a small skillet over medium-high heat. When the foam subsides, toss in the bread cubes and cook, turning, until the bread is coated with butter and starting to color lightly, about 2 minutes. Sprinkle over the sugar and continue to cook, stirring, until the sugar caramelizes and coats the bread, another 1 to 2 minutes. Scrape the bread into the bowl with the cocoa mix and stir. Allow the bread to cool to room temperature and crisp up.

Using a large chef's knife, very finely chop the caramelized bread into bits the size of pumpkin seeds. Set the crunch aside while you make the filling. (*The crunch can be made up to 1 week ahead and kept in a covered jar in a cool, dry place—not the refrigerator.*)

TO MAKE THE FILLING: Put the gelatin in a small microwave-safe bowl and pour over the cold water. Let sit for about 3 minutes, or until the gelatin is completely moistened and has begun to "bloom," or expand.

Meanwhile, whisk the sugar, cinnamon and salt together in a small bowl.

Heat the gelatin in a microwave oven for 15 seconds to dissolve it.

Working in the bowl of a stand mixer fitted with the paddle attachment, or in a medium bowl with a hand mixer, beat the cream cheese on medium-high speed until very soft and creamy, about 4 minutes. Pour in the cream and beat for 2 minutes more. Lower the mixer speed to medium, add the sugar mixture and beat for another 2 minutes. Beat in the vanilla. Stir a spoonful of this mixture into the gelatin, then add the gelatin to the filling. Raise the mixer speed to medium-high and beat for 1 minute more, or until smooth.

Immediately divide the filling among the 4 crusts. Smooth the tops and sprinkle over the crunch topping, pressing it down lightly with your fingertips.

Chill the tartlets for at least 2 hours before serving.

Tiramisu Tart

Makes 8 servings

SERVING: The tart, meant to be served straight from the refrigerator, needs no accompaniment, although finishing with an espresso is always nice.

STORING: The tart must be chilled for at least 3 hours so that the filling sets and grabs some of the espresso-rum flavor. Once it's set, you can keep it covered in the refrigerator overnight or wrap it very well and freeze it for up to 2 months.

SOMETIMES I WONDER if this simple Italian dessert is as popular in its native land as it is in France and the United States. I hope so, because it's a dessert that deserves its fame. It's wonderfully rich, but not too sweet. It's creamy, but its hallmark espresso-soaked ladyfingers keep the texture interesting. And it's boozy, but not too. The basics of tiramisu are straight-forward: There are two elements, the espresso-and-booze soaked ladyfingers and the cream, a mixture of mascarpone and eggs, layered, chilled and deco-rated with a dusting of cocoa powder. *Finito.* Or not. The sweet's simplicity seems to encourage variation, and I've seen tiramisu flavored with all kinds of liqueurs and fruits, its supple nature bent to become cupcakes and cream puffs, ice cream or coffee drinks. Of all the many ways I've seen tiramisu served, encasing the elements in a tart crust is my favorite. It not only gives the dessert a beautiful form and another layer of texture, it also makes it ele-gant. In this version, I've swapped the cocoa powder for chopped chocolate, which has more flavor and certainly more crunch.

A WORD ON THE EGGS: The eggs in this recipe are not cooked, so make sure to use very fresh ones, preferably organic.

¾ cup (180 ml) hot strong espresso (made fresh or with instant espresso powder)
2–3 tablespoons dark rum
½ pound (227 grams) mascarpone
2 very fresh large eggs, preferably organic, separated, at room temperature
Pinch of fine sea salt
½ cup (100 grams) sugar

1 fully baked 9- to 9½-inch tart crust made with Sweet Tart Dough (page 414) or Chocolate Tart Dough (page 418), cooled

About 12 savoiardi (store-bought crisp Italian ladyfingers) or homemade Ladyfingers (page 217)
Chopped semisweet or bittersweet chocolate, for topping

The soaking syrup for the ladyfingers needs to be strong. Pour the espresso into a loaf pan or wide shallow bowl and stir in 2 tablespoons of the rum. If it seems delicious but not knock-your-socks-off strong, stir in another tablespoonful or so of rum. Set aside to cool to room temperature.

Put the mascarpone in a large bowl and, using a flexible spatula, gently mash and stir it to soften and smooth it. (You never want to beat mascarpone, because it will seize and turn into butter.)

Put the egg whites in the bowl of a stand mixer fitted with the whisk attachment, or work in a medium bowl with a hand mixer. Add the salt and start beating the whites at medium-high speed. Once they've gone from foamy to opaque, gradually beat in ¼ cup of the sugar. Continue to beat until the whites are glossy and smooth; the meringue will look shiny and marsh-mallowy, and that's just right.

Scrape the whites into a small bowl and add the yolks to the mixing bowl. (There's no need to wash the bowl or the beater.) Add the remaining ¼ cup sugar and beat on medium-high speed for a couple of minutes, until the yolks thicken and lighten in color. Scrape the yolks into the bowl with the mascarpone.

Working with the spatula and a soft touch, stir the yolks into the mas-carpone, then add the meringue and gently stir and fold until blended. You might have a tiny lump here and there, and if you do, just leave it—a lump is better than a beaten-down mix.

Spread a thin layer of the mascarpone cream over the crust.

Before you start dipping the ladyfingers into the syrup, take a look at the tart and plan how you're going to arrange them: My choice is to make a horizontal row of cookies down the center, place a cookie vertically on either side and break cookies as needed to fill in the spaces. One by one, dip the cookies into the espresso and rum, dipping both sides. Do this quickly—5 seconds is probably enough; 10 will saturate the cookies and make them fall apart (especially if you've got homemade ladyfingers). Arrange the cookies in the tart shell, and don't worry if you've got a few uncookied spots. Spoon the rest of the mascarpone cream over the cookies and smooth the top with a spatula. Refrigerate the tart for at least 3 hours. (*The tart can be refrigerated for as long as overnight.*)

Right before serving, scatter the chopped chocolate over the top of the tart, pressing it lightly into the mascarpone cream with your fingertips.

Bonne Idée

CLASSIC TIRAMISU: If you'd like to make individual classic tiramisus without a crust, you can use the same cream. Build each tiramisu in a *verrine*, or short glass. You may need more or fewer cookies or more or less espresso, depending on how you arrange the layers.

Another Bonne Idée

ESPRESSO-ESPRESSO TIRAMISU: Dissolve 1½ tablespoons instant espresso powder in 2 tablespoons boiling water or espresso, cool and then add to the mascarpone and yolk mixture before folding in the meringue.

Cookies-and-Cream Tartlets

Makes 6 tartlets

SERVING: The tartlets are good cold and better after they've spent 20 minutes or so at room temperature. Just before serving, top each tartlet with some crème fraîche, whipped cream or yogurt.

STORING: Once the tartlets are filled, you can keep them covered in the refrigerator for up to 2 days or, wrapped airtight, in the freezer for up to 2 months; defrost overnight in the refrigerator. You can even serve the tartlets frozen—their texture won't be luxurious, but the crust will have crunch and the ganache will melt on your tongue, which is its own kind of wonderful.

WHILE IT'S HARD TO IMAGINE a dessert made with spice cookies as being anything but wonderful, some are more wonderful than others. This one is in the more-wonderful camp. It's also in the simple camp: The cookies are crushed and stirred into a bittersweet chocolate ganache, which is poured into fully baked tartlet crusts and chilled. The spicy chunks and crumbs that speckle the ganache and pop up intermittently are both a surprise and a pleasure. Adding to the pleasure, the tarts are good at room temperature, chilled or even almost frozen, meaning you can have a party-ready dessert just waiting for a party to turn up.

If you like surprises as much as I do, put a spoonful of Biscoff spread or Nutella in the bottom of each tartlet shell before you add the ganache.

6 fully baked 4-inch tartlet crusts made with Sweet Tart Dough (page 414), cooled (and still in their pans)	2 tablespoons (1 ounce; 28 grams) unsalted butter, cut into 4 pieces
¼ cup (74 grams) Biscoff or Nutella spread (optional)	4½ ounces (128 grams) bittersweet or semisweet chocolate, finely chopped
12 Biscoff or 8 LU Cinnamon Sugar Spice cookies (or about 3½ ounces; 100 grams)	Pinch of fleur de sel
½ cup (120 ml) heavy cream	Very lightly sweetened crème fraîche, softly whipped heavy cream or thick plain Greek yogurt, for topping
	Crushed cookies, shaved chocolate or cocoa nibs, for topping (optional)

Place the tartlet pans on a baking sheet lined with parchment paper or wax paper, to make it easy to move them around the kitchen.

If you'd like to have a layer of Biscoff or Nutella in the bottom of your tartlets—I do—divide the spread among the tartlet shells and use a small flexible spatula or the back of a spoon to spread it evenly in the crusts.

Crush the cookies by putting them between two sheets of parchment or wax paper and bashing them with a rolling pin, by putting them in a zipper-lock bag and squeezing them into bits or—this is what I do—by cutting them into small pieces with a serrated knife. If you cut them, you'll get some cookie dust and some crumb-like pieces, but you also get larger bits that give every mouthful a little more flavor and texture. Set the crushed cookies aside.

Put the cream and butter in a small saucepan and heat just until the cream reaches a boil, stirring to melt the butter (or do this in a microwave oven). Remove from the heat and add the chocolate. Wait about 30 seconds, then stir, starting in the center and making small, steadily increasing concentric circles; stay in the center of the pan until the ganache thickens and turns totally brown before moving outward. You should have a smooth, glossy ganache. Stir in the salt, then mix in the crushed cookies. If the ganache is very thin, let it sit for a few minutes to thicken just a little.

Divide the filling among the crusts, mounding it slightly in the center, and allow the ganache to set. The quickest way to set the filling is to put the tartlets in the fridge for about 30 minutes. (*They can stay there for up to 2 days; cover them when they're set.*)

Serve the tartlets topped with créme fraîche, whipped cream or yogurt and, if you'd like, sprinkled with cookie crumbs, chocolate shavings or cocoa nibs.

Lemon Meringue Tart
A New Way

Makes 8 servings

SERVING: If you can serve the tart right after the meringue has cooled, terrific; however, no harm will come to your dessert if it waits a while. I like the tart chilled, but others prefer it at room temperature—the choice is yours.

STORING: The lemon filling can be made up to 2 days ahead and kept covered in the refrigerator; whisk it well to smooth it before spooning it into the crust. Assembled to this point, the tart can be refrigerated for up to 8 hours. The meringue signals showtime: Once it's browned, it's best if you can serve the tart soon. If you can't, keep the tart in the refrigerator until you're ready for it.

JUST WHEN I THOUGHT I'd made lemon tarts every way possible, my friend Hélène Samuel handed me this recipe and said, "Wait until you taste the filling—it's as light as a flan." I doubted her until the first forkful. The recipe was almost identical to the one I use for pastry cream, so why would the texture be different? The reason is lemon juice—lots of it. It's there for the taste and tang, as always, but it also changes the way the pastry cream sets, the way it melts in your mouth and the way it jiggles in the crust. Hélène had nailed it: It's got all the best qualities of a flan and everything you want in a filling.

The recipe, which made guest appearances at Café Salle Pleyel, Hélène's Paris restaurant, came to me with instructions for an Italian (cooked-sugar) meringue topping, which is stable and can be held for a few hours. At the café, the crust was fully baked and filled with lemon cream and then, when an order for it came in, a slice was cut, squiggled with meringue and browned with a blowtorch. Of course you could do that at home, but chez moi, I'm more likely to make a simple uncooked meringue, swirl it over the whole tart and brown it under the broiler.

FOR THE FILLING

- ¾ cup (180 ml) freshly squeezed lemon juice (from about 5 lemons)
- ⅓ cup (43 grams) cornstarch
- ¾ cup (150 grams) sugar
- 4 large egg yolks
- 2 cups (480 ml) whole milk
  Finely grated zest of 1 lemon

- 1 fully baked 9- to 9½-inch tart crust made with Sweet Tart Dough (page 414), cooled

FOR THE MERINGUE

- 3 large egg whites, at room temperature
- ½ cup (100 grams) sugar

TO MAKE THE FILLING: Pour the lemon juice into a medium heavy-bottomed saucepan. Sift the cornstarch by pushing it through a strainer into the pan, then whisk until the mixture is smooth. Whisk in the sugar. One by one, beat in the yolks, followed by the milk and lemon zest. Put the saucepan over medium heat and, whisking constantly—make sure to get the tip of your whisk into the corners of the pan—cook until a bubble pops on the surface, at which point the cream will have thickened and the whisk will leave tracks. It can take 5 to 9 minutes to get tracks—it all depends on the dimensions of your pan and the level of heat you have under it. Lower the heat and continue to cook and stir without stopping for 1 minute more, insurance that the cornstarch won't taste raw.

Scrape the filling into a bowl, press a piece of plastic film against the surface to keep a skin from forming and refrigerate until cool (or for up to 2 days); you can speed things along by whisking every now and then if you're in the kitchen. (You can also put the bowl in a larger bowl filled with ice cubes and cold water and stir until the cream is uniformly chilled.)

When the filling is cool, give it a vigorous whisking to resmooth it and spoon it into the crust, leveling the top. You can either finish the tart with the meringue and serve it now or cover it and keep it in the refrigerator until you're ready. (*The tart can be refrigerated for up to 8 hours.*)

TO MAKE THE MERINGUE: If you don't have a kitchen torch, position a rack in the top third of your oven and preheat the broiler.

Put the whites in the bowl of a stand mixer fitted with the whisk attachment, or use a medium bowl and a hand mixer. In either case, make sure the bowl is squeaky clean (any fat in the bowl will impede the whites' rise). Beat the whites at medium-high speed until they're foamy and just opaque. Slowly and steadily, add the sugar, beating until the whites are glossy and form stiff peaks.

Cover the tart with the meringue. You can swirl it on with a knife, spatula or the back of a spoon, or you can put it in a pastry bag fitted with an open star tip and pipe out a creative design (I usually pipe a spiral starting at the center of the tart). Just make sure the meringue goes all the way to, even a little over, the edges. Meringue shrinks after it's browned, so you've got a better chance of keeping the lemon cream covered if you overshoot your mark. That said, tarts can be very attractive with peekaboo edges, so don't fuss about this.

If you have a kitchen torch, fire it up and brown the meringue. If you're using the broiler, put the tart on a baking sheet, slide it under the broiler and don't step away: Depending on the strength of your broiler, browning the meringue can take anywhere from 30 seconds to 3 minutes, and you want to be there when perfection hits.

Serve the tart at room temperature or chilled.

Smoothest, Silkiest, Creamiest, Tartest Lime Tart

Makes 8 servings

SERVING: The filling tastes tangier—and truer to the nature of limes—when it's cold, so give the tart time to chill and serve it straight out of the refrigerator. This tart would never, ever, ever be served with a margarita in France, but if you're in America . . .

STORING: The filling can be made up to 2 days ahead and kept tightly covered in the refrigerator. For the sake of the crust, it's best to assemble the tart no more than a couple of hours or so before you're ready to serve it. However, if you've got leftovers, they'll be better than fine the next day.

THIS IS A VERSION OF THE TART all of Paris fell in love with: The pastry chef Jacques Genin made lime the flavor of the moment when he introduced a tart that was at once rich and refreshing, so tart that it's north-wind sharp. The filling is really a crème anglaise made with fruit juice instead of the usual milk or cream. It's cooked (carefully and under constant surveillance) for a few minutes on the stove and then whirred in a blender for a few minutes more, during which time the magic ingredient is added: butter. Lots of it. It's the butter that gives the filling its remarkable texture.

I tasted this totally French tart and immediately thought of Key lime pie. And so, in a cross-cultural mash-up, I finished the tart with sour cream, the way many Key lime pies are. If you'd like to wave our flag a little more, you can skip the French crust and make the tart in a graham cracker shell.

A WORD ON THE CRÈME ANGLAISE: Crème anglaise is easy to make as long as you give it your full attention. You must stir without stopping and watch as the custard goes from thin to slightly thicker, from calm to just on the verge of boiling. If you've got an instant-read thermometer, pull it out. Ideally, you want to cook the custard to 180 degrees F, which takes about 8 minutes or so, depending on the heat you've got under the pan. If the temperature's a little lower (even as low as 160 degrees F), you'll still get a custard that will set because of the butter, but if you can get it to 180 degrees F, you'll get one in which the ingredients bond, the texture is silken and the flavor is deep.

FOR THE FILLING

1 cup (200 grams) sugar
6 bright green, juicy limes
4 large eggs
2 sticks (8 ounces; 227 grams) unsalted butter, cut into 16 pieces, at room temperature

1 fully baked 9- to 9½-inch tart crust made from Sweet Tart Dough (page 414), cooled

FOR THE TOPPING (OPTIONAL)

1 cup (240 grams) sour cream
1–2 tablespoons confectioners' sugar, sifted

Have a blender plugged in and ready to whir. Or set up a food processor, if that's what you've got.

TO MAKE THE FILLING: Pour the sugar into a heavy-bottomed 2- to 3-quart saucepan and grate the zest from the limes over it. Using your fingertips, rub the sugar and zest together until the sugar is moist and aromatic.

It will also be a lovely shade of pale green. Squeeze the juice of the limes into a measuring cup; you want ¾ cup. Add the eggs to the saucepan, whisking energetically as soon as the yolks hit the sugar (if you let them sit, the sugar will "burn" the yolks and a film will form over them). Whisk in the lime juice.

Place the saucepan over medium heat (medium-low if you've got a powerful burner), plant yourself in front of the stove and start whisking. You don't have to whisk vigorously, but you do have to whisk vigilantly—this is a nonstop job. For the first few minutes, you won't see much change in the custard, but keep at it, and you'll notice that soon it will take a full second for the custard to fill the space your whisk leaves at the bottom of the pan. Keep whisking, making sure to get into the corners of the pan, and after 7 to 9 minutes, the custard will thicken. If you stick a wooden spoon into it and then run your finger down the back of the spoon, the custard won't fill in the track you created. Here's the important sign: One bubble will pop at the surface. If you measure the temperature of the custard with an instant-read thermometer, it should be about 180 degrees F. When that bubble pops, immediately pull the pan from the heat and strain the crème anglaise into the blender; discard the zest and any bits of eggs that scrambled.

Allow the custard to sit in the blender for about 5 minutes, and pulse the blender on and off as you pass it, just to help the cream cool down. Turn the blender to high and start adding the butter 2 pats at a time. Keep whirring and tossing in the butter and then, when all the butter is in, whir for another minute. Scrape the shiny, voluptuously smooth cream into a bowl, press a piece of plastic film against the surface to keep a skin from forming (don't do this before you stick your finger in the cream for a first taste) and refrigerate the cream for at least 4 hours (or for up to 2 days). Alternatively, you can put the bowl of hot cream into a larger bowl filled with ice cubes and water and stir until the cream cools down. Even if you do this, it's good to give the cream some time in the refrigerator—the chilling time allows the butter to set more substantially and also gives the flavors time to develop.

About 2 hours before you're ready to serve the tart, remove the filling from the refrigerator, whisk it briefly and spread it evenly into the crust. If you'd like to finish the tart with the sour cream topping, stir the sour cream and confectioners' sugar together in a small bowl, just to blend. Then pour it onto the center of the tart and, using an offset icing spatula or the back of a spoon, spread it over the filling, working your way out, leaving a bare edge of lime cream visible.

Return the tart to the refrigerator for another 2 hours (or for up to 8 hours) before serving.

Bonne Idée
LIME AND BERRY TART: Fresh berries—raspberries, blueberries or blackberries—add color, surprise and another texture to this tart. If you'd like to use them, you can scatter the berries over the bottom of the crust before you add the chilled lime cream; you can arrange them randomly or in militarily precise rings on top of the lime cream; you can mound them in the center of the tart after you've spread the sour cream over the filling; you can serve a bowl of lightly sugared (or honeyed) berries alongside the tart; or you can make a berry sauce to pass in a pitcher at the table. So many choices, all lovely.

BABY CAKES
AND PETITE PASTRIES

Nutella Buttons

**Makes about
24 mini cakes**

SERVING: Good with tea or coffee, these are nice to put in a lunchbox or pack for a picnic.

STORING: These will keep for about 3 days in a covered container at room temperature.

YOU MIGHT THINK OF THESE as mini cupcakes or fairy cakes, but the French would think of them as *bouchées*, or "mouthfuls." Me? I think of them as surprise cakes that are more template than dictate. The cake itself is a white cake with an especially fine and springy crumb, and the surprise is anything you'd like it to be. I've filled them with Nutella, the spread the French like as much as we like peanut butter, but you can hide a dollop of jam, a bit of leftover ganache or some Biscoff speculoos spread in the center. Whatever you choose, you'll have a delicious mouthful—or two.

4   large eggs, at room
      temperature
1   cup minus 1 tablespoon
      (95 grams) confectioners'
      sugar, sifted
¾   cup (102 grams) all-purpose
      flour
¼   teaspoon baking powder
      Pinch of fine sea salt
½   teaspoon pure vanilla extract

Drop of pure almond extract
   (optional)
¾   stick (6 tablespoons;
      3 ounces; 85 grams)
      unsalted butter, melted and
      cooled to room temperature

About ¼ cup (74 grams)
   Nutella at room
   temperature

Center a rack in the oven and preheat the oven to 350 degrees F. The buttons can be baked in mini muffin tins or in foil-and-paper mini muffin cups. If you're using muffin tins, butter them or line them with paper cups; if you're using foil muffin cups, put them on a baking sheet.

Separate the eggs. Put the yolks in a small bowl and whisk them lightly, just to blend. Put the whites in the bowl of a stand mixer or in a large bowl.

Whisk the confectioners' sugar, flour, baking powder and salt together in a large bowl. Add the yolks, vanilla extract and almond extract, if you're using it, and blend with a flexible spatula; the mixture will resemble a paste. Pour in the melted butter, stir to combine and then give the batter a vigorous beating.

If you're working in the bowl of a stand mixer, fit it with the whisk attachment; if not, use a hand mixer. Beat the whites until they hold firm peaks but are still glossy. Using a flexible spatula, stir about one quarter of the whites into the batter to loosen it, then gently fold in the remaining whites. (*At this point, you can press a piece of plastic film against the surface of the batter and refrigerate it overnight, if you'd like.*)

It's hard to give exact measurements, because muffin tin sizes can vary, but the principle here is to put a small amount of batter, about 1 teaspoon, in the bottom of each mold or paper cup, add ½ teaspoon Nutella, and

Chocolate-Dipped Nutella Buttons

Bonne Idée

CHOCOLATE-DIPPED
NUTELLA BUTTONS:
If you'd like to dress these
up, dip either the bottoms
or tops in just-made
ganache (page 434) or,
more simply, in melted
white chocolate. Let
the buttons set at room
temperature or, if you're
as impatient as I usually
am, slide them into the
refrigerator for about 20
minutes, until the chocolate
firms.

then cover the Nutella with enough batter to fill the mold or paper cup just to the top. If you're using mini muffin tins and have some unfilled molds, put a spoonful of water into each empty one (this helps the buttons bake evenly). If you have more batter than muffin tins, refrigerate the batter until you're ready to bake it.

Bake for 15 to 18 minutes, or until the tops of the buttons are golden brown and springy to the touch and a toothpick stuck into the center of a button comes out clean. Remove the buttons from the muffin tins as soon as they come out of the oven; the buttons baked in cups can, of course, stay in their liners. Cool the buttons to room temperature on racks. If you have more batter, make sure that the muffin tins are cool before filling them with the remaining batter and Nutella.

Soft-Centered Chocolate Teacup Cakes

We Americans know these small sweets as molten chocolate or lava cakes: soft dark chocolate cakes with oozy, impossible-to-contain centers. They became a must-have sometime in the late 1980s and they're still adored.

As near as I can tell, the first cake of this kind was created by Michel Bras, an extraordinary chef from the central region of France. Bras is an innovator and, even though his Michelin-starred restaurant sits amid grazing pastures far from much else, you have to plan months ahead to nab a table. The original Bras cake—beautifully diagrammed in his published notebooks—was made with a thoroughly frozen small chocolate truffle in its middle. The cake baked, but the truffle didn't have enough time in the oven to melt and then resolidify, so it created the "molten lava" that flowed from the cake at first cut. It was genius, as every other chocolate-loving chef in the world recognized.

These little cakes use a similar technique to achieve their moltenness: They have chunks of chocolate in their centers, which melt while the batter bakes itself into a cake.

The success of the recipe depends on the chocolate: Choose one that makes you happy when you eat it straight up.

Makes 4 servings

SERVING: When these cakes are served in bistros, they arrive with nothing more than a spoon. But it's hard to beat a hot cake topped with a melting scoop of vanilla ice cream.

STORING: You can wait to serve the cakes until they reach room temperature, at which point their innards will be more fudgy than molten. You can even chill them. Yes, cold is the opposite of what they were created to be, but because you started with great chocolate, you'll end up with a great cold cake.

- Sugar, for dusting (optional)
- ½ stick (4 tablespoons; 2 ounces; 57 grams) unsalted butter, cut into chunks
- 5 ounces (142 grams) bittersweet chocolate, coarsely chopped, plus 2 ounces (57 grams) bittersweet or milk chocolate, cut into 8 pieces
- 3 large eggs, at room temperature
- ½ cup (60 grams) confectioners' sugar, sifted
- 2 tablespoons all-purpose flour or 1 tablespoon cornstarch

Center a rack in the oven and preheat the oven to 400 degrees F. Butter four 6-ounce ovenproof teacups or coffee cups or use ramekins or custard cups. If you'd like a teensy bit of crunch, dust the interior of the cups with granulated sugar. Place the cups on a baking sheet lined with parchment paper or a silicone baking mat.

Put the butter and the 5 ounces chopped chocolate in a heatproof bowl set over a pan of simmering water and heat, stirring occasionally, until the

butter and chocolate are melted but not so hot that they separate. When you stir them together, the mixture should be thick, smooth and shiny. Remove the bowl from the heat and set aside.

Working in the bowl of a stand mixer fitted with the paddle attachment, or in a large bowl with a hand mixer, whip the eggs and confectioners' sugar at medium-high speed for about 5 minutes, until the eggs are pale and have increased in volume. Reduce the mixer speed to low and blend in the flour or cornstarch. Switch to a flexible spatula and gently blend in the melted chocolate mixture, stirring until it's completely incorporated.

Divide half of the batter among the cups. Drop in the chocolate chunks (2 pieces in each cup) and top with the remaining batter.

Bake the cakes for 10 to 12 minutes: At 10 minutes, the edges, tops and a thin section of the bottoms of the cakes will be set and the centers will be super-runny. At 12 minutes, the set sections will be thicker and the centers will be just a tad less runny. The cakes are wonderful either way.

Transfer the cups to a rack and let the cakes rest for 5 to 10 minutes. You want them to be hot but not dangerous to eat.

Bonne Idée

MOLTEN SURPRISE CAKES: The technique of placing something that's slow to melt in the center of a chocolate cake is too good an idea not to riff on. Stuffing these cakes with white or milk chocolate chunks is one way to play with them. But you can also put juicy fruit in the center. Berries are perfect here: Mash them, freeze them and add a spoonful to each cake, or use frozen berry coulis. Or return to Chef Bras' original idea: Put a small frozen chocolate truffle (page 397) in each cake.

Limoncello Cupcakes

Makes 12 cupcakes

SERVING: These cupcakes are just as good served cold as they are at room temperature. The flavor is so strong that chilling doesn't dull it.

STORING: Covered, these will keep at room temperature or in the refrigerator for 2 to 3 days.

I MADE THESE CUPCAKES as a surprise for my friend Bernard Collet, who adores limoncello, a fact I discovered one evening when we went to a local pizza place. The owners poured us some limoncello after dinner and Bernard drank the frigid lemon liquor, licked his lips and declared that Italy was created so that limoncello could be invented! Spoken like a proud Frenchman, but one with an appreciation for the good things, don't you think?

These are definitely good things for adults. There's limoncello in the cupcakes, in the syrup used to soak the cakes and make them extra-moist, and more in the butter frosting. The flavor is powerful and it has an almost magnetic pull on all of us who love lemon.

I've given you a recipe for a French-style frosting, meaning there's enough to crown each cupcake with a modest swirl. If you'd like a more American-style swirl, meaning one that's generous and high, just double the recipe. My French friends would say it's de trop, but they'd be wrong: How could more of a good thing be too much?

A WORD ON TIMING: It's best to make the syrup as soon as you put the cupcakes into the oven so it has time to cool down a bit.

FOR THE CUPCAKES
- 1½ cups (204 grams) all-purpose flour
- 2 teaspoons baking powder
- ¼ teaspoon ground cardamom or a big pinch of cracked black pepper
- Pinch of fine sea salt
- ¾ cup (150 grams) sugar
- 1 lemon
- ½ cup (113 grams) plain Greek yogurt
- 3 large eggs, at room temperature
- 2 tablespoons limoncello
- ½ cup (120 ml) canola, safflower or other flavorless oil
- ¼ cup (80 grams) lemon or orange marmalade (optional)

FOR THE SYRUP
- 1½ tablespoons sugar
- 2 tablespoons water
- 1 tablespoon limoncello

FOR THE FROSTING
- ¾ stick (6 tablespoons; 3 ounces; 85 grams) unsalted butter, at room temperature
- 2 cups (240 grams) confectioners' sugar, sifted
- 2 tablespoons limoncello
- 2 teaspoons freshly squeezed lemon juice

TO MAKE THE CUPCAKES: Center a rack in the oven and preheat the oven to 350 degrees F. Fit a 12-mold muffin tin with cupcake liners or butter the molds.

Whisk the flour, baking powder, cardamom or pepper and salt together in a small bowl.

Put the sugar in a large bowl and finely grate the zest of the lemon over it. (Hold on to the lemon and use the juice for the frosting.) Rub the sugar and zest together with your fingertips until the sugar is moist and aromatic. Whisk in the yogurt. Add the eggs one by one, whisking well after each egg goes in. Whisk in the limoncello. Switch to a flexible spatula and add the dry ingredients, stirring only until the flour disappears into the batter. Gradually add the oil, folding and stirring until it is thoroughly incorporated. You'll have a smooth, heavy batter.

If you want to add marmalade to the center of the cupcakes, put a large spoonful of batter into each cupcake mold, drop a teaspoon of the marmalade into the center of the batter and cover with the remaining batter. If you're skipping the marmalade, just divide the batter among the cupcake molds.

Bake for 20 to 25 minutes, or until a skewer inserted into the center of a cupcake comes out clean. The cakes will dome a little and may crack in the center; they should be lightly golden around the edges. Transfer the tin to a rack.

MEANWHILE, MAKE THE SYRUP: As soon as the cupcakes go into the oven, put the sugar and water in a microwave-safe container and bring just to a boil. (You can do this in a saucepan, too, of course.) Stir to dissolve the sugar. Let the syrup cool for 10 minutes, then stir in the limoncello.

TO SOAK THE CUPCAKES: The cupcakes should be soaked as soon as they come out of the oven. Leave them in the muffin tin and, using a pastry brush, brush the tops with the syrup (or use a spoon). Allow the cupcakes to cool to room temperature before frosting.

TO MAKE THE FROSTING: Working in the bowl of a stand mixer fitted with the paddle attachment, or in a medium bowl with a hand mixer, beat the butter and confectioners' sugar together on low speed until the mixture comes together and wraps around the beater, about 4 minutes. Add the limoncello and lemon juice, raise the speed to medium and beat until the frosting is smooth, light and fluffy, another 3 to 5 minutes.

You can spread the frosting on the cupcakes with an icing spatula, a table knife or the back of a spoon, but I think the cupcakes look prettiest when the frosting is piped through an open star tube. No matter what you use to frost the cupcakes, allow them to sit at room temperature for 30 minutes, or until the frosting develops a slightly firm outer coating (my favorite part).

Tiger Cakes

ALTHOUGH THESE SOUND as if they might be a health food or energy bar, they're really a traditional French pastry made with egg whites, almond flour and lots of butter. The addition of finely chopped chocolate that melts and stripes the little cakes explains their name. It's hard not to fall for buttery almonds and chocolate, but it was the texture, as well as the flavor, of these that grabbed me: The cakes have a little spring in their crumb and just enough chew to make the flavor last and last.

Most pâtisseries finish tiger cakes with a dab of chocolate, usually a rosette of ganache, a nice flourish. My own preference is to dip the cakes in chocolate—although the glaze hides the tiger stripes, it intensifies the chocolate flavor—but it is entirely optional.

Makes 24 small cakes

SERVING: I enjoy these with a rich espresso or cappuccino, but they're good with tea and nice with ice cream.

STORING: Stored in a covered container, the cakes will keep at room temperature for about 2 days. If you'd like, you can pack them airtight and freeze them for up to 2 months. Also, the batter can be covered tightly and refrigerated for up to 3 days; use it directly from the fridge.

FOR THE CAKES

- 3 large egg whites, at room temperature
- 1 cup (100 grams) almond flour
- 2/3 cup (132 grams) sugar
- 3 tablespoons all-purpose flour
- 1/4 teaspoon fine sea salt
- 1/2 teaspoon pure vanilla extract
- 1 stick (8 tablespoons; 4 ounces; 113 grams) unsalted butter
- 3 ounces (85 grams) bittersweet chocolate, very finely chopped

FOR THE GLAZE (OPTIONAL)

- 2 ounces (57 grams) semisweet or bittersweet chocolate, finely chopped
- 1/4 cup (60 ml) heavy cream

TO MAKE THE CAKES: Center a rack in the oven and preheat the oven to 350 degrees F. Butter (or spray) the molds of two mini muffin tins. (You'll have enough batter to make 24 cakes.)

Put the whites in a medium bowl and whisk them just enough to break them up, then add the almond flour. Using a flexible spatula, stir until the flour is evenly moistened, then mix in the sugar, all-purpose flour, salt and vanilla.

Bring the butter to a boil in a small saucepan over medium heat, or do this in a microwave oven. Gradually add the melted butter to the batter, stirring with the conviction that all the butter will be absorbed—and it will be. You'll have a thick batter with a beautiful sheen. Stir in the chopped chocolate. (*If it's more convenient, you can cover the batter and keep it in the refrigerator for up to 3 days.*) Divide the batter evenly among the molds.

Bake the cakes for 15 to 18 minutes, or until they are puffed and golden and spring back when gently poked. A toothpick inserted into the center of a cake will come out clean. Transfer the pans to a rack and wait for 2 minutes,

then turn out the cakes. If you've got a few that are reluctant to pop out, rap the pan against the counter to free them. Cool the cakes until they are only just warm or, if you want to glaze them, until they reach room temperature.

TO GLAZE THE CAKES (OPTIONAL): Put the chopped chocolate in a small microwave-safe bowl and heat it for about 90 seconds at 50% power. You can melt it if you'd like, but what's most important is that it be warm and soft and that the bowl be warm too. (You've got so little chocolate and cream that you want to give it a head start toward ganachehood.)

Bring the cream to a boil in the microwave. Pour the cream over the chocolate, let it sit for 30 seconds and then gently stir the ganache, starting at the center of the bowl and working your way out, until you have a smooth, glossy glaze.

Line a baking sheet with parchment paper. One by one, dip the bottoms or the tops of the cakes into the ganache, twirling each one slightly as you lift it out of the chocolate, so that the excess drips back into the bowl, and place ganache side up on the baking sheet. Refrigerate for about 30 minutes, or just long enough to set the glaze.

Les Whoopies

**Makes about
24 small cakes**

SERVING: Since I've never seen a soul, young or old, drink a glass of milk in France, it's unlikely *les français* would enjoy *les whoopies* with milk. A shame, since the dark devil's food cake is so good with milk. I leave it to you, milk or not, and if not, I'd suggest a shot of espresso.

STORING: Best the day they're made, the whoopie pies—without the filling and glaze—can be wrapped airtight and frozen for up to 2 months. Defrost in the wrapper.

I KNEW THAT WHOOPIE PIES had made a successful transatlantic journey when they turned up front and center in the showcase of La Grande Epicerie's pastry department. La Grande Epicerie is to epicures what Disneyland is to kids: heaven. You could call it a supermarket, but you wouldn't be doing justice to its wine, meat, caviar, seafood, exotic fruit and extensive bread offerings. Or to its fabulous candy section. Or its selection of jams that goes on endlessly. Or its cutting-edge pastry stand. When something shows up there, you know it won't be long before it will be everywhere. And so it was with Les Whoopies.

Those whoopies—delicate cakes sandwiching thick, creamy fillings—reminded me of dainty Parisian macarons. Unlike so many others I'd seen, which were too large, fat and messy, they were small, elegant, precisely constructed and decorated with sophistication and restraint. Each was finished with a shiny chocolate glaze and some had little spots of color.

Like the whoopies that inspired me, the ones I make look Parisian—fashionably slim and properly glossed—but they cradle an American secret: a peanut butter filling. This is grown-up pleasure and childish delight, all in one package. Not bad for a cake the size of a bonbon.

A NOTE ON WHOOPIE PIE PANS: I use a whoopie-pie pan with twenty-four 2-inch-diameter indentations. You can use a pan with differing dimensions, but you may need to use a different amount of batter for each cake and your yield may differ.

FOR THE WHOOPIE PIES

- 2 cups (272 grams) all-purpose flour
- ½ cup (42 grams) unsweetened cocoa powder (preferably Dutch-processed)
- 1¼ teaspoons baking soda
- ¼ teaspoon baking powder
- ½ teaspoon fine sea salt
- 1 stick (8 tablespoons; 4 ounces; 113 grams) unsalted butter, at room temperature
- ½ cup (100 grams) sugar
- ½ cup (100 grams) packed light brown sugar
- 1 large egg, at room temperature
- ½ teaspoon pure vanilla extract
- 1 cup (240 ml) whole milk, at room temperature

FOR THE PEANUT BUTTER FILLING

- ¾ stick (6 tablespoons; 3 ounces; 85 grams) unsalted butter, at room temperature

½ cup (128 grams) creamy
peanut butter (not natural)

½ cup (60 grams) confectioners'
sugar

½ teaspoon pure vanilla extract

¼ teaspoon fine sea salt

FOR THE CHOCOLATE GLAZE
(OPTIONAL)

2 ounces (57 grams) bittersweet
or semisweet chocolate,
finely chopped

¼ cup (60 ml) heavy cream

TO MAKE THE WHOOPIE PIES: Center a rack in the oven and preheat the oven to 350 degrees F. Butter or spray a whoopie-pie pan; you might want to do this even if your pan is nonstick. Or if you're making whoopie pies without a pan, line a baking sheet with parchment paper.

Sift the flour, cocoa, baking soda, baking powder and salt together into a medium bowl.

Working in the bowl of a stand mixer fitted with the paddle attachment, or in a large bowl with a hand mixer, beat the butter at medium speed until soft and creamy. Add both sugars and beat until well blended, about 2 minutes. Add the egg and beat for 2 minutes. Beat in the vanilla. Reduce the mixer speed to low and add the dry ingredients alternately with the milk, adding the dry ingredients in 3 additions and the milk in 2 additions. Mix only until the dry ingredients are incorporated and you've got a thick, smooth, silky batter.

Using a small cookie scoop with a capacity of 2 teaspoons or a teaspoon measure (in which case you'll want to scoop out rounded spoonfuls), fill each of the whoopie molds with batter—don't bother smoothing it because it will spread under heat—or place dollops of batter on the baking sheet, making sure to leave about 2 inches of space between the mounds of batter. You'll have to work in batches, so cover the leftover batter and set aside.

Bake for 8 to 10 minutes, or until the cakes puff and spring back when poked lightly; a toothpick inserted into the center should come out clean. Transfer the whoopie pie pan to a rack and wait for 5 to 10 minutes, then gently lift the cakes out of the molds. Or, if you baked the cakes on parchment, slide the paper off the baking sheet onto a rack and let the cakes cool to room temperature before gingerly lifting them off the paper.

Continue to bake whoopie pies—always making sure the pan or baking sheet is cool—until you've used all the batter. Allow the cakes to cool to room temperature before filling them.

TO MAKE THE FILLING: Working in the bowl of a stand mixer fitted with the paddle attachment, or in a medium bowl with a hand mixer, beat all the ingredients together on medium-high speed until soft, fluffy and smooth, about 3 minutes.

TO FILL THE WHOOPIE PIES: Using a piping bag with a plain or star tip or a spoon, put about 1 tablespoon filling on the flat side of half the cakes. Top with the other halves, flat side down, twisting the tops gently just to make certain that the pieces are "glued" together.

TO GLAZE THE WHOOPIE PIES: This is an optional step, but it makes the pies look like a true French pastry. Put the chopped chocolate in a medium microwave-safe bowl and heat it for about 90 seconds at 50% power. Bring the cream to a boil. Pour the cream over the chocolate and let it sit for 30 seconds, then gently stir the mixture, starting at the center of the bowl and working your way out in ever-widening concentric circles, until you have a smooth, glossy ganache.

Line a baking sheet with parchment paper. One by one, dip the tops of the whoopie pies into the ganache, twirling each pie slightly as you lift it out of the chocolate, so that the excess drips back into the bowl, and place glazed side up on the baking sheet. When all your pies are dipped, refrigerate for about 30 minutes, or just long enough to set the glaze.

Bonne Idée
For a truly French whoopie pie, skip the peanut butter and go directly to the Salted Caramel Filling (page 436).

TICKTOCK . . . TREAT TIME

Bread is considered a daily necessity in France, and so the government regulates the price of a baguette, making it affordable to all. But pastry is a luxury, although it can seem like a daily luxury, especially in Paris—you can't go two blocks without coming across a pâtisserie. Temptation is never far away.

Yet the French think of sweets less as temptations (implying that the right thing to do would be to resist) and more as small pleasures. "Pleasure" (*plaisir*) is a word you hear several times a day in France, much more so than in America.

The French day can go something like this: croissant or brioche for breakfast; a custard, slice of tart or small chocolate after lunch; a financier or macaron (or three) as an afternoon pick-me-up; and dessert after dinner or, instead, a last small treat, maybe a piece of chocolate, a truffle or a cookie, before bed.

France's internal clock seems to run on sweets. It's almost reliable enough to set your watch by.

Pistachio and Raspberry Financiers

Makes about 36 mini cakes

SERVING: Financiers are the perfect sweet alongside tea or coffee. Whether or not you've used green tea in the batter, these are nice with green tea or Earl Grey.

STORING: You can keep the batter covered in the refrigerator for up to 2 days and bake these on demand. Once baked, they'll be good for about 2 days.

PISTACHIO IS A NOW-AND-THEN INGREDIENT in American baking, but in France, every pâtisserie seems to have at least one pastry featuring the nut, either as a colorful decoration or as a full-fledged flavor-bearer. And, more and more, pistachios are used in financiers, small cakes characterized by a base of ground nuts, the inclusion of egg whites and, especially, the addition of more butter than you'd think would be wise. It's the butter that makes financiers moist and luscious and as rich as their stockbroker namesakes (see page 205).

Even though there's only one raspberry plunked on top of each cake, when it bakes into the batter, its taste seems to intensify, and its acidity too. The berry is what pulls these cakes into balance and makes you reach for another one.

Traditional financier molds are rectangular—low-sided and narrow—and each has a capacity of about 3 tablespoons. If you have the molds, by all means use them. However, since they're not a usual piece of gear, I've given directions for baking the financiers in mini muffin pans. It's a different look, but it makes a delicious little cake.

A WORD ON TIMING: The batter should chill for at least 8 hours (and for up to 2 days), so plan ahead.

1½ sticks (12 tablespoons; 6 ounces; 170 grams) unsalted butter	⅔ cup (90 grams) all-purpose flour
	Pinch of fine sea salt
6 large egg whites, at room temperature	⅛ teaspoon matcha green tea (optional)
¾ cup (3½ ounces; 99 grams) shelled pistachios (raw and unsalted)	½ pint (1 cup; 123 grams) fresh raspberries
1 cup (200 grams) sugar	

Put the butter in a small saucepan and cook over medium heat until it melts and only just begins to take on a pale golden color. Pour the butter into a measuring cup with a spout and set aside.

Use a fork to stir the egg whites in a small bowl just enough to break them up; set aside.

Put the pistachios and sugar in a food processor and pulse until the nuts are ground. Don't overdo it—it's better to have a chunk here and there than to end up with nut paste. Add the flour, salt and matcha, if you're using it, and whir to blend. Transfer the mixture to a medium bowl.

Pour the egg whites into the bowl and, using a whisk or a flexible spatula, stir gently until they're blended into the nut mixture. If you're using the framboise, add it now, then gradually and gently blend the butter into the batter. You might think you've got so much butter that the batter won't be able to absorb it, but keep stirring lightly and you'll have a thick, shiny batter. Press a piece of plastic film against the surface of the batter and chill for at least 8 hours. (*The batter can be kept covered in the fridge for up to 2 days.*)

Center a rack in the oven and preheat the oven to 350 degrees F. Butter the molds of a mini muffin pan (each cup should have a capacity of 2 tablespoons), dust with flour and tap out the excess. Place the pan on a baking sheet. (If you want, you can bake more than one pan at a time.)

Fill each muffin cup to the halfway point with chilled batter. (Return any remaining batter to the refrigerator until you're ready to make the next batch.) Place 1 raspberry in the center of each cup.

Bake the financiers for 24 to 28 minutes, rotating the pan(s) at the midway point, or until they start to come away from the sides of the molds. Their tops should be springy to the touch and a toothpick inserted into the center of a financier should come out clean. Run a table knife around the edges of the cookies to detach them from the pan, then unmold them onto a rack. Turn them right side up to cool to room temperature.

Repeat with the remaining batter, if necessary, making certain that the pan is cool.

Bonne Idée

If you want to make a traditional financier, swap almonds or hazelnuts for the pistachios; add 1 teaspoon dark rum or vanilla and skip the raspberries (or don't; they're great in almost any version). If you want to see a Southern rendition, take a look at the financiers made with cornmeal and pecans (page 210).

FINANCIERS

I've always liked the story of how financiers came to be—it's a good example of creative entrepreneurship. Toward the end of the nineteenth century, Monsieur Lasne owned a pastry shop in Paris. It was very close to the stock exchange, and every afternoon the stockbrokers would rush in for a quick pick-me-up. What they wanted was what we now know as "grab and go," but it didn't exist until M. Lasne invented his version: a small, compact cake perfect for his clients. The original was made with a batter of nut flour, sugar and egg whites, enriched—and here the word is so appropriate—with melted butter, lots and lots of it. The cakes were baked in small rectangular molds and served with no decoration.

I'm not sure what Lasne had in mind, but I've always looked at the cakes and thought how clever he was to come up with a treat that was:

- As rich as his customers
- Shaped like a gold ingot, a commodity they knew well
- Meant to be eaten out of hand; no knives or forks needed (perhaps this *was* the original grab-and-go)

- Self-contained, so the brokers could return to work with no telltale crumbs on shirt, tie or jacket
- Named for his clients, *les financiers*

I don't know how quickly the recipe spread across Paris, but I do know that today you find it all over France, and America too, and it's not just enjoyed by stockbrokers. The batter for the cake hasn't changed much, but chefs everywhere have come up with their own takes on the classic.

Matcha Financiers

Makes 30 mini cakes

SERVING: Financiers of any stripe are traditionally served as a teatime sweet or as an after-dinner indulgence. These are also wonderful with hot chocolate. I love them warm and, because they're so quick to bake, I often pop some into the oven when I serve the main course so we can have freshly baked financiers for dessert.

STORING: The batter can be kept in the refrigerator for up to 3 days. The financiers are best the day they're baked, but they're still good a day later; store in a covered container. However, like brewed green tea that goes from green to yellow—the effect of oxidation—the financiers' color will change. If you'd like, you can freeze the baked financiers for up to 2 months—do that, and you might want to warm the thawed cakes briefly in a 350-degree-F oven before serving.

I T SEEMS SO APPROPRIATE to make a money-colored pastry named for the people whose job it is to make lots of money: *les financiers* of Paris. The small cakes' spring-green color comes from the Japanese powdered green tea, matcha, a tea that has become standard in many pâtissiers' pantries. I don't know who first baked with matcha, but Sadaharu Aoki, a famous French-trained Japanese pastry chef in Paris, has made an art of incorporating the tea into classics: éclairs and cream puffs, sablés, loaf cakes and even Opera cakes. It was his matcha financiers that inspired mine.

It wasn't until I started experimenting with matcha at home that I came to love it. As an assertive primary ingredient, it can be vegetal and bitter, so I use it as a subtle background flavor and in smaller doses than many pastry chefs do. In these almond (or hazelnut) financiers, matcha meets its perfect mates.

Matcha is a very expensive tea, and not one you're likely to find on every supermarket shelf. It comes in grades, and the highest grade is unnecessary for baking. Look for a culinary- or commercial-grade tea; I use Harney & Sons Matcha Culinary Grade.

If you're new to matcha's flavor, you might want to start small: Use just 1 teaspoon tea in the recipe. If you find yourself wishing there were more of it, increase the dosage the next time around.

Finally, as distinctive and bold as matcha is, it welcomes many other flavors into its fold. It's a natural with raspberries and red plums and lovely with chocolate, especially milk and white (see Bonne Idées).

1½ sticks (12 tablespoons; 6 ounces; 170 grams) unsalted butter, cut into chunks	Pinch of fine sea salt
⅔ cup (90 grams) all-purpose flour	1 cup (200 grams) sugar
1½ teaspoons matcha green tea (see above)	1 cup (100 grams) almond or hazelnut flour
	6 large egg whites, at room temperature, lightly beaten

Heat the butter in a small saucepan over medium heat until it starts to boil, then boil for 1 minute; it may color ever so slightly, but you don't want it to brown. Remove the pan from the heat and set it aside (you want the butter to be warm when you add it).

Whisk the all-purpose flour, matcha and salt together in a small bowl.

Using a flexible spatula, stir the sugar and nut flour together in a large bowl. Gradually add the egg whites, stirring to moisten the dry ingredients.

Bonne Idée

CHOCOLATE-CENTERED
MATCHA FINANCIERS:
You'll need 1 or 2 small
chunks of best-quality
milk or white chocolate for
each financier. Fill the mini
muffin molds halfway with
batter, put the chocolate
in the center of the batter
and then fill the molds
almost to the tops. Bake
as directed.

Another Bonne Idée

MATCHA TIGER CAKES:
Finely chop 5 ounces
best-quality milk or white
chocolate. After the butter
is incorporated into the
batter, stir in the chocolate.
Chill and bake as directed.

When all the whites are in, give the mix a few vigorous stirs. Stir in the all-purpose flour mixture, mixing only until it's evenly blended, then start adding the melted butter, a little at a time, folding and stirring the batter until all the butter is in, a feat that will seem miraculous. You'll have a pea-green batter with a sheen to it.

Press a piece of plastic film against the surface of the batter and refrigerate for at least 1 hour. (*The batter can be refrigerated for up to 3 days.*)

WHEN YOU'RE READY TO BAKE: Center a rack in the oven and preheat the oven to 400 degrees F. Butter the cups of a mini muffin tin (or tins; you can make as many or as few financiers as you want—there's enough batter for 30), dust with flour and tap out the excess (or use baker's spray, a mix of vegetable oil and flour).

Spoon the batter into the muffin cups, filling them almost to the top.

Bake the financiers for 12 to 14 minutes, or until they have crowned and feel springy to the touch; their tops may have cracked, and that's fine. They'll be browned around the edges (and on the bottom) and a beautiful green in the center.

Remove the tin(s) from the oven, wait 1 minute, then tap them against the counter to encourage the financiers to tumble out. Pry any stragglers from their molds with a table knife. Transfer the financiers to a rack and let cool until they are just warm or at room temperature.

Even if you speak French, speaking pastry can be confusing. Sometimes the same word can mean two different things. Here's a quick primer.

DESSERT: The French use the term *dessert* just as we do to refer to sweets after a meal, but among the pastry set, a *dessert* is a sweet that isn't made with dough. Custard is a *dessert*, and so are pudding, mousse, panna cotta, ice cream and fruit.

PÂTE: Literally, the word translates as "paste," but we'd say "dough." *Pâte sablée* and *pâte sucrée* are the doughs used to make sweet tarts; *pâte à choux* is used for cream puffs, and *pâte feuilletée* is puff pastry. Without *pâte*, there is no *pâtisserie*.

PÂTISSERIE: It means "pastry shop," but it also means "pastry."

PÂTISSIER: A man who makes pastry; a *chef-pâtissier* is a pastry chef (although most people just use the term *pâtissier*). A female pastry chef is a *pâtissière*, a word that has only recently gotten some use as more women started working in what was, for centuries, a man's world.

PASTRY: For the French, "pastry," or *pâtisserie*, refers to specific kinds of sweets. Originally anything with dough (or *pâte*) was pastry, but these days, small cakes are included too.

CONFISERIE: Like *pâtisserie*, the word *confiserie* has two meanings: It can refer to a candy shop or to candy itself. You can still find *confiseries* in Paris, and when you do, you'll find lots of hard candies, some from heirloom recipes; licorice of all kinds; mints; marshmallows; and the like. But you may or may not see many chocolates. Fine chocolates live in another domain (see below).

CHOCOLATERIE: A chocolate shop in which the bonbons are made by a *chocolatier*. Sometimes you'll find a small selection of cakes and tarts in a *chocolaterie*—all chocolate, of course—but the main attraction will be chocolate bonbons (or what we call "candy").

BOULANGER: A bread baker.

BOULANGERIE: A bread shop. Some *boulangeries* have a few sweets, and some *pâtisseries* have a few breads. Both are likely to have *viennoiserie* (see the next entry).

VIENNOISERIE: A special group of pastries, all of which include yeast and some sugar. Among the best known are croissants, brioche, *pain au raisin* (what we call raisin Danish) and kugelhopf. When guilds were in control of the crafts, permission was given for *viennoiserie* to be sold by both *boulangers* and *pâtissiers*, and the overlap still exists today.

Cowgirl Cornmeal-Pecan Financiers

Makes 48 mini cakes

SERVING: Financiers, Cowgirl or otherwise, are usually served as a teatime sweet or, in restaurants, as a *mignardise*, an "after-dessert dessert." These, however, seem perfect to serve at brunch; maybe it's the cornmeal. They're a sweet and surprising addition to a bread basket.

STORING: The batter can be made up to 3 days ahead and kept tightly covered in the refrigerator. You can use the batter straight from the fridge, although you might have to add an extra minute to the baking time. Once baked, financiers are best eaten the day they are made, although they're buttery enough to be held in a tin overnight.

THIS RECIPE COMES FROM my friend Ellise Pierce, best known as the Cowgirl Chef, a tall, talented American in Paris who's always seen in straight-from-Texas tooled boots. Like Ellise, the recipe has roots in two countries: The base is the French financier and the main ingredients are pure-American cornmeal and pecans. The cornmeal's sweetness is a great match for the ground toasted nuts and brown butter. It's a terrific take on tradition and a small pastry that's at home wherever it's served.

The recipe makes 48 small financiers (I make them in mini muffin tins), which is a lot. You can halve the recipe, if you'd like, but I never do: The batter will keep in the refrigerator for a few days and, since these are also good warm, it's fun to dip into the batter and make just enough for snacking whenever the urge strikes.

2 sticks (8 ounces; 227 grams) unsalted butter, cut into chunks	¼ cup (34 grams) all-purpose flour
1¼ cups (5 ounces; 142 grams) pecans, toasted	¼ cup (34 grams) fine cornmeal (do not use coarse)
⅔ cup (132 grams) sugar	½ teaspoon fine sea salt
	6 large egg whites, at room temperature

Melt the butter in a medium saucepan over low heat. When the butter starts to bubble, stay close: You want to make *beurre noisette*, or butter the color of hazelnuts (it'll smell nutty as well), and the butter can go from *noisette* to burned in seconds. Allow it to bubble away until it is the color of honey and you see toasty brown specks. Pour the butter—and the brown specks—into a liquid measuring cup or heatproof pitcher.

Toss the pecans and sugar into a food processor and pulse until the pecans are finely ground. This is another little task that requires vigilance: You want pecan meal or flour, not nut butter, so be careful not to overdo it.

Put the pecan mixture, flour, cornmeal and salt in a large bowl and whisk to blend. Use the whisk to break up the egg whites, then pour the whites into the bowl and whisk to blend. The aim here is to moisten the batter evenly, not to beat or aerate it. Gradually stir in the brown butter, whisking until fully incorporated. You'll have a thin, shiny batter. Press a piece of plastic film against the surface of the batter to create an airtight seal and refrigerate for at least 4 hours. (*You can use the batter immediately, but the financiers have a better texture if you give them a prebake chill. The batter can be refrigerated for up to 3 days.*)

WHEN YOU'RE READY TO BAKE: Center a rack in the oven and preheat the oven to 350 degrees F. Generously butter or spray a mini muffin tin or a couple of tins, depending on the size of the molds and the number of financiers you want to make. (My molds have a capacity of between 2 and 2½ tablespoons.)

Spoon enough batter into each little mold to fill it halfway.

Bake the financiers for 16 to 19 minutes, or until they are brown around the edges and golden and springy to the touch in the center; a toothpick inserted into the center of a financier will come out clean. If you tug gently at a financier, it should easily pull away from the sides of the mold. Rap the pan against the counter to send the financiers tumbling out; use a knife to loosen any stragglers. Cool them to only just warm or room temperature on a rack, either right side up or upside down—it's your choice.

Lemon Madeleines

SERVING: Generally served with tea, madeleines are good at any time of day or night, with anything from coffee to Cognac. They are a delight warm or at room temperature and even still nice when they're slightly stale—and perfect for dunking.

STORING: You can make the batter up to 2 days ahead and keep it covered in the refrigerator, but once baked, madeleines are best the day they're baked.

MADELEINES ARE THE NE PLUS ULTRA of tea cakes. Made with a buttery whole-egg sponge cake batter, spooned into shell-shaped molds and baked until they turn golden on their shell side and grow a large bump on their bellies, madeleines have long been a touchstone sweet among pâtissiers and pastry lovers.

I don't know if the *bosse*, the "bump" or "hump," was as iconic in the eighteenth century—the time when madeleines were first made—as it is today, but that dome has become the holy grail of madeleine bakers. And, like everyone else, I'm a seeker. I'd been making madeleines almost forever and then, in one year, mine took a giant leap, thanks to tips from two of Paris's most talented pastry chefs: Philippe Conticini of Pâtisserie des Rêves and Fabrice Le Bourdat of Blé Sucré.

Philippe taught me to bake the chilled batter in a cold pan on a very hot baking sheet—it mimics the heat of a baker's hearth oven, the way a pizza stone does. Because of this tiny but monumental tweak, my madeleines, which had always had respectable bumps, are now so bumpy they're in danger of rolling over from top-hump heaviness.

It was Fabrice who showed me how to glaze madeleines, accentuating the domes. It's true that the cakes are luscious unadorned and pretty with just a dusting of confectioners' sugar, but they're almost jewel-like and even more elegant when glazed.

Merci, mes chers pâtissiers.

FOR THE MADELEINES

- ⅔ cup (90 grams) all-purpose flour
- 1 teaspoon baking powder
- ¼ teaspoon fleur de sel or a pinch of fine sea salt
- ⅓ cup (67 grams) sugar
  Finely grated zest of 1 lemon
- 2 large eggs, at room temperature
- 1 tablespoon honey
- 1 teaspoon pure vanilla extract
- 1 stick (8 tablespoons; 4 ounces; 113 grams) unsalted butter, melted and still warm
- 2 tablespoons whole milk
  Confectioners' sugar, for dusting (optional)

FOR THE GLAZE (OPTIONAL)

- 1 cup (120 grams) confectioners' sugar, sifted
  About ¼ cup (60 ml) freshly squeezed lemon juice

TO MAKE THE MADELEINES: Whisk together the flour, baking powder and salt together in a small bowl; set aside.

Working in a large bowl, rub the sugar and lemon zest together with

your fingertips until the sugar is moist and fragrant. Add the eggs and whisk energetically. You want the egg-sugar mixture to thicken ever so slightly and pale just a little; this could take a couple of minutes (if you'd like, you can use a mixer). When the whisk leaves tracks, beat in the honey and vanilla. Using a gentler touch—and a flexible spatula, if you'd like—fold in the dry ingredients, folding only until they disappear into the batter. Finally, fold in the warm melted butter and, when it's incorporated, the milk. You'll have a smooth, shiny batter. Press a piece of plastic film against the surface of the batter and chill for at least 1 hour. (*The batter can be kept in the refrigerator for up to 2 days.*)

An hour or so before you're ready to bake, butter the molds of a 12-shell madeleine pan, dust with flour and tap out the excess. Even if you have non-stick or silicone madeleine molds, it's a good idea to give them the butter-flour treatment. (Alternatively, you can use baker's spray.)

Spoon the batter into the molds—don't worry about spreading it evenly; the oven's heat will take care of that—and refrigerate for 1 hour more. (You can cover the batter lightly with a sheet of wax or parchment paper, but inevitably some of the batter will stick, so I leave the pan bare.)

WEHN YOU'RE READY TO BAKE: Center a rack in the oven, put a large heavy baking sheet on the rack and preheat the oven to 400 degrees F.

Place the madeleine pan on the hot baking sheet and bake for 11 to 13 minutes, or until the cakes are golden and the big bumps on their tops spring back when touched. Remove the pan from the oven and immediately release the madeleines from the molds by rapping the edge of the pan against the counter. Gently pry any recalcitrant madeleines from the pan using your fingers or a table knife. Transfer to a cooling rack and allow them to cool to room temperature. (If you're not glazing them, you can serve them warm. Unglazed madeleines are nice with a dusting of confectioners' sugar.)

TO GLAZE THE MADELEINES: Center a rack in the oven and preheat the oven to 500 degrees F. Line a baking sheet with parchment or foil and put a cooling rack on it.

Put the confectioners' sugar in a bowl that's large enough to allow you to dip the madeleines into the glaze. Whisk in the lemon juice a little at a time until you get a glaze that's about as thick as heavy cream. (You'll have more glaze than you need, but it's hard to work with a smaller amount.)

One by one, dip (don't soak) the bump side of each madeleine in the glaze and put them bump side up on the cooling rack. Slide them into the oven, close the door and stay put: It takes 1 to 3 minutes for the glaze to melt and coat the madeleines, and you want to be there to pull them out of the oven at the first sign of a bubble in the glaze. Remove from the oven, lift the hot cooling rack with the cakes onto another cooling rack, to protect your countertop, and let cool to room temperature.

Black-and-White Marbled Madeleines

T HE FRENCH ARE MASTERS AT knowing how to take a good idea and spin it into another good idea—and another. These days they're playing around with madeleines. While the shell-shaped pastries are classically flavored with lemon (page 212) or vanilla, today a madeleine's batter might include green tea or Earl Grey, raspberry or rose, herbs or exotic spices. I think of these marbled tea cakes as straddlers, the placeholders between tradition and treats that go out on a limb. This batter is flavored with vanilla and not-so-classic lime zest, then half of it is mixed with melted milk chocolate (nice with the lime) and cocoa powder (great for color). With the chocolate grounding them a bit, the madeleines don't develop the hefty bump that their plainer relatives do. Nonetheless, their look is enchanting, their flavors true and, because of the marbling, each bite is different, a playfulness that's always welcome in a dessert.

These defy the golden rule of the madeleine: They don't have to be eaten almost as soon as they're made; they even taste great a day later.

Makes 12 madeleines

SERVING: Madeleines can be served moments out of the oven, just warm or at room temperature. While they're perfect the day they're made, these are also good, if a bit denser, the next day.

STORING: The madeleine batter can be spooned into the molds, marbled and kept refrigerated for up to 1 day; cover the batter when it firms. If you're keeping the madeleines overnight, pack them in a covered container. The tea cakes can also be wrapped airtight, frozen for up to 2 months and brought to room temperature before serving. Madeleines that have been frozen benefit from a quick warm-up in a 350-degree-F oven.

2/3 cup (90 grams) all-purpose flour	3/4 stick (6 tablespoons; 3 ounces; 85 grams) unsalted butter, melted and cooled
1 teaspoon baking powder	
Pinch of fine sea salt	
1/2 cup (100 grams) sugar	1/2 teaspoon pure vanilla extract
Finely grated zest of 1 lime	1 tablespoon unsweetened cocoa powder
2 large eggs, at room temperature	1 ounce (28 grams) best-quality milk chocolate, melted and still fluid

Butter the molds of a 12-shell madeleine pan, dust with flour and tap out the excess (or use baker's spray, a mix of vegetable oil and flour). Do this even if your pan is silicone or nonstick. Put the pan in the refrigerator while you make the batter.

Whisk the flour, baking powder and salt together in a small bowl.

Put the sugar in the bowl of a stand mixer, or put it in a large bowl and work with a hand mixer. Add the lime zest and use your fingertips to rub the zest and sugar together until the sugar is moist and fragrant. If using a stand mixer, fit it with the paddle and attach the bowl. Add the eggs to the bowl and immediately begin mixing at medium speed. (If you let the eggs and sugar sit, the sugar will "cook" the yolks and they'll develop a film.) Mix for 2 to

3 minutes, or until the mixture is pale and thick. Add the dry ingredients and, using a flexible spatula, stir and fold gently until the flour disappears into the batter. Add the butter in 3 additions, folding each one into the batter with a light touch. Pour half of the batter into another bowl.

Stir the vanilla extract into one half of the batter. Place a small sieve over the other bowl, drop in the cocoa and shake it over the batter. Then pour the melted chocolate into the bowl and gently stir and fold everything together with a flexible spatula until well blended.

Divide the vanilla batter evenly among the molds. Top with the chocolate batter. If you'd like, you can leave the madeleines like this and they'll bake with a dark bull's-eye—the chocolate batter doesn't budge much. For marbled madeleines, my preference, take a table knife and swirl it through the batters. Don't overdo it—2 or 3 squiggles are enough to get a little marbling.

Refrigerate the filled pan for at least 1 hour. (*The batter can be refrigerated for as long as overnight. Once the batter is firm, cover lightly with plastic film.*)

WHEN YOU'RE READY TO BAKE: Center a rack in the oven, put a large heavy baking sheet on the rack and preheat the oven to 400 degrees F.

Place the madeleine pan on the hot baking sheet and bake for 13 to 15 minutes, or until the madeleines are puffed, golden brown and springy to the touch. If you poke the shells at the edges, they'll pull away from the pan. Remove the pan from the oven and rap the edge of the pan against the counter—the madeleines should come tumbling out. Gently pry any recalcitrant cakes from their shells with a table knife or your fingers. If not serving immediately, transfer to a cooling rack.

Ladyfingers

*Makes about
24 ladyfingers*

WHETHER THEY'RE LONG AND THIN or short and fat, ladyfingers are the ultimate companion. As lovely as they are on their own, they're really made to play along with something else: something simple like Dark Chocolate Mousse (page 348), or something dramatic like a trifle with layers of Vanilla Pastry Cream (page 430), berries, whipped cream and ladyfingers, soaked in rum or kirsch or eau-de-vie or not. Unless you have a quintessential French pâtisserie on your corner, nothing will compare to the tender, light, sponge-cake ladyfingers you make at home. If you're accustomed to store-bought, these will be a revelation.

SERVING: If you'd like, give the ladyfingers a final sugar dusting before serving. The ultimate teatime sweet, ladyfingers can be served with whipped cream, mousse or jam, but I think plainness is a virtue with these little pastries.

STORING: Layered between sheets of parchment in a closed container and kept in a dry place, the ladyfingers will be good for about 1 week; even as they stale and dry a bit, they retain their charm.

1 recipe Ladyfinger Batter
 (page 424)

Confectioners' sugar,
 for dusting

The easiest way to make ladyfingers is to take a piece of parchment paper the size of your baking sheet and draw a template on it. Working the long way, draw two lines 4 inches apart; leave some space and draw another 4-inch-wide band. This will allow you to make ladyfingers that are 4 inches long, the perfect length. Flip the paper over—you'll still be able to see the lines— and use it to line a baking sheet. (Of course, you can always pipe freehand, making the ladyfingers as long or short, or as chubby or slim as you want.)

Fit a pastry bag with a plain ½-inch tip and fill it with half of the batter. Alternatively, you can use a zipper-lock bag to pipe—fill it and snip off a corner to make a ½-inch opening.

Working with a long side of the baking sheet toward you, pipe out fingers: Start at the top line of one of the template's bands and pipe to the bottom, making the fingers 4 inches long and about 1 inch wide. If you'd like, do what the pros do: Pipe the logs so close to one another that they almost touch; they'll bake together and you can separate them when they cool. Fill the bag with the remainder of the batter and continue to pipe.

Dust the tops of the fingers with confectioners' sugar and let them rest on the counter while you preheat the oven (or for at least 15 minutes).

Center a rack in the oven and preheat the oven to 400 degrees F.

Dust the ladyfingers once again with sugar and then slide the sheet into the oven. Bake for 8 to 10 minutes, or until the ladyfingers are a pale golden color—they shouldn't color much. Lift the parchment from the baking sheet onto a cooling rack and let the ladyfingers cool to room temperature.

When you're ready to use the them, run a long offset spatula under them to ease them off the parchment, then use a long sharp knife or a pizza wheel to cut into individual ladyfingers, if necessary.

Babas au Rhum

SERVING: I serve the babas in shallow bowls and pour the extra syrup around them. Just as they do in Paris bistros these days, I also put a bottle of dark rum on the table and let everyone douse and redouse the babas.

STORING: Unsoaked, the babas can be kept uncovered at room temperature for a day; if they are soaked, you can cover them and store in the refrigerator for up to 1 day. The syrup is a good keeper: Stow in the fridge for up to 1 week.

BABAS AU RHUM HAVE BEEN AROUND for about three hundred years, but I wonder if they've ever been as popular as they are today. At its simplest, the baba is a tight-grained yeast-raised cake that's soaked in a rum syrup. Serve it with whipped cream, and it's a baba au Chantilly; bake the dough in a ring mold, and it becomes a savarin. When I first started going to Paris, babas were in most pâtisseries, simply soaked in syrup and placed on little foil saucers to catch any excess. They're still there, but dolled up. Pierre Hermé has an entire collection of babas in flavors from chocolate and vanilla to rose and passion fruit. And Philippe Conticini's Pâtisserie des Rêves offers what might be called do-it-yourself babas: Each comes with a little container of whipped cream and a capsule of aged rum, so you can give your babas an extra soak chez you.

These days, chefs as grand as Alain Ducasse put babas on their menus. Order a baba in a restaurant today, and it might be surrounded by a shallow pool of syrup and accompanied by a bottle of exotic rum with a pouring spout. Or you might get a limoncello baba, or one soaked and served with Armagnac.

In order for the babas to be able to imbibe the warm syrup, they have to be dry—stale, really. You can dunk yours after they've come to room temperature, but they'll be so much thirstier and they'll drink up so much more rum syrup (the object of babas' existence) if you let them sit out longer, even for as long as 24 hours. My recipe for rum syrup produces enough for you to drench the babas and still have enough to serve in the bottom of the bowls. If that's too much for you, cut the recipe in half.

A WORD ON MIXERS: As with other yeast doughs, the baba dough calls for prolonged beating—this is a job best done with a stand mixer.

AND A WORD ON MOLDS: Babas are traditionally made in special cylindrical molds called timbales. For the sake of practicality, I make these in muffin tins.

FOR THE BABAS

2¼ teaspoons active dry yeast

⅓ cup (80 ml) warm water

1 tablespoon honey

¾ stick (6 tablespoons; 3 ounces; 85 grams) unsalted butter

1 cup (136 grams) all-purpose flour

¼ teaspoon fine sea salt

4 large eggs, at room temperature

FOR THE RUM SYRUP

1 moist, fragrant vanilla bean, split lengthwise, or 2 teaspoons pure vanilla extract

2½ cups (600 ml) water

1¼ cups (250 grams) sugar

½ orange (with rind), cut into 4
    pieces
    Small piece cinnamon stick
½ cup (120 ml) dark rum

FOR THE CREAM
¾ cup (180 ml) heavy cream

2 tablespoons sugar
1 teaspoon pure vanilla extract
    (optional)

Dark rum, for serving
    (optional)

TO MAKE THE BABAS: Put the yeast and warm water (check the yeast package for the correct temperature) in the bowl of a stand mixer. Stir in the honey and let stand for about 5 minutes, or until the yeast dissolves and becomes creamy; the mix may or may not bubble.

Meanwhile, cut the butter into chunks and toss it into a small saucepan. Melt the butter over medium heat and allow it to simmer until it turns a warm golden brown. Stay close—brown can quickly turn to black—and don't worry when you see specks on the bottom of the pan. Remove the pan from the heat.

Attach the bowl to the stand mixer, fit with the paddle attachment and pulse just to blend the yeast and water; add the flour. Working at medium speed, beat in the flour, then add the salt and beat until the dough forms a ball around the paddle, about 2 minutes. Add the eggs one by one, beating for 2 minutes after each egg goes in. Increase the mixer speed to medium-high and beat for another 2 minutes. Pour in the brown butter, scraping in the brown bits stuck to the bottom of the pan, and beat on medium-high speed for another 3 minutes. You'll have a thin, creamy dough with brown-butter flecks.

Cover the bowl with plastic film and set in a warm place (70 to 75 degrees F) for 30 minutes; the dough will rise, but it may or may not double in volume.

Generously butter a 12-mold muffin tin.

Stir the bubbly dough down with a flexible spatula and divide it evenly among the muffin molds; the dough will only come about halfway up the sides of the molds. Cover with a sheet of parchment or wax paper and set the pan in the warm spot. Allow the dough to rise until it comes about three quarters of the way up the sides, about 30 minutes.

While the dough is rising, center a rack in the oven and preheat the oven to 350 degrees F.

Remove the paper and bake the babas for about 25 minutes, or until they're golden brown. Transfer the tin to a cooling rack and let the babas rest for 3 minutes, then remove them from the tin. Let them cool on the rack for at least 2 hours, or leave them overnight (or for up to 24 hours), as some pastry chefs do—the drier they are, the more rum syrup they'll absorb.

TO MAKE THE SYRUP: Slide the back of a paring knife down the halves of the vanilla bean, to remove all the pulp. Toss the pulp and the pod into a

medium saucepan (if you're using vanilla extract, you'll add it at the end), add the water, sugar, orange pieces and cinnamon stick and bring to a boil. Cook for 1 minute, then pour the syrup into a large heatproof bowl. If you're using vanilla extract, stir it in now. Let the syrup cool for 20 minutes.

Remove the orange pieces, cinnamon and vanilla pod (if you used one) from the syrup and stir in the rum. The syrup is ready to be used now, or you can pour it into a jar, cover and refrigerate for up to 1 week. (If the syrup has been chilled, warm it gently before using.)

TO SOAK THE BABAS: Pour the syrup into a large bowl and drop in as many babas as will fit at a time. Turn the babas around in the syrup and leave them there for 1 minute—you want them to be thoroughly soaked—then transfer them to a large rimmed platter or a glass baking dish. If you made a full recipe of syrup, pour the remaining syrup into a pitcher and save it to pour around the babas when you serve them; if you made a half recipe and there's any syrup left over, pour it over the babas.

TO MAKE THE CREAM: Working in a cold bowl, beat the cream until it holds very soft peaks. Beat in the sugar and whip until the cream is firm. If you're using vanilla extract, beat it in.

TO FINISH THE BABAS: You can cut off the tops of the babas—cut about one third of the way down—pipe or spoon a generous amount of whipped cream onto the base of each baba and replace the tops. Or you can cut the babas in half down the center, stopping before you separate the halves, and pipe or spoon the whipped cream into the openings you've created. If you'd like, serve with a bottle of rum.

RUM, RUM, RHUM

France's affection for rum runs deep, a fact that surprised me when I first realized it. With all the wines and spirits that are produced within France, it seemed odd that an import would have such a cozy place in the Gallic heart—and pastry kitchen. I'd forgotten that some of the Caribbean islands, home to the world's finest rums, had once been part of the French Empire.

You'll find rum—*rhum* in French—in babas au rhum, for sure, but it's used often as a flavoring, just as vanilla is.

(Actually, the best combination in a dessert is rum *and* vanilla.) And the rum of choice is *rhum agricole*, an agricultural rum. Whereas most rums are made from molasses, *agricole* is distilled from sugarcane juice and is less sweet. It has a floral fragrance as beautiful as perfume. Like molasses-based rums, *agricole* can be light or dark; the darker, amber-colored rum works best in desserts. And if you can find an aged or vintage agricultural rum, you're in for an extraordinary experience.

Cannelés

*Makes about
45 mini cannelés*

SERVING: Cannelés
are traditionally served
alongside coffee or tea
and often turn up on trays
of *mignardises*, the small
sweets that are after-dessert
desserts.

STORING: The batter
needs to be refrigerated for
at least 12 hours, but it can
hold there for up to 3 days.
As for the baked cannelés,
they're perfect the day they
are made and still good,
but firmer and chewier, the
day after. Keep the cannelés
in a dry place at room
temperature. Lightly cover
them if you like.

IT'S THOUGHT THAT THESE LITTLE CAKES were first made centuries ago by cloistered nuns in Bordeaux; however, it's a fact that they're very beloved—and not just in Bordeaux, but in Paris, other parts of France, and in bakeries across America. They're a sweet completely different from any other, so it's easy to understand how they'd capture the imaginations of pastry lovers everywhere.

The name comes from the shape of the molds in which they're baked: *Cannelé* means "channeled," or "crenelated," and the molds, traditionally made of copper, are beautifully ridged, flat on the bottom and slightly indented on top. The cakes are made from a thin batter, like the kind you'd use for crêpes, which is highly flavored with rum and vanilla and left to rest in the refrigerator overnight. When the cannelés are baked, the exterior becomes dark and firm, and the interior, a fascinating cross between custardy and chewy, remains very moist. Pull one apart, and you'll find irregular pockets and holes—almost like the ones in a yeast cake, like babka or kugelhopf.

Traditionally, cannelés were made in copper molds brushed with beeswax, and they turned almost as dark as nuggets of coal. Today, most bakers use silicone molds and forego the beeswax. You can get that charred color with silicone and without beeswax, but I call them done when the bottoms are almost black and the sides a deep caramel. Silicone molds are available as minis, which I use, and large; if you use the large ones, you'll have to adjust the baking time (and, obviously, you'll get a different yield). Mini Bundt molds also make lovely cannelés.

This recipe was given to me by Joëlle Caussade, whose husband, Gilles, owns a lively Paris bistro, Le Petit Vendôme, where Joëlle makes the mini cannelés that are served with coffee.

A WORD ON TIMING: The batter needs to rest in the refrigerator for at least 12 hours, so plan ahead.

2 cups (480 ml) whole milk	1 large egg yolk
1¼ cups (250 grams) sugar	2½ tablespoons dark rum
2 tablespoons (1 ounce; 28 grams) unsalted butter	2 teaspoons pure vanilla extract
1 cup (136 grams) all-purpose flour	Melted unsalted butter, for the molds
2 large eggs	

AT LEAST 1 DAY BEFORE MAKING THE CANNELÉS: Bring the milk, ¾ cup of the sugar and the butter to a boil in a medium saucepan, stirring occasionally to make sure the sugar dissolves. Remove from the heat and let cool until

the mixture reaches 140 degrees F. (If you don't have a thermometer, cool the milk for 10 to 15 minutes; it should still feel hot to the touch.)

While the milk is cooling, put the flour and the remaining ½ cup sugar into a strainer and sift them onto a piece of parchment or wax paper. Keep the strainer at hand.

Working with a whisk, beat the eggs and yolk together in a large bowl until blended. Whisking without stopping, start adding the hot milk, just a little at first; then, when you've got about a quarter of the milk blended into the eggs, whisk in the remainder in a steady stream. Add the flour mixture all at once and whisk—don't be afraid to be energetic—until the batter is homogeneous. You might have a few lumps here and there, but you can ignore them.

Strain the batter into a large bowl or, better yet, a pitcher or a large measuring cup with a spout; discard any lumps in the strainer. Whisk in the rum and vanilla, cover the container tightly and refrigerate the batter for at least 12 hours. (*The batter can be refrigerated for up to 3 days.*)

Lightly brush the cannelé molds (see page 222) with melted butter and put the pan in the freezer. The pan only needs to be frozen for 30 minutes, but if you put it into the freezer right after you make the batter, you won't have to wait for it on baking day.

WHEN YOU'RE READY TO BAKE: Center a rack in the oven and preheat the oven to 450 degrees F. Line a baking sheet with parchment paper or a silicone baking mat. Put a cooling rack on the sheet and put the frozen cannelé molds on the rack.

Remove the batter from the fridge. It will have settled and formed layers, so give it a good whisking to bring it back together, then rap the container against the counter to debubble it a bit. Fill the cannelé molds about three quarters full.

Bake the cannelés for 30 minutes, then lower the oven temperature to 400 degrees F and bake for another 30 minutes or so. Cannelés are supposed to get very dark—black really—but if you're concerned that yours are darkening too fast or too much, place a piece of parchment or foil over the molds. When properly baked, the bottoms will be dark and the sides of the little pastries will be a deep brown—think mahogany. (I spear a cannelé with a bamboo skewer and pull it out of its mold to inspect it.) While the cannelés bake, they may puff above the tops of the molds, like popovers or soufflés, and then, as they continue baking, or when they're pulled from the oven, they'll settle down. Pull the whole setup from the oven and put it on a cooling rack.

Let the cannelés rest in their molds for 10 minutes, then turn them out onto a cooling rack. (Resting gives the tender pastries a chance to firm so they'll hold their shape when unmolded.) Be careful: Even though you've waited 10 minutes, because of the caramelized sugar and melted butter, cannelés are hotter than most other pastries. Let the cannelés cool until they are only slightly warm or at room temperature.

....

Without an oven, you can't bake; without getting to know your oven, you can't bake well.

Every oven has its own personality. I know this from experience: My oven in Paris—tiny, electric, perfectly level and with hardly a hot spot—couldn't be more different from my capacious, powerful gas ranges back home. Both types do a good job, but they do it in their own style. Although all my ovens seem to come to temperature in about the same amount of time, on the advice of an American oven repairman, I always wait about fifteen more minutes before baking. He said that even though the indicator light goes off, signaling that the oven has reached the right temperature, it usually hasn't. (I checked with my oven thermometer, and he was right.) He also said that this extra preheating time helps the oven maintain its temperature longer and cycle on and off less, something that's especially important if you're baking something for just a short time, like cookies.

No matter what your oven's quirks—or even if it's quirk-free—never bake without an oven thermometer. Even perfect ovens can go haywire, and it would be a shame to lose a beautiful gâteau just because you didn't check the thermometer.

Most ovens have their hot spots, so it's best to rotate your pans midway through the baking time. Rotate the pans from front to back and, if you're baking on two racks, from top to bottom.

Crackle-Top Cream Puffs

Makes about 24 puffs

SERVING: Unfilled cream puffs can be eaten when they are just slightly warm, but they're usually served at room temperature. Puffs that are going to be filled must be at room temperature. Warm or not, the puffs are good plain or with a berry coulis, chocolate sauce or caramel. The French style is to serve filled puffs with dessert forks and spoons.

STORING: You have many options. You can freeze the unbaked puffs and disks (freeze them on lined baking sheets, then transfer to containers when firm), then assemble and bake them straight from the freezer; you might have to add a few minutes to the baking time. Baked and kept at room temperature, the puffs are best eaten the day they are made. If you'd like, you can freeze the baked puffs and reheat them before serving; 5 to 8 minutes in a 375-degree-F oven does the trick.

'M NOT SURE WHEN PASTRY CHEFS started topping cream puffs with disks of sweet dough that crack as they bake, giving the puffs the look of having been crowned with streusel or cookie crumbs. But whenever it started, it's now happening from one end of Paris to the other. Gone are the glazes, the shiny fondant and the fuss; in their place there's a brown-sugar crackle, so transformative that it's only after you've eaten a few puffs that you realize there was no icing and that you didn't miss it either. If you opt to top the puffs with thin disks of Sweet Tart Dough with Nuts (page 415) rather than the crackle, they will be a little less sweet and no less delicious.

If you want to fill the puffs, use any of your favorite creams or mousses (try the Dark Chocolate Mousse, page 348). Pastry cream (page 430) is traditional; use it straight or mix it with a little whipped cream. Sweetened whipped cream will make these the classic *choux à la crème*; ice cream will turn them into Profiteroles (page 238); and a mix of lime cream (page 184) and whipped cream will render them ethereal.

FOR THE CRACKLE TOPS

4½ tablespoons (2¼ ounces; 64 grams) unsalted butter

½ cup (100 grams) lightly packed light brown sugar

Pinch of fine sea salt

½ cup plus 2 tablespoons (85 grams) all-purpose flour

¾ teaspoon pure vanilla extract

OR

1 recipe Sweet Tart Dough with Nuts (page 415)

FOR THE CREAM PUFFS

½ cup (120 ml) whole milk

½ cup (120 ml) water

1 stick (8 tablespoons; 4 ounces; 113 grams) unsalted butter, cut into 4 pieces

1 tablespoon sugar

½ teaspoon fine sea salt

1 cup (136 grams) all-purpose flour

4 large eggs, at room temperature

TO MAKE THE CRACKLE TOPS: Remove the butter from the refrigerator 10 minutes before you're ready to make the dough.

After 10 minutes, cut the butter into small cubes and toss it and the brown sugar and salt into a food processor. Process until almost blended. Add the flour and pulse until the dough forms moist curds. Pulse in the vanilla.

Scrape the dough onto a piece of parchment or wax paper and shape it into a disk. Cover with another piece of parchment or wax paper and roll the dough out so that it's about 1/16 th inch thick. Slide the dough, still between the paper, onto a cutting board and freeze it for at least 2 hours. (*The dough can be frozen for up to 2 months, in which case it should be wrapped airtight.*)

IF YOU'RE USING THE SWEET TART DOUGH: Roll and freeze the dough as for the crackle tops.

When the dough is cold and firm, use a 1½-inch round cookie cutter to cut out at least 24 rounds. Put them on a lined baking sheet (or return to the cutting board) and freeze for at least 30 minutes. (If you have more rounds, they can be frozen and used straight from the freezer next time or baked and enjoyed as cookies.)

MEANWHILE, MAKE THE CREAM PUFFS: Position the racks to divide the oven into thirds and preheat the oven to 425 degrees F. Line two baking sheets with parchment paper or silicone baking mats.

Bring the milk, water, butter, sugar and salt to a rapid boil in a medium heavy-bottomed saucepan over high heat. Add the flour all at once, lower the heat to medium-low and quickly start stirring energetically with a wooden spoon or sturdy heatproof spatula. The dough will come together and a light crust will form on the bottom of the pan. Keep stirring vigorously for another minute or two to dry the dough. The dough should be very smooth.

Turn the dough out into the bowl of a stand mixer fitted with the paddle attachment, or into a large bowl in which you can use a hand mixer or a wooden spoon. Let the dough sit for 3 minutes, then add the eggs one by one, beating until the dough is thick and shiny. Make sure that each egg is fully incorporated before you add the next, and don't be concerned if the dough falls apart; by the time the last egg goes in, it will have come together again. The dough should be used immediately.

The easiest way to divide the dough evenly is to use a medium cookie scoop (one with a capacity of 1½ tablespoons). Alternatively, you can portion out the dough with a tablespoon (use a rounded tablespoonful of dough for each puff) or pipe it with a zipper-lock bag (fill the bag, seal it and snip off a bit of one corner) or a pastry bag and large plain tip.

Scoop or pipe the dough onto the baking sheets, leaving 2 inches between the mounds. Place a frozen round of crackle top or tart dough on top of each puff.

Slide the baking sheets into the oven and immediately turn the oven down to 375 degrees F. Bake the puffs for 20 minutes, then rotate the pans from top to bottom and back to front and bake for another 10 to 15 minutes. When properly baked, the puffs will be golden brown, firm and feel hollow when tapped on their bottoms. Transfer to a cooling rack and allow them to cool to room temperature (although you might want to snatch one to eat when it's still warm).

TO FILL THE PUFFS (OPTIONAL; SEE PAGE 226): You can cut the puffs at the point where the crackle stops, fill the puffs and top them with the little caps. Or, if you're using a very creamy filling, such as Pastry Cream (page 430), fit a pastry bag with a small plain tip and fill it, then use the tip to poke a hole in the side of the puff and squeeze the filling in through the hole. Some people like to cut the puffs and pull out the custardy strands inside before filling them. It's a matter of personal preference; try it both ways and see which you like more.

CHOUQUETTES

That the French don't snack on *chouquettes* with the same exuberance we show for popcorn and chips is either a sign of generations of good breeding or a degree of discipline too frightening to contemplate. I met my first *chouquette* decades ago during a pastry course, and I've been forcing myself to enjoy them with restraint ever since. *Chouquettes* are mini choux puffs—cream puffs without the cream—usually the size of Ping-Pong balls. They're often more tender than cream puffs; they don't have to hold a filling and it's fine (even nice) if they collapse at first bite.

When I was a student at Ecole Lenôtre in Plaisir, France (it's impossible to imagine a setting with a better name), the days were long and strictly regimented. We came in early, changed into our chef coats and had breakfast in the dining room, then donned our tall toques, headed for the kitchen and just about saluted when the chef walked in. We'd work very quietly—you only spoke when you had to—and at midmorning, we'd break for coffee.

We were very well fed at Lenôtre: Breakfast had lots of bread and butter, signature Lenôtre jams and espresso that must have been especially blended to wake up sleepyheads (and shoo away hangovers); lunches were lavish and always included carafes of red and white wine; and the coffee break had everything I loved. The display of pastries was dazzling. It was the moment for *viennoiserie*, the slightly sweet, made-with-yeast treats that fall somewhere between bread and cake. And tucked among the croissants, pains au chocolat, raisin snails with vanilla pastry cream and swirled kugelhopfs, there was always a basket of my favorite, *chouquettes*.

There is no explanation for why *chouquettes* are so alluring, but it takes only one to convince you that reasons don't matter. Clearly I'm not the only one with a crush on the puffs: You find baskets of them in neighborhood pâtisseries, kids lining up for them after school and grown-ups buying them by the handful for tea or that wonderful midmorning coffee break.

To make *chouquettes*, follow the recipe for Crackle-Top Cream Puffs (page 226), but:

- Beat 5 (rather than 4) large eggs into the dough—this will make the choux more tender and the innards more custardy.

- Use a teaspoon to scoop the dough—you can make these any size you want, but small is traditional and so much more snackable.

- Brush the tops of the *choux* with egg wash (beat a large egg with a splash of cold water).

- Omit the crackle top and sprinkle the tops of the *choux* with coarse or pearl sugar.

- Bake until the *choux* are golden brown on their tops and bottoms and firm enough to accept a gentle squeeze without sagging.

Chouquettes are best enjoyed the day they're made, but, as with all cream puffs, you can freeze them as soon as you shape them and then bake as many as you'd like whenever you'd like—they go straight from the freezer to the oven.

Bubble Eclairs

Makes 16 éclairs

SERVING: There's no law that says you can't pass these around and let everyone eat them out of hand, but I think of them as knife-and-fork pastries. If you serve them with cutlery you might want to serve them with Bittersweet Chocolate Sauce (page 442) or Hot or Cold Salted Caramel Sauce (page 447).

STORING: Once the éclairs are filled, they're best served immediately (especially if they're filled with ice cream) or stored in the refrigerator and eaten the same day. However, as with most pastries made from pâte à choux, you can freeze the piped-out éclairs and then bake them straight from the freezer. You can also wrap the unfilled baked pastries and freeze them for up to 2 months. Defrost them in the refrigerator, warm them in a 350-degree-F oven for 10 minutes, cool and then fill them.

CLAIRS HAVE NEVER BEEN MORE PREVALENT in France or more paradoxical than they are today: Some are bold, frivolous and full of folly, some are spare and almost modest about the pleasures they hold within. Pastry chefs like Christophe Adam, whose shop in Paris is called L'Eclair de Génie, make fantastical éclairs with glazes portraying everything from the Mona Lisa to a wild zebra. Others who have taken minimalism to the max make their éclairs simple and sleek, perhaps giving them a crackle top (page 226), or not; perhaps showering them with sugar, or not; perhaps playing with their shape, or not. As easy as playing with the shape of the éclair is, it's the most heretical thing you can do to the pastry, since its name means "lightning," and its inventor, Carême, wanted its form to follow the slender line of a bolt.

I prefer the simplicity of the unglazed pastries, particularly because they're so easy to make at home. Sometimes I'll add a crackle top, streusel (see page 114) or coarse sugar, and almost every time I'll defy Carême and go for my favorite shape: three little puffs, scooped (or piped) so close that they bake together, like Siamese triplets.

Icing them would be a distraction, but filling them with abandon is just right. Think of these as the pastry version of an ice cream sundae with three bubbles that can hold fillings. Imagine all the fillings you can use—pastry cream, whipped cream, mousse, curd and fruits—then mix and match.

FOR THE ECLAIRS
1 recipe Cream Puff dough (page 226), just made and ready to use

Egg wash (1 large egg lightly beaten with a splash of cold water; optional)

CHOICE OF TOPPERS (OPTIONAL)
Double recipe Crackle Tops dough (page 226), rolled out, cut into 1-inch rounds and frozen

1 recipe Streusel (page 114)
Pearl sugar (available online or at Ikea)

CHOICE OF FILLINGS
Pastry Cream (page 430)
Whipped Cream (page 439)
Dark Chocolate Mousse (page 348)
Ice cream, slightly softened

Confectioners' sugar, for dusting (optional)

TO MAKE THE ECLAIRS: Center a rack in the oven and preheat the oven to 425 degrees F. Line a baking sheet with parchment paper or a silicone baking mat.

There are several ways to shape your bubble éclairs. Usually I portion the dough with a small cookie scoop (one with a capacity of 2 teaspoons), but you can pipe the dough from a pastry bag with a plain or open star tip, which makes squiggles and swirls that look lovely when baked. You might want to make it simple and just use a zipper-lock plastic bag as a piping bag.

No matter what you use, you want to scoop or pipe 3 balls of dough as close to one another as you can get them for each éclair. If you're scooping, scoop 1 ball, then crowd it with the second—giving it a little nudge—and then scoop out the last bubble, snuggling it up to the second ball of dough. When you've got 3 bubbles in a row, move on to the next éclair, making sure to leave at least 2 inches of puff-and-grow space between the clusters. If you're piping, the principle is the same.

Now you have to make some decisions about the topping. If you're going to top the bubbles with disks of crackle, there's no need to give them an egg wash. Just lay a circle of the crackle-top dough on each puff of dough.

If you'd like to top the éclairs with streusel or pearl sugar, then it's nice to give each puff a swipe of egg wash. Make an effort to keep the egg wash on the top of the puffs and not let it drip down the sides; it's not fatal, but it does hamper the even rise of the pâte à choux. If you're using streusel, break up the pieces with your fingertips and use a smidge on each puff—put it on and press it down very, very lightly. If you're using pearl sugar, go to town—it's nice to have that crunch.

Slide the baking sheet into the oven and immediately turn the oven temperature down to 375 degrees F. Bake the éclairs for 20 minutes without opening the oven door, then rotate the pan and continue to bake the pastries for another 10 to 15 minutes, or until they are golden on top and bottom and firm to the touch. Transfer the éclairs to a rack to cool to room temperature.

TO FILL THE ECLAIRS: There are two traditional ways to fill éclairs, both good and both fun. One is to fill a pastry bag with whatever you've chosen as a filling, use a medium plain pastry tip to poke a hole in the éclair—either in the bottom or in one side—nuzzle the tip into the hole and squeeze in enough filling to come to the edges of the hole.

The other way is to slice the éclairs horizontally, either in half or by cutting off the top one third. If you do this, you can scoop out the (inevitable) eggy innards. Some people love the custard interior, some don't, so know thyself (and thine audience). Pipe, spoon or scoop the filling into the bottom of the éclairs and cap with the tops.

No matter how you've filled the pastries, they should be served immediately or stowed in the refrigerator until needed.

If you haven't sugared or crackled your éclairs, you might want to give them a last-minute dusting of confectioners' sugar.

Chocolate Cream Puffs with Mascarpone Filling

Makes 15 puffs

FOR ABOUT TWENTY-FOUR HOURS, I thought I had invented chocolate pâte à choux, and those hours were pretty sweet. I'd never tasted chocolate cream puffs, I'd never seen them and I was so tickled that I'd made them. And then chocolate cream puffs seemed to pop up in books and magazines, pâtisseries and restaurants everywhere. Had I just never noticed?

While everything made with pâte à choux is dramatic, these are both dramatic *and* sexy. It's the magic of that vixen, cocoa. There's not much of it in the dough, but it's enough to transform the traditional cream puff, to turn it dark, dark brown and to give it a true chocolate flavor.

The puffs make wonderful Profiteroles (page 238) and they're fun with a crackle top (see page 226), but I like them most filled with something velvety, like chocolate mousse (page 348) or a mix of mascarpone and whipped cream, as in this recipe. Consider going totally romantic and adding a little rose extract (available online) to the mascarpone filling, maybe even tinting it pink, and then surprising your Valentine with a platter piled high with puffs.

SERVING: The puffs should be served at room temperature or slightly chilled. If you want to go deliciously overboard, you could pass some chocolate sauce (page 442) at the table.

STORING: The cream puffs can be scooped and frozen for up to 2 months before baking—bake them from the freezer, no defrosting necessary. And the cream filling can be made a few hours ahead and kept refrigerated. However, it's best to fill the puffs just before serving.

FOR THE CREAM PUFFS

½ cup (68 grams) all-purpose flour

1½ tablespoons unsweetened cocoa powder

⅓ cup (80 ml) water

¼ cup (60 ml) whole milk

½ stick (4 tablespoons; 2 ounces; 57 grams) unsalted butter, cut into chunks

1 tablespoon sugar

¼ teaspoon fine sea salt

2 large eggs, at room temperature

FOR THE FILLING

½ cup (113 grams) mascarpone, chilled

½ cup (120 ml) very cold heavy cream

2 tablespoons sugar

1 teaspoon pure vanilla extract or ½ teaspoon pure rose extract, preferably Star Kay White, or rose water to taste

Red food coloring (optional)

Confectioners' sugar, for dusting

TO MAKE THE PUFFS: Center a rack in the oven and preheat the oven to 425 degrees F. Line a baking sheet with parchment paper or a silicone baking mat.

Sift the flour and cocoa together into a small bowl.

Put the water, milk, butter, sugar and salt in a medium saucepan and bring to a boil over high heat. Add the flour and cocoa all at once, lower the heat to medium-low and, using a wooden spoon or sturdy heatproof spatula, stir like mad. The mixture will come together in a ball and there will be a film on the bottom of the pan, but don't stop stirring—give it another minute of energetic beating. Transfer the hot dough to the bowl of a stand mixer fitted with the paddle attachment, or a large bowl in which you can use a hand mixer, and let it rest for 2 minutes.

Beat the dough for 1 minute, then add the eggs one by one, beating very well after each egg goes in. You'll have a smooth, shiny dough.

Place mounds of dough on the baking sheets using a small cookie scoop (one with a 2-teaspoon capacity, my tool of choice) or dropping the dough by small spoonfuls; leave about 2 inches between them.

Slide the baking sheet into the oven, then immediately reduce the oven temperature to 375 degrees F. Bake for 25 to 30 minutes, rotating the sheet at the midway point, or until the puffs feel hollow and lift off the paper or mat easily. Cool to room temperature on a cooling rack before filling.

TO MAKE THE FILLING: Put the mascarpone in a medium bowl and, using a flexible spatula, stir it gently to loosen it. Beating makes mascarpone grainy, so go easy.

Whip the heavy cream in a small bowl just until it starts to thicken. Beat in the sugar and vanilla or rose extract and continue to whip until the cream holds medium peaks. If you're using red food coloring, add a drop and mix it in, then add more coloring, if needed. Continue to mix until the cream holds firm peaks. Stir a spoonful of the cream into the mascarpone to lighten it, then gently fold in the remainder. (*The cream can be made a few hours ahead and refrigerated.*)

TO FILL THE PUFFS: Just before serving, cut or carefully pull the cream puffs apart at their middles. If you'd like, you can hollow out the base of the puffs by removing the custardy interior. (I like the creamy center and always leave it.) Spoon or pipe some filling (using a pastry bag with a plain tip or a zipper-lock plastic bag from which you've snipped off a corner) into the base of each puff; replace the tops. If you'd like, the puffs can be chilled for about 30 minutes.

Dust the puffs with confectioners' sugar just before serving.

Profiteroles, Ice Cream and Hot Chocolate Sauce, Benoit Style (page 238)

Profiteroles, Ice Cream and Hot Chocolate Sauce, Benoit Style

Makes about 48 puffs

SERVING: At Benoit, six small puffs are arranged around a scoop of ice cream on a shallow dessert bowl and the chocolate sauce is served in a pitcher. It's quite beautiful, but it's just as beautiful served family style, with all the puffs in a mound, the ice cream in a bucket and the sauce in a jar.

STORING: Every component of this dessert can be made ahead. The puffs can be formed and frozen, unbaked, for up to 2 months, and baked and filled and refrigerated for up to 4 hours. The pastry cream can be made ahead, covered and refrigerated for up to 3 days—in fact, you want it chilled—and the chocolate sauce can be made ahead and warmed right before serving.

BENOIT STARTED A CENTURY AGO as a traditional bistro serving the butchers and fishmongers, bakers, farmers, artists and night owls who came to Les Halles, the huge food market that was the stuff not just of commerce, but of legend and literature. "The stomach of Paris" is what Emile Zola called it, but throughout the night and into the hours before dawn when the raucous market was at full tilt, it might just as well have been the city's heart. The market was demolished in 1971, but Benoit lived on, its exuberance never dampened, although its clientele changed. Benoit's cuisine is still traditional—and excellent—but these days the tables are filled with people who follow the Michelin Guide to fine dining rather than the weather in the Farmer's Almanac.

Benoit is famous for many of its dishes, but it's the bistro's profiteroles that I adore. Profiteroles are small cream puffs that are usually filled with ice cream and finished with hot chocolate sauce. Chez Benoit does the classic one better: They fill the puffs with vanilla pastry cream and serve them with vanilla ice cream, a silver pitcher of hot chocolate sauce and knives, forks and spoons. You can pour the sauce over the puffs and ice cream to make a kind of sundae, or you can spear a cream puff, dunk it in sauce and enjoy it with a spoonful of ice cream. Just because Benoit's gone luxe doesn't mean they don't remember how much fun it is to play with your food. (The photo is on pages 236 to 237.)

A WORD ON THE PUFFS: At Benoit, the puffs are plain, but if you'd like to make the profiteroles with a crackle-top (page 226), they will only be better.

FOR THE CREAM PUFFS AND FILLING	FOR SERVING
1 recipe Cream Puff Dough (page 226), just made and still warm	1 recipe Bittersweet Chocolate Sauce (page 442), warm and ready to serve
1 recipe Vanilla Pastry Cream (page 430), chilled and ready to use	1 pint (473 ml) vanilla ice cream, homemade (page 453) or store-bought

TO MAKE THE CREAM PUFFS: Position the racks to divide the oven into thirds and preheat the oven to 425 degrees F. Line two baking sheets with parchment paper or silicone baking mats.

You can make the puffs any size you'd like, but I prefer these tiny. I use a small cookie scoop (2-teaspoon capacity) to portion out the dough, but you can use a teaspoon (mound the dough on it) or pipe these out with a pastry bag (or a zipper-lock plastic bag). For me, the ideal size is that of a small walnut or a big cherry (of course, the finished puffs will be larger). Leave 2 inches of space between each scoop. (If you're making these crackle top (see previous page), place a frozen round of dough on top of each puff.)

Slide the baking sheets into the oven and immediately turn the oven temperature down to 375 degrees F. Bake the puffs for 25 to 30 minutes, rotating the sheets from top to bottom and front to back at the midway point, or until the puffs are golden brown, firm and feel hollow when tapped on their bottoms. Transfer the puffs to a cooling rack and allow them to come to room temperature.

TO FILL THE PUFFS: You can either cut the puffs at their midpoints and fill them with pastry cream, or you can fit a pastry bag with a small tip, fill it, then use the tip to poke a hole in the side of the puff and squeeze in the filling through the hole. It's best to fill the puffs shortly before you're ready to serve, but if that's not possible, cover the puffs and put them in the refrigerator until you're ready for them (or for up to 4 hours).

Serve with the ice cream and chocolate sauce.

Nun's Beignets

**Makes about
25 beignets**

SERVING: If you manage to get the beignets to the table, you might want to serve them with chunky jam, honey or a bowl of crème anglaise (page 441). The beignets are best hot, but they're surprisingly good at room temperature too—just be sure get to them within a couple of hours.

STORING: Beignets are best eaten the day they are made.

THE STORY ABOUT THESE BEIGNETS revolves around a young nun named Agnès and an abbess who, sometime in the eighteenth century, were preparing a feast for the archbishop. Agnès was fiddling with a piece of cream puff dough and listening to the older nun's instructions, when suddenly, a rat-a-tat was heard from beneath her robes. The *nonnette* was embarrassed to the point of trembling, and her hands shook so forcefully that the lump of dough she'd been holding fell into a cauldron of boiling oil, where it puffed and browned and turned into a golden ball. When the nuns tasted it, they called it a wonder and christened the beignets *pets de nonne*, translated so indelicately as "nun's farts."

Whatever you call them, they're wonderfully crisp on the outside and soft and eggy on the inside. They're the kind of sweet that draws people into the kitchen as you're making them, the kind that never lasts long enough to make it to a platter.

½ cup (120 ml) whole milk	3 large eggs, at room temperature
½ cup (120 ml) water	
2 tablespoons sugar	1 teaspoon pure vanilla extract (optional)
¼ teaspoon fine sea salt	
1 stick (8 tablespoons; 4 ounces; 113 grams) unsalted butter, cut into 4 chunks	Flavorless oil, such as canola or grape seed, for deep-frying
1 cup (136 grams) all-purpose flour	Sugar, cinnamon sugar or vanilla sugar, for dredging

Bring the milk, water, sugar, salt and butter to a rapid boil in a medium heavy-bottomed saucepan over high heat. Add the flour all at once, lower the heat to medium-low and quickly start stirring energetically with a wooden spoon or sturdy heatproof spatula. The dough will come together and a light crust will form on the bottom of the pan. Keep stirring vigorously for another minute or two to dry the dough. The dough should be very smooth.

Turn the dough out into the bowl of a stand mixer fitted with the paddle attachment, or into a large bowl in which you can use a hand mixer or a wooden spoon. Let the dough sit for a minute, then add the eggs one by one, beating until the dough is thick and shiny. Make sure that each egg is fully incorporated before you add the next, and don't be concerned if the dough falls apart; by the time the last egg goes in, the dough will have come together again. Beat in the vanilla extract, if you're using it.

TO FRY THE BEIGNETS: Pour about 4 inches of oil into a large Dutch oven, fit the pot with a deep-fat thermometer and heat the oil until it reaches 325 degrees F. (The beignets are best fried at between 325 and 350 degrees F.)

Meanwhile, set two soupspoons and a slotted spoon or small spider strainer near the stove. Line a plate or small baking sheet with a double thickness of paper towels and keep it near the stove as well. Put a generous handful of sugar, cinnamon sugar or vanilla sugar in a large bowl.

When the oil is at temperature, use a soupspoon to scoop up a rounded spoonful of dough about the size of a Ping-Pong ball, and use the second spoon to push the dough into the oil. Repeat to make more beignets: You want to give each ball of dough room to bob and turn, so don't crowd the pot; I usually fry 5 beignets at a time. Fry the beignets, adjusting the heat as needed, for 8 to 12 minutes, or until they've puffed to about three times their original size, turned deeply golden brown and split. The little split or fissure is important—it's a sign that the beignets have expanded sufficiently. As each beignet is done, lift it out of the oil with the slotted spoon or spider strainer (tap against the side of the pot to drain off the excess oil) and onto the paper towels. Turn the beignet around a couple of times to dry it slightly, then put it in the bowl of sugar. Using a spoon or your fingers, turn the hot beignets around to coat them generously with sugar, then transfer to a serving platter. Continue until you have used all the dough, always making sure that the temperature of the oil is in the right range.

Pailles

PAILLE MEANS "STRAW," and I knew nothing about these pastries until I saw them at my corner pâtisserie. They appealed to me instantly, in part because of the way the sandwiched pastries look: two rectangles of caramelized ridged puff pastry, which do, indeed, look like a lineup of drinking straws or piles of hay, trying their best (but failing) to contain a swath of berry jam. The pastries are and very brittle, and the sweet jam is very soft, so that when you bite into them, there's always a little ooze and a lot of crackle and crumbs.

You don't so much make *pailles* as you construct them. The process involves rolling and folding a sheet of puff pastry—brushing each roll and fold with egg and sprinkling it with sugar—and then, after freezing the dough, cutting it into small strips and pressing (or more likely smashing) the strips together so that when they bake, they expand sideways rather than upward. If you like to play with your food, you'll love making these.

A WORD ON QUANTITY AND SIZE: One sheet of puff pastry will make about 8 cookies, and that's usually all I bake at one time. However, you can roll and fold more sheets of pastry and keep them in the freezer to cut and bake later. My *pailles* are dainty, but there's no one right size for these. I've seen them small and I've seen them so big that they looked like lunch box jelly sandwiches. Once you understand the technique, you'll see that you can make them any size you want.

Makes 8 sandwich cookies

SERVING: These are ready to go as soon as they're filled and dusted.

STORING: The pastries themselves will keep for a couple of hours, but like almost everything made with puff pastry, they're best enjoyed as close to just-baked as possible. On the other hand, the rolled and folded dough can be wrapped airtight and kept in the freezer for up to 2 months. You can cut and bake the dough frozen; no defrosting needed.

- 1 large egg
- 1 sheet puff pastry, about 8 ounces (227 grams), ready to roll (defrosted if frozen, but still cold)

Sugar, for sprinkling
Thick jam, for spreading
Confectioners' sugar, for dusting

Line a baking sheet with parchment or wax paper. Beat the egg with a splash of cold water and set it and a pastry brush on the counter.

Flour a work surface. Grab a rolling pin, give the puff pastry a dusting of flour and roll it into a square that's about 16 × 16 inches. If you don't get the exact measurements, don't worry; if you get a rectangle and not a square, that's okay too. Bigger is better than smaller, but you'll be able to work with whatever you end up with. As you're rolling, turn the puff pastry over, so that you're rolling both sides, flouring it as needed; if it gets soft and sticky, chill the puff pastry for a few minutes and then carry on. If you end up with a rectangle, turn the puff pastry so that a short side faces you. Brush the flour off the puff pastry.

Brush the surface of the puff pastry with the egg wash, sprinkle with sugar—you want to coat but not bury the puff pastry—and fold it in half (the long way if you have a rectangle). Once again, brush off the flour, brush on the egg wash and sprinkle with sugar. Fold the puff pastry lengthwise again. Brush off the flour, brush on the egg wash and sprinkle with sugar. Slide the strip of folded pastry onto the baking sheet and freeze for at least 2 hours. (*Once the dough is frozen, you can wrap it and keep it frozen for up to 2 months.*)

WHEN YOU'RE READY TO BAKE: Center a rack in the oven and preheat the oven to 400 degrees F. Line a baking sheet with parchment paper or a silicone baking mat.

Remove the puff pastry from the freezer, leaving it on the paper, and slide it onto a cutting board. Keep a long side facing you. Using a ruler and a pizza wheel or sharp knife, cut the dough crosswise into ¼-inch-wide strips.

Now comes the fussy part: Place 1 strip of pastry on the lined baking sheet, with a cut side up so that the layers are visible. Line up 3 more strips next to it, cut side up, and then gently press them together. You don't want to squash them and pinch their layers, but you do want to get them so that they're touching one another and will bake together as one cookie. Repeat until you've used all the strips. Sprinkle the tops lightly with sugar.

Cover the pastries with a sheet of parchment paper and top with a large cooling rack. The pastries are meant to be flat and crisp, and the parchment and rack will help to make them that way.

Bake for 10 minutes. Remove the cooling rack and the top sheet of parchment, press the pastries down with a metal spatula and flip them over. Bake—no rack or parchment needed—for about 10 minutes more, or until golden brown. Transfer to a rack and cool to room temperature.

Just before serving, sandwich pairs of the pastries together with jam and dust them with confectioners' sugar. In many pâtisseries, a center band of the *paille* is covered with a strip of parchment before it is dusted, so that only the ends get coated with sugar. It's a nice look because that way, you can see the "straw" lines.

Merveilles

**Makes about
40 pastries**

SERVING: These are best
eaten as soon as they're
cool enough to bite into,
but they're also delicious
at room temperature. If the
sugar has melted into the
cookies, dust them again
before serving.

STORING: These are not
really keepers, and that's
not a bad thing, because
it's unlikely that you'll have
any left to keep. However,
if there are a few, you can
keep them overnight in a
dry place; don't refrigerate.

*M*ERVEILLE MEANS "MIRACLE," and the name is not hyperbole. Can sweet, brandied egg dough, fried until puffed and then sugared until it poses a threat to shirtfronts be anything less than a miracle? The pastry, a centuries-old sweet from France's Aquitaine, the region that claims Bordeaux as its capital, was traditionally made for Carnivale, but knowing a good thing when they see it, the Aquitaines now make it throughout the year.

In Provence, a similar dough is cut into squares and called *oreillettes*, or "pillows," and in the Lot, in the southwest, the dough is cut into bands, sandwiched and twisted. I've seen trapezoidal *merveilles* and pastries shaped into rings. Depending on the location, the recipe might or might not include yeast (I use baking powder); the fat for frying might be olive oil, goose fat, shortening, or grape seed or canola oil; and the spirit that flavors it might be rum, eau-de-vie, Armagnac or whatever is local.

With so much variety in their homeland, *merveilles* are yours to do with as you want. I usually cut the dough into long strips or small triangles with a fluted ravioli wheel. My oil of choice is canola or grape seed and my moment of choice is anytime there are a lot of people around. This is a party sweet and one that's the most fun—and the messiest—eaten when the dough is just shy of too hot.

1 cup (136 grams) all-purpose flour	2 tablespoons brandy or dark rum
½ teaspoon baking powder	1 teaspoon pure vanilla extract
¼ teaspoon fine sea salt	Cinnamon sugar and/or confectioners' sugar, for dusting
3 tablespoons sugar	
Grated zest of 1 orange	
1 tablespoon unsalted butter, at room temperature	
1 large egg, lightly beaten, at room temperature	Flavorless oil, such as grape seed or canola, for deep-frying

Whisk the flour, baking powder and salt together in a small bowl.

Put the sugar in a medium bowl and sprinkle the orange zest over it. Using your fingertips, rub the sugar and zest together until the sugar is moist and fragrant. Toss the butter into the bowl and work it into the sugar with a sturdy flexible spatula. Pour in the egg, brandy or rum and vanilla and stir to blend as best as you can. At this point, the mixture will look like egg drop soup—don't be discouraged. Add the dry ingredients and stir until the dough, which will be soft and moist and very much like a sticky muffin dough, comes together.

Turn out the dough, wrap it in plastic film and chill it for at least 2 hours. (*The dough can be refrigerated for as long as overnight.*)

When you're ready to roll and cut the dough, line a baking sheet with plastic film.

Cut the dough in half and return one half to the refrigerator. Flour your work surface well—this is a sticky dough and will need more flour than you might usually use—and flour the top of the dough. Roll it out, turning it over to make sure it's not sticking, rolling on both sides and adding more flour if necessary. Once the surface is properly floured and you've got the dough going, it's very easy to roll, and you'll be able to roll it until it's paper-thin, which is what you want. If you can roll it into a large rectangle, great; if it's more free-form, that's fine too.

Working with a fluted pastry wheel or ravioli cutter, a plain pizza wheel or a knife, cut the dough into long strips, squares, diamonds or any other shape that appeals to you. (I go for strips that are about 1 inch wide and 3 inches long; for more drama, you can go longer.) Place the strips on the lined baking sheet and cover with another piece of plastic film. Repeat with the remaining dough, cover with the plastic and chill for at least 1 hour.

WHEN YOU'RE READY TO FRY: Have a baking sheet lined with a triple thickness of paper towels near the stove. Have a skimmer, tongs or chopsticks (my favorite tool here), at hand as well. Fill a sugar duster or strainer (or two) with cinnamon sugar and/or confectioners' sugar. Pour 4 inches oil into a large deep saucepan (or use an electric deep fryer) and heat it to 350 degrees F, as measured on a deep-fat thermometer.

Drop 4 to 6 *merveilles* into the pan—don't crowd them—and fry until they're golden on both sides, 2 to 3 minutes. Lift them out of the oil with the skimmer or other tool, allowing the excess oil to drip back into the pan, then turn out onto the paper towel–lined baking sheet to drain. Pat the tops with more paper towels to remove surface oil, then dust both sides with sugar(s) while the cookies are still hot and slightly moist from the oil. Continue frying the remaining *merveilles*—making sure to keep the oil at 350 degrees F—draining, patting dry and dusting until all the dough is fried.

Palmiers

W HEN THESE PASTRIES ARE SMALL, like these, they're called palmiers, a nod to the palm tree (a name I've never really been able to understand); when they're large, they're called elephant ears (slightly more understandable); and when they're any size and made by anyone who loves puff pastry, they might also be called hearts or eyeglasses (even if they might look more like lorgnettes). No matter what they're called, they're all the same to their core: puff pastry, rolled out on sugar, folded from the long sides into the center, closed like a book, cut and then baked, so that the sugar caramelizes and the pastry puffs out more than up. French pastries don't come simpler, nor more beloved. Elephant ears are an after-school treat—seeing children lined up at a pâtisserie, coins in their fists and eyes on the big sweet, makes you think you've stepped into a Robert Doisneau picture. Smaller palmiers are a teatime indulgence or a last-of-the-night sweet in a restaurant. Beware: A well-made palmier will shatter at first bite, sending flakes and shards into the folds of ties and carefully knotted scarves.

Making palmiers is a rather free-form activity. I'm giving you "real" instructions, but I can't give you exact measurements, particularly when it comes to the sugar. The best I can tell you is to be generous: Roll the puff pastry out on a bed of sugar, keep the top sugared and then use more sugar after you've brushed the dough with some melted butter. Make these once, and you'll understand why. And you'll never need a recipe again.

You also might have your own *bonne idées* for flavoring your next batch. Think about mixing the sugar with cinnamon, ginger, a smidgen of cardamom, vanilla or lemon zest. Or go for cocoa (see Bonne Idée).

Makes about 24 palmiers

SERVING: Palmiers can be a snack, a nibble with coffee or tea or the additional crunch in a dessert: Top ice cream, pots de crème, panna cotta, rice pudding or any soft dessert with a palmier.

STORING: Kept in a dry place—moisture's the wrecker here—the palmiers will hold for about 5 days.

Sugar
1 sheet puff pastry (about 8 ounces; 227 grams), thawed (if frozen) and ready to roll

About 3 tablespoons unsalted butter (1½ ounces; 43 grams), melted and cooled

Dust your work surface generously with sugar. Place the puff pastry on the bed of sugar—if your pastry is folded, leave it that way—dust the top of the dough with sugar and start rolling. You're aiming for a 13-inch square (come close, and you'll be fine). As you're rolling, turn the dough over, so you're rolling both sides (which will help give you an even puff), and add more sugar as you go—you want to keep both sides sugared and moveable.

TO MAKE MINI PALMIERS: Brush the surface of the dough with melted butter and sprinkle with sugar to cover the dough. Imagine a centerline going from the top of the dough to the bottom; fold the left and right sides of the dough over so that they meet each other in the center. Brush the surface with butter, sprinkle with sugar and repeat the folding; you'll have 4 layers on each side. Then fold one side over the other—as though you were closing a book—and slide the dough onto a cutting board. Chill the dough while you preheat the oven.

TO MAKE LARGER (BUT NOT ELEPHANTINE) PALMIERS: Follow the same butter-and-sugar instructions as for minis, but bring the left and right sides of the dough only halfway to the centerline. Butter and sugar the folded-over strips and then bring those strips over to meet at the centerline. You will have 3 layers of dough on each side. Then fold over again like a book and chill while you preheat the oven.

TO BAKE THE PALMIERS: Center a rack in the oven and preheat the oven to 425 degrees F. Line a baking sheet with parchment paper or a silicone baking mat. (You can position the racks to divide the oven in thirds and bake two sheets of palmiers at a time, but since you have to flip the pastries halfway through baking, I find it easier to work with one sheet at a time.)

Cut the dough crosswise into strips that are ½ inch wide. Place the strips on the baking sheet, cut side up (so that the layers are visible), leaving at least 2 inches of puff space between them. Lightly cover the remaining dough and keep it in the refrigerator.

Bake the palmiers for about 10 minutes, flip them over with a metal spatula and bake for another 3 to 5 minutes, or until the bottoms are caramelized. Transfer the baking sheet to a cooling rack and let the pastries cool to room temperature on the sheet.

Repeat with the remaining dough, using a cool baking sheet.

Petite Apple Croustades

CROUSTADES, which tiptoe along the line that separates tarts and pastries, are beloved in many regions of France, but for me they'll always be Gascon, since I first learned about them and tasted them with a chef who was the pride of Gascony, the late Jean-Louis Palladin. It was the end of the 1980s, and Jean-Louis, who was the chef at the Watergate in Washington, D.C., was making food that was spinning the heads of every great chef in America and France. To say that he was avant-garde wouldn't put him far enough ahead of the pack. But the dessert that we were talking about was very old, and it was one he loved dearly.

For our croustade adventure, Jean-Louis chose Armagnac-soaked prunes (although he said that apples would be wonderful too) and, in place of the traditional dough that depended on fat from either ducks or geese, he used phyllo. He brushed each layer with butter and sprinkled it with sugar. Every two layers of stacked buttered-and-sugared phyllo were run under the broiler until caramelized. It was gorgeous.

Yet as gorgeous and delicious as it was, I never made it again—the process was too complicated. It wasn't until recently when I saw beautiful croustades in a neighborhood bakery in Paris that I tried my hand at them. Now, I make them just as they're done in the pâtisserie: simply. I cut strips of phyllo, butter and sugar them, stack them to make pouches, fill them with caramelized apples and seal them like beggar's purses. I bake them in muffin tins—the perfect molds.

A WORD ON SPIRIT AND SIZE: I use Armagnac to flavor the apples, but you can use brandy, Cognac, applejack or Calvados instead. You can also omit the alcohol. As for size, since the recipe is a construction, it's easy—and mathematically unchallenging—to adjust it for more or fewer.

Makes 6 servings

SERVING: Croustades are most delicious when they're warm, but they are still very good at room temperature. If you'd like, you can reheat them on a parchment-lined baking sheet for about 10 minutes in a 350-degree-F oven before serving. Depending on when you're serving them, perhaps as a midday snack or an after-dinner dessert, the croustades can be enjoyed plain, with ice cream or with Vanilla Crème Anglaise (page 441) poured around them.

STORING: You can make the apple filling up to 2 days ahead and keep it covered in the refrigerator. The croustades are best served shortly after they're made, but you can bake them a few hours ahead of serving—in which case, it's nice to reheat them briefly (see Serving).

FOR THE FILLING

1½ tablespoons (¾ ounce; 21 grams) unsalted butter

3 tablespoons sugar

3 apples (about 1½ pounds; 681 grams), such as Gala, Fuji or Golden Delicious, peeled, cored and cut into 1-inch cubes

1½ tablespoons Armagnac or 1½ teaspoons pure vanilla extract (optional)

FOR THE CRUST

½ stick (4 tablespoons; 2 ounces; 57 grams) unsalted butter, melted

9 sheets phyllo dough, each about 8 × 14 inches, thawed

Sugar, for sprinkling

Confectioners' sugar, for dusting

TO MAKE THE FILLING: Melt the butter in a medium skillet, preferably non-stick, over medium-high heat. Sprinkle the sugar over the butter and stay nearby. As soon as the sugar starts to color around the edges of the pan, grab a wooden spoon and begin making little circles all around the edges of the pan, blending in the colored sugar. Continue to make larger circles, drawing in the caramelized sugar, and soon you will have worked your way to the center of the pan. When the sugar is a pale caramel color, toss in the apples, turn the heat to high and stir and toss the apples until they are coated with mahogany-colored caramel and cooked through but not mushy, 5 to 7 minutes. Pour in the Armagnac, if you're using it, and cook until it evaporates. Or, if you'd like, you can flambé the Armagnac—just turn off the heat and stand back!

Scrape the apples into a heatproof bowl. If you're using vanilla extract, stir it in. Set the apples aside to cool until just warm or at room temperature. (*Once they are cooled, you can pack the apples into an airtight container and keep them in the refrigerator for up to 2 days; drain off the excess liquid and stir before using.*)

TO ASSEMBLE AND BAKE THE CROUSTADES: Center a rack in the oven and preheat the oven to 350 degrees F. If you have a 6-cup muffin tin, great; if not, use a 12-cup tin. Using the melted butter, coat 6 muffin cups. If you're making 6 croustades in a 12-cup tin, use every other muffin cup, so that you have extra room to lay out the phyllo strips and so the croustades will bake more evenly.

Put a large piece of plastic film on the counter, lay the sheets of phyllo on top and cover with another sheet of film. Keep the phyllo you're not working with covered like this.

Lay a few sheets of phyllo out on the counter, with a short side toward you, and, using a pizza wheel or a sharp knife, cut each sheet in half from top to bottom. Then cut each half in half again from top to bottom. You'll have 4 strips, each 2 × 14 inches, from each sheet.

You'll be using 6 strips for each croustade: Place one strip on the counter (I line the counter with a piece of parchment), brush it with melted butter and sprinkle it with sugar. Lay it in a muffin cup, buttered side up. Butter and sugar a second strip and lay it in the cup perpendicular to the first strip. Continue buttering and sugaring 4 more strips, laying them into the cup so that they crisscross each other and cover the sides completely. Spoon in a portion of the apples; they should come about three quarters of the way up the sides of the cup. Carefully reach under the overhanging strips and gather them together the way you would a bouquet, to enclose the filling. Squeeze the strips together and, if you'd like, give them a gentle twist. The phyllo is fragile, so the edges may break off—it's okay; ragged is very pretty. Brush and/or sprinkle the top of the croustade with melted butter—do the best that you can with the uneven top—and then dust with confectioners' sugar, using a sugar duster or strainer.

Repeat until all 6 croustades are assembled.

Bake for 25 to 30 minutes, or until the croustades are a gorgeous toasty brown. Transfer the muffin tin to a rack and let the croustades cool for about 5 minutes, then gingerly lift them out of the tin and place them on the rack. Cool to warm or to room temperature.

Banana-Chocolate Chaussons

Makes 8 turnovers

SERVING: These are really good when they're still warm. They're also good at room temperature—but only for a couple of hours. Bake them close to the time that you want to enjoy them. Although they are more of a breakfast treat, there's no rule that says you can't serve them as an after-school sweet.

STORING: The turnovers will keep for only a few hours, but you can assemble the pastries up to 2 weeks ahead of time, wrap them airtight and freeze them. When you're ready to bake, brush them with egg wash, sprinkle with sugar and bake, without defrosting.

THE FRENCH HAVE as much affection for turnovers—they call them *chaussons*—as we do. Usually made with puff pastry that flakes haphazardly at first bite, filled with fruit and baked until golden, *chaussons* have a permanent place in the canon of comfort sweets as well as in the cases of neighborhood pâtisseries. Yet as simple and homey as they are, I've never known a French person to bake one at home, which seems a shame, since the best turnovers are the ones you eat just a few minutes out of the oven.

It's most common to find a *chausson* filled with apples, but turnovers are too easy to make and too inviting to riff on not to shake up the status quo. One of my favorite plays on the filling is this combination: bananas, chocolate, brown sugar, a pinch of spice, some salt and, just for fun, either Nutella or peanut butter. It sounds like kid stuff, but don't be fooled—these turnovers are just right for the sophisticated brunch set.

1 sheet puff pastry (about 6 ounces; 227 grams), ready to roll (defrosted if frozen but still cold)

2½ ounces (71 grams) bittersweet or semisweet or milk chocolate, finely chopped

1½ tablespoons light brown sugar

1 tablespoon sugar

Pinch of freshly grated nutmeg or ground allspice

Pinch of sea salt, preferably fleur de sel

2 ripe but firm bananas

2 tablespoons (1 ounce; 28 grams) unsalted butter, cut into small pieces and chilled

1 large egg

Nutella or peanut butter, for filling (optional)

Sugar, for dusting

Line a baking sheet with parchment paper.

If your puff pastry came folded, leave it that way. Dust a work surface and the top of the dough with flour and roll the dough into a rectangle that's 8 × 16 inches. Using a pizza wheel or a knife, cut the dough in half the long way and then cut each long rectangle crosswise into 4 squares; you'll have a total of eight 4-inch squares. Place the dough on the baking sheet and freeze for at least 20 minutes.

Center a rack in the oven and preheat the oven to 425 degrees F.

Put the chopped chocolate, both sugars, nutmeg or allspice and salt in a medium bowl and stir to mix. Peel the bananas, slice them lengthwise in half and then cut them crosswise into chunks about ½ inch thick. Toss the bananas with the chocolate mix. Add the butter bits and stir to blend.

Using a fork, beat the egg with a splash of cold water in a small bowl.

Remove the pastry squares from the freezer. Divide the filling among the squares, placing a spoonful of filling just off center on each square and leaving a bare border of about 1 inch around it. If you want to add Nutella or peanut butter, top the filling on each square with a small spoonful. Brush all the borders with the egg wash and fold the dough over to form triangular turnovers. Use the tines of the fork to press down and seal the edges; make a snug seal, so that the filling won't seep out. Brush the tops of the turnovers with the egg wash, taking care not to let it drip down the sides of the pastries and onto the baking sheet (drips will glue down the pastries and keep them from rising). Sprinkle each turnover with some sugar.

Slide the baking sheet into the oven and immediately turn the oven down to 350 degrees F. Bake the turnovers for 30 to 35 minutes, or until golden brown on top and bottom. Transfer the turnovers to a rack and allow them to cool until they are just warm or they reach room temperature.

Bonne Idée
APPLE CHAUSSONS:
Instead of the banana-chocolate filling, toss
¼ cup sugar, 1½ teaspoons all-purpose flour and a pinch of ground cinnamon (optional) together in a medium bowl. Peel and core 2 apples (Fuji or Granny Smiths) and cut them into small cubes. Toss the apples into the bowl and stir to coat. Just before you close up the turnovers, dot with butter (you'll need about 2 tablespoons, cut into bits).

COOKIES AND BARS

Vanilla-Bean Sablés

I N THE AMERICAN WORLD OF COOKIES, the chocolate chip is the icon. In the French world, it's the sablé, a simple shortbread cookie notable for its fine texture—snappy around the edges, cakier in the center—its fresh butter flavor and, often, its bit of saltiness. While the French have hundreds of cookies, half a hundred of them are probably based on the sablé. Chocolate chip? Just add chips. Lemon? Orange? Hazelnut? Caramel? Ditto. It's the tabula rasa of French cookiedom. It also happens to be my favorite cookie.

Sablé, which means "sandy," is both the cookie's name and the adjective that best describes its characteristic texture. To get the sandy-ish shortbread texture, you need to mix the dough at low speed so you don't add air to it and, most important, once the flour goes in, you've got to work quickly and gently—you want to beat the dough as little as possible. Often I'll add the flour, pulse the mixer on and off to get the blending going and then do the rest of the mixing by hand. Whether you continue with the machine or with hand power, the key is not to overdo it.

⅓ cup (67 grams) sugar	½ teaspoon fine sea salt
2 moist, fragrant vanilla beans or 2 teaspoons pure vanilla extract	1 large egg yolk
	2 cups (272 grams) all-purpose flour
2 sticks (8 ounces; 226 grams) unsalted butter, at room temperature	FOR THE EDGING
⅓ cup (40 grams) confectioners' sugar, sifted	1 large egg yolk
	Sanding sugar

Put the granulated sugar in the bowl of a stand mixer fitted with the paddle attachment, or in a large bowl in which you can use a hand mixer. If you are using vanilla beans, cut them in half lengthwise and scrape the pulp over the sugar. (Save the pods for another use or stash them in a canister of sugar to make vanilla sugar.) Using your fingertips, rub the vanilla pulp into the sugar until it's fragrant. (If you're using extract, you'll add it later.)

Add the butter, confectioners' sugar and salt to the bowl and beat on low speed until the mixture is smooth and creamy (you don't want it to get light and fluffy), scraping down the sides and bottom of the bowl as needed. Drop in the egg yolk and beat for 1 minute. If you're using vanilla extract, beat it in now. Add the flour all at once and pulse the mixer on and off to start incorporating it into the dough. Mix on low speed just until the flour has disappeared (or do this last little bit by hand with a flexible spatula).

Turn the dough out onto a work surface and divide it in half. Shape each

SERVING: I think of these as tea biscuits, café cookies, after-school treats, grown-up nibbles and midnight snacks—I serve them anytime.

STORING: You can wrap the logs of dough airtight and keep them in the freezer for up to 2 months; coat them with the egg wash and sugar just before baking. Once baked, the cookies will keep at room temperature in a closed container for about 1 week.

half into a log about 9 inches long. (To learn how to get really tight logs, see page 61.) Wrap the logs in parchment or plastic film and refrigerate for at least 3 hours. (*If you'd like, you can wrap the logs airtight and freeze them for up to 2 months. Let the logs sit at room temperature for about 10 minutes before cutting and baking; no need to fully defrost.*)

WHEN YOU'RE READY TO BAKE: Position the racks to divide the oven into thirds and preheat the oven to 350 degrees F. Line two baking sheets with parchment paper or silicone baking mats.

Add a splash of cold water to the yolk and mix with a fork to blend. Brush each log with this egg wash and roll it in sanding sugar until it's evenly coated. Using a sturdy knife, trim the ends of the logs if they're ragged, then cut the dough into ½-inch-thick rounds. Place them on the baking sheets, about 2 inches apart.

Bake the cookies for 18 to 22 minutes, rotating the baking sheets from top to bottom and front to back at the midway point. The cookies are baked when they are brown around the edges and golden on the bottom. Carefully transfer them to a cooling rack and cool to room temperature. These really shouldn't be eaten warm; they need time to cool so that their texture will set properly.

Bonne Idées

This recipe can be the base of several other cookies or the recipe you can build your own cookie dreams on. Here are a few suggestions.

LEMON SABLÉS: Keep the vanilla bean or extract, and rub the grated zest of 1½ lemons into the sugar.

ORANGE SABLÉS: Keep the vanilla bean or extract, and rub the grated zest of 1 orange into the sugar.

COCOA SABLÉS: Reduce the amount of all-purpose flour to 1¾ cups and sift it with ¼ cup unsweetened cocoa powder. Use just 1 vanilla bean or 1 teaspoon pure vanilla extract and, if you'd like, mix in 2 ounces finely chopped semisweet or bittersweet chocolate once the flour is incorporated.

NUT SABLÉS: Lightly toast ½ cup hazelnuts (skin them while they are still warm), almonds, pistachios or other nuts, finely chop them and mix them into the dough once the flour is incorporated.

SPICE SABLÉS: Whisk your favorite spices into the flour before adding it to the dough. Try ½ teaspoon ground cinnamon, ¼ teaspoon ground ginger and a pinch of ground cloves for holiday cookies; or just use ¾ to 1 teaspoon ground cinnamon. Reduce the vanilla to ½ to 1 bean or ½ teaspoon extract.

Viennese Sablés

Makes about
24 cookies

FIRST LEARNED TO MAKE a nontraditional chocolate version of these cookies with Paris pâtissier Pierre Hermé, and he first learned to make the originals at Wittamer, the famed pastry shop in Brussels. At Wittamer, the cookies are flavored with vanilla and piped with an open-star tip into a tight W—the initial for both Wittamer and Wien (German for Vienna, where the cookies are thought to have been invented). As Belgian or Viennese as these may be, they're also found in French pastry shops. And every American I've ever given them to has said, "These taste exactly like those Danish butter cookies, the ones that come in the blue tin." And they do.

The cookies are butter-rich, sweet but not too sweet, perfectly salted and beautifully scented with vanilla. For me, it's their texture that makes them so winning: You get an initial crunch, a hit of flavor and then they melt in your mouth.

Although I stick to tradition and pipe a W onto my cookies, you can pipe any letter of the alphabet—or not. The cookies can be piped into circles, pretzel shapes, rosettes or free-form swirls. No matter the shape, the flavor and texture will still steal the show.

For a recipe for chocolate sablés, see Bonne Idée. The chocolate cookies are almost black because they are made with dark cocoa and, for the same reason, not as sweet as their vanilla sisters. They're also softer and just a bit denser.

SERVING: I love these with coffee or tea, and they also make a good accompaniment to ice cream, fruit salad or any kind of crème, from pots de crème to crème brûlée.

STORING: Packed airtight, the cookies will keep for at least 1 week; they can be frozen for up to 2 months. If you decide to freeze them, it's best not to dust them with confectioners' sugar.

9 tablespoons (4½ ounces; 128 grams) unsalted butter, very soft

½ cup (60 grams) confectioners' sugar

¼ teaspoon fine sea salt

1 large egg white, at room temperature

¾ teaspoon pure vanilla extract

1 cup plus 2 tablespoons (153 grams) all-purpose flour

Confectioners' sugar, for dusting (optional)

Position the racks to divide the oven into thirds and preheat the oven to 350 degrees F. Line two baking sheets with parchment paper or silicone baking mats.

I make this batter in the bowl of a stand mixer fitted with the paddle attachment, but you can make it by hand in a medium bowl using a flexible spatula or whisk. Put the butter in the bowl and sift the confectioners' sugar over it; add the salt. On low speed, or with the spatula or whisk, beat just until smooth but not fluffy. You want a homogeneous dough, but you don't want to beat air into it. Beat in the egg white. The white will make the dough

separate and it will be slick and slidey. Keep mixing for about 1 minute and, if the mixture curdles, don't be concerned; the flour will smooth it out. Beat in the vanilla and scrape down the bowl. Gradually add the flour, beating only until it disappears into the soft dough.

Fit a pastry bag with an open-star tip, one that's a scant ½ inch in diameter. (Alternatively, you can pipe plain cookies by filling a zipper-lock bag with the dough and snipping off one corner of the bag.) Scrape the dough into the piping bag.

Pipe the dough onto the lined baking sheets in tight W shapes that are about 2 inches wide and 1½ inches high, leaving about 2 inches of space between them—the dough will puff and spread under heat. You can make the cookies larger or smaller or in different shapes, but whatever you do, leave enough space between them to spread out.

Bake the cookies for 17 to 20 minutes, rotating the pans from top to bottom and front to back at the midway point. The cookies should be golden brown at their edges and on their bottoms and paler at the center. Allow the cookies to cool on the baking sheets for a few minutes, then transfer them to racks to cool to room temperature.

Dust with confectioners' sugar, if you'd like, just before serving.

Bonne Idée

CHOCOLATE VIENNESE SABLÉS: The method is almost the same as the one for the vanilla cookies, but the ingredients are slightly different and the baking time is shorter. Sift together 1 cup all-purpose flour and 2½ tablespoons unsweetened cocoa powder (the darker, the better; I use Valrhona) and set aside. Sift ½ cup confectioners' sugar over 9 tablespoons (4½ ounces) very soft unsalted butter in the mixing bowl. Add 2 tablespoons granulated sugar and ¼ teaspoon fine sea salt to the bowl and mix as directed. Beat in 1 large egg white, followed by the flour mixture. Pipe as directed. Bake for about 14 minutes, or until they are only just firm, then cool as in the recipe. Dust with confectioners' sugar, if you'd like, just before serving.

Toasted Buckwheat and Chopped Chocolate Sablés

*Makes about
40 cookies*

SERVING: Good on their own or with coffee, sablés are also terrific alongside fruit desserts—think poached pears—or ice cream. I think they're also really good with red wine.

STORING: Packed into a covered container, the cookies will keep at room temperature for at least 4 days; packed airtight, they'll be fine in the freezer for up to 2 months.

I OWE MY DISCOVERY OF the pleasures of toasted flour to the Michelin-starred chef Pierre Gagnaire, the scientist Hervé This and the writer Clotilde Dusoulier, all of whom experimented with the technique of toasting it in the oven the way you toast nuts. (See Bonne Idée for my first foray into toasted-flour land.)

Years later, I had the idea to toast buckwheat flour. It seemed so logical: Buckwheat is the flour of Breton crêpes, and the grain takes well to high heat. Buckwheat's flavor is deep and hearty, but also elusive. Every one of my friends who was born in Brittany recognized it in these cookies; not one of my Parisian friends could guess what gave them their flavor.

The addition of chopped chocolate was a last-second inspiration: Just when I was ready to take the dough out of the mixer bowl, I decided to toss it in.

A WORD ON TOASTING: To get the proportions right, you need to toast more flour than the recipe will use: The flour loses moisture in the oven, and you've got to compensate for this. You've also got to toast it until it is really hot and really fragrant. Trust your nose here, not your timer. And you want the flour to color just a little. The first time I made these, I was a timid toaster, and the cookies suffered for my tentativeness.

1¼ cups (150 grams) buckwheat flour	¾ cup (150 grams) sugar
1½ cups (204 grams) all-purpose flour	½ teaspoon fine sea salt
1½ sticks (12 tablespoons; 6 ounces; 170 grams) unsalted butter, cut into chunks, at room temperature	1 large egg, at room temperature
	4 ounces (113 grams) bittersweet, semisweet or milk chocolate, finely chopped

Center a rack in the oven and preheat the oven to 350 degrees F. Line a baking sheet with parchment paper or a silicone baking mat.

Spread the buckwheat flour out on the baking sheet, leaving a border of a few inches bare. Toast the flour for 5 minutes, then stir it with a table knife or a heatproof spatula. Continue to toast the flour, stirring every 5 minutes, for another 15 to 20 minutes. The flour is ready when it is a darker shade of beige and fragrant; it might even smoke around the edges. Let it cool to room temperature. Turn off the oven; you won't need it for a while.

Measure 1 cup of the cooled buckwheat flour into a medium bowl and add the all-purpose flour; whisk to blend.

Working in the bowl of a stand mixer fitted with the paddle attachment, or in a large bowl with a hand mixer, beat the butter at medium speed until it is soft and creamy. Add the sugar and salt and beat for another 2 minutes, or until the mixture is again smooth and creamy. Add the egg and beat for 1 minute more. The mixture may curdle; if it does, beat for another few seconds, and if that doesn't undo the curdling, adding the dry ingredients will. Reduce the mixer speed to low and add the flours in 2 or 3 additions, mixing until they disappear into the dough. Add the chopped chocolate and pulse the mixer on and off several times to incorporate it. Or, if you'd prefer, use a flexible spatula to stir the chocolate into the dough.

Turn the dough out onto a work surface and knead it gently, just so that it comes together. Divide the dough in half.

Working with half of the dough at a time, put the dough between two sheets of parchment or wax paper and roll until it is ¼ inch thick. (Check for thickness, not shape.) Slide the dough, still between the papers, onto a cutting board or a cookie sheet. Slide the second piece of dough on top of the first and put the dough in the freezer to firm for about 1 hour. *Alternatively, you can refrigerate the dough for several hours (or for up to 2 days).*

WHEN YOU'RE READY TO BAKE: Position the racks to divide the oven into thirds and preheat the oven to 350 degrees F. Line two baking sheets with parchment paper or silicone baking mats.

I like to use a 1¾-inch round cutter for the cookies, but you can use whatever you like, knowing that your yield and perhaps your baking time will change depending on the size of your cutter. Cut out as many cookies as you can from the first piece of dough and put them on a baking sheet, leaving an inch or so between cookies. Keep the cookies in the fridge or in a cool spot while you cut cookies from the second piece of dough. Combine the scraps, put them between two sheets of parchment or wax paper and roll out until it is ¼ inch thick; chill before cutting and baking.

Bake the cookies for 13 to 15 minutes, rotating the sheets from top to bottom and front to back at the midway point, until the bottoms and edges are a deep golden brown. Remove the baking sheets from the oven and let the cookies rest on the sheets for a few minutes, then transfer them to racks to cool to room temperature.

Bonne Idée
TOASTED FLOUR SABLÉS: Toast 2¼ cups all-purpose flour as directed, then measure out 2 cups of flour to use in the dough. Follow the instructions for the buckwheat cookies, but use the following ingredients: 2 cups toasted all-purpose flour, 1½ sticks (12 tablespoons; 6 ounces) unsalted butter, ½ teaspoon fine sea salt, ⅔ cup sugar and 1 large egg. If you'd like, you can sprinkle the tops of the cookies with sanding sugar before you bake them.

Another Bonne Idée
TOASTED FLOUR OR BUCKWHEAT SABLÉ SANDWICH COOKIES: Roll either dough out to a thickness of about ⅛ inch and cut out the cookies. If you'd like, dust half of the cookies with sanding sugar. Watch the cookies carefully as they bake, and pull them out of the oven as soon as they are light brown around the edges. When the cookies are cool, pair each plain cookie with a sugarcoated one (or a second plain one if you skipped the sanding sugar) and sandwiching them with jam (I opt for raspberry or apricot), a thin layer of chocolate ganache (page 434) or an equally thin layer of Nutella or Biscoff spread.

Green Tea Sablés

*Makes about
40 cookies*

SERVING: Just because they're made with tea doesn't mean these sablés aren't good with coffee—they are. In fact, they're especially good with espresso. And they're nice with wine too.

STORING: The unbaked logs of dough will keep in the refrigerator for up to 3 days and can be frozen for up to 2 months; cut and bake directly from the freezer. Baked, the cookies will keep in a sealed container for about 4 days at room temperature.

I CAN'T REMEMBER HOW MANY YEARS AGO green-tea sweets became the rage in Paris. For the most part, the tea that was used was matcha (it's still the pastry chefs' favorite), a powdered tea that dissolves in water rather than steeps. Matcha is bitter, vegetal and divisive—a love-it-or-leave-it flavor—which is why I created these shortbread cookies using a mild tea. My preference is for berry- or citrus-flavored green tea, Earl Grey green tea (which gets its charm from bergamot, a type of lemon) or a spiced green tea. If you sniff the tea and like the fragrance, you're bound to like the flavor.

Whether you make the cookie with loose-leaf tea or tea that you spill out of a tea bag, you'll get the most flavor if you pulverize it and then work it into the sugar and salt with your fingertips.

1 stick (8 tablespoons; 4 ounces; 113 grams) unsalted butter	¼ teaspoon fine sea salt
2½ teaspoons flavored green tea leaves	1¼ cups (170 grams) all-purpose flour
¼ cup (50 grams) sugar	Raw sugar, sanding sugar or granulated sugar, for rolling

Remove the butter from the refrigerator and leave it on the counter while prepare the other ingredients. You want the butter to be cool but pliable.

You can crush the tea with a mortar and pestle or you can put it between pieces of parchment or wax paper and crush with the bottom of a glass. Any way you do it, you want to end up with enough crushed tea to measure 1½ teaspoons.

Put the tea, sugar and salt in a large bowl and, using your fingertips, rub the ingredients together until you smell the aroma of the tea. Add the flour and stir everything together to mix well.

Cut the butter into 16 pieces. Drop them into the bowl, toss with your fingertips just to coat the pieces and then set to work rubbing the butter into the flour mixture to make a soft dough that will stick together when you press it between your fingers. Knead the dough gently to work it into a ball and then divide the ball in half.

Shape each piece of dough into a log about 7 inches long. Take care that the logs are solid—it's easy to end up with hollows (you can feel them), which will turn into holes in the cookies. (See page 61 for a nifty way to get solid logs.) Wrap the logs and refrigerate them for at least 3 hours, or freeze for at least 1 hour.

WHEN YOU'RE READY TO BAKE: Position the racks to divide the oven into thirds and preheat the oven to 350 degrees F. Line two baking sheets with parchment paper or silicone baking mats.

Sprinkle some raw, sanding or granulated sugar on the counter and roll the logs in it, just to coat the exterior. Trim the ends of the logs if they're ragged, then slice into rounds that are ⅓ inch thick. Put the cookies on the baking sheets, at least 1 inch apart.

Bake for 12 to 14 minutes, rotating the baking sheets from top to bottom and front to back at the midway point, or until the cookies are golden brown on the edges and bottom but still pale on top. Let the cookies cool on the sheets for a few minutes, then transfer them to racks to cool to room temperature.

Double-Butter Double-Baked Petit Beurre Cookies

Makes about 12 cookies

SERVING: I suggest you serve these cookies topped with something, so that when they crumble, they can add their flavor and marvelous texture to the rest of the dessert. Good toppings are ice cream and crushed berries, roasted rhubarb (page 335) and grapefruit curd and strawberries (page 384). Or serve them as is with tea or coffee.

STORING: The dough for these cookies can be kept in the freezer for up to 2 months, but the cookies themselves are best enjoyed within 2 days. Keep them in a covered container.

EVERY FEW YEARS IN FRANCE, and occasionally in French restaurants in America, I'd be served a dessert that included a butter cookie of such fragility that it would crumble as soon as it was touched. It was not meant to be picked up and eaten out of hand—that would have been impossible. In fact, many times it was served broken, almost like streusel (or the Cocoa Crumbs, page 426). It was invariably part of a more elaborate dessert, something with fruit and sorbet (or a sauce, a curd or a special cream). No matter the accompaniment, it was the cookie that kept me going back for more.

The cookie gets its singular texture and deeply rich flavor from an odd technique that involves making a sablé cookie dough, baking it like streusel, mixing it with more butter and then baking it again. What you get is a *petit beurre* cookie—the kind we know from LU biscuits—but with a lot more *beurre* ("butter"). It's the butter that holds the cookie together, but only just barely.

I've read that the original double-baked cookie recipe came from the nineteenth-century chef and pâtissier Urbain Dubois. My version, chunky and crunchy, is inspired by Dubois and others but is a little different: I beat my dough less and bake my cookies more than most. You can get a whole cookie onto a plate, if you'd like to serve it on its own, but look at it for more than a second, and it will crumble.

1½ cups (204 grams) all-purpose flour	2¼ sticks (9 ounces; 255 grams) unsalted butter, cut into tablespoon-sized pieces, at room temperature
1 cup (100 grams) almond flour	
½ cup (60 grams) confectioners' sugar	
¾ teaspoon fleur de sel or ½ teaspoon fine sea salt	

Center a rack in the oven and preheat the oven to 350 degrees F. Line a baking sheet with parchment paper or a silicone baking mat.

Put the flour, almond flour, confectioners' sugar and salt in the bowl of a stand mixer fitted with the paddle attachment, or in a large bowl in which you can use a hand mixer. Drop 10 tablespoons (5 ounces) of the butter into the bowl. Beat on medium speed until you have crumbs that resemble streusel, about 5 minutes. Turn the crumbs out onto the lined baking sheet and squeeze the crumbs here and there to create pieces of various sizes. This is not crucial—many people bake the mixture straight from the mixer—but I like the kind of textural variety you get if you scrunch the dough.

Bake for 15 to 17 minutes, turning the crumbs with a wide metal spatula every 5 minutes or so. You should have a pale golden brown streusel. Some spots will be darker than others—it's inevitable. Transfer the sheet to a cooling rack and cool the crumbs to room temperature.

When the crumbs are cool, use the parchment paper (or baking mat) they baked on as a funnel to transfer them to the mixer or mixing bowl. Add the remaining 8 tablespoons (4 ounces) butter and beat on medium speed until a dough forms around the paddle or beaters, 2 to 3 minutes. Don't overmix—you want a dough that you can roll, but it's nice if you can retain some of the original haphazard texture. Gather the dough together, shape it into a ball, and press it into a thick disk.

Roll the dough between two sheets of parchment or wax paper, flipping it over to roll both top and bottom and lifting the paper to check that it's not sticking, until it is about ⅓ inch thick (a scant ½ inch is fine too). Slide the sandwiched dough onto a cutting board or baking sheet and freeze it for at least 1 hour, or refrigerate for at least 2 hours. The dough has to be very firm before you can proceed.

WHEN YOU'RE READY TO BAKE: Center a rack in the oven and preheat the oven to 350 degrees F. Line a baking sheet with parchment paper or a silicone baking mat.

Using a 2-inch round cookie cutter, cut out as many rounds of dough as you can. It's almost a sure bet that the cold dough will crack. When it does, press it together; it will be fine when it's baked. Place the pucks of dough on the baking sheet, at least 2 inches apart, since they will spread considerably. Gather the scraps of dough together, put them between sheets of parchment or wax paper and roll out; chill before cutting and baking them.

Bake the cookies for 14 to 16 minutes, rotating the sheet from front to back at the midway point, or until they are golden brown at the center and a deeper brown around the edges. Transfer the baking sheet to a cooling rack and don't even think about trying to budge the cookies now; allow them to cool to room temperature.

Slide the cooled cookies, still on the baking sheet (and still untouched) into the refrigerator and let them chill for 1 hour, then use a wide metal spatula to loosen them and remove them from the sheet.

Palets de Dames, Lille Style

*Makes about
40 cookies*

SERVING: A cup of coffee,
a *palet de dames* and *la vie
est belle.*

STORING: Once the
icing is dry, the cookies
can be put in a covered
container; they'll keep
for up to 3 days at room
temperature. Because
of the icing, the finished
cookies can't be frozen.
However, if you'd like, you
can pack the undipped
cookies airtight and freeze
them for up to 2 months;
defrost and then ice them.

THE WORD *PALET* MEANS "PUCK," and you find it used most often by chocolatiers, who make pucks of ganache and enrobe them in chocolate. But the only thing puckish about these cookies is their adorableness. With wide, flat uppers iced in white, and rounded bottoms, they look like toy tops or open parasols. I saw these cookies in all sizes in every pâtisserie I visited in Lille, the northern French city that borders Belgium. Then I saw them finished with melted rose pralines, the red candies that are the sweet symbol of Lyon, the gastronomic capital of the Rhône-Alpes region. And everywhere I saw them, I bought them—the combination of cakeish cookie and sweet icing is irresistible.

While a plain icing made with confectioners' sugar is the tradition in Lille, there's no reason not to have a little fun with these. Think about adding food coloring to the icing or dividing the icing and creating a few tints. And to make these already festive cookies even more so, you can speckle the still-wet glaze with sanding sugar.

FOR THE COOKIES
- 9 tablespoons (4½ ounces; 128 grams) unsalted butter, at room temperature
- ⅔ cup (132 grams) sugar
  Pinch of fine sea salt
- 2 large eggs, at room temperature
- ¼ teaspoon pure vanilla extract
- 1¼ cups (170 grams) all-purpose flour

FOR THE ICING
- 1 cup (120 grams) confectioners' sugar, sifted
  About 1½ tablespoons whole milk
  A few drops of freshly squeezed lemon juice

TO MAKE THE COOKIES: Working in the bowl of a stand mixer fitted with the paddle attachment, or in a large bowl with a hand mixer, beat the butter on medium speed until smooth and creamy. Add the sugar and salt and beat for another 2 to 3 minutes, until the mixture is again smooth and creamy. Add the eggs one at a time, beating for 1 minute after each egg goes in. Don't be discouraged if the mixture curdles; it will be fine as soon as you add the flour. Beat in the vanilla extract. Reduce the mixer speed to low and add the flour in 3 additions, mixing only until it disappears after each addition. You'll have a very soft dough that might look more like a cake batter than a cookie dough. Scrape the dough into a bowl, press a piece of plastic film against the surface to create an airtight seal and chill the dough for at least 1 hour, or until it is firm. (*The dough can be wrapped airtight and kept in the refrigerator for up to 2 days.*)

WHEN YOU'RE READY TO BAKE: Center a rack in the oven and preheat the oven to 400 degrees F. Line a baking sheet with parchment paper or a silicone baking mat.

You need about 2 teaspoons of dough for each cookie. You can use a small (2-teaspoon capacity) cookie scoop—my favorite tool for this job—or you can use a spoon to scoop out rounded teaspoonfuls of dough, in which case it's best to roll the dough gently between your palms to form balls. Place the scoops or balls of dough about 2 inches apart on the baking sheet.

Bake for 7 to 9 minutes, or until the cookies are set and just slightly brown around the edges. Carefully transfer the cookies to a rack and allow them to cool to room temperature. Repeat with the remaining dough, cooling the baking sheet between batches.

TO MAKE THE ICING: Put the confectioners' sugar in a wide bowl and add 1 tablespoon milk and the lemon juice. Using a small whisk or a fork, stir until you have a smooth icing that forms a ribbon when the whisk or fork is lifted. If the icing is too thick to flow smoothly, add more milk; you might need even more than 1½ tablespoons milk total, in which case it's best to add the additional milk in nano-driplets.

One by one, pick up the cookies and dip one side into the icing, then lift the cookie up and give it a little twirl, so that the excess icing falls back into the bowl. Put the cookie icing side up on a rack and let the icing dry and firm at room temperature.

PARCHMENT PAPER

I didn't learn the joys of parchment paper until I moved to Paris, where wax paper isn't available, aluminum foil is a little wonky (it's more like Mylar) and my silicone baking mats were too big for the pans that fit into my little oven. Parchment paper is as easy to find in Paris as a baguette. I use it to line baking sheets and pans, and I've taken to rolling all my dough (whether tart, tourte, galette or cookie) between sheets of parchment, then using that paper to line the baking sheets.

Parchment is easy to use and makes sliding dough onto a pan or cutting board and into and out of the freezer or fridge a cinch. It's also the best material to use to shape and tighten a log of cookie dough (see page 61) and then to wrap it. You can buy already-cut parchment to line various sizes of pans and you can buy the paper in rolls in the supermarket. I buy large sheets online and cut them to the size I need.

But if you're not a fan, you can roll out dough between sheets of wax paper or plastic film and you can line your baking pans with silicone baking mats (which are expensive, but effective and endlessly reusable) or foil (nonstick is nice).

Jam-Filled Sandwich Cookies

T HESE ARE EVERYWHERE IN FRANCE: simple butter cookies filled with jam and sprinkled with sugar. They make grown-ups as happy as the kids who buy them after school. Because the dough is made with confectioners' sugar and cornstarch, it's soft and just a little fussy to work with. The refrigerator is your friend here—if the cookies are hard to lift off the counter and onto the baking sheet, give them a quick chill; it's the fix-all. The upside of working with this soft dough is that it produces cookies that are particularly tender—just the right texture for their jammy filling. I like raspberry and apricot jams for these cookies, but any of your favorites will work, including marmalade.

Makes about 12 sandwich cookies

SERVING: As pretty as these cookies look— dust them with the confectioners' sugar and they'll look even more festive—they don't need a special occasion to be enjoyed. Jam-Filled Sandwich Cookies can be a kid's after-school snack with milk or a grown-up's indulgence with tea.

STORING: The cookies will keep in an airtight container for up to 2 days at room temperature or in the freezer, well wrapped, for up to 2 months; defrost, still wrapped, overnight in the refrigerator. My preference, though, is to freeze the rolled-out dough, rather than the completed cookies. Wrapped airtight, the dough will keep for up to 2 months; let stand at room temperature for 5 to 10 minutes before cutting out cookies.

½ cup (60 grams) confectioners' sugar

1 stick (8 tablespoons; 4 ounces; 113 grams) unsalted butter, cut into chunks, at room temperature

1 tablespoon sugar

1 cup (136 grams) all-purpose flour

⅓ cup (43 grams) cornstarch

½ teaspoon baking powder

Pinch of fine sea salt

About ¾ cup (240 grams) jam, for filling

Sugar, for sprinkling

Confectioners' sugar, for dusting (optional)

Position a large strainer over the bowl of your stand mixer, or over a large bowl if you're going to use a hand mixer, and shake the confectioners' sugar through it. Drop the pieces of butter into the bowl, add the sugar and beat at low speed with the paddle attachment or hand mixer until smooth.

Put the strainer over the bowl again, add the flour, cornstarch, baking powder and salt, stir them around to combine and shake them onto the butter mixture. Pulse the mixer a few times, so you don't have flying flour, then beat on low speed until the dough comes together. You'll hit a stage where the dough is crumbly—mix on. In another minute or so, the dough will come together and just about clean the sides of the bowl, your signal to stop mixing.

Turn the dough out onto the counter and divide it in half. Shape each half into a disk, kneading the dough gently if necessary to pull it together and shape it.

Put one piece of dough between two sheets of parchment or wax paper and roll it to a thickness of about ⅛ inch. Don't worry about the shape of the dough. Slide the paper-sandwiched dough onto a cutting board or baking sheet. Repeat with the second piece of dough (you can stack the pieces). Refrigerate the dough for at least 2 hours. (*Wrapped well, the dough can be refrigerated for up to 2 days or frozen for up to 2 months. Defrost frozen dough for 5 to 10 minutes before cutting.*)

WHEN YOU'RE READY TO BAKE: Center a rack in the oven and preheat the oven to 350 degrees F. Line two baking sheets with parchment paper or a silicone baking mat.

Pull one piece of dough from the refrigerator and cut out cookies. (Leave the bottom piece of paper in place so that if the dough gets soft and needs a quick chill, you can easily transport it.) I use a 2-inch round cutter, but you can cut these a little larger, if you'd like (of course, the yield will be less). I don't advise making the cookies smaller than 2 inches because they'll be too difficult to fill. Place the cookies on the baking sheet, an inch or so apart, and refrigerate while you cut the second piece of dough. (Reserve the scraps.) Put the second set of cookies on the other baking sheet; refrigerate.

Gather the scraps from both pieces of dough, press them together and roll the dough until it's ⅛ inch thick, then chill until firm enough to cut and make more cookies.

Spoon a little jam onto the center of half of the chilled rounds—¼ to ½ teaspoon is sufficient for a 2-inch cookie. Dip your finger into a bowl of water and, one at a time, lightly moisten the edges of each round, top with an uncovered round and press gently to seal. Sprinkle the tops with sugar.

Bake for 15 to 17 minutes, rotating the pan at the midway point, or until the cookies are golden brown on the bottom and colored only around the edges. The tops may crack, and that's fine. Carefully transfer them to a cooling rack and let them cool to room temperature.

Bake the second sheet of cookies, then cut and bake the remaining dough, making sure the baking sheet is cool.

Dust with confectioners' sugar, if you'd like, right before serving.

Cat's Tongues

**Makes about
18 cookies**

SERVING: In France, small treats like these cookies are usually a snack with a mid afternoon cup of espresso or a go-along with ice cream, mousse or fruit desserts. They're never served as a dessert themselves, but sandwiched with ganache, I think they could make a play for stand-alone status.

STORING: Kept in a dry place—humidity is a *langue de chat*'s mortal enemy—the cookies will hold their flavor and texture for at least 5 days. If you wrap them airtight, they'll keep in the freezer for up to 2 months.

AT'S TONGUES ARE long, thin oval-shaped cookies that are characteristically browned around the edges and paler at the center. Their texture is mostly crisp with a little give, and their light vanilla flavor is sweet, sometimes lightly lemony and mild enough to share a table with coffee, tea, ice cream or mousse. (I think *langues de chat* were the inspiration for Pepperidge Farm Milano cookies, though I have no evidence for this.)

Since my go-to recipe from a baking class I attended more than thirty years ago has become inexplicably problematic—too floury and soft-textured in the center—I had to rework it. I lessened the amount of flour and then raised the oven temperature so the cookies would set better. When I peeked into the oven, some were squiggled and some were straight. Seeing them, a Parisian friend exclaimed, "*Que les cookies sont mignons* ('cute')!" And we both loved their crisp texture and their buttery flavor.

A COUPLE OF WORDS OF ADVICE: It's important that all the ingredients be at room temperature and that the butter be soft (not oily). The measurement for the flour is fussy, but it's what gives the cookies their *mignon* look.

½ stick (4 tablespoons; 2 ounces; 57 grams) unsalted butter, at room temperature

⅓ cup (67 grams) sugar

¼ teaspoon fine sea salt

½ teaspoon pure vanilla extract

2 large egg whites, at room temperature

⅓ cup plus 1 tablespoon (54 grams) all-purpose flour

Center a rack in the oven and preheat the oven to 425 degrees F. Line two baking sheets with parchment paper or silicone baking mats.

Working in the bowl of a stand mixer fitted with the whisk attachment, or in a large bowl with a hand mixer, beat the butter on medium speed until soft and creamy. Add the sugar, salt and vanilla and beat at high speed for 1 to 2 minutes, until the mixture is light and creamy. With the mixer on high, gradually add the egg whites, then beat for another minute after they are incorporated. (The batter may look curdled or unstable.) Reduce the mixer speed to low and add the flour in 2 additions. When the flour is incorporated, ramp up the mixer speed and give the batter one last fast spin; because you won't have much batter, make sure you scrape the bottom of the bowl.

Fit a piping bag with a plain ¼-inch tip and fill the bag with the batter. (Alternatively, you can fill a zipper-lock bag with the batter, push the batter into one corner and snip off the corner.) Using gentle pressure, pipe out cat's tongues that are about ½ inch wide and 3 inches long onto one of the baking sheets; leave at least 2 inches between the strips of batter.

Bake the cookies for 6 to 7 minutes, or until deeply browned around the edges and a very pale gold in the center. Your perfectly straight lines of batter may go all squiggly-wiggly in the oven—that's just the way this batter can be. Transfer the baking sheet to a cooling rack and let the cookies cool for a few minutes before carefully peeling them away from the paper. Cool to room temperature on the rack.

While the first batch is baking, pipe out the remaining batter on the second baking sheet, then bake.

Bonne Idée

MILANO-ISH SANDWICH COOKIES: Spread half of the cookies with chocolate ganache (page 293) and then sandwich them. For Mint Milano fans, add ⅛ teaspoon pure peppermint extract to the ganache; taste and add more, a drop at a time, until you get the intensity you like. If your cookies are too squiggly to sandwich, just spread one side of each one, or dip the ends in ganache; refrigerate to set the chocolate.

Stained Glass Cookies

SERVING: Put these on a white or clear glass plate so that their colors sparkle.

STORING: These will keep for 1 day in a cool, dry place. If you make plain cookies, they will keep for about 4 days—it's the candy that has a tendency to turn soft and sticky.

EVERY FEBRUARY you can count on two things being in the French news: pictures of pastries and chocolates for Valentine's Day; and pictures of the president petting a cow. February is when the *Salon de l'Agriculture* sets up in a huge convention space in Paris, and it's absolutely obligatory for the president to make an appearance with at least one farm animal and at least one made-in-France piece of farm gear. I wish you could have seen the always elegant M. Chirac with a cow.

I don't go to the fair for the animals or the heavy machinery (although every French schoolboy does); I go for the food, and there's so much of it that it's hard to take it all in. The Salon is where I saw a stained glass cookie that delighted me.

The "windows" of the stained glass cookies were made from heirloom candies and speckled with seeds and spices, and the parts of the cookies that weren't cut out were decorated with tiny bits of herbs. France has a long history of artisanal candy making—centuries ago, candies were made in monasteries and some still are—and old-fashioned candies continue to be cherished.

Back in New York, it became clear that heirloom wasn't going to be practical, and so that's when I started using Life Savers. I know they're not the same as violet candies from Flavigny, but . . .

I opt for simple—I cut the dough into small rounds and then cut out a smaller round to fill with crushed candy—but you can go wild with these, cutting out many windows in whatever shapes you like. Let your inner cathedral builder loose. This dough is also delicious baked into plain cookies.

FOR THE COOKIES	FOR THE DECORATION
2 sticks (8 ounces; 226 grams) unsalted butter, at room temperature	About 15 Life Savers or other hard candies
½ cup (100 grams) sugar	1 large egg, for glazing
½ teaspoon fine sea salt	Small seeds, such as poppy or flax (optional)
1 teaspoon pure vanilla extract	Fresh herb leaves, such as tarragon, thyme or cilantro (optional)
2½ cups (340 grams) all-purpose flour	Sugar, for sprinkling

TO MAKE THE COOKIES: Working in the bowl of a stand mixer fitted with the paddle attachment, or in a large bowl with a hand mixer, beat the butter, sugar and salt together at medium speed until smooth and creamy, about 3 minutes. Reduce the speed to low and beat in the vanilla. Add the flour all at once and pulse the mixer on and off a few times to start blending it in. With the mixer on the lowest speed, continue to mix in the flour, scraping the bowl as necessary, until you have what look like curds. Turn the dough out onto a work surface and finish blending the dough by pulling off small hunks of it and pushing each hunk across the work surface with the heel of your hand. Then gather the smooth dough into a ball, divide it in half and press each half into a disk.

Working with one piece of dough at a time, roll the dough between sheets of parchment or wax paper to a thickness of about ⅛ inch; thinner is better than thicker here. Slide the paper-sandwiched dough onto a baking sheet or cutting board (you can stack the pieces of dough) and freeze for at least 1 hour. (*The dough can be wrapped airtight and frozen for up to 2 months.*)

WHEN YOU'RE READY TO BAKE: Center a rack in the oven and preheat the oven to 350 degrees F. Line a baking sheet with parchment paper or a silicone baking mat.

The candies need to be pulverized. I do this with a mortar and pestle, but you can put them between sheets of parchment or wax paper and bash them with a rolling pin or skillet. Crush the candies by color—you don't want to blend colors.

TO CUT OUT THE COOKIES: I use a 2-inch round cutter—though you can cut these into any shape and size you want—and, to make the windows, a ¼-inch pastry tip.

Beat the egg with a splash of cold water.

Remove one piece of dough from the freezer and cut out cookies. As you cut them, place them on the lined baking sheet, about 1 inch apart. Use the pastry tip to cut out one or more windows in each cookie. Fill the cutouts with crushed candy, keeping the candy level with the cookie. (After I cut out the windows with the small end of the pastry tip and clean away the little plugs of dough, I insert the tip in each hole and use it as a funnel to fill the cutouts with the candy—it's a neat trick.) Sprinkle 2 or 3 seeds onto the candy in each window, if you're using them. Using a pastry brush, brush the dough very lightly with the egg wash, avoiding the candy. If you're using herbs, "paste" them onto the dough. Finally, lightly sprinkle the cookies with sugar. (Save the dough scraps to combine with the scraps from the other piece of dough.)

Bake for 8 to 9 minutes, or until the cookies are almost firm and the candy has melted but not turned brown. You'll want to bake these longer because the cookie part will be pale, but resist. (I've overbaked them so that every candy color went to brown. They weren't as attractive as they might have been, though the golden cookies were still good.) Transfer the baking sheet to a cooling rack and allow the cookies to cool until the candy hardens, then lift them off the sheet with an offset spatula and put on a rack.

Repeat with the remaining dough: Gather the scraps together, reroll them, chill and make more cookies, cooling the baking sheet before using it.

Bonne Idée

STAINED GLASS COOKIE DECORATIONS: If you'd like to use these cookies as ornaments for a Christmas tree, cut the cutouts larger and, right before you slide them into the oven, poke a small hole in the top of each cookie—I use a drinking straw to do this—so that you'll be able to run ribbons through the baked cookies.

Coco Rochers

Makes about 30 cookies

SERVING: In restaurants, *rochers* usually appear as an after-dessert dessert, a *mignardise* to be enjoyed with coffee or tea. At home, I think of them as an anytime nibble, good with coffee or tea no matter when and always good with ice cream.

STORING: The dough can be kept in the refrigerator for up to 5 days. Once baked, the cookies should be packed in a tin or plastic container; they'll keep for at least 3 days. They may get a little drier, but they won't get less delicious.

THIS IS A DOUBLE-O MACAROON. Not a delicate, colorful, filled-with-cream, Parisian one-O macaron (page 288), but a macaroon as most of us Americans know the little cookie: lightly browned and crunchy on the outside, pale and chewy on the inside and full of coconut inside and out. The cookies are called *rochers,* or "rocks," because of their shape, but they can be scooped (my preference), rolled between your palms into round rocks (easy and pretty) or pinched into pyramids, in which case they're sometimes called *congolais.*

The dough contains just four ingredients—shredded coconut, egg whites, sugar and vanilla—and it's cooked on the stove before the cookies are baked. This precook means that the *rochers* go into the oven primarily to dry and crisp up their outer crust. It also means that you can keep the dough in the refrigerator for a few days and scoop out and bake *rochers* on demand.

A WORD ON THE COCONUT: *Rochers* should be made with unsweetened coconut, preferably fine or medium shred—sweetened coconut won't give you the right texture.

2½ cups (200 grams) unsweetened shredded coconut	4 large egg whites
	⅔ cup (132 grams) sugar
	1 teaspoon pure vanilla extract

Put the coconut, egg whites and sugar in a medium saucepan and stir to mix well. Place the saucepan over medium-low heat and cook, stirring constantly, until the mixture is hot to the touch, 7 to 10 minutes. You want to heat the ingredients without coloring them.

Scrape the dough into a heatproof bowl and stir in the vanilla. Press a piece of plastic film against the surface and chill for several hours; overnight is best. (*The dough can be refrigerated for up to 5 days.*)

WHEN YOU'RE READY TO BAKE: Center a rack in the oven and preheat the oven to 300 degrees F. Use an insulated baking sheet or stack two baking sheets one on top of the other. Line the (top) sheet with parchment paper or a silicone baking mat (you need to double-pan these to properly bake the tops without burning the bottoms).

Scoop out mounds of dough using a small cookie scoop with a capacity of about 2 teaspoons, packing the dough into the scoop and then releasing it onto the baking sheet. Leave just ½ inch or so between the mounds—these don't spread much. Alternatively, you can scoop the dough with a spoon and press the mixture into balls between the palms of your hands. If you do this, you might want to wet your fingers lightly and gently pinch each mound to form a little pyramid.

Bake the *rochers* for 20 to 25 minutes, until they are lightly golden and feel slightly firm to the touch. It's hard to judge doneness with these cookies, since they are already cooked when you put them in the oven and all you're doing is drying them out and setting their texture. Transfer the baking sheet to a rack and let the cookies cool on the sheet.

Basque Macarons

*Makes about
40 cookies*

SERVING: These are a
perfect accompanying
cookie, good with ice
cream, sorbet, fruit and
creamy desserts, but I
like them best with strong
coffee or hard cider.

STORING: If you are going
to keep these for a few
days, put them in a cool,
dry place—humidity will
make them not just chewy,
but sticky. If your house
is dry, leave them out in a
basket. If the cookies get
too soft, try bringing them
back by warming them
for a few minutes in a
350-degree-F oven.

YOU FIND MACARONS almost everywhere you go in France, and everywhere you find them, the people of that region are pretty much convinced that theirs are the best or the most authentic—or the best *and* the most authentic. I can't vouch for the authenticity of this recipe from the Pays Basque, where the cookies are called *muxuak*, but I can stand behind the buttonish sweets' full almond flavor and wonderful texture, which is both crisp and chewy, inching closer to totally chewy as time passes.

With the exception of the sugar, which is granulated, not confectioners', this recipe mimics smooth-topped Parisian Macarons (page 288), but you'd never know it to look at them or even to taste them.

Since these simple macarons aren't filled and sandwiched the way their slicker cousins are, think about adding a little ground spice to the sugar-almond mixture to give them a spot more flavor. (I often add cinnamon.) Alternatively, you can rub grated lemon or orange zest into the sugar before you stir it together with the almonds.

3 large egg whites, at room temperature	1 cup (200 grams) sugar
1¼ cups (125 grams) almond flour	½ teaspoon ground cinnamon or other spice (optional)
	Pinch of fine sea salt

Center a rack in the oven and preheat the oven to 400 degrees F. Line two baking sheets with parchment paper or silicone baking mats.

You need to divide the egg whites in half. I think the easiest way to do this is to weigh the 3 whites (I weigh them in grams, because it makes the math easier) and then to divide them by weight. Another way is to put the whites in a Pyrex measuring cup. Stir gently, just to break them up and then divide them. Put half of the whites in the bowl of a stand mixer fitted with the whisk attachment, or in a medium bowl in which you can use a hand mixer. Set aside.

Whisk the almond flour, sugar and cinnamon or spice, if you're using it, in a large bowl. Add the remaining egg whites and, using a sturdy flexible spatula or wooden spoon, mix until the dry ingredients are evenly moistened. This is easier said than done. You'll find yourself not so much mixing as mashing, and you'll end up with a very firm, compact mixture. It's not pretty, but it's right.

Add the salt to the egg whites in the bowl and whip the whites until they're stiff but still glossy. Scoop about one quarter of the whites onto the dough and stir, cutting into the dough, to incorporate the whites and lighten the dough a little. Turn the rest of the whites out onto the dough and stir and fold and mix as best as you can; you'll have a moist but still heavy batter.

You can spoon these macarons out or pipe them using a piping bag fitted with a ¼-inch plain tip (or a zipper-lock bag—fill it, seal it and snip off a corner). But I prefer using a small cookie scoop, one with a capacity of 2 teaspoons.

Scoop, spoon or pipe the dough out, about 2 teaspoons at a time, so that the mounds are about 2 inches apart. Fill both baking sheets, though you'll bake just one sheet at a time.

Bake the cookies for 8 minutes, then open the oven door briefly to let some of the moisture out and rotate the baking sheet. Turn the oven temperature down to 350 degrees F and bake for another 3 to 4 minutes, until the cookies are golden all over and deeply golden around the edges. Transfer the baking sheet to a cooling rack, but don't try to budge the macarons yet. Return the oven's temperature to 400 degrees F and when it comes to temperature, bake the second batch.

Allow the macarons to rest on the baking sheets for 15 minutes before peeling them off the paper or mat. Finish cooling the cookies on a rack.

Parisian Macarons (page 288)

Parisian Macarons

**Makes about
45 sandwiched
macarons**

SERVING: Macarons
are usually served as an
afternoon treat with tea
or coffee or after dinner
or sometimes even after
dessert. Take them out of
the refrigerator about
30 minutes before serving.

STORING: You must keep
the macarons refrigerated
for 1 day before serving,
and they can stay in the
fridge for up to 4 days. They
can also be frozen, packed
airtight, for up to 2 months;
defrost, still wrapped,
overnight in the refrigerator.

ABOUT TWENTY YEARS AGO my friend Anne Noblet brought me a box of beautiful chocolates from her home in Angers, in the Loire Valley, and told me that the chocolatier was also a pastry chef, a very good one. I quickly asked if he made wonderful macarons, and she just as quickly answered, "Macarons! Only Parisians care about them!" She was right then, but wouldn't be at all right now. The macaron craze has spread across France and even jumped to America.

These are not double-O macaroons (see page 282 for a recipe for those), not Passover macaroons, coconut macaroons or even amaretti types. They are small, sweet almond meringue cookies that, when properly made, puff into a smooth-topped matte round with a craggy ring on the bottom, referred to as "the foot." The foot is the grand prize of macaron making and, like the smooth, uncracked top, it's a sign of a job well done. There's one more sign, which only becomes visible when you break into the cookie: a chewy interior beneath that outer shell.

The shells themselves—made of confectioners' sugar, almond flour, egg whites and a sugar syrup—are always beautifully and fancifully colored but never have much taste. Taste is not their primary job. They were created to look pretty, provide crunch and sandwich a filling, the star of the show and an element that invites fantasy and fun. Some pâtissiers have dozens of flavors, and no matter how many there are, each week there are new ones. Go wild with these—everyone else does.

This recipe is long, not because there's so much to do or because what you have to do is difficult, but because there are so many things to look for. I've provided the best instructions I can, but you still might have to make these a couple of times to get them just right. You've got to learn about the batter and your oven. Much of what you have to do goes against established practice, so experience and trust are your best guides. Happily, most less-than-perfect macs still taste good. The photograph is on pages 286 to 287.

A WORD ON EGG WHITES: Some pros leave their egg whites at room temperature for a few days before using them—you get a better meringue with old (more liquidy) whites. I leave them out overnight. If that makes you uncomfortable, separate the eggs and leave the whites in the refrigerator for a day or two.

A WORD ON ALMOND FLOUR: The almond flour has to be absolutely free of lumps, so you must sift it or press it through a sieve. Never skip this step—it's imperative.

A WORD ON MEASURING: If you have a scale, use it to measure the ingredients for this recipe. You want equal weights of almond flour and confectioners' sugar. You also want 150 ml of egg whites. That's about 5 whites.

Just turn your glass measuring cup around to the metric side, you'll have an easy time of it. It's also easier to use the metric measure should you have to divide the egg whites in half.

A WORD ON TOOLS: Because you have to beat the egg whites and, at the same time, pour hot sugar syrup into the bowl, it's best to work in the bowl of a stand mixer. You'll also need a candy thermometer. And while you can certainly bake the macarons on parchment-lined baking sheets, this is a case in which silicone baking mats do a better job.

AND FINALLY, A WORD ON TIMING: Filled macarons need to soften in the refrigerator for at least 1 day. Sorry, it's the rule.

FOR THE MACARONS

2 cups (200 grams) almond flour (made from blanched almonds)

1²/₃ cups (200 grams) confectioners' sugar

150 ml egg whites (about 5 large egg whites; see previous page), at room temperature

Food coloring (optional)

1 cup (200 grams) sugar

¼ cup (60 ml) water

CHOICE OF FILLING

Chocolate Ganache (page 434) or White Chocolate Ganache (page 435)

Salted Caramel Filling (page 436)

Thick jam

Lime Cream (page 184)

TO MAKE THE MACARONS: If you are going to bake the macarons on baking sheets lined with parchment paper, you might want to make a template. Using a cookie cutter as your guide, trace circles about 1½ inches in diameter on each sheet of paper, leaving about 2 inches between them, then turn the papers over on the baking sheets. If you're using silicone mats, there's nothing to do but line the baking sheets with them. Fit a large pastry bag with a plain ½-inch tip. (Alternatively, you can use a zipper-lock bag—fill the bag, seal it and snip off a corner.)

Place a strainer over a large bowl and press the almond flour and confectioners' sugar through the mesh. This is a tedious job, but much depends on it, so be assiduous. Then whisk to blend.

Put half of the egg whites in the bowl of a stand mixer fitted with the whisk attachment.

Add food coloring, if you're using it, to the remaining egg whites, stir and then pour the whites over the almond flour and confectioners' sugar. Using a flexible spatula, mix and mash the whites into the dry ingredients until you have a homogeneous paste.

Bring the granulated sugar and water to a boil in a small saucepan over medium heat. If there are spatters on the sides of the pan, wash them down with a pastry brush dipped in cold water. Insert a candy thermometer and cook the syrup until it reaches 243 to 245 degrees F. (This can take about 10 minutes.)

Meanwhile, beat the egg whites on medium speed until they hold medium-firm peaks. Reduce the mixer speed to low and keep mixing until the sugar syrup comes up to temperature.

When the sugar syrup reaches the right temperature, take the pan off the heat and remove the thermometer. With the mixer on low speed, pour in the hot syrup, trying to pour it between the whirring whisk and the side of the bowl. You'll have spatters—it's impossible not to—but ignore them; whatever you do, don't try to incorporate them into the meringue. Raise the mixer speed to high and beat until the meringue cools to room temperature, about 10 minutes—you'll be able to tell by touching the bottom of the bowl.

Give the almond flour mixture another turn with the spatula, then scrape the meringue over it and fold everything together. Don't be gentle here: Use your spatula to cut through the meringue and almond mixture, bring some of the batter from the bottom up over the top and then press it against the side of the bowl. The action is the same as the one you used to get the egg whites into the almonds and sugar: mix and mash. Keep folding and mixing and mashing until when you lift the spatula, the batter flows off it in a thick band, like lava.

If you want to add more food coloring, do it now.

Spoon half of the batter into the pastry bag (or zipper-lock bag) and, holding the bag vertically 1 inch above one of the baking sheets, pipe out 1½-inch rounds. Don't worry if you have a point in the center of each round—it will dissolve into the batter. Holding the baking sheet with both hands, raise it about 8 inches above the counter and let it fall (unnerving but necessary to de-bubble the batter and promote smooth tops). Refill the bag, pipe batter onto the second sheet and drop it onto the counter.

Set the baking sheets aside in a cool, dry place to allow the batter to form a crust. When you can gingerly touch the top of the macarons without having batter stick to your finger, you're ready to bake. (Depending on room temperature and humidity, this can take 15 to 30 minutes, sometimes more.)

While the batter is crusting, center a rack in the oven and preheat the oven to 350 degrees F.

Bake the macarons, one sheet at a time, for 6 minutes. Rotate the pan and bake for another 6 to 9 minutes, or until the macarons can be lifted from the mat or can be carefully peeled away from the paper. The bottoms will feel just a little soft. Slide the silicone mat or parchment off the baking sheet onto a counter and set aside to cool to room temperature.

Repeat with the second baking sheet of macarons.

Peel the macarons off the silicone or parchment and match them up for sandwiching.

TO SANDWICH THE MACARONS: Line a baking sheet with parchment paper. You can use a teaspoon or a piping bag to fill the macarons. It's up to you to decide how much filling you'll want to use; some pastry chefs use enough filling to form a layer about half as high as one of the shells and others make the filling as tall as a shell, so they've got equal layers of shell, filling and shell. Spoon or pipe some filling onto the flat side of a macaron and sandwich it with its mate, gently twisting the top macaron until the filling spreads to the edges. Repeat with the remaining macarons and filling, then put the macarons on the baking sheet and cover with plastic film. (Or, if it's easier for you, pack the macs into a container.) Chill for at least 24 hours, or for up to 4 days.

Macaron Biscotti

Makes as many as you want.

SERVING: These simple cookies are so grown-up that they should be served with Champagne, sherry, a dessert wine or strong espresso.

STORING: Like other biscotti, these are good keepers. In a cool, dry place, they'll be fine for at least 1 week.

I BOUGHT A BAG OF DOUBLE-BAKED MACARONS from Sadaharu Aoki in Paris not knowing what they were, just because they looked so snackable. A couple of bags later, I learned how the small, buttonish cookies were made: Macaron shells—the cookies before they're sandwiched—are dipped in butter and then baked again. What you get are crunchy almond cookies that crack at first bite. It's hard to find a name for them, but biscotti is close.

This is not really a recipe, because there are no real quantities to give. All you need are some unfilled macarons and some butter. Having a little Champagne or sherry on hand is nice too.

Unsalted butter
Macaron shells (page 288),
    freshly baked or days old

Center a rack in the oven and preheat the oven to 325 degrees F. Line a baking sheet with parchment paper. (Parchment is better than a silicone baking mat here.)

You need enough melted butter to dip and coat the macarons, so take a guess at the amount and put it in a small saucepan or skillet (to melt it on the stovetop) or in a microwave-safe bowl (to melt it in the microwave). Melt the butter. (Clarified butter would be ideal, because it won't give you specks of milk solids on the shell. I leave it to you to clarify or not. I don't; I bet Sadaharu Aoki does.)

One by one, dip the mac shells into the melted butter to coat them completely and place on the baking sheet.

Bake for 15 to 20 minutes, or until the macs are golden brown and firm. There's really no overbaking here, just overbrowning, but if you underbake them, they'll be uninteresting. Transfer the sheet to a rack and let the biscotti cool to room temperature. As they cool, you'll see that they absorb any butter that might have been bubbling around their craggy feet when they were in the oven.

Cocoa Crunch
Meringue Sandwiches

THESE FALL SOMEWHERE BETWEEN traditional meringues and dacquoise, the French meringue made with nut flour. Instead of nut flour, I opt for chopped toasted nuts and end up with a cocoa meringue that's airy (as it should be) and crunchy (as I always want it to be). While you can certainly make these in the classic kiss shape so popular for meringues, I prefer to pipe the batter into dainty disks and then sandwich them together with a thick layer of creamy dark chocolate ganache. Done this way, the sandwiches might remind you of another member of the meringue family: macarons.

If you're having a party, you can double (or even triple) this recipe.

FOR THE MERINGUES
- ¼ cup (30 grams) confectioners' sugar
- 2 tablespoons unsweetened cocoa powder
- 2 large egg whites, at room temperature
- Pinch of fine sea salt
- 2 tablespoons sugar

- ¼ cup (30 grams) almonds or walnuts, lightly toasted, cooled and very finely chopped

FOR THE FILLING
- 2 ounces (57 grams) bittersweet or semisweet chocolate, finely chopped
- ¼ cup (60 ml) heavy cream
- 1 tablespoon unsalted butter

Makes 8 meringue sandwiches

SERVING: These are best served cold. They're lovely as part of a pastry sampler and thoroughly satisfying on their own.

STORING: The cookies are really at their finest the day they're made—if you keep these in the fridge too long, they become soft and sticky. As with all meringues, these should be kept in a dry place.

TO MAKE THE MERINGUES: Center a rack in the oven and preheat the oven to 250 degrees F. Trace sixteen 2-inch circles on a piece of parchment paper, flip the paper over and use it to line a baking sheet. It will be your template for piping the meringues.

Sift the confectioners' sugar and cocoa together onto a sheet of parchment or wax paper.

Pour the egg whites into the bowl of a stand mixer fitted with the whisk attachment, or into a large bowl in which you can use a hand mixer. Add the salt and beat the whites on medium speed until they start to turn opaque. Still beating, gradually add the sugar, then turn up the mixer speed to medium-high and beat until the whites hold stiff, glossy peaks.

Add the cocoa mixture to the meringue and, with a flexible spatula, start to fold the cocoa mixture into the meringue. When you've got half of the mixture in, add the nuts and continue to fold until everything is well incorporated. Take a peek at what's happening at the bottom of the bowl; if something's lurking there, fold it in.

Spoon half of the batter into a pastry bag fitted with a ½-inch tip (or use a zipper-lock bag; seal it and then cut a ½-inch-wide opening from one of the corners) and pipe out circles onto the template. Start in the middle of a circle and work your way out in a spiral. Alternatively, you can spoon out mounds of meringue.

Bake for 90 minutes without opening the oven door. Turn off the oven and let the meringues stay for another hour with the door closed.

Transfer the baking sheet to a cooling rack. When you're ready to make the sandwiches, peel the paper away from the meringues.

TO MAKE THE FILLING: Put the chocolate in a heatproof bowl. Bring the cream and butter to a boil in a microwave oven or on the stovetop. Pour the hot cream over the chocolate and wait for 30 seconds, then, using a whisk, begin stirring the ingredients together, starting at the center of the bowl. Stir in gradually widening concentric circles until you have a dark, smooth, glossy ganache. Set the ganache aside to firm at room temperature—a process that could take 1 hour or more—or quick-chill it: Put the bowl in a larger bowl filled with ice cubes and water and stir the ganache until it firms enough to spread or pipe, 5 to 10 minutes. (You can also refrigerate the ganache for about 15 minutes; just make sure you check on it so it doesn't get too firm.)

TO ASSEMBLE THE SANDWICHES: Fit a small pastry bag with an open or closed star tip (or use a snipped zipper-lock bag) and fill it with the ganache. Turn half of the meringues bottom side up and pipe a rosette or spiral of ganache on each. Top each with another meringue, bottom side down, and twist until the ganache spreads and glues the sandwich together. (You can also spoon the ganache onto the meringues.) Refrigerate until firm.

Almond Stripes

SERVING: If you'd like, you can dust the cookies with more confectioners' sugar just before serving. Dusted or not, the cookies are nice with coffee or tea or as part of a cookie plate.

STORING: Packed into a container with sheets of parchment or wax paper between the layers, the cookies will keep for at least 3 days at room temperature.

Bonne Ideé

Dip one or both ends of each cookie into melted bittersweet or semisweet or white chocolate, let the excess drip back into the bowl, dunk the ends into sprinkles, if you like, and then put the cookies on a baking sheet lined with parchment or wax paper. Refrigerate until the chocolate is set.

YOU FIND THESE PIPED COOKIES in small-town pâtisseries, the old-fashioned kind where nothing is fancier than an apple tart. They're plain looking, but they have a lingering flavor of butter and a hint of sweetness that makes them as addictive as potato chips.

A WORD ON THE EGG WHITE: I know how fussy it is to give a measurement for just a spoonful of egg white, but that's what you need.

7 tablespoons (3½ ounces; 99 grams) unsalted butter, at room temperature	1 tablespoon egg white, lightly beaten
¾ cup (75 grams) almond flour	1 cup (136 grams) all-purpose flour
½ cup (100 grams) sugar	
Pinch of fine sea salt	Confectioners' sugar,
Pinch of ground cinnamon (optional)	for dusting

Center a rack in the oven and preheat the oven to 350 degrees F. Line two baking sheets with parchment paper or silicone baking mats.

Working in the bowl of a stand mixer fitted with the paddle attachment, or in a large bowl with a hand mixer, beat the butter, almond flour, sugar, salt and cinnamon, if you're using it, on medium speed for about 3 minutes, or until you have a smooth, creamy mixture. Scrape down the bowl and add the bit of egg white, beating until it is incorporated. Reduce the mixer speed to low and add the all-purpose flour, mixing only until it disappears. You'll have a soft dough.

Fit a piping bag with an open-star tip—I use a tip that's a scant ½ inch in diameter—and spoon in half of the dough. (If you don't have a pastry bag, fill a zipper-lock bag with the dough, seal it and snip off a corner. You won't have stripes, but you'll have a good cookie.) Squeeze out cookies that are about 2½ inches long onto one of the baking sheets, leaving at least 1½ inches of space between the ribbons of dough. Dust the cookies lightly with confectioners' sugar.

Bake the cookies for 8 to 10 minutes, or until golden, particularly around the edges. Leave the cookies on the sheet for a minute or two, until they are firm enough to safely transfer to a cooling rack; transfer to the rack and cool to room temperature.

While the first batch of cookies is in the oven, pipe the remaining dough onto the second baking sheet. When you remove the first batch, slide the second sheet into the oven to bake.

The baking ingredients I stock up on for baking in France are almost the same as those I always have on hand in America—butter, flour, sugar, eggs—but there's one big exception: nut flour. The French use almond and hazelnut flour much more than we do—so much that you can buy it in cellophane packets even in late-night convenience stores. It's a staple, not a specialty, and the only explanation I can come up with is that nut flour took precedence over wheat centuries ago, when fine-ground wheat, like sugar, was a luxury, but I have no proof of that.

When I began baking years ago, getting almond flour wasn't easy. I could order it freshly ground from a Hungarian market in New York City, but most of the time, I made my own, grinding nuts in a food processor with a little sugar to keep them from turning into butter. But ever since Bob's Red Mill almond meal/flour started appearing on supermarket shelves, I've been a steady customer and I keep a stash in my freezer. (Bob's Red Mill also makes hazelnut meal/flour, which you can use instead of almond flour if you prefer.)

The company uses the words "meal" and "flour" interchangeably, so when a recipe specifies almond flour, as mine do, almond meal will be just fine. All my recipes will work with homemade nut flour as well.

Excellent nut flours are also available from the King Arthur catalog. Look for them online.

Edouard's Chocolate Chip Cookies

SERVING: The cookies are good warm or at room temperature; good with coffee, good with tea and terrific with milk (a beverage I've never seen a grown French person sip); and even good with Armagnac.

STORING: The best way to maintain the cookies' chewiness is to store them in a zipper-lock plastic bag; they'll stay fresh for about 3 days. You can keep them longer, of course, just know that they'll get a little firmer as time passes. Or pack them into an airtight container and freeze them for up to 2 months.

WHEN EDOUARD BOBIN, the co-owner of one of the sweetest small bistros in Paris, Le Pantruche, said he would give me the recipe for his favorite hazelnut cookie, I knew the minute I read the one-word title, Cookies, that chocolate chips would be involved. See the word *cookies* (or "*les cookies*") in France, as you do nowadays in glossy magazines, modern bakeshops and trendy cafés, and it's a pretty risk-free bet that the sweet will turn out to be a chocolate chipper. If there are nuts, they may be hazelnuts, pecans, walnuts or macadamias; there may even be a few M&M's-type candies pressed into the dough; and the chocolate can be any kind. Whatever the case, the basic cookie is always a play on the American chocolate chip.

And so it was with Edouard's cookies. In fact, as I looked at the recipe, I thought it was the standard back-of-the-bag recipe. It had the American mix of baking powder and baking soda (the French mostly use packets with the two leavening agents already combined), the same amount of chocolate chips as you get in a U.S. bag and the same number of eggs as in the classic American recipe. I'd hoped for something new, and I didn't think this was going to be it.

But I hadn't noticed a couple of important differences: Edouard called for almost half again as much flour (by weight) as the classic recipe, and the nuts were ground not chopped, acting even more like flour. The cookies were chubby and chewy and just a little soft at the center—altogether great. If this is what the French think of as American cookies, we Americans can be proud.

3½ cups (476 grams) all-purpose flour	1 cup (200 grams) packed light brown sugar
1¼ teaspoons fine sea salt	1½ teaspoons pure vanilla extract
¾ teaspoon baking soda	2 large eggs, at room temperature
½ teaspoon baking powder	12 ounces (340 grams) semisweet or bittersweet chocolate, coarsely chopped (or 2 cups chocolate chips)
2 sticks (8 ounces; 226 grams) unsalted butter, at room temperature	
1 cup (200 grams) sugar	1½ cups (150 grams) hazelnut or almond flour

Whisk the flour, salt, baking soda and baking powder together in a medium bowl.

Working in the bowl of a stand mixer fitted with the paddle attachment, or in a large bowl with a hand mixer, beat the butter on medium speed for about 1 minute, until smooth. Add both sugars and beat for another 2 minutes or so, until well blended. Beat in the vanilla. Add the eggs one at a time, beating for a minute after each egg goes in. Reduce the mixer speed to low and add the dry ingredients in 4 or 5 additions, mixing only until each addition is just incorporated. (Because you're going to add more ingredients after the flour, it's good not to be too thorough.) Still on low speed, mix in the chocolate and nut flour.

Divide the dough in half, wrap each piece in plastic film and refrigerate for at least 2 hours. (*The dough can be refrigerated for up to 3 days. Or, if it's more convenient for you, you can scoop the dough now and freeze it in balls. You won't need to defrost the cookies, but you will need to bake them a little longer.*)

WHEN YOU'RE READY TO BAKE: Center a rack in the oven and preheat the oven to 350 degrees F. Line two baking sheets with parchment paper or silicone baking mats.

Edouard says to scoop the dough into mounds the size of golf balls. A medium cookie scoop with a capacity of 1½ tablespoons is just right here, but you can also spoon the dough out using a rounded tablespoon of dough for each cookie. Place the dough on the lined sheets, about 2 inches apart.

Bake the cookies one sheet at a time for 8 minutes and then, using a metal spatula, gently press each mound down just a little; rotate the baking sheet. Bake for another 7 minutes or so, until the cookies are pale brown. They'll still be slightly soft in the center, but that's fine—they'll firm up as they cool. Pull the sheet from the oven and allow the cookies to rest for 1 minute, then, using a wide metal spatula, carefully transfer them to racks to cool to room temperature.

Repeat with the remainder of the dough, always using a cool baking sheet.

The Rugelach
That Won Over France

AFTER I HAD BAKED RUGELACH IN A HURRY to use up on-hand ingredients before flying to Paris one year, my husband, Michael, offered a few to the French flight crew, and we were treated like royalty for the next seven hours. The rugelachs' natural deliciousness and the combination of coconut, peanuts, milk chocolate and dried cherries were the main attractions, but what fascinated them was that the cookies were made with cream cheese, an ingredient they thought was reserved only for cheesecakes and bagels. They had no idea that it could make dough so tender, light and flaky. As an attendant on the Air France flight said after I wrote out the recipe for her, "I thought you'd made puff pastry. I can't believe you use cream cheese and that it's this easy."

Makes about 48 cookies

SERVING: Tea, preferably black tea—it's what's right with these.

STORING: The rugelach will keep for a couple of days in a closed tin, but I think the cream cheese dough really shows off its best qualities the day it's made. Like puff pastry, which it resembles, it has a tendency to lose its flakiness and become a tad heavy after day one. Happily, the unbaked rolls, the unbaked but sliced cookies and even the baked rugelach can be wrapped airtight and frozen for up to 2 months. You can bake them straight from the freezer.

FOR THE DOUGH

- 4 ounces (113 grams) cold cream cheese
- 1 stick (8 tablespoons; 4 ounces; 113 grams) cold unsalted butter
- 1 cup (136 grams) all-purpose flour
- ¼ teaspoon fine sea salt

FOR THE FILLING

- ¾ cup (90 grams) sweetened shredded coconut
- ½ cup (60 grams) lightly toasted pecans, chopped
- 3 ounces (85 grams) milk or semisweet chocolate, finely chopped
- ⅓ cup (about 55 grams) plump, moist dried cherries or raisins, chopped or snipped
- 2 tablespoons (1 ounce; 28 grams) unsalted butter, melted and cooled
- 3 tablespoons sugar mixed with ¼ teaspoon ground cinnamon, or more to taste
- 1 large egg, for glazing
  Sanding or granulated sugar, for dusting

TO MAKE THE DOUGH: Take the cream cheese and butter out of the refrigerator 10 minutes before you're ready to start cooking and cut each into 4 chunks. You want them to be slightly softened but still cool.

Put the flour and salt in a food processor, scatter over the pieces of cream cheese and butter and pulse the machine 6 to 10 times, until the flour coats the chunks. Process, scraping down the sides of the bowl often, until the dough forms large curds. Stop at the curd stage; you don't want the dough to form a ball.

Turn the dough out onto a work surface, gather it into a ball and divide it in half. Shape each half into a square, wrap the squares in plastic film and chill for at least 2 hours. (*The dough can be refrigerated for up to 1 day.*)

If you discover that you like
rugelach, you'll discover
lots of different fillings. For
many years, my favorite
filling was warmed jam,
cinnamon sugar, nuts,
raisins or currants and bits
of chocolate, but you can
make wonderful cookies
without the jam and/or
chocolate. Because the
dough itself isn't sweet, you
can use it to make savory
rugelach: Think hot pepper
jelly, tapenade, pesto or
grated cheese and crispy
bacon.

TO MAKE THE FILLING: Mix the coconut, pecans, chocolate and cherries in a small bowl; set aside.

Working on a lightly floured surface, flour the top of one piece of dough and roll it into a square that's about 12 inches on a side; don't worry if it's not exactly the right size or if it's more rectangular than square. Lift and turn the dough frequently, flouring the counter as needed, so that it doesn't stick. (This dough is an easy roller that's fun to work with. Interestingly, unlike most doughs, it doesn't do well rolled between sheets of parchment paper.) You'll have a very thin dough. If it seems sticky and you think it might be hard to work with, slide it onto a cutting board or cookie sheet and chill it while you roll out the other piece of dough.

Cut one square of dough in half (so that you have 2 pieces about 12 × 6 inches). Brush each half with some of the melted butter and sprinkle with some cinnamon sugar. Working with one piece at a time, sprinkle one quarter of the filling over the dough, arranging it so that there's a slim bare border at the long ragged (rolled-out) side of the dough and a bare border about ⅓ inch wide on the straight (cut) side. Gently pat one quarter of the toppings into the dough. Starting from the ragged long side, carefully roll the sheet up snugly, ending with the neat edge on the bottom of the roll. This is easier to read than to do, but just go slowly and cut yourself some slack when the stuffing pops out the ends—it'll all be fine.

Slide the roll into the freezer and fill and roll the other rectangle, then repeat the whole process with the remaining dough and toppings.

It will be easiest to slice the dough if it's had an hour's rest in the freezer, but if you're impatient, just keep the rolls in the freezer for the amount of time it takes you to preheat the oven. (*If you'd like, you can wrap the rolls airtight and keep them frozen for up to 2 months; slice and bake directly from the freezer.*)

WHEN YOU'RE READY TO BAKE: Position the racks to divide the oven into thirds and preheat the oven to 400 degrees F. Line two baking sheets with parchment paper or silicone baking mats.

Beat the egg lightly with a splash of cold water.

Remove the rolls from the freezer, brush the top of each roll with egg glaze and then sprinkle with sugar. Using a slender knife and a gentle sawing motion, cut each roll into slices at least ½ inch thick (it's easier if you slice the rolls thicker, but then the yield changes—it's a matter of personal preference) and place them seam side down on the baking sheets.

Bake for 15 to 17 minutes, rotating the sheets from top to bottom and front to back at the midway point, or until the cookies are golden brown. Because these cookies are rolled and therefore have several layers, I think it's better to overbake than underbake them; if you don't bake them enough, you'll have a smidgen of not-quite-cooked dough at the center. Don't worry about burned cherries—they're inevitable and are usually polite enough to fall off and remain on the baking sheet. Transfer the cookies to racks and allow them to cool to room temperature.

TOASTING, ROASTING OR BROWNING NUTS

....

Warming and browning nuts in the oven—by toasting or roasting them—greatly increases their flavor and slightly decreases their oiliness. Some nuts, like hazelnuts, always need to be toasted. In the case of hazelnuts, toasting is the most efficient way to remove their stubborn skins. In addition, untoasted hazelnuts are somewhat bland, whereas toasted hazelnuts are unmissable in any dish. Other nuts, like almonds and walnuts, are fine added to a dessert untouched, but they too double up on flavor when toasted. Even roasted peanuts can benefit from a few minutes in the oven.

The most common way to toast nuts is to put them on a baking sheet (lined with parchment paper, a silicone baking mat or a piece of foil) and slide them into a 350-degree-F oven. I hesitate to give you an exact time for toasting because this is a case in which your nose is a better alert than a clock. When you start to smell the nuts, it's time to open the oven. I usually check every 3 minutes and shake the baking sheet or turn the nuts over with a spoon to help them brown evenly. You want the nuts to be lightly golden and fragrant. You can usually count on about 8 minutes in the oven. You can also toast nuts in a heavy skillet—no oil needed—or in a microwave, in which case I advise you to stay next to it and turn the nuts early and often. No matter what method you use, allow the nuts to cool before you add them to your recipe.

Many French recipes specify a much longer roasting time, until the nuts are brown to their core. My own preference is to stop just a little short of that, but I leave it to you to find the degree of toastiness that suits you best.

Cocoa Linzer Cookies

*Makes about 20
sandwich cookies*

SERVING: Classic Linzer
cookies are tea cookies,
but adding cocoa and
spice changes the game
and makes these right
for strong coffee or even
stronger Armagnac.

STORING: The dough can
be wrapped airtight and
frozen—cut into circles or
just rolled out—for up to
2 months; bake directly
from the freezer. Once
baked, the cookies will keep
for about 3 days in a closed
container. If you'd like, the
sandwich cookies can be
packed airtight and frozen
for up to 2 months; defrost
overnight in the container.

THAT ALSACE HAS BEEN TOSSED BACK AND FORTH between France and Germany over the centuries is evident in ways big and small, and especially in the region's food. Choucroute—sauerkraut and sausages—is an Alsatian specialty, as are pretzels, *leckerli* (spice cookies that age from summer to Christmas) and gingerbread that could draw in Hansel and Gretel. And then there are the members of the Linzer family.

Linzer dough goes heavy on ground almonds or hazelnuts and always includes cinnamon. The dough has been made in some form since the late seventeenth century and it gets its name from the city of Linz in Austria, a country without a border to France. That makes me think it might have been carried to the region by a talented German baker.

I've never met a Linzer tart I didn't like or a Linzer sandwich cookie I didn't love. There's something about the proportion of the spice cookie to the traditional jam filling that makes the smaller sweets perfect. For this version, I've held on to the nuts and cinnamon, but I've added cocoa, allspice, black pepper and, for a slight crunch, a few tablespoons of cocoa nibs (crushed bits of cacao beans; you can substitute chopped chocolate, if you'd like). I've also embellished the filling. While I sometimes sandwich the cookies with jam, at other times I fill them with chocolate ganache and often I go big and use both. For a Classic Linzer recipe, see Bonne Idée.

A WORD ON TECHNIQUE: After years of making Linzer cookies with a stand mixer, I now make the dough in a food processor—it's easy, fast and neat. If you'd rather use a mixer, whisk the dry ingredients together, then beat the butter and sugar together in the mixer bowl. Add the egg and vanilla, and when they're well blended in, add the dry ingredients all at once and mix just until they're incorporated into the dough. Then add the cocoa nibs (or chocolate).

FOR THE COOKIES

1¾ cups (175 grams) almond flour

1⅓ cups (181 grams) all-purpose flour

3 tablespoons unsweetened cocoa powder

1 teaspoon ground cinnamon

½ teaspoon ground allspice

¼ teaspoon freshly ground black pepper

Tiny pinch of ground cloves

½ teaspoon fine sea salt

1 stick (8 tablespoons; 4 ounces; 113 grams) unsalted butter, at room temperature

⅔ cup (132 grams) sugar

1 large egg, at room temperature

½ teaspoon pure vanilla extract

2½ tablespoons cocoa nibs, or 1½ ounces (43 grams) bittersweet or semisweet chocolate, finely chopped

2 ounces (57 grams) bittersweet
  or semisweet chocolate,
  finely chopped
¼ cup (60 ml) heavy cream

About ½ cup (160 grams)
  raspberry, cherry or apricot
  jam

Confectioners' sugar,
  for dusting

TO MAKE THE COOKIES: Pulse the flours, cocoa powder, spices and salt together in a food processor just until thoroughly blended. Turn the mixture out onto a sheet of parchment paper or into a bowl. There's no need to clean the work bowl now.

Cut the butter into chunks and toss them into the processor, along with the sugar. Whir until the butter and sugar are smooth, then drop in the egg and process until it's blended in. Add the vanilla and pulse a few times. Add the dry ingredients and pulse about 20 times, or until the dough comes together in moist clumps and curds. If you squeeze a bit of the dough, it should hold together nicely. Add the cocoa nibs or chocolate and pulse just to mix.

Turn the dough out onto a piece of parchment or wax paper and knead it once or twice to bring it together, then divide it in half. Roll each piece of dough out between two sheets of parchment or wax paper to a thickness of ⅛ inch, making sure to turn the dough over, so that you roll both top and bottom, and lifting the paper from time to time so you don't roll it into the dough and form creases. Slide the dough onto a cutting board or baking sheet (you can stack the pieces of dough) and refrigerate for at least 3 hours, or freeze for at least 1 hour. (*The dough can be wrapped airtight and frozen for up to 2 months.*)

WHEN YOU'RE READY TO BAKE: Position the racks to divide the oven into thirds and preheat the oven to 350 degrees F. Line two baking sheets with parchment paper or silicone baking mats.

Working with one piece of dough at a time and using a 2-inch round cookie cutter, cut out rounds of dough. (Of course you can use a different-sized cutter, and it needn't be round.) Place the circles of dough on the baking sheets, about 1½ inches apart. If you'd like peekaboo cookies—it's the way I always want them—cut out small circles of dough from the center of half of the cookies. I do this with a ½-inch piping tip, but you can use a small cookie cutter—the size of the opening is up to you. Gather the scraps together so that you can reroll and chill, then cut and bake them.

Bake for 11 to 13 minutes, rotating the baking sheets from top to bottom and front to back at the midway point, or until the cookies feel almost firm to the touch. Allow them to remain on the baking sheet for 5 minutes, then carefully transfer them to a cooling rack to cool to room temperature.

Repeat with the remaining dough, making sure to cool the baking sheets between batches.

Follow the directions for
Cocoa Linzers, using:
1½ cups all-purpose flour,
1⅓ cups almond flour,
1¾ teaspoons ground
cinnamon, ½ teaspoon
fine sea salt, 1 stick
(8 tablespoons; 4 ounces)
unsalted butter, ½ cup
sugar, 1 large egg,
2 teaspoons dark rum
and ¼ teaspoon pure
vanilla extract. Traditionally
these are filled with
raspberry jam, but the
chocolate filling would also
be delicious.

TO MAKE THE CHOCOLATE FILLING, IF USING: Put the chopped chocolate in a microwave-safe bowl and heat it for about 90 seconds at half power, just to soften it; or, if you'd like, melt it in a double boiler on the stove. Bring the cream to a boil. Pour the cream over the chocolate and let it sit for 30 seconds, then gently stir the mixture, starting at the center of the bowl and working your way out, until you have a smooth, glossy ganache. Chill the ganache for about 30 minutes, stirring it every 5 minutes, until it's just thick enough to pool when you drop it from a spoon.

TO MAKE THE JAM FILLING, IF USING: Put the jam in a microwave-safe bowl, stir in a splash of water and bring to a boil in the microwave. Allow the jam to cool and thicken just a little before using.

TO SANDWICH THE COOKIES: Turn the whole cookies over (if you made peekaboo cookies; otherwise, turn half of the cookies over), so that the bottoms are facing up. Put a small spoonful of either ganache or jam on each cookie (if you want, you can use both fillings—put the ganache on first, let it firm for a few minutes and top them with a dab of jam) and then top with the cut cookies (or the remaining cookies), jiggling the top cookies slightly to spread the filling and "glue" the sandwiches. If you want to set the cookies quickly, put them in the refrigerator for about 20 minutes; otherwise, leave them at room temperature until the filling sets.

Dust the cookies with confectioners' sugar just before serving.

Fruit and Nut Croquants

THE WORD *CROQUANT* can be both an adjective and a noun. As an adjective, it's easy: It means "crunchy." As a noun, it can be confusing: It usually refers to a cookie, but there are bunches of cookies that carry the appellation and, depending on who's making them and where, the cookies can vary in size, shape, flavor and degree of *croquant*-ness. Say *croquant*, and most French cookie lovers think of the ones from the south of France, which are usually studded with whole almonds and flavored with orange-flower water.

However, the *croquants* that really caught my attention came from a small bakery in Lyon. The Lyonnaise cookies weren't flavored with orange-flower water—in fact, I didn't detect any flavoring at all—and in addition to lots of almonds, they had other nuts and dried fruits. They looked similar to biscotti or mandelbrot, the Eastern European version of the double-baked sweet, and while they were called *croquant*, they didn't quite live up to their name (or their nickname: *casse-dents*, which means "tooth breakers")—they were crunchy on the outside and just a little softer and chewier on the inside.

I've flavored these with vanilla, but if a whiff of orange-flower water appeals to you, go ahead and add it. When I've got oranges in the house or, better yet, tangerines or clementines, I add some grated zest whether I'm using vanilla or orange-flower water, or a combination of both. As for the nuts and dried fruits, I leave their selection up to you, although I think you should go heavier on the nuts than the fruit. For sure you should have whole almonds (preferably with their skins on), but you can also use cashews, walnuts, (skinned) hazelnuts, macadamias or pistachios. Similarly, while I often add golden raisins, there's no reason not to consider dried cherries, pieces of dried apricots or even slim wedges of dried figs.

Makes about 30 cookies

SERVING: It's hard to resist dunking these cookies, so don't. They're great with coffee, tea, red wine or dessert wine.

STORING: Moisture and crunch don't mix, so find a dry place for these. A cookie jar, tin or storage tub works well, but because they're meant to be hard, I just keep them in an uncovered bowl or basket. Yes, they get firmer, but I'm fine with that. If your cookies lose their crunch, heat them in a 350-degree-F oven for about 10 minutes.

- 2 large eggs, at room temperature
- 1 large egg white, at room temperature
- 2 teaspoons pure vanilla extract
- ¼ teaspoon pure almond extract (optional)
- Finely grated zest of 1 tangerine or orange (optional)
- ¾ cup (150 grams) sugar
- 2 cups (272 grams) all-purpose flour

- 1 teaspoon baking powder
- ½ teaspoon fine sea salt
- ¼ teaspoon freshly grated nutmeg (optional)
- Pinch of ground cloves (optional)
- 8 ounces (227 grams) dried fruits and whole nuts (see above)

- Sugar, for sprinkling

Center a rack in the oven and preheat the oven to 350 degrees F. Line a baking sheet with parchment paper or a silicone baking mat.

Put the eggs and egg white in a liquid measuring cup, add the vanilla and the almond extract, if you're using it, and beat the eggs lightly with a fork, just until they're foamy.

If you're using grated zest, put it in the bowl of a stand mixer, or in a large bowl in which you can use a hand mixer. Add the sugar and, using your fingertips, rub the sugar and zest together until the sugar is moist and fragrant (or just add the sugar to the bowl). Add the flour, baking powder, salt and spices, if you're using them. Fit the stand mixer with the paddle attachment, set the bowl on the stand and turn the mixer to low, just to blend the ingredients. If you're using a hand mixer, just use a whisk to combine the ingredients.

With the mixer on low, steadily pour in the eggs. Once the dough starts to come together, add the dried fruits and nuts and keep mixing until the dough cleans the sides of the bowl. You'll probably have dry ingredients in the bottom of the bowl; use a flexible spatula to stir them into the sticky dough.

Spoon half the dough onto the lined baking sheet a few inches away from one of the long sides, and use your fingers and the spatula to cajole the dough into a log that's 10 to 12 inches long and 2 to 2½ inches wide. The log will be rectangular, not domed, and pretty rough and ragged. Shape a second log with the remaining dough on the other side of the baking sheet. Leave space between the logs—they will spread as they bake. Sprinkle the logs with sugar.

Bake the logs for 45 to 50 minutes, or until browned and firm to the touch. (If you want the *croquants* to be softer and chewier, bake them for 40 minutes.) Place each log on a cutting board, wait 5 minutes and then, using a serrated knife and a gentle sawing motion, cut into slices about ½ inch thick. Transfer the slices to a rack and allow them to cool to room temperature.

Croquets

*Makes about
36 cookies*

SERVING: I think these are particularly nice with ice cream, fruit desserts or anything creamy that can use a crackly companion.

STORING: Stored at room temperature in a dry place, these cookies will keep for at least 2 weeks. You can store them in a tin, if you'd like, or, if it's not humid, you can just put them in a basket and cover them with a kitchen towel. Since they're so crunchy to begin with, having them get crunchier is not a concern; only moisture can spoil them.

THESE MIGHT WIN THE PRIZE for being the crunchiest cookies in the French canon. They are my friend Bernard Collet's favorite cookies, so I try to make them for him often when I'm in Paris. And every time I do, I eat more of them than I should, and Bernard, normally a moderate man, eats cookie after cookie, making an oh-how-I-love-these sound each time he reaches for another. These cookies have that effect, even on grown men.

Croquets are unusual. They seem as if they are made of equal parts egg whites and air, but the dough for them is quite heavy, rather like a sticky nougat. For the nuts, I like to use unblanched almonds, but you can use hazelnuts (they should be skinned), macadamias or cashews. You want a nut with some body and crunch and, to keep that crunch, you want to chop the nuts into chunks—not little bits.

The dough is patted out into two logs, like biscotti. And, just like biscotti, when the dough is baked, you wait a few minutes and then cut the logs. But here's where the similarities end: *Croquets* are not twice-baked and they're not as well behaved as biscotti either. When you cut them, they're bound to crack some, and you're sure to end up with cookies that are every shape in the universe. Their imperfection is part of their charm.

A WORD ON THE DOUGH: It's very heavy and very sticky, so if you have a stand mixer, break it out. If you're using a hand mixer, you might do best to beat the egg whites and sugar together with the mixer and then switch to a wooden spoon and some muscle to work in the nuts and flour.

2 large egg whites, at room temperature	macadamias, cashews or hazelnuts, very coarsely chopped
1¼ cups (250 grams) sugar	¾ cup plus 2 tablespoons (119 grams) all-purpose flour
Pinch of fine sea salt	
4 ounces (113 grams) whole almonds, preferably unblanched, or	

Center a rack in the oven and preheat the oven to 350 degrees F. Line a baking sheet with parchment paper or a silicone baking mat.

Working in the bowl of a stand mixer fitted with the paddle attachment, or in a large bowl with a hand mixer, beat the egg whites, sugar and salt together at medium speed for about 2 minutes. The mixture will turn pure white and look like a thick, heavy meringue frosting. (If you're using a hand mixer, you might want to switch to a sturdy wooden spoon for the next step.) Reduce the speed to low and mix in the nuts. Still on low speed, add the flour, mixing

until it is fully incorporated. The dough will be very heavy and very sticky and it will ball up around the paddle—I told you it was a misbehaver. It will look more like nougat candy than cookie dough.

Using a flexible spatula (or your wooden spoon), transfer half of the dough onto one long side of the lined baking sheet and spread it, as best as you can, into a log that's about 12 inches long. Repeat with the other half of the dough, placing it on the other side of the baking sheet. Use your fingertips to flatten the logs to a thickness of about ½ inch.

Bake the logs for 25 to 30 minutes, until light brown, puffed, cracked and speckled with caramelized sugar. Transfer the baking sheet to a cooling rack and let the logs cool for 10 minutes.

If it looks as though the logs have stuck to the lined baking sheet, slide an offset spatula under them to loosen them, then carefully transfer them to a cutting board. Using a long serrated knife and a sawing motion, slice each log into cookies ½ to ⅔ inch thick. Some of the slices might break so you're bound to have lots of crumbs and shardish pieces—they're inevitable, so just snack on them while you work. Allow the cookies to cool fully and crisp even more—about 1 hour—before serving.

Lavender Galettes

Makes about 25 cookies

SERVING: These are good with fruit desserts, ice cream and puddings, but I think they are best with tea (hot or cold) or wine (they're as good with red wine as they are with white).

STORING: The cookies, which are fragile and very sensitive to humidity, should be eaten the day they are made. If your kitchen is cool and dry, you can leave them out; if not, pack them in a covered container, separating the layers with parchment or wax paper.

THIS BEAUTIFUL COOKIE was inspired by the famed French (by way of Ireland) cookbook author Trish Deseine. Called galettes, a name often used for thick cookies, these are so thin and crunchy that they're almost crackers. Flavored with orange zest, olive oil, vanilla and lavender, they're unusual no matter what you call them.

Lavender is a tricky business in the kitchen—a smidge too much can be overbearing when baked. If you're not sure you like it, use a little less; if you adore it, don't be tempted to up the amount—even just a bit more could end your love affair with the flower. The first time I made these, I took some of them to Au Petit Suisse, our neighborhood café, to share with the manager. Before he bit into one, he said, "I don't really like lavender." Then, he declared: "I like these!" It's all about the type of lavender you use. If you leave the buds whole or crush them just a bit, the recipe's quantity will be just right. If the lavender is ground, start with ½ teaspoon and adjust the amount if necessary the next time you make them.

A BONUS: Because the cookies have so little sugar, they turn out to be just as good with wine as they are with tea. If you've got a little wine left from dinner, finish it with the cookies—the combo is great.

3 tablespoons sugar	1 teaspoon baking powder
Grated zest of 1 orange or tangerine	½ teaspoon fine sea salt
1½ teaspoons edible dried lavender flowers, very lightly crushed or coarsely chopped (see above)	½ cup (120 ml) olive oil
	4 teaspoons pure vanilla extract
	¼ cup (60 ml) ice water
2¼ cups (306 grams) all-purpose flour	1 large egg white
	Sugar, for dusting

Center a rack in the oven and preheat the oven to 400 degrees F. Have two baking sheets handy. I've made these several different ways and the easiest seems to be to cut a little parchment rectangle for each cookie to roll it out and bake it on. The step is fussy, but in the end neater, and the best way to work with dough that's sticky when raw and fragile when baked. Cut 26 pieces of parchment paper, each about 7 × 6 inches.

Put the sugar, zest and lavender in a large bowl and use your fingertips to rub the ingredients together until the sugar is moist and fragrant. Add the flour, baking powder and salt and whisk to blend.

Mix the olive oil and vanilla extract together and pour them over the dry ingredients. Working with a sturdy flexible spatula and determination, stir

and mash until the dry ingredients are evenly moistened; you'll have a bowl full of lumpy dough. Pour the ice water over the dough and mix until the dough smooths out. Knead the dough in the bowl a few times to bring it all together, if necessary.

Scoop out 1 tablespoon dough, roll it into a ball between your palms and place it in the center of a parchment rectangle. Press to flatten it a little, cover with another parchment rectangle and roll the dough until it is about 5 inches long. It will be vaguely oval—or not; the edges will be ragged, and that's fine. You want to roll the dough to a thickness of about $\frac{1}{16}$ inch—thin, but not so thin that the top sheet of parchment will stick to it. Peel off the top piece of paper—save it: you'll use it to roll all of the galettes—and transfer the wafer, on its parchment rectangle, to one of the baking sheets. Continue until you've filled the sheet—I usually get about 8 to a sheet.

Whisk the egg white in a small bowl until it holds soft peaks (this is a quick job to do by hand), then brush a little of the white over each galette. Sprinkle with sugar.

Bake 8 to 10 minutes, rotating the pan after 5 minutes, until the cookies are golden brown; they won't brown evenly. Let the galettes cool on the sheet for about 5 minutes, then carefully transfer them—still on their papers—to a cooling rack to cool to room temperature.

Meanwhile, roll out the next batch of cookies and put them on the second baking sheet. If the egg white has gone liquidy, just whisk it back to soft peaks before using it. Bake the second sheet when the first one comes out of the oven, then repeat until you've used all the dough—just remember that the baking sheets have to cool before you can put more galettes on them.

Olive Oil and Wine Cookies

THAT THESE COOKIES are made with olive oil and wine is not surprising when you realize that they're a specialty of the Languedoc-Roussillon region in the south of France—it's one of the non–butter regions of the country and one known for its vast vineyards. But if the mix of oil and wine isn't surprising, just about every other thing about these cookies is: Their shape is long, plump in the middle and pointy at the ends, and they have a sophisticated flavor—first a little sweet and then a little tangy and finally wonderfully mysterious. Right after they're baked, their texture is crunchy at the tips and cakey in the center—wait a day or so, and the chubby middle dries and starts to resemble a great tea biscuit. In fact, I like these best after they've had a little time to age and develop a crunchier texture and a more mellow flavor.

You can use any white wine or even any rosé you have on hand, but if you use a sweet or off-dry wine, you'll come closer to the original cookies, which are made with Muscat de Rivesaltes, a Roussillon star.

Makes about 36 cookies

SERVING: This is the kind of cookie that might come to a French table as the go-along with a fruit salad, but they're also great with coffee or tea—their shape and texture just about call out "Dunk, dunk." Although it's not at all traditional, I serve them with white wine in the summer. They're sweeter than the usual aperitif cracker, but they're much more surprising.

STORING: Of course you can serve these cookies as soon as they reach room temperature, but I think they're better a couple of days later. Packed into a container, they will keep at room temperature for at least 5 days.

2¾ cups (374 grams) all-purpose flour
½ cup (100 grams) sugar
½ teaspoon baking powder
¼ teaspoon fine sea salt
½ cup (120 ml) olive oil, extra-virgin or not, preferably fruity

½ teaspoon pure vanilla extract
½ cup (120 ml) white wine, preferably sweet (see above)

Sugar, for dredging

Position the racks to divide the oven into thirds and preheat the oven to 350 degrees F. Line two baking sheets with parchment paper or silicone baking mats.

Whisk the flour, sugar, baking powder and salt together in a large bowl. Pour in the olive oil, switch to a flexible spatula and stir to incorporate—you don't have to be thorough now. Pour the vanilla extract into the wine, then pour the wine mixture into the bowl and mix until you have an easy-to-work-with dough. It will be smooth on the outside, but peek inside, and you'll see that it looks like a sponge; when you pinch and pull it, you'll be surprised at how stretchy it is.

Divide the dough into pieces about the size of a large cherry or small walnut and roll each one into a ball. Next, roll each ball under your palm to shape it into a short sausage. When you've got the sausage shape, press on the ends with your thumb and pinkie (don't press the center), and roll up and back a few times to form a cookie about 4 inches long that is just a little

In the Languedoc-
Roussillon, these cookies
are often flavored with
orange-flower water
(instead of vanilla, which
was my idea) or enriched
with anise seeds. My
favorite addition is grated
orange (or tangerine or
clementine) zest. To get the
most out of the zest, first
put the sugar in the mixing
bowl, sprinkle over the zest
and use your fingers to rub
the sugar and zest together
until the sugar is moist
and aromatic. Add the rest
of the dry ingredients and
continue with the recipe.

plump in the center and tapered at the ends. Dredge each cookie in sugar
and arrange the cookies on the baking sheets. (*The cookies can be shaped, but
not rolled in sugar, frozen on the lined baking sheets and then, when firm, packed
airtight and kept in the freezer for up to 2 months. There's no need to defrost before
baking.*)

Bake the cookies for 20 to 22 minutes, rotating the baking sheets from top
to bottom and front to back after 10 minutes, until the cookies have brown
tips and bottoms and golden bellies. (If baking from frozen, dredge the cookies in sugar and bake a minute or two longer.) Cool the cookies on the baking
sheets and, if you can stand it, wait at least a day before serving.

Canistrelli

*Makes about
25 biggish or
60 bite-sized
cookies*

THE FIRST TIME I MET LAËTITIA GHIPPONI, who is everyone's favorite server at Bistrot Paul Bert, a Paris restaurant I adore, I was so taken with her that I told my husband, Michael, "I bet *Laëtitia* means 'happiness.'" And guess what? It means "joy." In my Laëtitia's case, it might also mean a person who knows, loves and can make really good food, particularly the foods of Corsica, her homeland.

It was when we were talking about dessert one evening that she asked if I knew how to make *canistrelli* and offered me her recipe. *Canistrelli* dough is made without butter or eggs. The little fat it has comes from oil (preferably olive) and the big flavor comes from white wine and Pastis, the anise liqueur of France's south. You mix the dough in a big bowl with a table fork, pat it out on the counter with your palms and cut it into pieces with a dough scraper or a knife. You can make the nuggets big or small, and you can make them all one size and one shape or go rogue. These are homey and rustic in every way.

When the cookies come out of the oven, they'll be thick and chunky yet light (it's the baking powder), and both crunchy and a little cakey. What they won't be is sweet. Their closest cousin is the Olive Oil and Wine Cookie (page 315)—you'll see the family resemblance, but you'll know they were raised in different parts of the country.

SERVING: I can't think of anything these cookies wouldn't be good with, from coffee or tea to wine—white, sparkling or rosé—to Pastis, of course.

STORING: Kept in a tin away from heat and humidity, these will stay crunchy for about 1 week.

1¾ cups (238 grams) all-purpose flour

½ cup (100 grams) sugar

1 teaspoon baking powder

¼ teaspoon fine sea salt

¼ cup (60 ml) olive oil

⅓ cup plus 2 tablespoons (110 ml) white wine

2½ tablespoons Pastis or other anise- or licorice-flavored liqueur

Sugar, for coating

Center a rack in the oven and preheat the oven to 350 degrees F. Line a baking sheet with parchment paper or a silicone baking mat. (If you're going to make bite-sized cookies, you'll need two sheets and you should position the racks to divide the oven into thirds.)

Put the flour, sugar, baking powder and salt in a large bowl and stir with a fork to mix. Make a well in the center and pour in the oil, wine and Pastis. Working with the fork (or a flexible spatula), and starting in the center of the bowl, stir the dry ingredients into the wet. Within a minute or so, you should have a soft dough. It might be pockmarked or look like a biscuit or spongy scone dough, and that's fine. Use your hands to gently fold and knead the dough in the bowl about 4 times—the purpose is not really to knead, but to pull the dough together, so don't overdo it.

Flour a work surface and turn the dough out onto it. Lightly flour the top of the dough or your hands and use your palms to pat the dough into a circle or square that's ½ inch thick and about 7 inches across. Precision is not important—I'm giving you these measurements only as indicators.

Pour some sugar into a medium bowl.

Using a bench scraper or a knife, cut the dough into pieces. You can make any shape you like or many shapes, and you can make them big or small. I usually stay in the 1½- to 2-inch range, but truly anything goes. As you cut the pieces—you'll see how spongy they are inside—drop them, a few at a time, into the bowl of sugar. Turn them in the sugar, lift them out, toss them from hand to hand to shake off the excess and then put them on the baking sheet(s), at least 1 inch apart (the cookies will puff and spread).

Bake small cookies (1 to 1½ inches) for about 30 minutes, larger cookies for 40 to 45 minutes. No matter the size, the cookies should be golden on their tops and bottoms. Rotate the sheet(s) during baking if the cookies aren't browning evenly. The *canistrelli* can cool to room temperature on the baking sheet(s) or on a rack.

Bonne Idée

COCKTAIL CANISTRELLI: Since these are so close to being savory, it doesn't take much to tip them over the edge. If you'd like a "cookie" to serve with cocktails, salads or even cheese, increase the fine sea salt to ½ teaspoon and add 1½ teaspoons herbes de Provence to the dry ingredients.

Speculoos

SERVING: Speculoos
are coffee's soul mate,
but they're also really nice
with tea and fine with
mulled wine.

STORING: The logs of
dough can be kept frozen
for up to 2 months. There's
no need to defrost them,
just let them soften enough
so that you can slice and
bake them. Stored airtight,
the baked cookies will keep
at room temperature for up
to 4 days.

THERE ARE PROBABLY as many different recipes for speculoos as there are bakers, but all have cinnamon, brown sugar and a fragrance that puts you in mind of Christmas. Mine have plenty of nutmeg too, and you can use them in any of the recipes that call for store-bought speculoos or LU Cinnamon Sugar Spice Cookies.

I shape these into logs and make slice-and-bake cookies, but you can roll them out and cut them with cookie cutters, if you'd like. Since these are as good on their own as they are turned into a crumble, crust or crumb, you might want to brush the logs with a beaten egg and roll them in sanding sugar before slicing and baking. In Belgium, where speculoos were born, the cookies celebrate Saint Nicolas and are, by definition, holiday treats. But if you love spice as much as I do, you'll make these year-round—deliciousness isn't seasonal.

2 cups (272 grams) all-purpose flour	½ cup (100 grams) packed light brown sugar
1 tablespoon ground cinnamon	¼ cup (50 grams) sugar
¾ teaspoon ground ginger	2 tablespoons mild (light) molasses
½ teaspoon freshly grated nutmeg	1 large egg, at room temperature
⅛ teaspoon ground cloves	1 teaspoon pure vanilla extract
½ teaspoon fine sea salt	
1 stick (8 tablespoons; 4 ounces; 113 grams) unsalted butter, at room temperature	

Whisk the flour, spices and salt together in a medium bowl.

Working in the bowl of a stand mixer fitted with the paddle attachment, or in a large bowl with a hand mixer, beat the butter at medium speed until smooth, about 2 minutes. Add both sugars and the molasses and beat until the mixture is smooth again, about 3 minutes. Beat in the egg and when it's incorporated, add the vanilla and mix for another 2 minutes. Add the dry ingredients all at once and pulse a few times, then mix on low speed just until the flour disappears into the dough and the dough cleans the sides of the bowl.

Scrape the dough out onto a work surface and divide it into thirds. Using the palms of your hands, roll each piece of dough into an 8-inch-long log (see page 61). Don't worry about the diameter: Get the length right and the diameter will be perfect. Wrap the logs tightly in plastic film and freeze for at least 3 hours. (*The dough can be frozen for up to 2 months.*)

WHEN YOU'RE READY TO BAKE: Position the racks to divide the oven into thirds and preheat the oven to 375 degrees F. Line three baking sheets with parchment paper or silicone baking mats.

Using a long, slender knife, slice off a sliver of dough from the end of one log to even it and then cut the log into ¼-inch-thick rounds. Place them on one of the lined baking sheets and stow the sheet in the freezer while you cut the remaining logs. (The cookies hold their shape better if you bake them when they're cold.)

Bake the first two sheets of cookies for 11 to 13 minutes, rotating the sheets from top to bottom and front to back after 6 minutes, or until they are uniformly golden brown and almost firm at the center. Transfer the cookies to racks and cool to room temperature. Bake the third sheet of cookies.

Chocolate-Cherry Brownies

Makes 25 squares

SERVING: Serve the brownies alongside espresso or port. Because of the wine and dried fruit, you can chill the brownies and they'll never get really hard—you can enjoy them straight from the fridge.

STORING: Wrapped in plastic film, the brownies will keep for at least 4 days at room temperature or in the refrigerator. Packed airtight, they'll keep for up to 2 months in the freezer.

IT'S A FINE LINE BETWEEN *les brownies* and *les moelleux*, France's beloved soft-in-the-center chocolate cakes (page 191), and sometimes all that separates the two is size.

When I bake these in France, I use dried cherries, cut them teensy and call them pastries. When I make the brownies in America, I cut them into hearty portions and I often make them with dried cranberries, which are so readily available here. On both sides of the ocean, I add a hit of black pepper and use very good, very dark chocolate—it makes a big difference.

This is a one-bowl recipe: Everything is mixed in the bowl you use to melt the chocolate and butter. It's a simple recipe, but even simple recipes have rules. For the brownies to be the best they can be: Melt the butter and chocolate together in a large bowl set over simmering water and stay close (remove the bowl when the chocolate is just melted or even only almost melted). Leave your eggs in the refrigerator until you're ready to use them (cold eggs give you a smoother batter). And don't overbake the brownies—it's better to remove the pan from the oven a minute too early than a minute too late. Because of the chopped chocolate in the batter, the brownies won't set until they cool, so a tester needn't come out completely clean and dry.

- 2 tablespoons fruity red wine or ruby port
- 2 tablespoons water
- 1 cup (160 grams) moist dried cherries or dried cranberries
- 10 ounces (283 grams) bittersweet or semisweet chocolate
- 5 tablespoons (2½ ounces; 71 grams) unsalted butter, cut into pieces
- ¾ cup (150 grams) sugar
- 2 large cold eggs
- ½ teaspoon fine sea salt
- ¼ teaspoon freshly ground black pepper
- ⅓ cup (45 grams) all-purpose flour

Center a rack in the oven and preheat the oven to 325 degrees F. Line an 8-inch square pan with parchment or foil and butter it.

Pour the red wine and water into a small saucepan and bring to a boil. Add the cherries or cranberries and cook over low heat until the fruit is plump and the liquid has been absorbed, about 3 minutes. Turn the fruit into a bowl and set aside to cool.

Measure out 6 ounces of the chocolate and coarsely chop it. Finely chop the remaining 4 ounces.

Put the butter in a large heatproof bowl set over a saucepan of simmering water and scatter over the coarsely chopped chocolate. Heat the mixture until the chocolate is just on the verge of melting completely; you don't want to heat the chocolate and butter so much that they separate. Remove the bowl from the saucepan and stir; you'll have a thick, shiny mixture.

Working with a flexible spatula, beat in the sugar. Don't be discouraged when the batter goes grainy; it ends up fine. When the sugar is incorporated, beat in the eggs one at a time—give the eggs a little elbow grease and you'll have a heavy batter that will have regained some of its glossiness. Mix in the salt and pepper, then gently stir in the flour, mixing only until it disappears into the batter. Stir in the cherries or cranberries and any liquid that has accumulated, then add the finely chopped chocolate. Scrape the batter into the pan and smooth the top as best as you can.

Bake the brownies for 27 to 29 minutes, or until the top is uniformly dull; a knife inserted into the center will come out almost clean. Transfer the pan to a rack and cool until the brownies are just warm or until they reach room temperature.

To unmold, invert the brownies onto a cutting board and peel away the parchment or foil. Turn the brownies over and cut into 25 small squares.

THE FRUIT AND NUT MAN

The French and I share an affinity for dried fruits. No matter what market I go to, no matter what the neighborhood, I always find a vendor with a vast display of dried fruits: prunes, for sure; raisins, golden and black, and tiny currants, too; dates and figs, sometimes several kinds of each; occasionally cranberries and blueberries; and almost always cherries. Since the vendors who sell dried fruit usually also sell nuts, another of my many weaknesses, I never leave the stand empty-handed. The fruit-and-nut man at the Tuesday and Friday markets on the Boulevard Raspail knows my soft spots and plays to them. As soon as he sees me coming, he beckons with an outstretched scoop and samples ready to be tasted. I'm crazy about his dark dried cherries. They're large, plump, meaty, just on the near side of tangy and almost black. (I tell him that they remind me of the best Michigan cherries, but he doesn't know where Michigan is.)

The most extravagant displays of fruit are reserved for Christmas. While there are wonderful dried fruits and beautiful nuts from all over (in French, nuts are referred to as *fruit secs*, "dried fruit"), the most stunning fruits are *glacéed*, or "candied." Laid out prettily, whole kumquats and mandarins, chestnuts and cherries, red and green, look like so many jewels. Their prices are almost as stunning as the fruits themselves, but still there are lines to buy them. It's a holiday tradition—and Christmas comes but once a year.

Crispy-Topped
Brown Sugar Bars

Makes 16 bars

SERVING: When you cut these into bars, they're a snack or a good dessert to pair with ice cream. Cut into smaller squares, they go from everyday to party fun. I leave it to you to decide at what temperature to serve these—I like them cold and my husband likes them at room temperature.

STORING: Covered, these will keep in the refrigerator for up to 5 days. They can also be wrapped airtight and frozen for up to 2 months, unless you've topped them with Caramelized Rice Krispies: The candied cereal doesn't hold up in the freezer.

AN AMERICAN-IN-PARIS FRIEND tasted one of these bars and declared: "This is what Rice Krispies Treats would have been had they been born in France." Indeed. Where the confection of our American childhoods was chubby and tooth-achingly sweet, these bars are supermodel slim, chic and bittersweet. Their thin, chewy cookie base is spread with melted chocolate and then topped with Rice Krispies. Sometimes I pour the cereal straight from the box, but most often I take a few extra minutes to make it extra special by caramelizing it and pressing the brittle-like bits into the chocolate. Other great toppers besides Rice Krispies include Crunchy Granola (page 408), large-flake coconut, popcorn, Cracker Jack, mixed nuts and dried fruits or, around holiday time, slivers of Candied Orange Peel (page 459).

THE BASE

- 1 stick (8 tablespoons; 4 ounces; 113 grams) unsalted butter, at room temperature
- ¼ cup (50 grams) packed light brown sugar
- 2 tablespoons sugar
- ¼ teaspoon fine sea salt
- ½ teaspoon pure vanilla extract
- ¾ cup (102 grams) all-purpose flour

FOR THE TOPPING

- 3½ ounces (99 grams) semisweet or bittersweet chocolate, finely chopped
- ½ recipe Caramelized Rice Krispies (page 428) or 1 cup (26 grams) Rice Krispies (see above for other options)

TO MAKE THE BASE: Center a rack in the oven and preheat the oven to 375 degrees F. Line an 8-inch square pan with parchment paper, leaving an overhang on two opposite sides so you can lift the cookie out of the pan. Butter the paper.

Working in the bowl of a stand mixer fitted with the paddle attachment, or in a large bowl with a hand mixer, beat the butter, brown sugar, sugar and salt together on medium speed until smooth, light and creamy. Beat in the vanilla. Add the flour all at once and then pulse the mixer on and off about 5 times to blend in the flour. If the flour isn't completely incorporated, mix on low speed until it disappears into the heavy, sticky dough.

Scrape the dough into the lined pan and, working with a flexible spatula and your fingers, spread the dough over the bottom of the pan in an even layer. The dough is sticky and may put up a fight—show it who's boss.

Bake for about 22 minutes, or until it puffs and puckers and has turned golden brown. Put the pan on a rack and immediately top the bars.

TO MAKE THE TOPPING TO FINISH THE BARS: Scatter the chopped chocolate evenly over the base and return the pan to the turned-off oven for 1 to 2 minutes, or until the chocolate is melted. Immediately, spread the chocolate evenly over the base, using a small offset spatula or the back of a spoon.

If you're using Caramelized Rice Krispies, break off pieces of the brittle and lightly press them into the chocolate until you've completely covered the top. If you're using plain Rice Krispies (or any other kind of crunchies), sprinkle them evenly over the chocolate and press them into place with your fingertips. Cool to room temperature on a rack and then, if the chocolate is still fluid (as it probably will be), put the pan in the refrigerator for 20 minutes to set it.

Remove the pan from the refrigerator, lift the cookie out of the pan with the parchment handles and transfer it to a cutting board. Using a long knife, cut the cookie into sixteen 2-inch squares.

Lemon Squares, French Style

SERVING: People are split on the question of serving temperature: One camp likes the squares at room temperature, when the crust is almost as tender as the filling; the other likes them chilled, when all the elements are firm but the filling melts in your mouth. I leave it to you to decide.

STORING: Well wrapped, the squares will keep in the refrigerator for about 5 days; wrapped airtight, they can be frozen for up to 2 months. Defrost the squares, still wrapped, overnight in the refrigerator.

THESE LEMON SQUARES ARE THE PROOF that if you use fine ingredients and take the time to do everything right, even the most commonplace dessert can be eye-opening. Each of the three components is the best that it can be. The filling in the middle is a classic pucker-tart curd, made with whole eggs, freshly squeezed lemon juice, grated zest and a generous amount of butter it needs for shine, flavor and verve. Then there's the crust and—unusual for these squares—the crumble topping. Both are made from the same butter-rich almond cookie dough. For the crust, the dough is pressed into the pan and prebaked, so that it has the texture of excellent shortbread; for the topping, it's rubbed and pinched so that it becomes a streusel. With each bite, you get crunch and cream and tender cookie. These are a revelation and a world beyond bake-sale lemon squares.

FOR THE CURD FILLING

- 4 large eggs
- 1½ cups (300 grams) sugar
  Finely grated zest of 2 lemons
- ⅔ cup (158 ml) freshly squeezed lemon juice (from 4–5 lemons)
- 2 sticks plus 2 tablespoons (9 ounces; 255 grams) unsalted butter, cut into small chunks

FOR THE CRUST AND CRUMBS

- 2 sticks plus 2 tablespoons (9 ounces; 255 grams) unsalted butter, at room temperature
- 1¼ cups (250 grams) sugar
- ½ teaspoon fine sea salt
- 1 teaspoon pure vanilla extract
- ¾ cup (75 grams) almond flour
- 2⅓ cups (317 grams) all-purpose flour
- ⅓ cup (43 grams) coarsely chopped slivered almonds or finely chopped blanched whole almonds

TO MAKE THE FILLING: Working in a heavy-bottomed medium saucepan, whisk the eggs and sugar together until well blended. Whisk in the zest and lemon juice, then drop in the chunks of butter. Put the saucepan over medium heat and start whisking, taking care to work the whisk into the edges of the pan. If your whisk is too big to get into the edges, switch to a wooden spoon or silicone spatula. Whisk without stopping and, in 8 to 10 minutes, the buttery curd will thicken. It won't get terribly thick—it thickens more as it chills—but you'll notice that your whisk leaves tracks. The sign that the curd is ready is a bubble or two burbling to the surface, then popping. Immediately remove the pan from the heat and scrape the curd into a heatproof bowl.

Before you can use the curd, it has to chill. You can either place a piece of plastic film against the surface and refrigerate the curd until it's cold all the way through or you can put the bowl into a larger bowl filled with ice cubes and cold water and stir until the curd is cold. (*Packed airtight, the curd can stay in the fridge for a couple of weeks.*)

WHEN YOU'RE READY TO BAKE: Center a rack in the oven and preheat the oven to 375 degrees F. Butter a 9-×-13-inch baking pan, line the bottom with parchment paper and butter the paper.

TO MAKE THE CRUST AND CRUMBS: Put the butter, sugar, salt and vanilla in a food processor and whir until the mixture is blended. Add the almond flour and blend until smooth. Add the flour and pulse, stopping as needed to scrape the bowl, until you've worked the flour into the other ingredients and have moist, bumpy curds of dough. If the dough holds together when you pinch it, it's ready.

Turn the dough out onto the counter and knead it gently to gather it together. Cut off one third of the dough, cover it with plastic film and set it aside (refrigerate the dough if your kitchen is very warm). Press the rest of the dough evenly into the bottom of the lined pan. If you want to be fussy about it—I sometimes am—take a small glass and use it as a mini rolling pin, rolling it along the pressed-in dough to even it out. Prick the dough all over with a fork.

Bake the crust for 15 to 18 minutes, or until it's pale golden all over. It will puff a bit and still feel soft to the touch, so judge its readiness by its color. Transfer the pan to a cooling rack and let the crust cool to room temperature.

If you've turned off the oven, heat it to 375 degrees F again.

Stir the curd to get it moving and then, using a long offset spatula or the back of a spoon, spread the filling evenly over the crust. Pinch off small pieces of the reserved dough and scatter them over the filling; you'll have enough dough to almost completely cover the curd. Finish by strewing over the chopped almonds.

Bake the lemon squares for 35 to 45 minutes, rotating the pan after about 20 minutes. The lemon curd will puff—it should puff all the way to the center and caramelize around the edges (my favorite part); and the crumbs and almonds will be golden brown. Transfer the pan to a cooling rack and let stand for at least 2 hours (and up to 6 hours) before cutting.

Run a table knife around the edges of the pan, making certain that the knife goes all the way down to the crust. Turn the cake over onto a cutting board or rack, carefully peel away the paper and invert the cake onto the cutting board. Using a long, slender knife, cut the cake into 24 squares, about 2¼ inches on a side.

Bonne Idée

LEMON-BERRY SQUARES: As long as I was playing around with the classic, I decided to treat the squares the way I might a tart and add more fruit to the mix. Scatter 1 cup blueberries and/or raspberries over the prebaked crust and then gently cover the berries with the curd; finish with the crumbs and slivered almonds. When the squares bake, the berries may pop up here and there and peek through the curd and crumble. When that happens, it gives this crowd-pleaser a look that's more peasant than pâtisserie.

Granola Energy Bars

Makes 20 bars

SERVING: Cut the bars into bite-sized pieces and serve them alongside tea. If you'd like to turn these snacks into a great gift, wrap them in cellophane and bundle a few together with a ribbon.

STORING: Wrapped in parchment and then in plastic and kept in a cool, dry place, the bars will keep for at least 1 week at room temperature.

THESE BETTER-THAN-STORE-BOUGHT SNACKS have all the ingredients I love in my Crunchy Granola (page 408), but they're baked into bars. When I started making them, a friend advised using brown rice syrup instead of honey and brown sugar, and I've been grateful to her ever since. Available at supermarkets and natural food shops, the syrup does the best job of binding the nuts and oats—and getting the ingredients to bind is the most common problem with homemade granola bars.

As with my granola, there's no real hard-and-fast formula. You want to keep the 2 cups of old-fashioned oats as your base and to keep the total quantity of nuts, seeds and fruits at about 2 cups as well—these are the proportions that work best with the amount of syrup. Choose whatever fruits and nuts you like most or have on hand. And, if you'd like to add chopped chocolate or cocoa nibs, pieces of candied fruit or chopped crystallized ginger, do it.

2 cups (160 grams) old-fashioned (not quick-cooking) oats	snipped apricots and/or cherries
½ cup (60 grams) slivered almonds	½ cup shredded coconut, sweetened (60 grams) or unsweetened (40 grams)
¼ cup (31 grams) raw sunflower seeds	¼ teaspoon fine sea salt
¼ cup (35 grams) raw pumpkin seeds	⅔ cup (158 ml) brown rice syrup
1 cup (about 160 grams) plump, moist dried fruit, such as raisins, cranberries,	2 tablespoons (1 ounce; 28 grams) unsalted butter
	1 tablespoon pure vanilla extract

Center a rack in the oven and preheat the oven to 325 degrees F. Line a 7-×-11-inch baking pan (I use Pyrex) with parchment paper, allowing the edges to extend up all four sides of the pan, and butter the paper.

Toss the oats and almonds together on a rimmed baking sheet and bake for 5 minutes. Add the sunflower and pumpkin seeds, give everything a stir and bake for another 3 to 5 minutes, or until the nuts and oats are lightly toasted. Transfer to a large bowl and stir in the dried fruit, coconut and salt.

Bring the brown rice syrup and butter to a boil in a small saucepan over medium heat. Pour the hot mixture into the bowl, add the vanilla and stir until the granola is evenly moistened. Turn the sticky granola into the lined pan and, using a flexible spatula, firmly press it into a tight, even layer.

Bake for 25 to 30 minutes, or until the surface of the granola is golden brown and shiny; if you gently poke the granola in the middle of the pan, it should still feel a little soft. Transfer the pan to a cooling rack. Using a silicone spatula or the back of a wide metal spatula, press down with authority, making sure to press against the entire surface. Cool for at least 3 hours.

Turn the granola out onto the rack, peel away the parchment and flip the granola onto a cutting board. Using a long heavy knife, cut crosswise into 10 strips, then cut each strip in half to make bars.

FRUIT, CREAMS, FROZEN DESSERTS AND CANDIES

Laurent's Slow-Roasted Spiced Pineapple

LAURENT TAVERNIER ISN'T EVEN MY HAIR STYLIST, but he knows that I love food, and so whenever I'm in the salon for a cut, he takes time to chat with me about what he's made over the weekend. When he gave me this recipe, I didn't wait for the weekend to try it. The dessert is simple enough: a slow-roasted ripe pineapple with a thick aromatic sauce. As it roasts, it's basted with orange juice, booze, jelly and a mix of spices until it is fork-tender and almost confited, or candied. How much juice? "Oh, about this much," Laurent said, making finger measurements that wavered. How much booze? "About the same amount." And what kind? "Whatever you've got." And the jelly? "Oh, you know, apple or quince or apricot or, no matter." (Two tries later, Laurent told me that I should use a whole jar of jelly.) And the spices? "Again, whatever you've got—even a hot pepper!"

I've given you a real recipe (kind of), but my inclination is to tell you to take a leaf from Laurent's book and let inspiration and whatever you've got in the cupboard guide you. Having made this so many times with so many combinations, I can now say with confidence what Laurent told me when he first described the dish, "You'll love it."

A WORD ON SIZE AND SERVINGS: In Paris, I make these with the small pineapples known as Victorias. They're squat and compact and one fruit serves two to four, depending on what else is on the dinner menu and who's around the table. In the United States, where pineapples are much larger, I figure one for six to eight people, usually eight. If you'd like, you can roast two pineapples at a time—the syrup multiplies easily.

1 ripe pineapple

½ cup (120 ml) freshly squeezed orange juice (from about 2 oranges)

½ cup (120 ml) Cognac, brandy, Scotch, Grand Marnier, bourbon, rum or other liquor (or an equal amount of orange juice)

1 jar (about 12 ounces; 340 grams) apple or quince jelly, apricot jam or orange marmalade

1 moist, fragrant vanilla bean, split lengthwise (optional)

Whole spices, lightly bruised, such as a few each of star anise, cardamom, coriander, pink peppercorns, allspice or cloves (no more than 3); fresh ginger slices; a cinnamon stick (broken); a small hot pepper (just 1 or a piece of 1); and/or black peppercorns (just a few)

Makes 6 to 8 servings

SERVING: I like to cut the pineapple into triangles and serve the fruit and syrup in small bowls with cookies on the side. My favorite go-along is Lemon Madeleines (page 212), because you can dip the small sponge cakes into the syrup. Of course you can serve the fruit with ice cream, whipped cream or crème fraîche, but I don't think it needs any extras.

STORING: If you've got leftovers, you can keep them covered in the refrigerator overnight and serve them chilled, at room temperature or warmed briefly in a microwave oven. Leftover syrup can be heated until it thickens slightly; then drizzle it over ice cream, pancakes or waffles.

Center a rack in the oven and preheat the oven to 300 degrees F.

Cut the top and bottom off the pineapple. Stand it upright and, using a sturdy knife, peel it by cutting between the fruit and the skin, following the contours of the pineapple. With the tip of a paring knife, remove the "eyes" (the tough dark spots). Cutting from top to bottom, quarter the pineapple and then cut away the core. Place the pineapple in a baking dish or small roasting pan that holds it snugly while still leaving you enough room to turn and baste the fruit.

Whisk the juice, liquor and jelly, jam, or marmalade together. Don't worry about fully incorporating the jelly—it will melt in the oven—you just want to break it up. Pour the mixture over the pineapple, toss in the vanilla bean, if you're using it, and scatter over the spices.

Bake the pineapple for about 2 hours, basting and turning it in the syrup every 20 minutes or so, until it is tender enough to be pierced easily with the tip of a knife. The fruit should have absorbed enough of the syrup to seem candied. Allow the pineapple to cool until it is comfortably warm or reaches room temperature. Laurent strains the syrup and discards the spices, making the dish more elegant, but I leave them in because I love the way they look speckling the sauce; if you're going to strain the syrup, do it while it's hot—it's easier.

The temperature you serve this at is, like so much of this recipe, up to you—warm or room temperature is best, but chilled is also good.

Roasted Rhubarb with Bitters

I T WAS ONLY AFTER I EXPERIMENTED with adding Angostura bitters to roasted rhubarb that I discovered that in the new and knowing cocktail culture, rhubarb bitters are actually trendy. The flavors are so completely complementary that you wonder why they don't double-date more often.

In France, rhubarb compote, which is what the French would call rhubarb that has been cooked down until it is almost a sauce, would be served over ice cream or fromage blanc or yogurt for a simple, quick and pretty weeknight dessert. Although I like this chunkier rhubarb over all of those things, I also like it mixed with other fruits—strawberries are a natural, but the last of the season's pears make a good match too.

If you are a bitters aficionado, play with other flavors (I think grapefruit, orange, or cherry bitters could be wonderful). But if bitters are not for you, omit them—the rhubarb has enough flavor to go it alone.

1 pound (454 grams) trimmed rhubarb

½ cup (100 grams) sugar
About 1 tablespoon Angostura bitters (if you use other bitters, experiment with the amount)

1 tablespoon grenadine (optional)
Honey or freshly squeezed lemon juice, if needed

Makes 4 servings

SERVING: The rhubarb is good warm, cold and every temperature in between, on its own or with cake or cookies or cream of any kind. It's delicious spooned over simple cakes, like the Gâteau de Savoie (page 11) or Plain and Simple Almond Cake (page 18). Or try this: Crumble some Double-Butter Double-Baked Petit Beurre Cookies (page 270) over or under the rhubarb and finish with a spoonful of whipped cream or crème fraîche. This last combo is quick enough for a school night and chic enough for a dinner party.

STORING: The rhubarb can be refrigerated in a covered container for up to 1 week.

Center a rack in the oven and preheat the oven to 400 degrees F.

Cut the rhubarb into pieces about 1½ inches long and toss them into a large bowl. Stir in the sugar, 1 tablespoon bitters and the grenadine, if you're using it, and let rest for about 10 minutes, stirring a few times, until a syrup starts to develop.

Transfer the rhubarb to a baking dish—I use a Pyrex pie plate—and cover with foil. Roast the rhubarb, gently stirring after 10 minutes, for 15 to 20 minutes, or until the sugar is melted. Remove the foil and roast for another 5 to 10 minutes, or until the syrup is bubbly. (The total roasting time is about 30 minutes.)

Using a slotted spoon, carefully transfer the rhubarb, which will be very tender, to a heatproof bowl. Taste the syrup. If you want to concentrate the flavors—I often do—boil the syrup in a microwave oven (or in a saucepan on the stovetop) for 2 minutes or so, just until it thickens slightly. Pour the syrup back over the rhubarb. When the rhubarb and syrup have cooled, taste a piece of rhubarb with some syrup. If it isn't sweet enough, add a minuscule amount of honey; if it is too sweet, squeeze in a splash of lemon juice. And if you think you'd like more bitters, add more, a little at a time, tasting all the way.

Serve warm, at room temperature or chilled.

Apple Speculoos Crumble

Makes 4 servings

SERVING: If you want to re-create the crumble of Le Bistrot des Colonnes, you need to serve it warm and top it with ice cream, but if the timing doesn't work for you, don't worry: The crumble is very good at room temperature, with or without something creamy on top or alongside.

STORING: Although the crumble is best the day it is made, it is still awfully good the next day, even straight out of the fridge. If you're a fan of warm crumbles, you can reheat it in a microwave oven—just don't overdo it.

I CAN'T THINK OF A SINGLE TIME when someone has proposed eating anything with speculoos cookies that I haven't said, "Yes, please!" Whether it's a cellophane-wrapped single serving that comes with coffee at the corner café (or on a plane), a dusting of crumbled cookies on an ice cream sundae or a crust, top or bottom, made with speculoos crumbs, I'm eager for it. It's probably the mix of brown sugar and cinnamon, but it might also be the cookies' sandy texture and their Christmas-is-just-around-the-corner aroma.

Although I do bake my own Speculoos (page 320), like most French home cooks, I usually buy them in the supermarket. In France, the most popular brand is Lotus; in America, it's Biscoff (the same company and the same cookies); and in both countries you can find a speculoos spread—like Nutella, only spiced and caramel flavored. The cookies are so popular that recipes using them turn up regularly in French food magazines, and Philippe Conticini, one of the country's best pastry chefs, has written an entire cookbook showcasing the sweet.

Not that most people follow the recipes—they're more likely to take a traditional and beloved recipe and slip speculoos into it, which is what the cook at Le Bistrot des Colonnes near Paris's stock exchange, from whom I got this recipe, seems to have done. Le Bistrot des Colonnes is more café than bistro, and definitely more a neighborhood spot than a destination. When the waitress, Caroline, mentioned that the dessert du jour was a speculoos crumble (the French actually say *un crumble*), of course I couldn't say no. And that's how we ended up with a terra-cotta gratin dish filled with apples and topped with a nubby layer of buttery crumbled store-bought speculoos: no flour, oats, nuts or dried fruit. At Le Bistrot des Colonnes, the crumble was accompanied by a big scoop of rapidly melting vanilla ice cream. I suggest that it should always be brought to the table that way.

A LAST WORD ON THE COOKIES: If you can't find Biscoff brand, look for LU Cinnamon Sugar Spice cookies. Because they are bigger and thicker than the other speculoos, you'll need fewer.

1½–2 pounds (6 or 7; 700 to 900 grams) apples, peeled, cored and cut into 1- to 2-inch chunks	1 package (about 8 ounces; 227 grams) Biscoff or other speculoos (or homemade speculoos, page 320)
1 tablespoon sugar, or more to taste	1 stick (8 tablespoons; 4 ounces; 113 grams) unsalted butter, cut into small chunks, at cool room temperature
3 tablespoons plump, moist raisins or dried cherries or coarsely chopped nuts (optional)	

Center a rack in the oven and preheat the oven to 375 degrees F. Butter an 8-inch round cake pan or a baking dish that holds 4 to 5 cups. Put the pan or dish on a baking sheet lined with parchment paper or a silicone baking mat.

In a large bowl, toss the apples with the sugar and dried fruit or nuts, if you're using them. Set aside, but stir the apples occasionally as you make the crumble topping.

Break the cookies into pieces in a large bowl. I crush them with my hands, trying not to make too many teensy crumbs but never succeeding. Add the butter and toss, turn and press the cookies and butter with your fingers, working them together until you have a fairly well-blended ball. Don't worry about being too thorough—you just want the cookies to stick together.

Give the apples a last stir, then spoon them into the pan and pour over whatever juices have accumulated in the bowl. Pull off bits of the crumble mixture and strew them over the apples—you'll have enough to almost cover the fruit.

Bake the crumble for 35 to 40 minutes; cover it with a foil tent if the topping browns too quickly. You'll know the crumble is baked when the topping is deeply brown and the fruit is bubbling. Transfer the crumble to a rack and let it cool until it is just warm or it reaches room temperature.

Bonne Ideé
Any fruit that goes well with cinnamon (which means almost all fruits) can be used as the base of this crumble. In summer, try it with peaches (which should be peeled), nectarines (which don't need peeling), plums, cherries or berries. In winter, in place of the apples, think about pears, bananas, pineapple (or, better yet, bananas and pineapple) or a holiday mix of cranberries, apples, dried fruits and nuts. There's plenty of leeway for you to make your own house version.

Strawberry Shortcakes
Franco-American Style

Makes 6 servings

SERVING: In true Franco-American style, this dessert is just as good with wine—try it with a sparkling wine or a sweet wine, like a Muscat de Beaumes de Venise—as it is with lemonade.

STORING: All of the shortcakes' components can be made ahead, but once they are assembled, it's best to serve them immediately, or within 1 hour.

I CALL THESE SHORTCAKES for lack of a truer name. They're a hybrid: part French, even if they've never been seen in this form in Paris or Gallic points beyond; and part American, even if the only biscuits in sight are *biscuits à la cuillère*—ladyfingers. Consider them indies, a dessert for both the Fourth of July and the Fourteenth, Bastille Day.

There's little about these shortcakes that's short, since I sandwich a thick swirl of whipped cream between thin disks of ladyfinger cake and top the chubby flying saucer sweets with rosettes of cream and either a tumble of sweetened strawberries or an avalanche of them. And just for fun, I sometimes slip in a spoonful of Roasted Strawberries—a surprise and a treat.

The shortcakes start out ooh-la-la lovely and then, with the first spoonful, collapse, so that everyone ends up scraping their plates for the last bit of cream and the inevitable runaway berry.

FOR THE CAKES

1 recipe Ladyfinger Batter
   (page 424)
   Confectioners' sugar,
   for dusting

FOR THE FILLING AND
TOPPING

1 pound (454 grams) ripe,
   fragrant strawberries,
   hulled and cut into
   spoonable chunks

1–2 tablespoons sugar,
   or as needed

1½ cups (360 ml) very cold
   heavy cream

¼ cup (30 grams) confectioners'
   sugar

2 teaspoons pure vanilla extract
   Finely grated lemon or
   lime zest (optional)
   Roasted Strawberries
   (page 458) and/or
   fresh strawberries

TO MAKE THE CAKES: Draw twelve 3-inch circles on a large piece of parchment paper, flip the paper over and use it to line a baking sheet. This will be your template for piping out the ladyfinger batter.

Fit a pastry bag with a plain ½-inch tip (or use a zipper-lock bag to pipe—fill it and snip off a corner to make a ½-inch opening). Fill the bag with half of the ladyfinger batter and pipe out circles, starting at the center of each circle and spiraling your way out to the edges. The disks will be thin. If there are spaces between the spirals, run an offset spatula over them to smooth and fill them. Fill the bag with the remainder of the batter and continue to pipe until you've filled all 12 circles. If you have leftover batter, you can pipe out more

disks for another use or pipe out some ladyfingers in the open spaces or on another parchment-lined baking sheet—you'll be happy to have them as a baker's nibble later in the day.

Dust the tops of the disks lightly with confectioners' sugar and let them rest on the counter for 15 minutes while you preheat the oven.

Center a rack in the oven and preheat the oven to 400 degrees F. (Divide the oven into thirds if you have two baking sheets.)

Dust the cakes once again with confectioners' sugar and then slide the sheet(s) into the oven. Bake for 8 to 10 minutes, or until the disks are a pale golden color; these shouldn't color much. Lift the parchment from the baking sheet onto a cooling rack and let the cakes cool to room temperature.

When you're ready to use the cakes, run a long offset spatula under them to ease them off the parchment. (*You can make the disks up to 1 week ahead and keep them layered between sheets of parchment paper in a sealed container.*)

TO MAKE THE FILLING AND TOPPING: Stir the berries and sugar (the amount depending on the berries' sweetness and your taste) together in a bowl. Set aside, stirring from time to time, while you whip the cream. (*You can macerate the berries 1 to 2 hours ahead and keep them covered in the refrigerator; remove them from the fridge at least 15 minutes before serving.*)

Pour the heavy cream into the bowl of a stand mixer fitted with the whisk attachment, or work with a hand mixer in a large bowl. Sift over the confectioners' sugar and start beating the cream on low speed. As it begins to thicken, increase the speed and beat the cream until it's firm enough to hold its shape on a spoon. Beat in the vanilla. (*If you're not ready to construct the shortcakes, cover the bowl and refrigerate the cream for up to 6 hours; whisk vigorously before using.*)

TO ASSEMBLE THE SHORTCAKES: Taste the cut berries and add more sugar if needed. Stir in the zest, if you're using it. Fill a pastry bag fitted with an open-star tip with the whipped cream (or use a spoon).

Place one ladyfinger disk, flat side up, on each of six dessert plates. Pipe (or spoon) a swirl of cream on each disk—be generous and pipe high. If you're using the roasted strawberries, put a spoonful in the center of each mound of cream. Top with the remaining 6 cakes, right side up, and pipe a rosette of cream in the middle of each one. Finish the shortcakes with the roasted and/or fresh berries. Serve immediately or, if you must, refrigerate for no longer than 1 hour.

Apple Matafan

YEARS AGO, I LEARNED ABOUT the potato *matafan*, the galette that in older times (and probably only on farms) was meant to stave off morning (*matin*) hunger (*faim*, which sounds a lot like *fan* in French). You can only imagine my delight as a card-carrying dessert lover when I discovered that the savory snack has a sweet sib: this large apple pancake. The sweet *matafan* is a cross between a crêpe and a griddle cake. Thick, completely unfussy, chunky and chock-full of apples, it's extremely satisfying whether you have it for breakfast, brunch or a pick-me-up on a chilly afternoon. For sure it's hearty and would certainly have served its hunger-curbing purpose. It would also have made everyone who ate it happy, as it still does today.

The *matafan* is best made in a 10-inch skillet. My preference is for non-stick, but you'll be fine using a well-seasoned cast-iron pan or your favorite regular skillet.

Makes 6 servings

½ cup (120 ml) whole milk

2 tablespoons (1 ounce; 28 grams) unsalted butter

1⅓ cups (181 grams) all-purpose flour

1 teaspoon baking powder

¼ teaspoon fine sea salt

½ cup (100 grams) sugar

3 large eggs, at room temperature

1 tablespoon brandy, Calvados, applejack or apple cider

1 teaspoon pure vanilla extract

3 medium apples, such as Gala or Fuji, peeled, cored and thinly sliced

Flavorless oil, for the pan

Confectioners' sugar, for dusting

Maple syrup, for serving (optional)

SERVING: In France, the *matafan* would be served with just its shower of sugar, but my husband believes that anything that resembles a pancake should have maple syrup, so he drizzles more than a little over his wedge, and these days, so do I—it's a nice match, as is honey. A spoonful of jam is good too.

STORING: The *matafan* is meant to be eaten hot or warm on the day it is made. However, I've covered it and left it on the counter overnight and enjoyed snacking on it the next day.

Heat the milk and 1 tablespoon of the butter in a small saucepan until the butter melts and the milk is barely simmering; set aside.

Whisk the flour, baking powder and salt together in a small bowl.

Working in a large bowl, whisk the sugar and eggs together vigorously for a minute or two, until the mixture thickens a bit. Stir in the liquor or cider and vanilla. Whisk in the dry ingredients in 3 additions, stirring gently to keep the mixture smooth. Pour in the warm milk and butter and stir— the whisk will leave tracks and you'll have a smooth, shiny batter. Switch to a flexible spatula and stir in the apple slices, making sure that each slice is coated with batter.

Put the remaining 1 tablespoon butter and about ½ tablespoon oil in a 10-inch skillet and place over medium heat. When the butter has melted and the bubbling has subsided, pour in the batter. Immediately turn the heat down to its lowest setting, cover the pan (if you don't have a lid, just put a heatproof plate over the pan) and cook for 15 to 20 minutes, or until the bottom is deeply browned and the top is puffed, just starting to set and speckled with bubbles that have popped and stayed open. After about the first 10 minutes, check that the *matafan* isn't sticking or burning: Run a heatproof spatula around the sides and under the pancake. When the *matafan* is loosened, carefully slide it out of the pan and onto a plate. If the pan is dry, add a bit more oil and heat it. Slip the *matafan* back into the pan, uncooked side down, and cook until the bottom is brown and a knife inserted into the center of the *matafan* comes out clean, about 8 minutes.

Slide the *matafan* onto a serving platter and dust with confectioners' sugar. Serve with maple syrup, if you'd like.

Bettelman

*B*ETTELMAN, "BEGGAR" IN ALSATIAN, is sometimes translated as "bread pudding," but it's unlike any bread pudding most of us know. Its texture falls somewhere between a cake and a pudding. Its base, crumbled soft bread made even softer by a soak in hot milk, is held together by a custard similar to the one you'd use for an American bread pudding, except it's often flavored with rum, Calvados or juice. The pudding has chunks of apples and some raisins—and this is the part that changes it all—the egg whites are beaten until stiff and then folded into the mixture, so the finished pudding is light and almost fluffy.

A WORD ON STALE BREAD: If you don't have old bread in the house, you can stale fresh bread quickly by tearing it into small pieces and putting it on a baking sheet in a 300-degree-F oven for about 5 minutes, or until it feels dry.

Makes 8 servings

SERVING: A bettelman is traditionally served warm, but I think it's better after it's had a few hours—or even a day—to settle and gather itself. (Its texture will be a bit more compact after a day.) It's even good straight out of the refrigerator.

STORING: The bettelman will keep, loosely covered, at cool room temperature for 1 day or in the fridge for 2 or 3 days.

8 ounces (227 grams) stale soft bread, such as Brioche (page 421), challah or cinnamon-swirl or potato bread, torn into small pieces	1½ tablespoons dark rum, Calvados or apple or orange juice (optional)
2¼ cups (540 ml) whole milk	2 large apples, such as Rome, Cortland or Fuji, peeled, cored and cut into cubes 1 to 2 inches on a side
4 large eggs, separated, at room temperature	¼ cup (40 grams) plump, moist raisins (optional)
¾ cup (150 grams) sugar, plus 2 tablespoons	Pinch of fine sea salt
1 teaspoon ground cinnamon	1 tablespoon unsalted butter, cut into bits
1 teaspoon pure vanilla extract	

Put the bread in a large, wide heatproof bowl. Bring the milk to a boil and pour it over the bread, poking down any unsubmerged pieces with a spoon. Set aside for 30 minutes to soak. (*If it's more convenient, you can cover the bowl and set it aside for up to 2 hours.*)

WHEN YOU'RE READY TO BAKE: Center a rack in the oven and preheat the oven to 400 degrees F. Generously butter a 9½-inch deep-dish pie plate or another pan that holds at least 7 cups and can double as a serving dish (a gratin pan is good). Place the pan on a baking sheet lined with parchment paper or a silicone baking mat.

Stir the bread around in the bowl with a fork, mashing it as you go; it will be mushy, and that's what you want.

In another bowl, whisk together the egg yolks and ¾ cup of the sugar, beating until thick and well blended. Whisk in the cinnamon, vanilla and liquor or juice, if you're using it. Pour over the bread, switch to a sturdy flexible spatula or wooden spoon and stir to blend. Add the apple pieces and raisins, if you're using them, and stir so that you've got a homogeneous batter.

Working in the bowl of a stand mixer fitted with the whisk attachment, or in a large bowl with a hand mixer, beat the egg whites and salt at medium-high speed until the whites are foamy and opaque. Gradually add the remaining 2 tablespoons sugar and continue to beat until the whites form medium-stiff peaks. (If you end up with stiff peaks, don't worry about it.) Using a flexible spatula, stir one quarter of the whites into the batter to lighten it a bit. Add the rest of the whites and fold them in. Go easy; it's better to have a few specks of white than to overmix. Scrape the batter into the pan—it may look as if it will overflow the pan, but it will be okay. Scatter the bits of butter over the top.

Bake for 60 to 70 minutes, or until the bettelman is puffed at the center, golden brown and slightly crusty; a knife inserted into the center should come out clean. If, after about 30 or 40 minutes, the pudding looks as if it's getting too brown too fast, cover it lightly with a foil tent. When it's done, transfer the bettelman, still on the baking sheet, to a rack and let cool until it is just warm or reaches room temperature before serving.

Pistachio and Berry Gratins

Makes 6 servings

Hear the word "gratin," and your thoughts are likely to turn to potatoes or melted cheese or maybe both, but gratins are not just savory. And they're not just hearty winter fare either, and here's the proof: berries topped with pistachio cream and baked until everything is so hot that the fruit bubbles and the cream puffs, browns and bubbles too. If you're lucky, some of the fruit and cream will bubble over the edge of the cups. It's a bit messy and a lot beautiful.

In some ways this is an inside-out fruit tart in the long tradition of tarts that are filled with almond cream, topped with fruit and baked until golden. But in this gratin, there's no crust and the fruit goes in before the cream. And the cream is made with pistachios. Of course, you can stick to the classic Almond Cream (page 432) or use hazelnuts.

Because there's no crust required and because the individual gratins can be assembled and refrigerated until you're ready to bake, this is an ideal dessert for a casual weekend dinner with friends. And, as you've probably surmised, it's endlessly variable. Whatever's fresh, juicy and colorful in the market will make a good gratin (see Bonne Idée). When winter comes along, you can swap apples, pears, pineapple, oranges or even kumquats for the berries.

I usually make these in custard cups, but they're just right in the dishes you'd use to make crème brûlée and they're fine in teacups, too. In fact, they're even more fun when you mix and match containers.

SERVING: This spoon dessert needs no accompaniment, decoration or garnish, but it is good (and just a tad messier) served warm with a scoop of ice cream.

STORING: The gratins are meant to be enjoyed the day they are baked, but you can keep the unbaked gratins covered in the refrigerator for up to 1 day before baking them.

2½	cups (375 grams) fresh blueberries or mixed fresh berries	(page 432), with pistachios substitued for almonds, chilled and ready to use
1	lemon or lime	Pistachios, shelled and
	About 2 teaspoons sugar	coarsely chopped, for
1	recipe Pistachio Cream	topping (optional)

Center a rack in the oven and preheat the oven to 350 degrees F. Line a baking sheet with parchment paper or a silicone baking mat (this is your drip catcher, since drips are guaranteed). Lightly butter six custard cups, crème brûlée dishes or other containers with a capacity of 6 to 8 ounces and place them on the baking sheet.

Put the berries in a medium bowl and finely grate the zest of the lemon or lime over them. Add 1½ teaspoons sugar, mix everything together and let sit, stirring occasionally, for 5 to 10 minutes, until a little syrup has developed.

Stir and taste the berries; if you think you want the mix a bit sweeter, add a little more sugar. If you want more pucker, add just a squirt or two of lemon or lime juice. Divide the fruit evenly among the cups.

Soft stone fruits make wonderful gratins, but you've got to chop the fruit or cut it into cubes. I like to use (peeled) peaches or nectarines (no need to peel), apricots, plums or cherries. Pit the fruit, chop it coarsely or dice it, and give it the same sugar-zest-and-juice treatment as above. To make it even juicier, think about adding a couple of berries to each gratin.

Another Bonne Idée

ONE BIG GRATIN: Mix the fruit together in an 8- or 9-inch pie plate or small baking pan and then, when the juices have developed, stir everything together again, taste for sugar and juice and cover with the pistachio cream.

Spoon an equal amount of pistachio cream over each portion of fruit and use a small offset spatula or the back of a spoon to smooth it as evenly as you can over the berries. (If there are bare patches here and there, leave them.) Scatter over the chopped pistachios, if you're using them.

Bake for 30 to 35 minutes, or until the gratins are golden and the fruit is bubbling. The pistachio cream may have sunk into the fruit and it might have run over the rims of the cups, but that's fine. Transfer the gratins, still on the baking sheet, to a cooling rack and let cool until they are warm or reach room temperature before serving.

Dark Chocolate Mousse

Makes 8 servings

SERVING: The mousse can be served elegantly in small cups or bowls, topped with a rosette of unsweetened whipped cream, or family style, as it's often served in French homes.

STORING: The mousse can be covered tightly and kept in the refrigerator for up to 1 day.

WHEN YOU NEED A LUSCIOUS MOUSSE to fill a layer cake, to scoop or pipe into cream puffs or éclairs or to serve to chocolate lovers, this is the recipe you'll turn to. It is everything a mousse should be: creamy, full flavored and rich, without seeming heavy. In other words, impossible to resist. It came to me from Pierre Hermé and it's a pro's recipe. Translation: It's a cooked-sugar-syrup mousse for which you'll need a candy or instant-read thermometer and about 25 uninterrupted minutes to make the sugar-syrup mousse. Anytime you're boiling sugar, you've got to pay attention. The temperature creeps up so slowly and then—whoosh—it speeds up, and you've got to be there at the precise moment.

Because you have to beat the eggs and syrup together until they cool to room temperature—a process that can take up to 10 minutes—a stand mixer is my tool of choice here (although a hand mixer will do the job too).

1¾ cups (420 ml) very cold heavy cream	10 ounces (283 grams) bittersweet chocolate, coarsely chopped
2 large eggs, at room temperature	½ cup (100 grams) sugar
4 large egg yolks, at room temperature	3 tablespoons water

Working in the bowl of a stand mixer fitted with the whisk attachment, or in a large bowl with a heavy-duty hand mixer, beat the cream until it holds medium-firm peaks. If you're working in a stand mixer, transfer the cream to another bowl and rinse and dry the mixer bowl and whisk. Cover the whipped cream and refrigerate.

Put the eggs and yolks in the mixer bowl and fit the machine with the whisk attachment, or work in another large bowl with the hand mixer. Beat the eggs at low speed just to break them up. Set aside while you prepare the chocolate and syrup.

Melt the chocolate in a microwave oven or in a heatproof bowl set over a saucepan of simmering water, making sure that the heat isn't too high and that the chocolate remains thick and shiny. If necessary, scrape the chocolate into a bowl that's large enough to hold all the ingredients for the mousse; set aside. The chocolate must cool (114 degrees F is the ideal temperature) so that when you fold in the cold whipped cream, it doesn't seize and clump.

Bring the sugar and water to a boil in a small heavy-bottomed saucepan. Swirl the pan to mix the ingredients as they start to heat, and if some of the sugar spatters on the sides of the pan, wash it down with a silicone pastry brush dipped in cold water. Cook the sugar over high heat until it reaches

257 degrees F on a candy or instant-read thermometer, about 8 minutes (or maybe a little more, depending on the dimensions of your pan and the heat you have under it).

Back to the eggs: Beat the eggs on the lowest speed, just to get them moving again, then very slowly pour in the hot sugar syrup in a thin stream. Try to pour the syrup between the side of the bowl and the whirring whisk. Please be careful—this is *soooooooo* hot and sticky! No matter how careful you are, you'll get spatters and you should just leave them—trying to scrape them into the eggs will only produce lumps. When all the syrup is in the bowl, up the mixer speed to high and beat until the eggs are pale and more than doubled in volume, about 5 minutes. If the eggs have doubled but still feel warm, lower the mixer speed to medium and keep beating until they reach room temperature.

Pull the whipped cream from the refrigerator and give it a couple of rounds with a whisk, just to bring back the medium-firm peaks. Working with a large flexible spatula, fold about one quarter of the whipped cream into the chocolate to lighten it, then gently fold in the rest of the cream. Now, using the spatula and your lightest touch, fold in the whipped eggs. Your voluminous eggs will deflate some, but be gentle and the texture of your mousse will be lovely.

Use the mousse now if you're filling a cake with it, but if you want to pipe it, it's best to cover and chill it for at least 1 hour. And if you are serving it on its own, chill it.

Mascarpone Mousse

Makes 4 servings

SERVING: Serve with fruit or just serve as is. Not that it wouldn't be good with a Cat's Tongue (page 278) or three, a couple of Desert Roses (page 391) or even a teensy square of the Chunky Chocolate Fruit-and-Nut Bars (page 394).

STORING: The mousse is best eaten the day it's made, although you can hold it in the refrigerator for another day or two.

THE FIRST TIME I MADE THIS MOUSSE, inspired by a dessert from the Provençal chef Reine Sammut, I had a mini aha moment. With the first spoonful, I understood why a mousse is called a mousse: The dessert is as light as foam, which is what the word means. That this mousse is so airy is a triumph of beaten egg whites over dense, creamy mascarpone. While the mousse's bubbles vanish as quickly as foam on the shore, the flavor lingers. You catch the tang of the mascarpone and the warmth of the honey, and then you're ready for another spoonful. There's a bit of sugar in the mousse and a pinch of salt, but what you taste is the purity of mascarpone, cream and honey.

And because the flavor is so clean, you have choices. You can serve the mousse neat or you can pair it with fruits. Sammut suggests poached peaches, and I like that idea. But I also like tossing berries with a little honey (or sugar or maple syrup) and either hiding them under the mousse or arranging them prettily on top. In winter, I team the mousse with finely diced Candied Orange Peel (page 459), putting the peel in the bottom of the glasses and drizzling some of the syrup on top.

If you make this in summer, you might want to do what Sammut does: Finish the mousse with sugarcoated rose petals (page 461).

½ teaspoon unflavored gelatin	2 tablespoons honey
1½ tablespoons cold water	3 large egg whites, at room
8 ounces (227 grams)	temperature
mascarpone	Pinch of fine sea salt
⅓ cup (80 ml) heavy cream	3 tablespoons sugar

Put the gelatin in a microwave-safe bowl, pour over the cold water and let the gelatin sit for about 3 minutes, or until it is completely moistened and has begun to "bloom," or expand. Then heat the gelatin in a microwave oven for 15 to 20 seconds to liquefy it.

Scrape the mascarpone into a large bowl—one with a pouring spout, if you've got one—and gently stir to loosen it.

Pour the cream and honey into a small saucepan, put over medium heat and bring just to a boil. (If you prefer, you can do this in the microwave.) Allow the liquid to cool for 5 minutes, then pour some into the gelatin and stir until smooth. Stir the contents of the gelatin bowl into the remaining cream and then pour everything into the bowl with the mascarpone. Use a whisk or flexible spatula to blend gently.

Working in the bowl of a stand mixer fitted with the whisk attachment, or in a large bowl with a hand mixer, beat the egg whites and salt together on medium-high speed until the whites just begin to turn opaque. Little by little, add the sugar and keep beating until the whites are marshmallowy—they'll be smooth, glossy and white and, when you lift the whisk, they'll form tipsy peaks.

Turn the whites out onto the mascarpone mixture and, using the whisk or flexible spatula, lightly fold them in. Thoroughness is less important than gentleness here.

Pour or spoon the mousse into four 1-cup-capacity goblets, stemless wineglasses, lowball glasses or bowls. Cover the mousse with plastic film and refrigerate for at least 3 hours before serving, making sure to keep it away from foods with strong odors.

Honey-Yogurt Mousse

Makes 4 servings

SERVING: The mousse can go to the table with nothing more than a spoon or it can be accompanied by a topping or a few cookies. Because I think it's always nice to serve something crunchy with something smooth, I like to serve it with Croquets (page 310).

STORING: Covered and refrigerated, the mousse will keep for up to 2 days.

DESSERTS LIKE THIS ARE THE KIND that make French hosts look like geniuses. They're elegant in their simplicity, flavorful, open to flourishes and easy to make. I use Greek yogurt here and because it's so thick and will become even thicker after it's drained, I choose nonfat yogurt. If you need to save time and are not going to hold the mousse overnight, you can just dash ahead and skip the draining, but you get more flavor and better texture if you press out the yogurt's water, a process that takes a couple of hours. My house yogurt is plain and so it's what I use in this mousse, but if there's a flavored yogurt that you think would be good with honey, use it. (Depending on the flavor, you might or might not want to add the vanilla extract.)

Choose whatever honey you like or have at hand. My preference is for one with character, since the flavor of the dessert depends on it. If you're going to top the mousse—think berries (in summer, I toss fresh strawberries with a little sugar and grated lemon zest), chocolate shavings or Cocoa Crumbs (page 426)—you might want to serve it in martini glasses; their flared shape gives you room to play.

1 cup (225 grams) plain Greek yogurt (see above; nonfat is fine)	½ cup (120 ml) very cold heavy cream
¾ teaspoon unflavored gelatin	½ cup (170 grams) honey
2 tablespoons cold water	2 teaspoons pure vanilla extract

At least 2 hours (and up to 1 day) ahead, line a strainer with a double thickness of dampened cheesecloth and set it over a bowl. (In a pinch, I've used a triple layer of paper towels.) Spoon the yogurt into the strainer, draw up the edges of the cheesecloth to cover the yogurt and put a heavy bowl (one that fits inside the strainer) on top of the yogurt. (If the base of the bowl doesn't cover the surface of the yogurt, you'll have to move it every once in a while to press the yogurt evenly.) Leave the yogurt on the counter to drain or, if you're going to drain it for more than 2 hours, refrigerate it.

When you're ready to make the mousse, discard the liquid and spoon the yogurt into a medium bowl.

Put the gelatin in a small microwave-safe bowl and pour over the cold water and let the gelatin sit for 3 minutes, or until it is completely moistened and has begun to "bloom," or expand. Then heat the gelatin in the microwave oven for 15 seconds, just to liquefy it.

Working in the bowl of a stand mixer fitted with the whisk attachment, or in a small bowl with a hand mixer, beat the heavy cream just until it holds soft peaks.

Whisk the honey into the yogurt and then add the vanilla. Pour in the hot gelatin and immediately start whisking so that it blends without forming strands or lumps. Fold in the whipped cream.

Spoon the mousse into four small bowls or glasses and refrigerate for at least 2 hours before serving.

Double-Mint Milk Chocolate Mousse and Gelée

Makes 4 servings

SERVING: It's nice to have a dollop of crème fraîche, sour cream or yogurt—something creamy and just a bit tangy—with the mousse, but it's not necessary. Because the mousse and the gelée both have mint in them, a sprig on the plate for color and a clue of what's in store is a good addition.

STORING: You can keep the mousse for 1 day in the refrigerator—and you want to keep it there for a while so that the mint flavor can develop—but the longer you refrigerate it, the denser it will become.

EVEN I HAVE BEEN KNOWN to just say no at the end of a meal. And that's what I said after a very good meal with friends at L'Hédoniste, one of Paris's new-style bistros. But I must not have said it loud enough, because minutes later I was sharing a *verrine* (a slender tumbler) of milk-chocolate mousse with my friend Christian, who was the first to discover that it had a secret. "Make sure you push your spoon all the way to the bottom," he said. And, when I did, the treat was revealed. There, beneath the layer of light and foamy mousse, was a layer of jiggly mint gelée. It was delicious, but it was also smart: It brought another texture to the dessert, and it brought pop. The gelée is mintier than the mousse, and so you get what I think of as a progression of coolness. Top this with crème fraîche (or even yogurt), and the flavors and textures will be even bolder.

A WORD ON TIMING: The mousse and gelée are good as soon as they're both set, but the flavors get deeper if you wait a few hours.

FOR THE GELÉE

- ½ cup (120 ml) water
- ¼ cup (50 grams) sugar
- Leaves from 3 sprigs fresh mint, finely chopped
- 1 tablespoon cold water
- 1 teaspoon unflavored gelatin
- Squirt of fresh lemon or lime juice

FOR THE MOUSSE

- ⅓ cup (80 ml) heavy cream
- 5 sprigs fresh mint

- 6 ounces (170 grams) best-quality milk chocolate, finely chopped
- 4 large egg whites, at room temperature
- Pinch of fine sea salt
- 3 tablespoons sugar

- Crème fraîche, store-bought or homemade (page 440), plain Greek yogurt or sour cream, for topping (optional)

TO MAKE THE GELÉE: Put the water, sugar and chopped mint in a small saucepan and bring to a boil. Stir to dissolve the sugar and allow the syrup to boil for 1 minute; remove from the heat.

Pour the 1 tablespoon water into a small microwave-safe bowl, sprinkle over the gelatin and let it sit for about 3 minutes, until the gelatin has absorbed the water. Heat the gelatin in the microwave for 15 seconds to liquefy it. Scrape into the syrup, stir well and then add the lemon or lime juice.

Divide the gelée among four custard cups, tumblers, martini glasses or wineglasses and refrigerate.

TO MAKE THE MOUSSE: Pour the cream into a microwave-safe bowl or a small saucepan, toss in the mint and bring to a boil in the microwave or on the stovetop. Remove from the heat and allow the cream to steep for 30 minutes. Bring back to a boil before continuing.

Melt the chocolate in the microwave or in a heatproof bowl set over a pan of simmering water. Strain the cream over the chocolate; discard the mint. Gently stir the cream into the chocolate until smooth.

Working in the bowl of a stand mixer fitted with the whisk attachment, or in a large bowl with a hand mixer, beat the egg whites and salt just until they turn opaque. Gradually add the sugar and continue to beat until they hold firm, glossy peaks. Using a flexible spatula, stir one quarter of the whites into the chocolate to lighten it, then gently but thoroughly fold in the remaining whites.

Spoon the mousse evenly over the gelée and chill for at least 4 hours (or for as long as overnight). When the mousse is set, cover tightly with plastic film—anything with cream and egg whites is a magnet for refrigerator odors.

Serve topped with crème fraîche, yogurt or sour cream, if you'd like.

Marquise au Chocolat

Makes 8 to 10 servings

THE SEVENTEENTH AND EIGHTEENTH CENTURIES were good times for French pastry chefs. Kings still reigned, aristocrats were scattered around the country and everyone with a title who could afford sugar and a chef wanted special sweets. It's likely that the Marquise au Chocolat comes from this period. A frozen chocolate mousse, it starts off as a simple sweet, but in the hands of someone's chef, it could become baroque. Even at home, the possibilities for getting fancy with this sweet are just about limitless.

Traditionally, the marquise is packed into a loaf pan, frozen and then sliced just before serving. This is exceedingly practical, since you can make the dessert weeks ahead; use what you need and keep the rest in the freezer for the next dinner party. The mousse also lends itself to being made in mini loaf pans or even small ramekins—when unmolded, these look very professional.

Similarly, the marquise can be plain or surprising. Often you'll find pieces of Petit Beurre or Biscoff (speculoos) cookies inside it, or the mousse might rest on a cookie or crumb base. Truly, anything that goes with chocolate (and that can stand up to freezing) is fair game for an addition.

A WORD ON THE EGGS: The yolks in this recipe are not cooked, so it's important to use very fresh eggs, preferably organic and/or from a trusted local source.

SERVING: The best way to slice the marquise is to use dental floss or a warm knife—run a long-bladed knife under hot water and wipe it dry. Cut the marquise into slices that are a scant 1 inch thick. If you can serve the slices on cold plates, so much the better. Traditionally the marquise is served with vanilla crème anglaise (page 441), a lovely match. If you're rushed for time, you can serve it with faux crème anglaise: melted premium-quality vanilla ice cream. It is also good with whipped cream or crème fraîche.

STORING: Wrapped airtight, the marquise will keep in the freezer for up to 1 month.

- 1 stick (8 tablespoons; 4 ounces; 113 grams) unsalted butter, cut into 16 pieces
- 13 ounces (369 grams) bittersweet chocolate, coarsely chopped
- 4 very fresh large egg yolks, preferably organic, at room temperature
- ⅓ cup (67 grams) sugar, plus 3 tablespoons sugar
- ¼ teaspoon fleur de sel or a pinch of fine sea salt
- 1½ cups (355 ml) very cold heavy cream

Line an 8½-×-4½-inch or 9-×-5-inch loaf pan with plastic film, leaving some overhang to make unmolding easier.

Put a large heatproof bowl over a pot of simmering water. Drop in the pieces of butter, cover with the chocolate and heat slowly, stirring occasionally, until the ingredients have melted; don't let the chocolate get too hot. When the chocolate and butter have melted, you should have a thick, velvety mixture. Transfer the bowl to the counter and let cool for 15 minutes.

Working in the bowl of a stand mixer fitted with the whisk attachment, or in a large bowl with a hand mixer, beat the yolks, ⅓ cup of the sugar and

If you'd like to add another texture to the marquise, you can include some cookies in the mousse. Petit Beurre (homemade, page 270, or store-bought), LU Cinnamon Sugar Spice, Biscoff and arrowroot cookies all work well. Use a knife to cut them into pieces of any size and, as you're spooning in the mousse, scatter in some cookie bits. If you'd like, you can be more orderly and make layers of cookies and layers of marquise. Or make a base for the marquise: After the mousse is in the pan, use a spatula to smooth the top and lay or sprinkle cookies or graham crackers, graham cracker crumbs, homemade Petit Beurre crumbs or Cocoa Crumbs (page 426) over the mousse, pressing gently to secure them.

Another Bonne Idée

To give this grown-up dessert a kid-like finish, pour some hot Hard-Crack Chocolate Sauce (page 445) over the loaf or bring a pitcher to the table and let your guests pour as much as they'd like over their own portions. Do that and they'll have the fun of watching it harden as soon as it hits the frozen dessert.

the salt at medium speed until the mixture pales and thickens slightly, about 2 minutes. Turn the yolk mixture out onto the chocolate and butter and, with a flexible spatula or a whisk, gently fold together. Don't worry about being thorough now; you're going to fold again soon.

Wipe out the mixer (or mixing) bowl and pour in the heavy cream. Whip the cream until it shows the first sign of thickening, then slowly and steadily add the remaining 3 tablespoons sugar and beat until the cream holds firm peaks. Spoon it onto the chocolate and very gently fold it in.

Spoon the mousse into the prepared pan, pushing it into the corners and smoothing the top. Fold the edges of the plastic film over the mousse and then wrap the pan in more plastic film. Freeze the marquise for at least 6 hours. (*The marquise can be frozen for up to 1 month.*)

To unmold, unwrap the pan, pull the edges of the plastic film away from the marquise and tug on the plastic to release the marquise. If the marquise is recalcitrant, dip the bottom of the pan in hot water for about 15 seconds, then try again. Turn the marquise over onto a platter or cutting board and serve immediately. (If it's more convenient for you, you can unmold the marquise and return it to the freezer for a few hours before serving.)

Lavender–White Chocolate Pots de Crème

Makes 6 to 8 servings

SERVING: These pots de crème are meant to be served cold, making them perfect for entertaining. If you'd like, you can pipe a little rosette of whipped cream on top of each custard—it's pretty but not at all necessary.

STORING: Covered tightly and kept away from foods with strong aromas, the pots de crème will keep in the refrigerator for up to 2 days.

THERE'S SOMETHING SO WINNIE-THE-POOH about pots de crème, and something so utterly grown-up and sophisticated too. Baked custards are classic comfort food, a quickly made dessert that every French home cook knows how to put together and a sweet that, depending on the flavors you choose and the *pots* you use, can coddle a baby or delight a knowing bon vivant.

The dessert was all the rage in the nineteenth century, when hostesses collected pots de crème sets: elaborately decorated porcelain cups with dainty covers that came on matching trays. The sets are still available—I'm tempted to buy one every time I go to the flea market at Clignancourt in Paris—but these days the crèmes are more likely to be made in teacups, ramekins or even canning jars. Just about any heatproof cup that you're happy to serve in will do.

What's most important about this simple dessert is your choice of ingredients, particularly the chocolate: You must use excellent white chocolate. White chocolate contains no cocoa solids and, if it doesn't have at least 30% cocoa butter, its flavor will be more sugar than chocolate—check the label. For these pots de crème, you're relying on the chocolate to give the dessert a warm chocolate-vanilla flavor and to contribute to the crème's thick, velvet-like texture.

The lavender is the other star player and you have to be as fussy about it as you are the chocolate. Choose edible lavender buds (not ground lavender). It's sometimes called culinary lavender and you should sniff it before you use it—the scent should make you think of warm days in Provence. Because lavender's strength varies—and because too much lavender can quickly tip the dessert from dreamy to dreadful—make the custard for the first time with 1 tablespoon of lavender. Then you can increase or decrease the amount the next time you make it.

A WORD ON SERVING SIZES: I usually use 1-cup ramekins and make 6 servings, but you can use smaller cups and make more portions; just keep in mind that the baking time might be less.

2 cups (480 ml) heavy cream	4 ounces (113 grams) best-quality white chocolate, finely chopped
1 cup (240 ml) whole milk	
⅓ cup (67 grams) sugar	
1 tablespoon edible dried lavender flowers	1 large egg
	4 large egg yolks
1 fat strip orange or lime zest (optional)	Pinch of fine sea salt
	½ teaspoon pure vanilla extract

Put 1½ cups of the heavy cream, the milk, sugar, lavender and zest, if you're using it, in a small saucepan and bring to a boil over medium heat. Stay close—milk has a nasty habit of boiling over. Turn off the heat, cover the pan and allow the mixture to steep for about 20 minutes.

Meanwhile, center a rack in the oven and preheat the oven to 300 degrees F. Place six to eight heatproof ramekins (see previous page) in a roasting pan lined with a double thickness of paper towels. Bring a kettle of water to a boil.

Put the white chocolate in a small heatproof bowl. Bring the remaining ½ cup heavy cream to a boil (you can do this in a microwave oven), pour the cream over the chocolate and let it sit for 30 seconds. Using a small flexible spatula or whisk and starting in the center of the bowl, stir the cream and chocolate together in increasingly wider circles until you have a smooth ganache.

Bring the lavender cream back to a boil, then immediately turn off the heat. Strain the cream and discard the lavender.

Working in a large heatproof liquid measuring cup (I use a 2-quart one) with a spout, a pitcher or a large bowl, whisk the egg and yolks together with the salt until smooth. Very slowly, dribble a bit of the hot cream over the eggs and then whisk like mad. Add about one quarter of the cream in this drizzle-and-whisk fashion—insurance against cooking the eggs. Whisk some of the hot cream into the white chocolate ganache, then add the ganache to the eggs. Then, in a steadier stream and using a gentler touch, whisk in the remaining cream. Stir in the vanilla extract.

If you've got lots of bubbles, skim them off with a spoon as best as you can, but don't worry about being meticulous. Divide the mixture among the ramekins. (If your mix doesn't look smooth, strain it into the ramekins.) Pour enough hot water into the roasting pan to come about halfway up the sides of the ramekins.

Bake the custards for 40 to 60 minutes (the time will depend on the size of your ramekins): When you tap the sides of the ramekins, the custard should be completely set except, perhaps, for a small circle in the center that will still shimmy. Transfer the roasting pan to a cooling rack and leave the setup intact for 10 minutes, then carefully lift the ramekins onto a rack to cool to room temperature.

Cover the custards and refrigerate for at least 2 hours before serving.

Bonne Idée

MINT–WHITE CHOCOLATE POTS DE CRÈME: Omit the lavender and steep the cream, milk and sugar with ½ cup (loosely packed) fresh mint leaves. If you'd like to use zest in this recipe, I'd suggest lime. Also omit the vanilla extract—with this version, you want to accentuate the bright flavors and gently tone down the warm ones.

Chocolate Crème Caramel

AS FANCY AS IT SOUNDS, LOOKS AND TASTES, crème caramel has just two elements: some cooked sugar that's spooned into the bottom of the ramekins and a quickly made custard that's poured over it. The magic occurs after the custards are baked and chilled. That's when you get to turn each ramekin upside down and watch as the custard shimmies its way out onto the plate and emerges cloaked in shiny caramel. While I consider each unmolded sweet a triumph, crème caramel is so basic that most cafés, hardly bastions of haute pâtisserie, have it on their menus every day at both lunch and dinner.

The classic crème caramel, sometimes called *crème renversée* because it's turned upside down to serve, is vanilla, often made with milk and cream, and sometimes with a combination of whole eggs and yolks. Since this chocolate crème is made with just milk and a couple of eggs, I think of it as "lite."

You can use milk, semisweet or bittersweet chocolate, and the custard can be infused with spice, if you'd like. I skip the spice when I'm using bittersweet chocolate and go for an infusion when I've got milk or semisweet. Fresh mint leaves (about 8) are nice with milk chocolate, ditto Earl Grey tea (about 1 teaspoon or 1 tea bag). Crushed cardamom pods (about 5), a (2-inch) cinnamon stick or coarsely chopped coffee beans (about ¼ cup) are good with semisweet.

⅓ cup (67 grams) sugar	2 ounces (57 grams) milk, semisweet or bittersweet chocolate, finely chopped
1¼ cups (300 ml) whole milk	
Spice, herb or other flavoring (optional; see above)	2 large eggs

Center a rack in the oven and preheat the oven to 300 degrees F. Line a roasting pan or a 9-×-13-inch baking pan with a double thickness of paper towels. Have it and four 6- to 8-ounce ramekins at hand. Bring a kettle of water to a boil.

Reserve 2 tablespoons of the sugar and sprinkle the remaining sugar over the bottom of a small skillet or saucepan, preferably nonstick, and put the pan over medium-high heat. When you see the sugar start to melt around the edges, begin stirring it in small circles, making your way around the edges and then going deeper into the center of the pan, until all the sugar is melted, blended, bubbling and, most important, a medium amber color; stay with the caramel, because the color changes in seconds. You can check the color by dropping a bit on a white plate. As soon as it's the right color, pull the pan from the heat and, being very, very careful (caramel is ferociously hot and sticky), divide it among the ramekins. Hold the ramekins by their tops and swirl to coat the bottoms with caramel. You'll never get the caramel perfectly even, and that will never matter. Place the ramekins in the roasting pan.

Bonne Idée

CLASSIC CRÈME CARAMEL:
For eight 4-ounce custards,
double the amount of
caramel and use it to line
eight ramekins. Bring
2 cups heavy cream and
1 cup whole milk to a boil.
Whisk together 2 large
eggs, 5 large egg yolks and
⅓ cup sugar until slightly
thickened. Slowly (first
in dribbles and then in a
steadier stream) stir in
the hot liquid. Pour the
custard into the caramel-
lined cups. Bake in a water
bath as directed for 35 to
40 minutes.

Put the milk and the reserved 2 tablespoons sugar in a small saucepan and bring to a boil. If you decide to flavor the milk, drop in the ingredient you've chosen, turn off the heat, cover the pan and let it steep for 15 minutes; before using the milk, bring it back to a boil and strain it.

Put the chopped chocolate in a heatproof bowl and pour the hot milk over it. Let stand for about 5 minutes to melt.

Meanwhile, put the eggs in a medium bowl and whisk them for about 1 minute; they'll pale a bit. Using a heatproof spatula, stir the chocolate and milk together until smooth. Then, stirring the eggs without stopping, gradually pour the hot chocolate milk over the eggs and stir until blended. You'll have bubbles on top of the crème, don't worry: You're going to turn the custards over and no one will ever see the bottoms.

Divide the custard among the ramekins. Pour enough hot water into the roasting pan to come halfway up the sides of the ramekins. Carefully slide the pan into the oven.

Bake the custards for 35 to 45 minutes, or until they are firm around the edges and just jiggly in the center. Remove the roasting pan from the oven and carefully place the ramekins on a cooling rack. Leave the ramekins at room temperature for about 20 minutes, then transfer them to the refrigerator. Chill for at least 4 hours, or until they are thoroughly cold before serving. (*You can make these 1 day ahead; cover and keep refrigerated.*)

When you're ready to serve, run a table knife around the edges of the ramekins, then turn the custards over onto small plates with raised rims. You might have to shake the ramekins a little or tap them gently against the plate to cajole the custards to come out, but fear not—they won't stick.

EGGS, LARGE AND SMALL, FRESH AND EXTRA-FRESH

....

When you want eggs in France, there are two places you can get them: the supermarket and the *fromagerie*. Most cheese shops stock all things dairy, so that in addition to cheese, you can find milk, cream, crème fraîche, butter (unsalted and salted) and eggs. *Chez la fromagerie*, eggs come singly or in packs, and in two sizes: medium and large. Because I always bake with large eggs in the U.S., I initially chose those in France, only to discover they were too big for my recipes; medium is the size I need there.

The eggs I use in my recipes have whites that weigh a little more than 1 ounce (30 grams) and yolks that weigh about 0.7 ounce (20 grams).

Once I'd figured out the sizes, the rest of the distinctions were easy: *Bio* is like our organic; *plein air* means "free range;" and *label rouge* indicates that the eggs have passed a certain test of quality. I thought I had it all sussed out until the day the *fromager* asked me if I wanted fresh eggs or extra-fresh eggs. Of course, I said extra-fresh: If fresh is good, fresher is better.

But then he asked what I was going to use them for. When I told him about the cake I had in mind, he pulled a box of eggs from a different stack and said, "Take these—if you're going to bake with eggs, why pay for extra-fresh?"

It was then that I got the lowdown. In addition to being labeled with the date that they were laid, French eggs are marked, as ours are, with a best-by date. And there's an additional sticker—a separate label that indicates how long the eggs will be extra-fresh, a date that is usually about 2½ weeks before their best-by time.

In the land of high-quality ingredients, in the country where people spend more money on their food than most other people do, the *fromager* wouldn't allow me to buy the extra-fresh box because I'd be wasting my money and the eggs' best qualities. "Buy these when you want to eat raw or only slightly cooked eggs. That's when they're worth it," he said. The next day, I brought him a piece of fresh cake to thank him for his lesson.

Caramelized-Coffee Bean Pots de Crème

Makes 6 servings

SERVING: While I often serve pots de crème chilled, I think these are nicest about 15 minutes out of the refrigerator. I also think they're nicest served with a cookie—I vote for Toasted Flour Sablés (page 267)—and a small squiggle of whipped cream.

STORING: Well covered, the custards will keep in the refrigerator for 1 day.

FOR THE FIRST FIVE YEARS that we lived in our Paris apartment near the Luxembourg Gardens, we'd pass the restaurant on our corner at least once a day, and at least once a day we'd peek in. There was a long bar that filled half of the restaurant and every morning, around 11:00, there'd be a small group of men drinking together. Yes, it might have been a little early for Calvados, but I looked at it as a show of camaraderie—the French workingman's answer to the coffee klatch. Down a few steps was the dining room, a plain room whose tables were covered with red- and white-checked cloths, whose chairs were a little rickety but serviceable and whose coatracks looked as if they were made to hold heavy wool coats, mufflers and well-worn hats. Depending on my mood and the amount of sunlight on the street, the place looked either dreary or delightful.

At last we went for dinner. And at last the mystery was solved—it was not delightful, but it wasn't dreary either: It was old-fashioned and pleasant. The food was what the French would call *correct*—there was nothing to find fault in or to get excited about. It was neither so good nor so bad that it would get in the way of conversation. And so we chatted with our friends all through dinner and never commented on any of the dishes—until dessert. The dessert, coffee pots de crème, was the best thing on the menu.

The custard was served in big white bowls—the kind with lions' heads on either side, usually used for onion soup; its texture was slippy-slidey; and the coffee flavor, while not robust, was good enough that we polished off every spoonful of the dessert, after exclaiming that the bowls were way too big.

A chat with the chef revealed that he'd flavored the custard with a popular French coffee extract, Trablit. "But you can use coffee beans, if you'd like," he said. And so I did—strong, aromatic espresso beans. And to give the beans even more gusto, I caramelized them in sugar. The result is more than pleasant and more than *correct*: It puts a pause in the conversation.

1½ cups (360 ml) whole milk	½ cup (100 grams) sugar
1 cup (240 ml) heavy cream	2 large eggs
½ cup (42 grams) espresso beans (regular or decaf)	5 large egg yolks
	Pinch of fine sea salt

Have the milk and cream measured and on the counter before you start.

To get the most flavor out of the espresso beans, you need to crack or crush them—not grind them—and the best way to do this is to put them in a mortar and give them a few taps with the pestle or to spread them out between sheets of parchment or wax paper and use the bottom of a skillet to bash them until they break.

Put the cracked beans and ¼ cup of the sugar in a heavy-bottomed saucepan. (I use a tall 3-quart pan.) Turn the heat to medium and start stirring with a wooden spoon. Within a couple of minutes, the sugar will start to melt and change color. Keep stirring without stopping as the color deepens and the sugar begins to smoke. Smoke—a fair amount of it—is part of the process, so you might want to have the exhaust fan going and the windows open. When the sugar is a strong amber color, stand away and pour in the milk and cream. The mixture will bubble furiously and the sugar may seize. Continue to stir until it smooths out, a matter of seconds. Pull the pan from the heat, cover and let steep for at least 20 minutes (or for up to 1 hour).

Center a rack in the oven and preheat the oven to 300 degrees F. Place six ramekins or coffee cups (with a capacity of at least 6 ounces; mine hold 1 cup) in a roasting pan lined with a double thickness of paper towels. Bring a kettle of water to a boil.

Bring the mixture back to a boil, then immediately turn off the heat. Strain the cream and discard the espresso beans.

Working in a large (at least 2-quart) heatproof liquid measuring cup with a spout, a pitcher or a large bowl, whisk together the eggs, yolks, the remaining ¼ cup sugar and the salt until smooth. Very slowly pour a bit of the hot milk and cream over the eggs and then whisk like mad. Once you've drizzled and whisked in about one quarter of the liquid and the risk of scrambling the eggs has passed, you can whisk in the remainder in a steadier stream.

Skim off any bubbles on top and divide the mixture among the ramekins. Pour enough hot water into the roasting pan to come about halfway up the sides of the ramekins.

Bake the custards for 35 to 40 minutes. When you tap the sides of the ramekins, the custards should be set except, perhaps, for a small circle in the center that will still shimmy; the rims of the custards will be dark. Transfer the roasting pan to a cooling rack and leave the setup intact for 10 minutes; then carefully lift the ramekins onto a rack to cool to room temperature.

Cover the custards and refrigerate for at least 2 hours before serving.

Tea and Honey Pots de Crème

Makes 6 to 8 servings

SERVING: The pots de crème should be cold through and through at serving time. They don't really need any dressing up, but if you want a flourish, you can top them with a rosette of whipped cream and/or a sugarcoated rose petal (page 461).

STORING: Tightly covered and kept away from foods with strong aromas, the pots de crème will keep in the refrigerator for up to 2 days.

COULD RIFF ON POTS DE CRÈME FOREVER and never run out of ideas. It's a classic culinary basic, a simple recipe with a generous spirit—it accepts new flavors and ingredients with open arms.

This version came to me when I was longing for spring. The weather in Paris was cold and wet and while the calendar said the season was here, there was nothing outdoors to prove it except the colorful hothouse flowers that lined the paths of the Luxembourg Gardens—but even they shivered. And so I came up with this pot de crème, a dessert that's part winter coziness—the honey and tea—and part breath of spring—the rose flavoring.

I like using rose-scented tea here—my favorite is Kusmi Rose Green Tea—but any very aromatic tea will work, rose or not, loose or in tea bags. I also add pure rose extract, but you needn't if it doesn't appeal to you. Rose has been *the* Parisian flavor for a few years now and its popularity shows no signs of waning, but it's not a flavor beloved by all.

Play with this and find the tea, honey and flavoring that make you happiest. And if you want to play even more, see Bonne Idée for a basic recipe to set you on your way.

A WORD ON SERVING SIZES: I usually use 1-cup ramekins and make 6 servings, but you can use smaller cups and make more portions, just keep in mind that the baking time might be less.

2 cups (480 ml) heavy cream	2 large eggs
1 cup (240 ml) whole milk	5 large egg yolks
¾ cup (150 grams) sugar	¼ cup (85 grams) honey
3 tablespoons loose rose tea (or 3 tea bags); or tea of your choice	1½ teaspoons pure vanilla extract
	½ teaspoon pure rose extract (I prefer Star Kay White)

Put the cream, milk, ½ cup of the sugar and the tea in a small saucepan and bring to a boil over medium heat, stirring to dissolve the sugar. Stay close—it can bubble over fast and make a mess. Turn off the heat, cover the pan and allow the mixture to steep for about 10 minutes.

Meanwhile, center a rack in the oven and preheat the oven to 300 degrees F. Place six to eight heatproof ramekins (see above) in a roasting pan lined with a double thickness of paper towels. Bring a kettle of water to a boil.

Bring the cream back to a boil, then immediately turn off the heat. Strain the cream and discard the tea.

Working in a large heatproof liquid measuring cup (I use a 2-quart one) with a spout, a pitcher or a large bowl, whisk the eggs, yolks, honey and the remaining ¼ cup sugar together until smooth. Drop by drop, pour a bit of the hot cream over the eggs and whisk vigorously. Add about one quarter of the cream in this drizzle-and-whisk fashion—insurance against cooking the eggs. Once the eggs are safely acclimatized to the heat, or tempered, you can pour in the remaining cream in a steadier stream, still whisking. Stir in the vanilla and rose extracts.

If you've got lots of bubbles, skim them off with a spoon as best as you can, but don't worry about being meticulous. Divide the mixture among the ramekins. Pour enough hot water into the roasting pan to come halfway up the sides of the ramekins.

Bake the custards for about 45 minutes (the time will depend on the size of your ramekins). When you tap the sides of the ramekins, the custards should be completely set except for, perhaps, just a tiny, jiggly circle in the center. Transfer the roasting pan to a cooling rack and leave the setup intact for 10 minutes, then carefully lift the ramekins onto a rack to cool to room temperature.

Cover the custards and refrigerate for at least 2 hours before serving.

Bonne Idée

VANILLA POTS DE CRÈME: This is the basic recipe from which all other pots de crème derive: Bring 1½ cups heavy cream, 1 cup whole milk and ¼ cup sugar to a boil. Whisk together 2 large eggs, 5 large egg yolks, ¼ cup sugar and a pinch of fine sea salt. Add the hot liquid to the eggs in drizzle-and-whisk fashion and finish with 4 teaspoons pure vanilla extract. The baking is as directed. Or, if you would like to use vanilla beans, omit the extract, split and scrape 2 beans and add the pods and pulp to the pot with the cream mixture; bring to a boil, cover and set aside to infuse for 20 minutes, then reheat and carry on.

CHOCOLATE POTS DE CRÈME: Bring 1½ cups heavy cream and 1½ cups whole milk to a boil. Pour the hot mixture over 4 ounces finely chopped bittersweet chocolate and stir to make a ganache. Whisk together 1 large egg, 5 large egg yolks, ¼ cup sugar and a pinch of fine sea salt. Add the hot ganache to the eggs using the dribble-and-whisk technique. The baking is as directed.

CARAMEL POTS DE CRÈME: Bring 2 cups heavy cream and 1 cup whole milk to a boil. Meanwhile, caramelize ½ cup sugar: Put the sugar in a large skillet, preferably nonstick, over medium-high heat and when the sugar starts to color around the edges of the pan, start stirring the colored sugar in small circles, stirring your way into the center of the pan as the sugar caramelizes. (See page 362 for fuller instructions.) When the sugar is a deep amber color, stand back and pour in the hot liquid, stirring until the seething mixture settles down and is smooth again. Whisk 2 large eggs, 5 large egg yolks, ¼ cup sugar and a pinch of fine sea salt together in a bowl. Add the hot caramel slowly as directed, and bake the custards as directed.

Vanilla-Mango Panna Cotta

Makes 4 servings

SERVING: The panna cotta should be served directly from the refrigerator. If you'd like, pass a plate of cookies at the table.

STORING: Although the panna cotta is best served the day it is made, you can keep it tightly covered in the refrigerator for up to 1 day—it will be fine, but its texture won't be as refined.

ITALY'S PANNA COTTA seems as popular in France these days as *grand-mère*'s mousse, and it's little wonder: In so many ways, this milk and cream mixture set with gelatin is the perfect dessert. It's spare—in the most elegant way; it's simple—the basic recipe has just three ingredients; it's voluptuous—the taste is rich and the texture luxurious; and it's versatile—you can layer flavors, ingredients and textures or play up its lovely plainness.

The core of this recipe is a barely sweet panna cotta strongly flavored with vanilla, a warm flavor, set on top of a cool mango and lime puree. The contrast only sounds extreme; the flavors, both tropical, have a natural affinity for one another.

Because of the mango puree, this panna cotta cannot be unmolded, so I like to serve it in chunky lowball or bistro glasses, jars or coupes, but ramekins and bowls are fine too. (If you make just the vanilla panna cotta though, you'll be able to serve it freestanding; see Bonne Idée.)

A WORD ON THE VANILLA: The recipe is minimal, so the vanilla flavor is front and center: Choose your best and purest. I prefer to use a vanilla bean for this panna cotta, but you can use extract—just make certain its fragrance is powerful.

FOR THE MANGO PUREE

- 1 large ripe mango or 8 ounces (227 grams) frozen mango cubes (no need to thaw)
- 1 juicy lime, halved
  Honey (optional)

FOR THE PANNA COTTA

- 1 cup (240 ml) heavy cream
- 1 cup (240 ml) whole milk
- ¼ cup (50 grams) sugar
- 1 moist, fragrant vanilla bean or 1 tablespoon pure vanilla extract
- 2¼ teaspoons unflavored gelatin
- 3 tablespoons cold water

TO MAKE THE PUREE: Peel the mango and cut all the fruit away from the pit. Put the mango in a food processor (a mini one is good here) or blender and squeeze over a little lime juice. Process the fruit to a puree. If it's grainy and you'd prefer it smoother, strain it. Taste and add more lime juice—I like it tart—or a little honey, if you want to round it out. Divide the puree among four glasses or bowls.

Slide the glasses or bowls into the freezer for 30 minutes, or until the puree is just firm. It doesn't need to be solid, but you do want it to stay where you put it when you pour over the hot panna cotta mixture.

TO MAKE THE PANNA COTTA: Pour the cream, milk and sugar into a small saucepan. If you're using a vanilla bean, slice it in half lengthwise,

Bonne Idée

FREESTANDING VANILLA PANNA COTTA: If you'd like to unmold the panna cotta, choose bowls, ramekins or disposable aluminum muffin molds. Omit the mango puree. Lightly oil the molds with flavorless oil, such as canola, before you pour in the hot cream. At serving time, run a table knife around the edges of each panna cotta to break the seal and turn it out onto a dessert plate. Serve with berries, whole or crushed, or with Spiced Hibiscus Syrup (page 450) or Chestnut-Vanilla Syrup (page 172.)

and, using the tip of your knife, scrape out the pulpy interior seeds. Put the seeds and bean into the saucepan and bring to a boil. (If you're using vanilla extract, you'll add it later.) Remove the pan from the heat, cover and allow to steep for at least 20 minutes.

When you're ready to finish the panna cotta, put the gelatin in a microwave-safe liquid measuring cup that holds at least 2 cups or in a small bowl. Pour over the cold water and let the gelatin sit for about 3 minutes, or until it is completely moistened and has begun to "bloom," or expand. Heat the gelatin in a microwave oven for 20 seconds to liquefy it.

Return the cream mixture to a boil, remove the bean (you can wash and dry it and use it to make vanilla sugar) and pour the cream over the gelatin. Stir to make certain that the gelatin is completely dissolved in the cream. If you're using vanilla extract, add it now. Allow the panna cotta to sit for 20 minutes to cool slightly.

Remove the glasses or bowls from the freezer and divide the panna cotta among them. Refrigerate until the panna cotta is set, at least 2 hours, before serving.

VANILLA

In addition to being America's favorite flavor, vanilla, like salt (see page 407), is a team player: It doesn't run roughshod over a recipe's other ingredients, it bolsters them. It blends with butter, rounds the flavor of eggs, gives depth to sugar, particularly when it's been caramelized, and makes nuts taste even more nuttish. You need just a little vanilla to produce these effects, but my motto with vanilla runs along the lines of "in for a penny, in for a pound": If I'm using vanilla, I like to know it's there.

Most French recipes call for vanilla beans. If you have access to high-quality beans, use them. A good vanilla bean is powerfully fragrant. Touch it, and it might be sticky—a good

thing; bend it, and it should be pliable. You want that suppleness and a certain moistness; a brittle bean won't give you much flavor. The best thing to do with brittle beans is to break them up and whir them in a blender or food processor with granulated sugar to make vanilla sugar, which you can use in recipes, stir into coffee or sprinkle over buttered toast (so good when the toast is brioche).

Most often you'll be using the pulpy seeds from the bean, but if you're infusing cream or another liquid, you'll use the pod too. To get at the seeds, lay the bean on a cutting board and, using a very sharp paring knife, slice it in half lengthwise. Open the bean, and you'll see a dark, sticky mass— the precious seeds. Use the tip

or the back of the knife to scrape out the pulp.

I always have vanilla beans in the house, but my go-to for vanilla is pure extract, one made without sugar, so that the flavor and fragrance is strong. Except in cases where only a bean will do, I used extract in these recipes.

It's hard to give an exact equation for substituting beans for extract (or vice versa), since everything depends on the quality of the ingredients, but here's a rule of thumb: 2 teaspoons pure extract is the equivalent of 1 vanilla bean. If you're using vanilla paste (vanilla-bean seeds suspended in a sweet, viscous syrup), use it as you would extract.

Hot Chocolate Panna Cotta

THE FIRST TIME I MADE THIS PANNA COTTA, I immediately thought of hot chocolate. Specifically, the hot chocolate I'd had years ago at Le Flore en l'Ile, a café on Paris's Île Saint-Louis. Yes, it's odd that something cold and jelled should remind me of something hot and liquid, but memories aren't bound by the laws of physics.

Whether this panna cotta conjures up old memories or creates new ones, it's a wonderful dessert. I make it straight, but it's easy to infuse the cream and milk with another flavor. In the winter, particularly at Christmastime, you could steep a little sachet of dampened cheesecloth that included a cinnamon stick, a small piece of fresh ginger, a couple of cloves, some allspice berries and a few peppercorns in the hot milk and cream for about 20 minutes. At other times, use Earl Grey tea, coffee beans or mint. However you decide to flavor the panna cotta—or not—it's important that you start with a chocolate you'd be content to snack on.

2 cups (480 ml) heavy cream	4 ounces (113 grams) bittersweet chocolate, finely chopped
½ cup (120 ml) whole milk	
3 tablespoons sugar	
2 tablespoons unsweetened cocoa powder	2¼ teaspoons unflavored gelatin
¼ teaspoon fine sea salt	3 tablespoons cold water

Pour the cream, milk, sugar, cocoa powder and salt into a small saucepan and bring just to a simmer; bubbles around the edges but not in the center are just fine. Remove from the heat.

Melt the chocolate in a heatproof bowl set over a pan of simmering water, or do this in a microwave oven.

Put the gelatin in a microwave-safe liquid measuring cup—you'll need one that holds at least 1 quart—or a small bowl. Pour over the cold water and let the gelatin sit for about 3 minutes, or until it is completely moistened and has begun to "bloom," or expand. Heat the gelatin in a microwave oven for 20 seconds to liquefy it.

Pour a little of the hot milk and cream over the gelatin and whisk gently, then pour the mixture into the pan with the rest of the hot milk and cream. Whisk to blend completely. Rinse the measuring cup and set aside.

Strain the hot liquid over the melted chocolate and, using a small whisk or heatproof spatula, gently stir to blend completely. Strain the panna cotta back into the measuring cup, discarding whatever remains in the strainer.

Pour the panna cotta into six glasses or bowls. Refrigerate at least 3 hours, or until set, before serving.

Makes 6 servings

SERVING: The panna cotta should be served directly from the refrigerator. If you'd like, pass a plate of cookies at the table. I'm partial to panna cotta with Cat's Tongues (page 278) or Croquets (page 310).

STORING: Panna cotta is really best served the day it is made, but if you cover them tightly and keep them in the refrigerator, they'll be good for another 2 days. At the 2-day mark, the texture won't be as refined, but the dessert will still be very enjoyable.

Bonne Idée
FREESTANDING HOT CHOCOLATE PANNA COTTA: If you'd like to unmold the panna cotta, use bowls or ramekins and lightly coat them with flavorless oil (such as canola). Increase the gelatin to 2¾ teaspoons. Refrigerate the panna cotta for at least 4 hours. At serving time, run a table knife around the edges of each one to break the seal and turn them out onto dessert plates. Unmolded panna cotta is good with berries, coulis, sauces and syrups. Try this one with Chestnut-Vanilla Syrup (page 172).

Nutella-Banana Panna Cotta

Makes 6 servings

....

SERVING: Panna cotta should be served cold. Whether it's unmolded or served in glasses, sprinkle the top with chopped hazelnuts and/or chopped chocolate, if you'd like. If the panna cottas are freestanding, it's nice to circle them with a little of the chocolate sauce; if they're in glasses, you can pass a small pitcher of the sauce—not necessary, but so good.

STORING: Panna cotta is best enjoyed the day it is made, but it can keep in the refrigerator for up to 2 days as long as the ramekins are well wrapped.

NUTELLA AND BANANA are a match made in heaven, and it's a match made countless times a day at crêpe stands across Paris. I prefer my Nutella and bananas creamy and cold, which is why I make this panna cotta. I think of it as Nutella and banana on summer vacation.

Like all panna cottas, this one is easy to make, but to have it turn out perfectly smooth, you must be certain to strain it and resist the temptation to push every little lump through the mesh. To get the most flavor out of the pairing, choose a banana that's ripe but not banana-bread mushy. You want to be able to mash it to a puree and not have it be mealy.

No matter how you serve the panna cotta, it's sigh-inducing, but I love the drama of serving it unmolded. To unmold, oil the cups, glasses or ramekins first. If you decide not to unmold, think about making the panna cotta in martini glasses or wineglasses.

Flavorless oil, such as canola (optional)	Coarsely chopped toasted hazelnuts and/or finely chopped bittersweet or
1 tablespoon unflavored gelatin	semisweet chocolate,
3 tablespoons cold water	for serving (optional)
1½ cups (360 ml) whole milk	Bittersweet Chocolate Sauce
1 cup (240 ml) heavy cream	(page 442), for serving
1 ripe but firm banana	(optional)
¾ cup (223 grams) Nutella, at room temperature	

Choose six custard cups, teacups, ramekins, tumblers or stemmed glasses for the panna cottas. If you're going to unmold the desserts, rub a little flavorless oil inside whichever containers you've chosen.

Put the gelatin in a small microwave-safe bowl and pour over the cold water. Let the gelatin sit for about 3 minutes, or until it has begun to "bloom," or expand. Heat the gelatin in a microwave oven for 20 seconds to liquefy it.

Bring the milk and cream just to a simmer in a small saucepan; no need to have more than bubbles around the edges of the pan.

Meanwhile, peel the banana, cut it into pieces and put the pieces in a large heatproof bowl or liquid measuring cup. Using a fork, mash the banana until it is smooth. (You should have about ½ cup banana puree—a little more or a little less is fine.) Add the Nutella and, using the fork or a sturdy flexible spatula, mash and mix and stir until homogeneous; it will look a little lumpy because of the banana, and that's okay.

Pour some of the hot milk and cream over the gelatin and stir until the gelatin is completely blended into the liquid. Pour the liquid back into the pan and whisk to incorporate it thoroughly.

Pour one third of the liquid over the Nutella and banana and whisk slowly and gently until you have a smooth, shiny mixture—think Nutella ganache. Whisk in half of the remaining liquid until blended, then pour in the rest of the liquid and whisk until smooth.

Place a strainer over a 1-quart or larger heatproof liquid measuring cup or pitcher and pour the panna cotta through the strainer. (If you're steadier than I am, you can strain the panna cotta directly into the cups.) Press lightly on the strainer to get all the liquid through the mesh, but don't push hard—you'll have a fair amount of gelatin and mush in the strainer, and it's best to discard it.

Divide the panna cotta evenly among the molds and refrigerate for at least 3 hours; cover them with plastic film once they cool down.

If you want to unmold the desserts, just before serving, run a table knife around the edges of each mold to break the seal and turn the mold over onto a plate. Shake the mold gently and the panna cotta will jiggle its way out.

Serve sprinkled with chopped nuts and/or chocolate, if you'd like, and with the chocolate sauce, if desired.

Bonne Idée

SPECULOOS PANNA COTTA: Biscoff spread, with all the flavors of too-delicious Biscoff speculoos cookies, is nipping at the heels of Nutella's popularity in France and, like Nutella, it makes a luscious panna cotta. Omit the banana and Nutella and use 1 cup Biscoff spread. Speculoos panna cotta, like its Nutella cousin, is good with chocolate sauce and, not surprisingly, also good with Biscoff cookies.

Cold Chocolate Crémeux, Wine-Poached Cherries and Lots of Crumbs

Makes 6 servings

SERVING: At Fish, the dessert was served in small shallow bowls, with a scoop of *crémeux* on one side of each bowl and cherries with syrup next to it. A generous amount of cocoa crumbs was sprinkled over the *crémeux*, dusted over the cherries and spooned into a mound next to them. It was perfect like that and I see no reason to change it.

STORING: You can make the *crémeux* a day or two ahead and keep it covered in the fridge; ditto the cherries and syrup. The crumbs can be kept covered in the refrigerator for up to 2 weeks or packed airtight and frozen for up to 2 months.

CRÉMEUX MAY HAVE EXISTED YEARS AGO, but if it did, I don't remember seeing it. Yet today it's in Parisian pâtisseries everywhere and on restaurant dessert menus. Seductively dense, it's a little like mousse, a little more like ganache, very much like pudding and, above all, creamy, which is the definition of the word *crémeux*. Think of it as a crème anglaise thickened with gelatin or a pastry cream in which the cornstarch is replaced by gelatin. A *crémeux* can be a filling for a cake or tart, the creamy layer of a trifle or, as in this recipe, the centerpiece of a dessert, my version of a sweet I enjoyed at one of my favorite Paris bistros, Fish La Boissonnerie. The *crémeux* was scooped like ice cream and served alongside red wine–poached cherries and crunchy cocoa crumbs. I had it in early summer, when cherries are abundant, but it is too good to be a once-a-year treat. Think about serving the *crémeux* and cocoa crumbs with prunes (poached exactly like the cherries), fresh raspberries or bananas (no need to poach these or have a syrup), or pair the fruit and cream with a scoop of vanilla ice cream or a little crème fraîche.

FOR THE *CRÉMEUX*

- 5 ounces (142 grams) semisweet or bittersweet chocolate, finely chopped
- ¾ cup (180 ml) whole milk
- ¼ cup (60 ml) heavy cream
- 2 large egg yolks
- 2 tablespoons sugar
- 1 tablespoon cold water
- ½ teaspoon unflavored gelatin

FOR THE CHERRIES

- 1 cup (240 ml) full-bodied, fruity red wine, such as Syrah or Zinfandel
- 2 tablespoons honey
- 2 tablespoons sugar
- 1 long, fat strip orange zest
- 8 ounces (227 grams) fresh sweet cherries, halved and pitted

Cocoa Crumbs (page 426), for topping

TO MAKE THE *CRÉMEUX*: Put the chocolate in a medium heatproof bowl. Heat the milk and cream in a small saucepan until bubbles form around the edges of the pan.

Meanwhile, put the egg yolks in another bowl, add the sugar and immediately begin to whisk energetically until the mixture thickens and the color

HURRY, HURRY, DON'T-
LET-IT-SET CHOCOLATE
SAUCE: If you grab the
crémeux when it's a
few minutes out of the
saucepan and not quite
cool, you'll have a chocolate
sauce that's good over
ice cream.

pales a bit. (It's important to whisk as soon as sugar hits yolks so that the sugar doesn't cause the yolks to develop a film.) Still whisking, dribble in some of the hot liquid—you don't want to add too much at once; the idea is to acclimatize the eggs to the heat, so they won't scramble. When you've got a few tablespoons of hot liquid mixed in, you can whisk in the rest in a steadier stream. Pour the mixture back into the saucepan, put the pan over medium heat (or medium-low, depending on the power of your burner) and, using a heatproof spatula and stirring without stopping, cook the custard until it just starts to thicken. You'll see one bubble pop at the surface (or you might see a few around the edges) and if you run your finger down the center of the spatula, the custard won't run into the track you've created. Give the custard a good last stir before pouring it over the chopped chocolate. Allow it to sit for 30 seconds and then gently, starting from the center of the bowl and working outward, stir the custard into the chocolate.

Pour the tablespoon of cold water into a small microwave-safe bowl, sprinkle over the gelatin and let sit for a couple of minutes, until the gelatin has absorbed the water. Then heat in the microwave for 15 seconds, or until the gelatin is completely liquefied. Pour the gelatin into the center of the chocolate and stir it in gently, just as you stirred in the custard.

You could let the *crémeux* come to room temperature, stirring often, and then chill it, but it's better to speed the cooling and setting by putting the *crémeux* bowl into a larger bowl filled with ice and cold water. Stir now and then until it is cool—it will set softly and begin to form lovely swirls and mounds when you stir and lift it. If you're not going to serve the dessert now, cover the *crémeux* tightly and refrigerate until needed.

TO MAKE THE CHERRIES: Put a strainer over a large bowl (you'll use it to drain the cherries). Stir the wine, honey and sugar together in a medium saucepan, add the orange zest and bring to a boil. Boil for 1 minute, then add the cherries and boil for 1 minute. Turn the cherries out into the strainer, then pour the liquid back into the pan and boil for 7 to 12 minutes, or until syrupy; you should have about ½ cup syrup. Discard the orange peel. Cool the cherries and syrup separately.

If you're not ready to serve the dessert, combine the cherries and syrup and keep them covered in the refrigerator.

Serve the *crémeux* with the cherries and cocoa crumbs.

CAFÉ GOURMAND

Gourmand is a word that can trip up the French almost as easily as it befuddles us. At its most flattering, the word is associated with loving food. At its most basic, it's translated as "greedy," but greedy in two ways: There's cute greedy, as in taking a second helping of a delicious dessert made by your host and proclaiming yourself *très gourmand*; and not so cute greedy, when more is too much more. It can also mean "glutton," a word that's hard to like in any language.

And gourmand's sister word, *gourmandise*, is caught in the same bind, sometimes being translated as "gluttony" and sometimes being used (as a noun) for an exquisite culinary creation, usually a sweet one.

The *café gourmand*, a restaurant trend that's taken over the country, draws on *gourmand*'s best qualities. In a land where coffee isn't served until dessert is finished, the *café gourmand* is a combo plate: a cup of coffee (espresso, actually) served on the same platter as two or three mini sweets. To me it seems almost American!

But it also seems like a very *bonne idée*, one anyone with a sweet tooth can have fun with. The *café gourmand* welcomes everything small and pretty—part of its appeal is that you're having just a tidbit of something rich and lovely. Some restaurants offer custards, like crème brûlée or pots de crème; small cakes, like mini madeleines or financiers; tiny pastries, like pinkie-sized éclairs; and, of course, cookies.

Many things that French restaurants do are completely beyond the skills of home bakers, but not *café gourmand*—this is something we can all pull off.

Rice Pudding, Strawberries and Spiced Hibiscus Syrup

Makes 4 servings

SERVING: Whether you serve the pudding family style or in individual dishes that you dress in the kitchen, both the pudding and the syrup should be chilled and the berries plentiful. As homey as rice pudding is on its own, that's how festive it is with the syrup and strawberries—so festive that it's nice to serve this dessert with sparkling wine. If you've got a rosé, reach for it.

STORING: The pudding will keep tightly covered in the refrigerator for up to 4 days; stir before serving.

As MUCH AS WE AMERICANS love rice pudding, I'd bet that the French love it even more—and serve it a lot more often. There are almost as many kinds of ready-to-eat rice puddings for sale in French supermarkets as there are butters. Lots of rice pudding mixes too. Like tapioca (page 382), rice pudding is having a renaissance, particularly in the best bistros in Paris, where it's on menus no matter the season. Sometimes it comes to the table in a canning jar, sometimes it's layered with fruit in a lowball glass (called a *verrine*), and sometimes it's served in a bowl, nursery style.

Most of the time, I serve rice pudding family style, the way it was served to us in a cozy ski lodge in Megève. After a day in the snowy mountains, we had a hearty meal that finished with a big, earthenware bowl placed in the center of our table and the instructions "Eat as much as you'd like." At other times, I go with the ever-trendy *verrines*, filling them halfway with pudding and then piling on fruit. One of my favorite recipes for a topping is fresh strawberries and jewel-red hibiscus syrup.

A WORD ON THE RICE: Most of the rice puddings I've had in France have been made with short-grain rice, such as Arborio. However, I've made good puddings with jasmine, basmati, Texmati and other kinds of rice. The cooking time will vary with the rice.

3 cups water
1 teaspoon fine sea salt
½ cup (92 grams) short-grain rice, such as Arborio
4 cups (960 ml) whole milk
⅓ cup (67 grams) sugar
½ moist, fragrant vanilla bean, split

Fresh strawberries, hulled and quartered, for topping
Spiced Hibiscus Syrup (page 450), for topping

Put the water in a 4-quart saucepan, add salt and bring to a boil. Add the rice and boil for 10 minutes, then drain.

Rinse the saucepan, add the milk and sugar and bring to a boil, stirring to dissolve the sugar. Stay at the stove—milk boils over quickly (and unexpectedly); as the milk bubbles up, stir it down. Then lower the heat to a simmer and stir in the rice.

Scrape the pulp from the vanilla bean and add it, as well as the pod, to the pan. Another word of warning: Until some of the milk has cooked away and the ingredients have settled into a simmering rhythm, there's still the threat of bubble-overs, so stay close. Stir regularly, especially at the beginning and toward the finish, and cook the rice for 30 to 40 minutes, until it is very tender, the pudding has thickened a little and most of the milk has been absorbed. Don't cook until all of the milk is gone, or you'll end up with an unpleasantly stiff pudding. (It's hard to give you an exact cooking time because the time will depend on the rice, the pan and the heat beneath it. Just stay with it.)

Scrape the pudding into a bowl and remove and discard the vanilla pod. Cover the pudding with a piece of plastic film, pressing it against the surface to prevent a skin from forming. Or, if you'd prefer, you can spoon the pudding into four individual serving dishes and cover them. Cool to room temperature, then refrigerate until chilled.

If the pudding is in a large bowl, you can spoon it into small dishes or cups and top each serving with berries and some syrup, or you can put out the pudding, berries and syrup and let everyone make their own rice pudding sundae. If the pudding is in individual serving dishes, top with berries and the syrup.

Coconut Tapioca

Makes 4 servings

SERVING: Tapioca pudding is often served plain or with a spoonful of whipped cream, but it really comes into its own when it's paired with fruit. Pineapple is a natural with it, and my favorite topping for this dessert is small chunks of Laurent's Slow-Roasted Spiced Pineapple (page 333) and a spoonful of its syrup. I'm also crazy about the pudding with strawberries and Spiced Hibiscus Syrup (page 450).

STORING: Packed into a covered container, the tapioca will keep in the refrigerator for up to 3 days.

WHEN I WAS A CHILD, tapioca was the dreaded dessert on the cafeteria menu, the one most likely to be passed over by even the most sugar-starved schoolkid. While I always liked the sound of the word *tapioca*—it made me think of a dance involving colorful ruffled skirts—I could never muster an affinity for the stuff.

And then I met Pierre Hermé and tasted his tapioca pudding. Cue the fireworks. His tapioca had texture and style, and I thought it shouldn't even be called tapioca—and it wasn't. The French refer to tapioca as *perles du Japon*, or "Japanese pearls," and when you see "pearled" tapioca, you realize that the name is perfect.

Tapioca is a starch from the plant known as manioc, cassava or yuca, and it's prized for its thickening properties. Finely ground and sold in American supermarkets as instant tapioca (which is what I had as a child), it's an alternative to cornstarch as a thickener in pies. But the tapioca of today's best desserts (found right next to the instant stuff) is opalescent and shaped like pearls. It also starts out as hard as pearls, so it must be soaked before using.

Cooked gently with coconut milk—proving again that what grows together goes together—the tapioca becomes a pudding, its pearls turning translucent and their texture becoming soft and slightly chewy. The bubble-pearls don't pop in your mouth as their looks might lead you to expect, but if you're someone who plays with your food, you'll want to discreetly press them against the roof of your mouth and let them become even softer before they finally dissolve. As for their taste, like the rice in rice pudding, tapioca is more about texture than flavor, more about carrying other flavors than staking a claim of its own, which is why it's so lovely with coconut and vanilla. And why tapioca lends itself so nicely to other additions and almost any kind of topping, especially fruit.

A WORD ON PLANNING AHEAD: Sadly for those of us who get cravings in need of instant gratification, pearl tapioca must soak for at least 8 hours, or overnight, before you can cook it.

½ cup (80 grams) large-pearl tapioca

2 cups cold water

1¾ cups (one 13½-ounce can; 399 ml) unsweetened coconut milk (not light)

1 cup (240 ml) whole milk

⅓ cup (67 grams) sugar

1 teaspoon pure vanilla extract, or more to taste

At least 8 hours and up to 1 day ahead, put the tapioca in a medium bowl, pour in the cold water, cover and refrigerate.

When you're ready to make the pudding, drain the tapioca and put it in a small pot, along with the coconut milk, whole milk and sugar. Put the pot over medium heat and cook, stirring, until the sugar dissolves and the milk comes to a boil. Stay nearby because milk has a sneaky way of boiling over. Reduce the heat to low and simmer, stirring often, until the milk has cooked down and thickened slightly. The pudding will have the texture of (non-Greek) yogurt; the pearls will be translucent and some will have popped; and there'll be a top layer of milk with the pearls floating just under the surface. I'm giving you these visual cues because it's hard to tell you how long it will take to reach this stage—depending on your pan and what "low" is on your stove, it might take as little as 12 minutes or as long as 20. Turn on some music, relax and enjoy the Zen of stirring your pudding.

Scrape the pudding into a heatproof bowl and stir in the vanilla extract. Cover the tapioca with plastic film, pressing it against the surface, and cool to room temperature. I serve the pudding cold, but there are room-temp fans—taste before you chill; you might be one of them.

Springtime Cookies and Curd

Makes 6 servings

SERVING: Once the dessert is assembled, it should go to the table immediately. No further accompaniments required.

STORING: The cookies, curd and rhubarb can be made a few days ahead; only the strawberries should be prepared last minute.

SAD TO REPORT, BUT APRIL IN PARIS is not the idyllic place that the famous song makes it out to be. Apparently Yip Harburg, the lyricist, knew this, but he needed a two-syllable month and just couldn't stretch May. The weather in Paris, always unpredictable, is particularly capricious in the spring and, for those of us who love food, the intermittent chill and gloom of April can create experiences that border on the surreal. I can't tell you how many times I've shopped the outdoor market on the Boulevard Raspail in the spring and been struck by the fact that the stands have mountains of ripe, aromatic and almost still-warm strawberries from Provence while I'm wearing a down vest and muffler and taking the berry from the vendor with a gloved hand.

There are those moments in April, and even into May and June, when the vegetables and fruits are so much more seasonal than the weather and, in the same way that I can't decide what to wear, I have trouble deciding what to serve. How springish can you be when you've just turned up the heat in the apartment?

This dessert is my answer. It's a straddler: The Double-Butter Double-Baked Petit Beurre Cookies (page 270) that sit at the bottom of the bowls are from any season; the grapefruit curd in the middle is a holdover from winter; the Roasted Rhubarb with Bitters (page 335), optional but lovely over the curd, hints at spring; and the strawberries that top the dessert hold the promise of warmer days.

Everything but the berries needs to be made ahead, which means that when dessert time rolls around, all that's left for you to do is to layer the elements. I usually serve this in small glass bowls, but you can crumble the cookies—they're made for crumbling—and construct the dessert in glasses or goblets. The only must is spoons long enough to dip down through all the layers.

FOR THE GRAPEFRUIT CURD	FOR THE STRAWBERRIES
4 large egg yolks	24 ripe strawberries
½ cup (100 grams) sugar	Sugar
Juice of ½ grapefruit (pink or yellow)	Kirsch (optional)
Juice of ½ lemon	
¾ stick (6 tablespoons; 3 ounces; 85 grams) unsalted butter, cut into 12 pieces, at room temperature	FOR FINISHING THE DESSERT
	6 Double-Butter Double-Baked Petit Beurre Cookies (page 270), plus 1–2 more if you want to top the dessert with crumbs (optional)
	Roasted Rhubarb with Bitters (page 335; optional)

TO MAKE THE CURD: Put the yolks and sugar in a medium heavy-bottomed saucepan and immediately start whisking (leaving sugar on yolks "burns" them). Whisk in the grapefruit and lemon juices and put the pan over medium heat. Continuing with the whisk or using a heatproof spatula, cook, stirring constantly. At first the mixture will be foamy and then, as the foam subsides, the mixture will thicken a bit. Don't worry if the curd starts to boil lightly— just keep stirring, making sure you get your whisk or spatula into the edges of the pan. After 8 to 10 minutes, the foam will be gone and the curd's color will be sunshine yellow. Dip a spoon into it and run your finger down the back of it—the curd shouldn't run into the track your finger created.

Scrape the curd into a heatproof bowl and allow it to sit on the counter for 10 minutes.

The butter needs to be blended into the curd while the curd is still very warm but not straight-from-the-stove hot. There's not enough curd to do this in a regular blender, so use an immersion blender or a whisk. Add the butter to the curd piece by piece, blending after each chunk goes in. When the butter is incorporated you can either press a piece of plastic film against the surface of the curd to keep a skin from forming and refrigerate it for at least 4 hours, or until it's thoroughly cold, or you can put the bowl of curd in a larger bowl filled with ice cubes and water and quick-chill it, stirring frequently. Either way, the curd will thicken but will always be pourable rather than spreadable, and that's just right.

TO MAKE THE STRAWBERRIES: About 10 minutes before you're ready to assemble and serve the dessert, hull the berries, slice them into spoonable pieces and sprinkle them lightly with sugar. Stir and set aside to allow the sugar to dissolve and form a little syrup. If you'd like, add a splash of kirsch.

TO FINISH THE DESSERT: For each serving, place a cookie in the bottom of a bowl or glass; you can leave the cookie whole or break it. Now start layering: Add a generous spoonful of grapefruit curd, top with some rhubarb and its pink syrup, if you're using it, and then finish with the strawberries and their syrup. If you'd like, crush another cookie or two and give each dessert a shower of crumbs.

Esquimaux Pops for Grown-Ups

Makes 6 to 8 Esquimaux (depending on your molds)

SERVING: This is less about serving and more about snacking.

STORING: The Esquimaux can be kept in the freezer for up to 3 days. Of course they'll keep longer, but they're really best when they're fresh.

WE MAY OWE THE MANY PLEASURES OF ice cream on a stick to America—the first chocolate-covered ice cream pop, the Eskimo Pie, was patented in the U.S. in 1922—but it would be tough to find a French kid who'd think that, since l'Esquimau can be found all over the country, in markets big and small and in kiosks from Cannes to the beaches of Brittany. L'Esquimau is a national icon and pretty much the name for any chocolate-covered pop, no matter the brand or the flavor.

My French friends might call these pops Esquimaux, but for sure they've never bought Esquimaux with booze—these pops depend on a splash of it not just for flavor, but to keep them from freezing rock hard.

My Esquimaux come from the land of Fudgsicles, a favorite of mine from childhood. These have a mild chocolate flavor, a hint of liqueur and, just for fun, speckles of dark chocolate. You can eat them right out of the molds or you can coat them with hard-crack chocolate (page 445).

If you don't have ice-pop molds, you can freeze the mixture in any kind of mold or even in a container from which you can scoop out portions. Do this, and it's nice to have Bittersweet Chocolate Sauce (page 442) to pour over each serving.

A WORD ON THE LIQUEUR: You can choose any liqueur that you like to drink with chocolate. I'm a fan of chocolate and crème de cassis (the liqueur best known for its use in Kir, the famous French aperitif), but crème de menthe is also really good, as is Kahlúa, Malibu rum or amaretto.

AND A WORD ON THE EGGS: The eggs in this recipe are not cooked, so it's important to choose those that are very fresh. Organic eggs are best, and organic eggs from a local source are even better.

4 ounces (113 grams) semisweet or bittersweet chocolate	1 tablespoon confectioners' sugar, sifted
2 very fresh large eggs, preferably organic, separated, at room temperature	3 tablespoons liqueur (see above)
	2/3 cup (158 ml) very cold heavy cream

Have your ice-pop molds at the ready. They should be clean and dry—drops of water will freeze and make it hard for you to unmold your Esquimaux.

Cut 2 ounces of the chocolate into small chunks and melt it in a microwave oven or in a heatproof bowl set over a small pan of simmering water; set aside. Chop the remaining 2 ounces chocolate into teensy pieces or, if you'd like, coarsely grate it; set aside separately.

Working in the bowl of a stand mixer fitted with the whisk attachment, or in a large bowl with a hand mixer, whip the egg whites until they're opaque and hold soft peaks. If you're using a stand mixer, scrape the whites into another bowl. Set aside. (There's no need to clean the mixer bowl or whisk.)

Beat the yolks and sugar together in the mixer bowl or a medium bowl until they turn pale and thicken slightly, about 3 minutes. Using a flexible spatula, stir in the melted chocolate and liqueur, then scrape the mixture into a large bowl if you used the stand mixer. (Again, there's no need to clean the mixer bowl now.)

If the whites need a little fluffing up, whisk them. Working with the spatula, stir a spoonful of whites into the chocolate mixture to lighten it, then gently fold in the rest. Don't worry about being too thorough at this stage—you've got more to fold in soon.

Finally (I know this recipe uses a lot of bowls—sorry), whip the heavy cream in the mixer bowl or a small bowl just until it holds soft peaks. Scrape the whipped cream into the bowl with the chocolate mixture and sprinkle the finely chopped or grated chocolate over the cream. With the spatula, fold everything together, being gentle and thorough.

Spoon the mixture into the molds, insert ice-pop sticks or the sticks that came with your molds, and freeze until completely solid, about 5 hours.

Bread and Chocolate
Coffee Can Brioche
Ice Cream Sandwiches

Makes 4 sandwiches

SERVING: Of course you can eat the plain ice cream sandwiches out of hand, but then you'd miss the caramel and that would be a shame.

STORING: You can make the sandwiches ahead, wrap them very well and freeze them for up to 1 week; leave them at room temperature for 5 to 10 minutes before serving. They'll certainly be good, though not as wonderful as when the bread is freshly toasted and soft in the center.

TWENTY YEARS AGO, at the first Chocolate Salon in Paris, the country's top pastry chefs, chocolatiers and chocolate companies gathered to share the best of what they were doing. Everything was glossy and sophisticated, elaborate and perfectly crafted. And then there was a table with no pastry on it, no bonbons and nothing that required the precision of a pâtissier. Standing at the table was Lionel Poilâne, France's most renowned bread baker, wearing his habitual gray baker's coat and his signature bow tie, and in front of him he had just three ingredients: his fabulous and famous *miche*, a 5-pound round of hearty, rustic bread; excellent butter; and a mound of short, slender bars of bittersweet chocolate (*bâtons*). For French people of a certain age, a bite of chocolate tucked between two pieces of buttered bread was the taste of childhood, the treasured after-school treat of so many and the raison d'être of today's popular chocolate croissants. Of all that I tasted and saw at that fête, what I remember most is my late friend, Lionel, and his bread and chocolate.

Of course I remembered him when I made this offbeat dessert. It's basically bread and chocolate, but the bread is a rich homemade brioche, the chocolate is ice cream and the flourish is warm caramel sauce. It's part ice cream sandwich and part ice cream sundae, part childhood and part very grown-up.

The best brioche for these sandwiches is one you make in a coffee can (page 421), so that you can cut perfect rounds. And the best way to fill the sandwiches is to make ice cream pucks the size of the brioche slices and freeze them. The best way to eat the sandwiches when they're covered with the caramel is with a knife and spoon. And the best time to eat them is anytime.

1 pint (473 ml) chocolate ice cream, homemade (page 455) or store-bought	a coffee can or store-bought brioche
1 Brioche (page 421), made in	Hot Salted Caramel Sauce (page 447), warmed

If the ice cream isn't soft enough to scoop and smush, leave it out for a few minutes. Divide it into 4 portions and, working on a piece of parchment or wax paper, shape each portion into a 3-inch-diameter puck. I use a pancake ring as a mold, but you can do this freehand. Slide the paper onto a cutting board or baking sheet and freeze the ice cream until it's firm, or until you're

ready to assemble the sandwiches. (*Well wrapped, the pucks can be kept in the freezer for up to 2 months.*)

When you're ready to serve, cut 8 slices of brioche, each about ¼ inch thick. If you're using a coffee-can loaf, you're good to go—just save the remainder for another snack. If you're using a regular brioche loaf, you might want to cut each slice into a circle about the same size or slightly larger than the ice cream pucks.

Toast the bread very lightly, so that the slice is ever so slightly crisped but the inside remains soft. Let the bread cool for 5 minutes.

Remove the ice cream pucks from the freezer. Using an offset spatula, slide each puck onto a piece of toast; sandwich with another piece of bread.

Place each sandwich in the center of a dessert plate, drizzle over some of the caramel sauce and pass the rest of the sauce at the table.

Desert Roses

Here's one more thing to add to the list of things I love about the French: The same people who invented the macaron, the mille-feuille and the iconic tarte Tatin not only invented the Desert Rose, but love it, a feat that seems as impossible as holding two opposing thoughts in your mind at the same time. Despite the evocative name, *roses des sables*, "desert" or "sand roses," are not at all related to anything botanical; instead, they come from the same mold as our Rice Krispies treats. They're made with cornflakes, chocolate (of any type) and butter and have been in the French repertoire for years. (I give you both dark and white chocolate versions here; see Bonne Idée for white chocolate Desert Roses.)

When I served these at a party in Paris, my friends were as delighted as sophisticated Americans would be had you capped off a swell dinner with penny candy or Rice Krispies treats. Everyone ate them. Everyone loved them. And everyone laughed. But when I mockingly scolded my friends for not telling me about the recipe, they all had the same response: It had never occurred to them. Desert Roses were just a part of their childhoods, like bicycle riding and roast chicken on Sunday. Their defense: They're not even baked! Hadn't I said I was collecting recipes for a book about baking in France? And the recipe was easy to find—well, not so easy now, but it first appeared on the back of a cornflakes box—so why would they bother with it? Then they went back to eating them: making a racket as they bit into them.

The confections, named for their resemblance to the spiky clumps of gypsum that form in the desert, can be made in any size or shape you'd like. I usually opt for scooping them out into mini muffin paper liners or spooning them into pancake rings or muffin pans, pressing them down and then, when the pucks are chilled, eating them like cookies.

As you'll see, I've added dried apricots and cherries and toasted slivered almonds—keep them, omit them or toss in your own favorites.

Makes about 40 mini candies

SERVING: *Roses des sables* are the perfect after-school treat, but they're just as perfect served with coffee after a grown-up meal, plain or fancy; think of them as whimsical truffles.

STORING: The roses will keep in the refrigerator for up to 4 days. Once the chocolate is firmly set, you can transfer them to a closed container.

- 1 stick (8 tablespoons; 4 ounces; 113 grams) unsalted butter, cut into chunks
- 12 ounces (340 grams) bittersweet or semisweet chocolate, finely chopped
- 4 cups (112 grams) cornflakes
- ⅓ cup (40 grams) sweetened shredded coconut
- ⅓ cup (53 grams) plump, moist dried cherries or dried cranberries, chopped
- ⅓ cup (53 grams) plump, moist dried Turkish apricots, chopped
- ⅓ cup (40 grams) toasted slivered almonds or walnuts, coarsely chopped
- Pinch of fleur de sel or fine sea salt

Line a baking sheet with parchment or wax paper, a silicone baking mat or aluminum foil. If you'd like to scoop the roses into paper liners or mold them into circles, have the liners or pancake rings at hand. I use a medium cookie scoop (one with a capacity of 1½ tablespoons) to shape the roses, but they're perfectly spoonable—neatness and uniformity mean nothing here.

Put the butter in a heatproof bowl set over a saucepan filled with a few inches of simmering water. Cover the butter with the chopped chocolate and heat, stirring occasionally, until the chocolate and butter are melted, thick and creamy; you don't want to heat the butter and chocolate so much that they separate.

Toss the rest of the ingredients into a large bowl and stir them around, then pour over the hot butter and chocolate. Gently mix everything together. Some of the cornflakes will break, but keep stirring until all is coated in chocolate.

Scoop or spoon the mixture onto the prepared baking sheet or into the paper liners. Alternatively, you can press the mixture into pancake rings, so that you've got little pucks. Of course, the number of roses you'll get will depend on the size of your sweets.

Slide the sheet into the refrigerator and chill until set, about 30 minutes.

Bonne Idée

WHITE CHOCOLATE DESERT ROSES: Use ¾ stick (6 tablespoons; 85 grams) butter and 12 ounces best-quality white chocolate.

Another Bonne Idée

CRUNCHY ICE CREAM SANDWICHES: Scoop the *roses des sables* mixture into pancake rings (put the rings on a lined baking sheet) or muffin cups, making a layer that's about ¼ inch thick. Chill or freeze the disks until they are set, then sandwich softened ice cream between them. Put the sandwiches on a lined baking sheet and freeze until firm, then wrap them airtight in plastic film and freeze. Let the sandwiches soften just a tad before you serve them—nuts, raisins and chocolate can get tooth-breakingly hard in the freezer.

Chunky Chocolate
Fruit-and-Nut Bars

*Makes about
12 servings*

SERVING: The candy is
meant to be served straight
from the refrigerator. It's
not the easiest thing to
cut cleanly, but if you use
a sharp chef's knife and
a firm downward stroke,
you'll get nice pieces. If
I'm serving it alongside
coffee, as I often do after
a big dinner, I'll cut small
squares; if I'm serving it as
a snack, I'll cut long bars
and let everyone break off
a piece. As I said, there are
no rules with this treat.

STORING: Wrap the candy
well, and you'll be able to
keep it in your refrigerator
for up to 2 weeks.

THINK OF THIS AS NOUGAT'S CRUNCHY COUSIN—it's just as jam-packed with chewy dried fruits and toasted nuts, but everything's held together with dark chocolate instead of honey and meringue. It's like an old-fashioned Chunky bar with more and better chunklets.

You can choose whatever dried fruits you like most or have on hand, but I think the bars are best when one of the fruits is the creamy beige dried figs that come pressed together in a circle: The seeds are a wonderful surprise in the mix. And while I always add almonds and a smaller amount of walnuts, my favorite add-in is the pistachios, as much for their bright color as for their flavor.

If you've got Candied Orange Peel (page 459), include it; drain it well, pat it dry and cut it into small cubes. Or add some pop with a little candied ginger (the kind that comes in syrup; treat it the way you would the orange peel) or slivers of crystallized ginger.

There are very few rules about how to make these bars—this is the perfect recipe to become your own house special—and no rules about how to serve them. Snack or snazzy small dessert? It's your choice.

Unsweetened cocoa powder,
for dusting

5 ounces (142 grams) mixed
nuts (it's nice to include
some salted nuts)

8 ounces (227 grams) plump,
moist mixed dried fruit,
such as figs, apricots,
cherries, cranberries
and/or raisins

1 tablespoon diced candied
orange peel, homemade
(page 459) or store-bought,
and/or slivered crystallized
or candied ginger (optional)

¼ cup (15 grams) unsweetened
shredded coconut
(optional)

Pinch of fine sea salt
(optional)

7 ounces (198 grams)
semisweet or bittersweet
chocolate, coarsely chopped

Center a rack in the oven and preheat the oven to 350 degrees F. Line a baking sheet with parchment paper or a silicone baking mat. Lightly spray an 8-inch (or slightly smaller) square baking pan with cooking spray (or use a little oil), line the pan with parchment or wax paper and dust the paper sparingly with cocoa powder.

Spread the nuts out on the baking sheet and bake for 6 to 10 minutes, stirring a couple of times, until they are lightly toasted. You don't need much color here, so when you catch a whiff of warm nuts, you've probably baked them enough. Cool them on the sheet for a few minutes, then transfer them to a cutting board and coarsely chop them. Toss them into a large bowl.

If you're using figs and/or apricots, they'll need to be cut into smaller pieces, a job most easily done with scissors. Toss all the dried fruit into the bowl with the nuts, add the orange peel and/or ginger, if you're using it, and give everything a good stir. Stir in the coconut, if using, and, if the nuts weren't salted, add some salt now, if you'd like.

Melt the chocolate in a microwave oven or in a bowl over a pan of simmering water. However you melt the chocolate, don't overheat it; you want the chocolate to be thick, smooth and velvety.

Pour the melted chocolate over the fruit and nuts and, using a heatproof spatula or a wooden spoon, stir to coat everything with chocolate. You might think you don't have enough chocolate, but you do—just keep stirring. When everything is coated with chocolate, scrape the mixture into the lined baking pan, push it into a fairly even layer with the spatula and dust the top lightly with cocoa powder. Take another piece of parchment paper, lay it over the top and press with your palms to level it as best you can. It's always going to be bumpy; you just want to try to get it even. Refrigerate the bar for at least 4 hours (or for up to 1 day).

When the bar is solid, peel away both pieces of parchment paper and, if you're not going to serve it right away, wrap it in a clean sheet of parchment or wax paper and give the candy a final wrap with plastic film or aluminum foil. Return it to the fridge until ready to serve.

Chocolate Truffles

**Makes about
36 truffles**

SERVING: These truffles are meant to be served cold—they'll soften and melt in your mouth. Of course they're good with espresso, which is how they're most often served in French restaurants, but they're also good with Cognac, Scotch or Armagnac.

STORING: Truffles, ready to shape or already shaped, can be refrigerated for at least 3 days. If you've rolled them in cocoa, the cocoa will have melted into the chocolate, so give them a fresh dusting. If you'd like to freeze the truffles, pack them airtight; they'll hold for up to 2 months.

CHOCOLATE TRUFFLES, perfectly round and coated in shiny shells of tempered chocolate, live in the rarefied world of professional chocolatiers. But truffles rolled between your palms, coated with cocoa and bumpy, uneven and looking like the rare black truffles they were named for are the homemade stuff of French hostesses and kids' after-school projects.

At their hearts—and truffles are all heart—the bonbons are ganache, a basic mixture of chocolate and cream. They are usually rolled in cocoa powder to resemble the soil that clings to the freshly dug fungi. But truffles are also delicious coated with confectioners' sugar (or a combination of confectioners' sugar and cocoa), chopped nuts (it's nice if they're toasted), sprinkles, finely chopped coconut, cookie crumbs, graham cracker crumbs or chopped chocolate. For a very special truffle coating, use the salted chocolate from the Carrément Chocolat (page 52). And just as you can play with the coating, you can play with the flavor of the truffle itself (see Bonne Idées).

10 ounces (283 grams) bittersweet chocolate, finely chopped

1 cup (240 ml) heavy cream

½ stick (4 tablespoons; 2 ounces; 57 grams) unsalted butter, at room temperature

1 tablespoon light corn syrup

About ½ cup (42 grams) unsweetened cocoa powder, for coating

Line an 8-inch square pan with plastic film.

To get the smoothest blend, you want to melt—or mostly melt—the chocolate before adding the other ingredients. You can melt the chocolate in a bowl set over a pan of simmering water, or you can put it in a microwave-safe bowl and heat it at medium power, stirring every minute, until most of the chocolate is melted.

Bring the cream to a boil in a saucepan on the stove, or do this in the microwave.

Pour the cream over the chocolate and let it sit for a minute. Using a flexible spatula or whisk and starting in the center of the bowl, stir in tiny circles until the ingredients are blended, then stir in wider concentric circles until the ganache is thick, smooth and shiny.

With a flexible spatula or the heel of your hand, smear the butter across a cutting board—you want to make sure that it's soft and pliable. Then stir the butter into the ganache in 4 or 5 additions, stirring gently until the ganache is once again smooth and shiny. Stir in the corn syrup. (If you are making any of the variations, stir those ingredients in now.)

Pour the ganache into the plastic-lined pan and press another piece of plastic film against the surface. Refrigerate for at least 3 hours, or until the ganache is firm all the way through. (*If it's more convenient, you can keep the ganache in the refrigerator for up to 3 days.*)

When you're ready to form the truffles, line a baking sheet with parchment or wax paper. Put the cocoa in a medium bowl.

Turn the ganache out onto a cutting board and remove the plastic. Cut the chocolate into small cubes or scoop out rounded teaspoonfuls. One by one, roll the pieces of ganache between your palms to make compact balls. Don't worry about molding perfect spheres—truffles are meant to be haphazard. As the balls are formed, drop them one by one into the bowl of cocoa powder, turning to make sure they're covered, then toss them from hand to hand to get rid of the excess cocoa; put them on the lined baking sheet.

Return the truffles to the refrigerator to firm before serving.

Bonne Idées

TRUFFLES OF MANY FLAVORS: Just about anything that goes with chocolate can be stirred into the ganache after you add the corn syrup, so just let your imagination race.

RUM-RAISIN TRUFFLES: Pour ¼ cup dark rum over 1 cup plump, moist raisins, cover and soak for 1 hour. Add the raisins and any remaining liquid to the ganache.

TEA-RAISIN TRUFFLES: Pour ¼ cup hot Earl Grey tea over 1 cup plump, moist raisins, cover and soak for 1 hour. Add the raisins and any remaining liquid to the ganache.

COCONUT TRUFFLES: Add 1 cup sweetened shredded coconut, lightly toasted, and 1 tablespoon Malibu rum (optional) to the ganache.

APRICOT-AMARETTO TRUFFLES: Pour ¼ cup amaretto (or brandy or orange juice) over 1 cup finely diced plump, moist dried Turkish apricots. Cover and soak for 1 hour. Add the apricots and any remaining liquid to the ganache.

MOCHA TRUFFLES: Make a paste of 1 tablespoon boiling water, 1 teaspoon ground cinnamon (optional) and 2 teaspoons instant espresso powder and add it to the hot cream.

PEPPERMINT TRUFFLES: Add 1 teaspoon pure peppermint extract or oil to the ganache. These are nice at Christmas, especially if you coat them in very finely crushed candy canes.

COOKIE-CRUMB TRUFFLES: Add 1 cup finely chopped cookies to the ganache. My favorites are Biscoff (speculoos), cinnamon cookies or graham crackers.

Honey-Nut Nougat

Makes 12 servings

SERVING: Nougat is a high-low treat. Handmade nougat is often served in expensive restaurants as part of a *mignardises* tray—a sampling of small pastries and confections that comes after the main dessert—and commercial nougat is just as often served at a corner café with espresso. In both cases, the idea is the same: to offer something small and delicious at a moment when you can most appreciate it. That said, I respect no hours or traditions when it comes to nougat—if it's in the house, it's mine.

STORING: If you keep your nougat well wrapped in a cool, dry place, it will be perfectly luscious for about 3 weeks (and just plain luscious for a week or so after that).

DEPENDING ON WHERE YOU ARE IN FRANCE, to toss off nougat as mere candy, or to call it taffy, would be the equivalent of a Frenchman disparaging apple pie and motherhood. The candy, a combination of toasted nuts and dried fruit embedded in a base of soft, sticky, stretchy honey and meringue, is so beloved in the south of France that there are *confréreries* of nougat lovers, societies dedicated to keeping the sweet alive and appreciated.

Nougat is usually made with a light honey, such as acacia or orange blossom, but medium honeys are nice as well. Because there is so much honey in this recipe, even if you use a pale honey, your nougat may not be white—a fact that has never bothered me, but if you're used to commercial nougat, you might take notice. Similarly, Marcona almonds are the almonds of choice among nougateers, but you can use slivered or sliced almonds, which are easier to find, and still produce praiseworthy nougat.

I don't make nougat very often, mostly because this is a sweet that defeats my limited self-control. I always cut the bar in half and give away one piece immediately, but knowing that there's nougat in the house, I nibble at it. I cut a sliver and cut the sliver into small pieces and I eat them one by one. And then, even though I've had enough, I go back for more. It's the flavor of the honey and the chewiness of the nougat that draws me in, but it's the contrasting texture of the fruits and nuts that keeps me coming back. The combination has the same effect on me that the sirens' call had on Odysseus's crew.

Before you set to work, make sure you have all your ingredients and gear, including a candy thermometer, prepped and ready to go. You'll be working with hot sugar and rapidly changing temperatures, and you're going to want to be nimble.

A WORD ON TRADITION: Authentic nougat is sandwiched between pieces of edible rice paper. Some people love the paper; others don't. Like it or not, it makes pressing the nougat into shape and serving it neater. You can find rice paper in baking supply stores, online or in some craft shops. If you don't have rice paper, you can use cornstarch and confectioners' sugar in its place—the nougat will be a little less prim looking, but no less seductive.

2 8-x-4-inch sheets edible rice paper (optional; see above)
   Flavorless oil or cooking spray
2 tablespoons cornstarch (if not using rice paper)
2 tablespoons confectioners' sugar (if not using rice paper)

8 ounces (227 grams) mixed nuts, such as almonds, cashews, pistachios, hazelnuts, pecans and/or walnuts (if you'd like, you can use just one kind)
2/3 cup (224 grams) honey

1 cup (200 grams) sugar, plus
   1 tablespoon
2 tablespoons water
1 large egg white, at room
   temperature
   Pinch of fine sea salt

½ cup (about 75 grams) plump,
   moist dried fruit, such
   as cherries, cranberries,
   apricots or figs, coarsely
   chopped or snipped

Center a rack in the oven and preheat the oven to 350 degrees F. If you're using edible rice paper, put the sheets on a baking sheet and set aside. If you don't have rice paper, use oil or cooking spray to lightly oil an 8-inch square baking pan. Line the pan with parchment paper, leaving an overhang on two opposite sides, and lightly oil or spray the paper. Whisk the cornstarch and confectioners' sugar together and sift half of it evenly over the parchment paper; reserve the remainder.

Line a baking sheet with parchment paper or a silicone baking mat and spread the nuts out on a rimmed baking sheet and bake for about 8 minutes, or until they are just barely colored. Transfer the nuts to a cutting board and turn off the oven; don't wash the baking sheet.

Chop the nuts very roughly—you want big pieces. (Actually, you could leave the nuts whole if you wanted to, it just makes it a little harder to guarantee that everyone's hunk of nougat is chock-full of nuts.) Return the nuts to the baking sheet and keep them in a warm place. If it's convenient, you can keep them in the oven with the door ajar. (You don't want to toast them any more, but you do want them to be warm when you add them to the nougat.)

Put the honey, 1 cup of the sugar and the water in a small heavy-bottomed saucepan and stir just to blend (I use a high-sided 2-quart saucepan). Position a candy thermometer in the pan so that the bulb doesn't touch the bottom of the pan and the numbers are clearly visible. Put the pan over medium heat and bring the mixture to a boil. There's no need to stir but every reason to stay near by: Once the mixture reaches a boil, it has a tendency to bubble up furiously—a dangerous condition, since the honey is both hot and sticky. Regulate the heat as needed and keep the mixture going at a nice burble. You want to cook the honey and sugar until the thermometer reads 300 degrees F (or just a few degrees less), a process that can take 10 to 15 minutes, depending on your pan and the heat under it.

When you've got the honey under control, start on the meringue. Working in the bowl of a stand mixer fitted with the whisk attachment, or in a large bowl with a sturdy hand mixer (a deep bowl is best and it is safest to steady it on the counter by wrapping a towel around its base), beat the egg white and salt together until firm. Add the remaining tablespoon of sugar and continue to mix. If the honey mixture hasn't hit temperature yet, either keep the stand mixer going at the lowest speed or use the hand mixer to fluff up the meringue every few minutes.

As soon as the honey mixture reaches 300 degrees F, remove the pan from the heat (remove the thermometer), set the mixer speed to medium and, using extreme caution and a good potholder, pour the hot syrup into the mixing bowl in a steady stream. Don't be slow—you want to get the syrup into the bowl while it's just the right temperature. Try to pour the syrup between the beater and the side of the bowl, but don't be discouraged when the syrup spatters. It's inevitable and you should leave it—don't try to scrape the hardened beads of syrup into the nougat. When the syrup is fully incorporated, turn the mixer speed to medium-high and beat for another 4 to 6 minutes, until the nougat is pale.

Grease a wooden spoon or very sturdy silicone spatula with oil or cooking spray and stir the warm chopped nuts and chopped dried fruit into the nougat. Scrape the nougat out onto one sheet of rice paper or into the prepared pan. If you're using a pan, scrape the nougat as much to one side as you can. (You want some height, so it's better to mold the nougat into half of the pan than to spread it across the entire pan.)

Oil or spray the palms of your hands, then press and mold the nougat into a block that's about 8 × 4 inches. Don't worry about getting it perfectly smooth or even, but do try to build it up. If you're using rice paper, place the second sheet of paper over the top of the nougat and press it down to smooth it across the top. If you're working in a pan, sift the remaining cornstarch mixture evenly over the top of the nougat. Set aside to cool at room temperature and finish firming up, about 2 hours.

If you used rice paper, just put the nougat on a cutting board. If you used a baking pan, dust off the cornstarch and sugar from the top of the nougat, turn the nougat out onto a cutting board, peel away the parchment and dust off the other side. The nougat will be very firm—it will soften in your mouth (one of the candy's many pleasures)—so choose a strong knife. Some people like a long serrated knife for this job; others a chef's knife (my preference). Score the top of the nougat and then work with determination: My choice is to cut long slices that are 1 inch wide and wrap the pieces in plastic film, then cut them into smaller pieces as needed. If you want to do all the cutting in one fell swoop, slice long strips and then cut each strip into pieces 1 to 1½ inches long; wrap these smaller pieces in plastic film or cellophane.

Chocolate-Covered
Toffee Breakups

Makes 12 servings

SERVING: Once the chocolate is set, crack, break or cut the toffee into pieces that are about 2 inches across. Neatness not only doesn't count here, it's just about impossible to achieve. Serve the toffee as a solo treat or alongside coffee. When you're down to the last of it, crush what you've got left and sprinkle the bits over ice cream.

STORING: The toffee will keep for about 1 week in a cool, dry place. Pack it into a container, putting parchment or wax paper between the layers.

THIS CHOCOLATE-COVERED nut-studded caramel toffee might be as close as you can get to a Heath Bar without being sued for some kind of trademark infringement. At least that's what my American friends say; my French friends say the candy reminds them of Daim, small hard caramel candies that taste like the Heath Bar's next of kin. What I know for sure is that the candy is great fun to make and that everyone I've ever made it for on either side of the Atlantic has not only loved it, but has asked for the recipe so that they can make it themselves. I think of the recipe as a chain letter that's never been broken.

The first link in the chain was my friend Nick Malgieri, the cooking teacher and cookbook author, who gave me the recipe about fifteen years ago, right before I was leaving for Christmas in Paris. No sooner had I arrived in Paris than I began toffeeing. I made toffee as after-dinner treats for friends who came to our house, and I made toffee as holiday gifts for just about everyone I knew. That's when the please-give-me-the-recipe requests began and the chain grew longer.

You don't need to be a pro candy maker to succeed with this toffee, but you do need a candy thermometer for cooking the sugar.

2 sticks (8 ounces; 227 grams) unsalted butter	almonds or other nuts, coarsely chopped, at room temperature
1½ cups (300 grams) sugar	12 ounces (340 grams)
3 tablespoons light corn syrup	semisweet or bittersweet
3 tablespoons water	chocolate, melted
½ teaspoon fine sea salt	Maldon sea salt or fleur de
2 cups (about 8 ounces; 227 grams) toasted	sel, for topping (optional)

Butter a 12-x-17-inch rimmed baking sheet, line it with parchment paper and butter the parchment. Have two large cutting boards and some more parchment or wax paper on hand—you'll need them when you're coating and flipping the candy.

Melt the butter in a medium saucepan. Remove the pan from the heat and, using a heatproof spatula or a wooden spoon, stir in the sugar, corn syrup and water. Position a candy thermometer in the pan so that the bulb doesn't touch the bottom of the pan. Cook the mixture over medium-high heat, stirring occasionally, until it reaches 300 degrees F, a process that can take 10 minutes or so, depending on your pan and the heat under it. At this point,

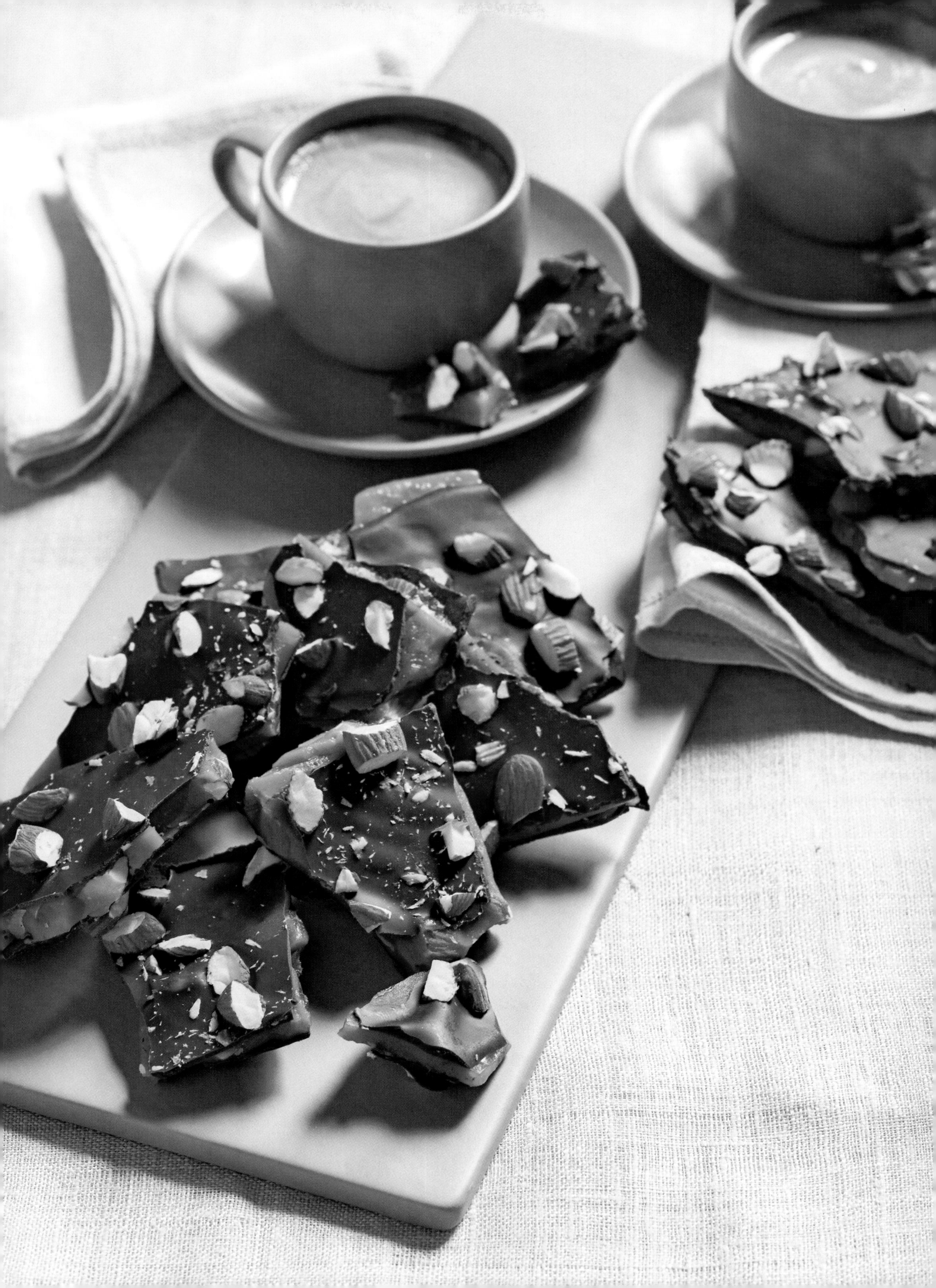

the toffee will be caramel colored and bubbling. Take the pan off the heat, remove the thermometer and stir in the salt and 1 cup of the nuts.

Cautiously pour the hot, sticky caramel into the parchment-lined pan. Immediately and with a sense of purpose, use the back of a spoon or an offset spatula to spread the toffee over the bottom of the pan. It's okay if you have a ragged oblong or an odd shape. Don't feel as if you have to push the toffee all the way to the edges of the pan, but you do have to work fast because the toffee hardens quickly.

When the candy is just firm enough to handle—in about 20 minutes—cover one of the cutting boards with parchment or wax paper and turn the toffee out onto it. Peel off the parchment on top and let cool completely.

For the chocolate to coat the toffee properly, the surface of the candy has to be dry, so use a damp paper towel to wipe away any excess butter or moisture. Let the toffee dry for a minute or so.

Use a small offset spatula or a table knife to quickly spread half of the melted chocolate over the toffee. Scatter ½ cup of the nuts over the chocolate. Cover the toffee with a sheet of parchment or wax paper and place the second cutting board on top. Holding both cutting boards, flip the setup over. Remove the top board and paper and quickly spread the remaining chocolate over the toffee. Scatter over the remaining ½ cup nuts, cover with a piece of parchment and lightly press the nuts into the chocolate; remove the paper. Sprinkle on a little sea salt, if you're using it.

Refrigerate the candy until the chocolate is set, about 30 minutes, before breaking it up or cutting it.

Soft Salted-Butter Caramels

CARAMEL CANDIES ARE NOT NEW IN FRANCE, but the word *caramélier*, "caramel maker," is not only a recent addition to the lexicon, it's one that's trademarked. Henri Le Roux gave himself the name and trademarked it, an act that most caramel lovers are just fine with, since he's the person credited with making *caramel au beurre salé*, or CBS (also trademarked)—caramel made with the famous salted butter of Brittany, his birthplace.

Soft caramel, called *caramel mou*, is sometimes sold in small squares and often in small cylinders (rather like Tootsie Rolls), each wrapped in cellophane, twisted firecracker style at the ends. If you go to the right cafés, you might get a *caramel mou* on the saucer with your espresso. And if you go to the right restaurants, you just might find a few caramels on the tray with your bill. (When we do, I slip them into my purse and save them for the walk home or for a last bite before bed.)

Like macarons, *caramel mou* has become a kind of obsession. Not that you'll find them made at home, but you will hear conversations in which people mention them with sighs and their eyes rolled heavenward.

Caramels are so much on Parisians' minds that when a friend of mine and her boyfriend hit a rough patch, she became so frustrated that she summed it all up by saying, "You are not an easy person!" He didn't even take a breath before volleying back, "Well, you're not exactly a *caramel mou*!" Miss Soft Caramel couldn't stay angry while laughing.

The classic soft caramel is flavored with vanilla and seasoned with fleur de sel from Brittany. In America, I use regular unsalted butter and add fleur de sel; in France, I use butter that's very salty and speckled with fleur de sel. No matter where I am, I never tackle caramel without a candy thermometer—it's your best friend when it comes to cooking sugar.

As with so much in life, good things come to those who wait. You need to give the caramel a few hours to cool down and firm; overnight in a cool, dry place is best.

A WORD ON WRAPPING: The caramels are best wrapped in cellophane. Second choice is wax paper, and parchment is by far a third choice. If you don't wrap the candies, they'll stick to one another. Another possibility is to leave the caramel in one piece, wrapped in parchment, and cut it as you need it.

Makes about 50 caramels

SERVING: Caramels are an anytime candy, very good with coffee and excellent with French Cognac or American bourbon.

STORING: Keep the caramels in an airtight container in the refrigerator. Let the candies sit at room temperature for a few minutes before serving. The caramels will keep for about 3 weeks in the refrigerator.

1–2 moist, fragrant vanilla beans or 1 tablespoon pure vanilla paste or extract	1 cup (240 ml) heavy cream
1½ cups (300 grams) sugar	3 tablespoons (1½ ounces; 43 grams) unsalted butter, at room temperature
¼ cup (60 ml) light corn syrup	1¼ teaspoons fleur de sel or ½ teaspoon fine sea salt
2 tablespoons water	

Line an 8-inch square baking pan with parchment paper, leaving an overhang on two opposite sides. Spray the paper and the exposed sides of the pan lightly with cooking spray and set aside on a cooling rack, trivet or potholder. (When you pour the caramel into the pan, it's going to be extremely hot, so you'll want to protect your counter.)

If you're using vanilla beans, cut each bean in half lengthwise and use the top of the knife to scrape out the pulpy seeds; set aside. Save the pods to flavor syrup or to make vanilla sugar.

Choose a deep saucepan with a capacity of 3 to 4 quarts—the sugar will bubble up furiously, and you need to be prepared and protected. Put the sugar, corn syrup and water in the saucepan and stir to mix. Have a brush—preferably a silicone brush—and a bowl of cold water nearby; you'll use them to wash down the sides of the pan.

Pour the cream into a small saucepan and bring it to a boil on the stove, or do this in a microwave oven. Have the hot cream, soft butter and salt near your stovetop, as well as a heatproof spatula or wooden spoon.

Place the saucepan with the sugar over medium to medium-high heat. You won't be stirring this now, but as sugar spatters on the sides of the pan, you should wash it down with water. When the sugar dissolves and the mixture starts to boil, position a candy thermometer in the pan so the bulb doesn't touch the bottom of the pan. You want to cook the caramel without stirring until it reaches 300 to 310 degrees F. (Don't go any higher.) It will take a while for the temperature to mount and then it will speed along—don't leave the stove! If the sugar starts to color (it might or it might not), swirl the pan gently to mix. When you've hit temperature, take the pan off the heat.

Off the heat, using the heatproof spatula and standing away from the pan, slowly add the hot cream and stir to mix. Drop in the butter and then the salt and stir. "Seething" is the word that will come to mind as the ingredients go in. Keep calm and stir on.

Put the pan back over medium-high heat and keep cooking, without stirring, until the caramel reaches 260 degrees F on the candy thermometer. Pull the pan from the heat and stir in the vanilla (pulp, extract or paste), then remove the thermometer and pour the bubbling caramel into the prepared pan; don't scrape out anything that sticks to the bottom. If necessary, shimmy the pan to level the caramel, then put the candy in a cool, dry place. Allow it to cool to room temperature and then wait a few hours more (preferably overnight) before cutting.

TO CUT THE CARAMEL: Turn the caramel out onto a parchment- or wax paper–lined cutting board, peel away the paper from the bottom of the caramel and then flip the candy over (or just leave it). The caramel is easiest to cut with a long chef's knife or a sturdy bench scraper. If you find that either sticks to the candy, rub the blade with a little oil. Cut the candy into 1-inch squares. Place each piece on a cellophane (or wax or parchment paper) rectangle and either wrap it as a square or do as I do: Roll the candy into a little log and twist the wrapper at both ends to seal it.

Salt is as important in sweets as it is in savories. It boosts the flavors of other ingredients and makes their tastes last longer.

Here and there you'll find recipes where I've called for a pinch of salt, but usually a pinch is not enough for me. Since I think of salt as a seasoning, I want to taste it—I rarely want anything to be salty, but I do want to know that the salt is there.

My everyday salt is fine sea salt, but I also keep a stash of "finishing salts" on hand and am never without fleur de sel, a moist, slightly coarse, hand-harvested sea salt from France (I prefer fleur de sel from Guérande), and Maldon, a flaky sea salt from England. These are expensive—don't pour them into your pasta water!—but you won't be using much of either in any one recipe.

You'll notice that sometimes I use fleur de sel in a recipe instead of fine sea salt. That's because fleur de sel is less salty than regular salt and it retains an ever-so-slight crunch even after it bakes—a nice surprise.

Once you're hooked on finishing salts—as I know you will be—you'll want to experiment with others. To get started, try Himalayan pink salt or Hawaiian black lava salt as sprinklers over chocolate mousse, anything caramel, a butter cookie or a tart made with ganache. Try some smoked salt over the Brown Sugar Tart (page 174), with or without the bacon. Or swap the fine sea salt for something crunchier in the streusel that tops the Cherry Crumb Tart (page 148).

Crunchy Granola

Makes about 10 cups

SERVING: Chez moi, granola is a morning-to-midnight treat. We have it with milk and fruit for breakfast, sprinkled over salad at lunch and on top of yogurt, ice cream or pudding for dessert. We also peck at it, small handfuls at a time. Actually, pecking's how we like it most.

STORING: If you keep the granola dry, it will stay fresh and crispy for 2 to 3 weeks at room temperature. Don't refrigerate or freeze it; the honey will cause it to go soggy.

WHEN I FIRST STARTED TO VISIT PARIS REGULARLY and began to have friends there and to be invited to dinner parties, I was often stumped about what to bring. I took my share of flowers and candles, but I felt that I should be bringing something made in America. I just wasn't sure what it should be. And then I hit on made-in-my-kitchen granola.

The idea was almost perfect: The perfect part was that granola was very popular in America and almost unknown in France. The less than perfect part was the oddity of a grown woman making her own gift. Arts and crafts and homemade gifts are common among French children, less common and a little less appreciated among sophisticated French adults. But, as it often does, goodness trumped everything else: One crunch, and my hosts were won over.

Even though you can now buy granola in the cereal section of every French supermarket, my friends still clamor for mine. Yes, I've given them the recipe. Yes, I've even given them packets of ingredients. But no, they never make it themselves. "We like it best when you make it for us," they say. It might be a cover-up for laziness, or it might be some well-practiced form of French flattery, but I take it as a compliment, and so I've been making granola for them for decades. Granola Cake and Granola Energy Bars too (pages 54 and 328).

Like so many of my favorite recipes, this lends itself to many, many variations. As long as you keep the amount of oatmeal steady, ditto the liquids, you can play around with which nuts and dried fruits to add. Sometimes I swap the slivered almonds for chunks of unblanched almonds; sometimes I go luxe and add pistachios or pecans; and sometimes I go tropical and add slivers of dried mango, pieces of dried banana and macadamias. The recipe makes a lot of granola, but it seems foolish to make less when it keeps so well and makes such a good gift.

A LAST WORD: You'll get the crunchiest granola if you make it on a day when humidity isn't an issue.

¾ cup (255 grams) honey	½ teaspoon fine sea salt
½ cup (100 grams) packed light brown sugar	About 5½ cups (454 grams) old-fashioned (not quick-cooking) oats
½ stick (4 tablespoons; 2 ounces; 57 grams) unsalted butter, cut into 4 chunks	1¾ cups (217 grams) raw sunflower seeds
1 tablespoon pure vanilla extract	1 cup (160 grams) raw pumpkin seeds

1½ cups (180 grams) slivered almonds	1 cup (about 150 grams) plump, moist dried fruit, such as raisins, cranberries, snipped apricots and/or cherries
1 cup shredded coconut, sweetened (120 grams) or unsweetened (60 grams)	

Center a rack in the oven and preheat the oven to 325 degrees F. Have two 9-×-13-inch Pyrex baking pans at hand.

Pour the honey into a small saucepan, add the brown sugar (run it between your fingers so that it's free of lumps) and butter and bring to a boil over medium heat, stirring frequently. Lower the heat and simmer—stirring often—until both the brown sugar and the butter are melted. Off the heat, stir in the vanilla and salt.

Toss the oats, seeds and nuts into a large bowl and mix everything together thoroughly with your hands. Pour over the warm liquid, grab a big wooden or silicone spoon and stir until everything is evenly moistened. You'll think that there isn't enough liquid to coat all the dry ingredients, but keep stirring, and every little flake of oat and nut will be coated with honey. Divide the mixture between the two pans.

The total baking time for the granola is 45 to 60 minutes, with lots of turning and scraping. After 20 minutes in the oven, use a big spoon to turn everything over, making sure to scrape up anything that's stuck to the pans. Do this again after another 20 minutes, but this time sprinkle an equal amount of the coconut over the granola in each pan and stir it in. Bake, scraping and turning, for another 5 to 15 minutes. You want the oats and nuts to be a burnished golden brown, and while the granola will be soft and sticky, you should be able to see each individual flake of oat or piece of nut. If you think it needs to be a tiny bit browner, bake it for a few minutes more.

Scrape the granola into a big bowl and stir in the dried fruit. When the granola has come to room temperature, use your hands to break up the many clumps that will have formed.

Real Hot Chocolate

Makes 2 servings

SERVING: Offer the chocolate in cups or mugs, as is or topped with a puff of whipped cream, a dusting of cinnamon or a marshmallow or two.

STORING: The chocolate mixture can be kept covered in the refrigerator for up to 2 days. When you're ready to serve it, gently bring it back to a boil and whir it for 1 minute with a blender.

Bonne Idée

COLD HOT CHOCOLATE: Make the hot chocolate following the recipe, then chill it thoroughly. When you're ready to serve it, pour it into a pitcher, add ¼ cup cold water and whir it for 1 minute with an immersion blender (or use a regular blender). Serve over a couple of ice cubes.

THERE'S SOMETHING NOSTALGIC about hot chocolate. Think of it, and you see kids with pink-tipped noses just coming in from the cold, or ice-skating parties sipping hot chocolate around a bonfire. But that's a very American picture of hot chocolate. In France, hot chocolate isn't a kids' drink, it's not reserved for warming you at a sports event and it isn't a winter-only beverage. It isn't even a special treat. It's an everyday drink, an alternative to coffee or tea and available in every café. The best hot chocolate—made with good chocolate and milk or cream—is served in the best cafés and tea salons. Angelina, perhaps the most widely known tearoom in Paris, is famous for its hot chocolate, which is so rich and thick that you might be able to stand a spoon up in it.

My preference is for a less dense, less rich hot chocolate, one that can either serve as dessert or be sipped along with a dessert. I make my hot chocolate with real chocolate, of course, but I use milk, not cream, and I add water to the milk. I love the consistency: still thick, still luxurious, but not cloying. And I love the flavor: chocolate, pure chocolate. If you'd like, you can chill the chocolate, thin it a bit more, whir it with a blender and serve it cold over ice (see Bonne Idée).

Use your favorite chocolate. I use bittersweet, but semisweet or even fine-quality milk chocolate will make a great drink; adjust the sugar to balance the sweetness. And, yes, marshmallows are great on this hot chocolate. I knew you were wondering.

2 cups (480 ml) whole milk	4 ounces (113 grams) bittersweet, semisweet or best-quality milk chocolate, melted and still warm
⅓ cup (80 ml) water	
2–5 tablespoons sugar	
Pinch of fleur de sel or fine sea salt	

Bring the milk, water, sugar and salt to a boil in a small saucepan over medium heat. Stir to be certain that the sugar is dissolved. Remove the pan from the heat and scrape in the melted chocolate.

Set the pan over medium heat and, whisking all the while, cook to blend the chocolate into the milk. Stop when you see bubbles rising to the surface.

Pour the chocolate into a heatproof pitcher and whir it for 1 minute with an immersion blender (or use a regular blender). Serve immediately.

BASICS

Sweet Tart Dough

*Makes one 9- to
9½-inch crust*

STORING: Well wrapped,
the dough can be kept in
the refrigerator for up to
5 days or frozen for up to
2 months. While the fully
baked crust can be packed
airtight and frozen for up
to 2 months, I prefer to
freeze the crust fitted into
the pan but not baked and
then to bake it directly
from the freezer—it will
have a fresher flavor. Just
add about 5 minutes to the
baking time.

USED BY SO MANY FRENCH PASTRY CHEFS for so many French tarts, this is the dough that I turn to automatically when I've got a tart on my mind. Known as *pâte sablée*, it's really a sweet cookie dough, the one you'd use to make a tender sablé or shortbread cookie.

I always prebake the crust even if it's going to get another long bake with the filling, because I like the resulting color, flavor and texture—and the fact that the bottom won't be soggy.

I use a fluted tart pan with a removable base. If all you've got is a pie plate, don't let that stop you.

A WORD ON ROLLING VERSUS PRESSING: You can roll the crust out and fit it into the tart pan or just press it in. I roll the dough. Rolling gives you a thinner crust than pressing, so if you press, you might occasionally find yourself with a little filling left over.

1½ cups (204 grams) all-purpose flour	9 tablespoons (4½ ounces; 128 grams) very cold unsalted butter, cut into small pieces
½ cup (60 grams) confectioners' sugar	
¼ teaspoon fine sea salt	1 large egg yolk

TO MAKE THE DOUGH: Put the flour, confectioners' sugar and salt in a food processor and pulse a couple of times to blend. Scatter the pieces of butter over the dry ingredients and pulse until the butter is cut in coarsely—you'll have some pieces the size of oatmeal flakes and some the size of peas. Stir the yolk just to break it up and add it a little at a time, pulsing after each addition. When the egg is incorporated, process in long pulses—about 10 seconds each—until the dough, which will look granular soon after the egg is added, forms clumps and curds. Just before you reach this clumpy stage, the sound of the machine working the dough will change—heads-up. Turn the dough out onto a work surface.

To incorporate the butter more evenly and to catch any dry ingredients that might have escaped mixing, separate small amounts of dough from the pile and use the heel of your hand to smear each piece a few inches across the counter. In French this is called *fraisage*, and it's the ideal way to finish blending a dough.

TO MAKE A ROLLED-OUT CRUST: Shape the dough into a disk and put it between two sheets of parchment or wax paper. Roll the dough out evenly, turning it over frequently and lifting the paper often so that it doesn't roll into the dough and form creases. Aim for a circle that's at least 3 inches larger than the base of your tart pan. The dough will be ⅛ to 1/16 inch thick, but it's the diameter, not the thickness, that counts. Slide the rolled-out dough, still between the papers, onto a baking sheet or cutting board and refrigerate for 2 hours or freeze it for 1 hour. (*The dough can be refrigerated overnight or frozen for up to 2 months; wrap it airtight to freeze.*)

When the dough is thoroughly chilled, put it on the counter and let it rest for about 10 minutes, or until it's just pliable enough to bend without breaking. Remove the dough from the paper, fit it into a buttered tart pan and trim the excess dough even with the edges of the pan. (If you'd like, you can fold the excess over and make a thicker wall around the sides of the tart.) Prick the crust all over with a fork and freeze for at least 30 minutes, preferably longer, before baking.

TO MAKE A PRESS-IN CRUST: Butter the tart pan and press the dough evenly over the bottom and up the sides of the pan. You won't need all of the dough if you want to make a thin crust, but I think it's nice to make a thickish one so that you can really enjoy the texture. Press the pieces of dough in so that they cling to one another and will knit together when baked, but don't use a lot of force—working lightly will preserve the crust's shortbread texture. Prick the crust all over with a fork and freeze for at least 30 minutes, preferably longer, before baking.

WHEN YOU'RE READY TO BAKE: Center a rack in the oven and preheat the oven to 400 degrees F. Butter the shiny side of a piece of aluminum foil (or use nonstick foil) and fit the foil snugly into the crust. If the crust is frozen, you can bake it as is; if not, fill it with dried beans or rice (which you can reuse as weights but won't be able to cook after they've been used this way).

TO PARTIALLY BAKE THE CRUST: Bake for 25 minutes, then carefully remove the foil (and weights). If the crust has puffed, press it down gently with the back of a spoon. Transfer the crust to a cooling rack (keep it in its pan).

TO FULLY BAKE THE CRUST: Bake the crust for 25 minutes, then carefully remove the foil (and weights). If the crust has puffed, press it down gently with the back of a spoon. Bake the crust for another 7 to 10 minutes, or until it is firm and golden brown. Transfer the crust to a cooling rack (keep it in its pan).

Bonne Idée

SWEET TART DOUGH WITH NUTS: Reduce the all-purpose flour to 1¼ cups and add ¼ cup almond or hazelnut flour (or very finely ground pecans or pistachios). Proceed as directed on the previous page.

For most of my life, I have followed instructions like a good student. This has meant that I made the dough—pie dough, tart dough, cookie dough, most any dough—gathered it into a ball, pressed it into a disk and refrigerated it for an hour (usually longer), so that the roughly handled dough could settle down before I had to rough it up again by rolling it out.

Gone are those days! As a woman of a certain age, I've rebelled and the dough and I are both better for it.

Dough fresh from the fridge is a bear to roll out. You have to leave it at room temperature until it's supple enough to roll or, if you're impatient, as I often am, you have to bash it with a rolling pin until it's soft enough to roll without cracking. These days, I no longer beat or bash: I roll the dough as soon as it's made, when it's softest and most compliant.

When the dough comes out of the mixer or food processor, I form it into a ball, divide it (if necessary), flatten it into a disk (or disks) and place it between sheets of parchment paper. And then I roll. And rolling is a breeze.

The key is to turn the dough over and roll on both sides and to lift the paper often, so that you don't roll creases into the dough.

When the dough is the thickness you want, slide it, still sandwiched between the papers, onto a cutting board or baking sheet and chill it for at least 1 hour (or for as long as the recipe instructs). If the dough is destined to be a pie or tart crust, you'll need to remove it from the fridge and let it warm up a bit before you can fit it into the pan. Not so if the dough is heading to cookiedom—you can usually cut that dough immediately. In both cases, it's best to rechill or even freeze the crust or cutout cookies while you preheat the oven—something I do no matter how I've rolled out the dough.

Chocolate Tart Dough

Makes one 9- to 9½-inch crust

STORING: Well wrapped, the dough can be kept in the refrigerator for up to 5 days or frozen for up to 2 months. While the fully baked crust can be packed airtight and frozen for up to 2 months, I prefer to freeze the crust fitted into the pan but not baked, and then bake it directly from the freezer—it will have a fresher flavor. Just add about 5 minutes to the baking time.

THE ONLY THING BETTER THAN some chocolate is more chocolate, so here's a recipe to make a chocolate shortbread dough, a dough that is just as delicious baked as cookies as it is as a tart shell for custard or ganache fillings, pastry cream or fruit.

You can use this recipe anywhere you would use the Sweet Tart Dough (page 414).

1¼	cups (170 grams) all-purpose flour	¼	teaspoon fine sea salt
¼	cup (21 grams) unsweetened cocoa powder	9	tablespoons (4½ ounces; 128 grams) very cold unsalted butter, cut into small pieces
¼	cup (30 grams) confectioners' sugar	1	large egg yolk

TO MAKE THE DOUGH: Put the flour, cocoa powder, confectioners' sugar and salt in a food processor and pulse a couple of times to blend. Scatter the pieces of butter over the dry ingredients and pulse until the butter is cut in coarsely—you'll have some pieces the size of oatmeal flakes and some the size of peas. Stir the yolk just to break it up and add it a little at a time, pulsing after each addition. When the egg is incorporated, process in long pulses—about 10 seconds each—until the dough, which will look granular soon after the egg is added, forms clumps and curds. Just before you reach this clumpy stage, the sound of the machine working the dough will change—heads-up. Turn the dough out onto a work surface.

To incorporate the butter more evenly and catch any dry ingredients that might have escaped mixing, separate small amounts of dough from the pile and use the heel of your hand to smear each piece across the counter. The French call this *fraisage*, and it's the ideal way to finish blending a dough.

TO MAKE A ROLLED-OUT CRUST: Shape the dough into a disk and put it between two sheets of parchment or wax paper. Roll the dough out evenly, turning it over frequently and lifting the paper often so that it doesn't roll into the dough and form creases. Aim for a circle that's at least 3 inches larger than the base of your tart pan. The dough will be ⅛ to 1/16 inch thick, but it's the diameter, not the thickness, that counts. Slide the rolled-out dough, still between the papers, onto a baking sheet or cutting board and refrigerate it for 2 hours or freeze it for 1 hour. (*The dough can be refrigerated overnight or frozen for up to 2 months; wrap it airtight to freeze.*)

When the dough is thoroughly chilled, put it on the counter and let it rest for about 10 minutes, or until it's just pliable enough to bend without breaking. Remove the dough from the paper, fit it into the buttered tart pan and trim the excess dough even with the edges of the pan. (If you'd like, you can fold the excess over and make a thicker wall around the sides of the tart.) Prick the crust all over and freeze for at least 30 minutes, preferably longer, before baking.

TO MAKE A PRESS-IN CRUST: Butter the tart pan and press the dough evenly over the bottom and up the sides of the pan. You won't need all the dough if you want to make a thin crust, but I think it's nice to make a thickish one so that you can really enjoy the texture. Press the pieces of dough in so that they cling to one another and will knit together when baked, but don't use a lot of force—working lightly will preserve the crust's shortbready texture. Prick the crust all over with a fork and freeze for at least 30 minutes, preferably longer, before baking.

WHEN YOU'RE READY TO BAKE: Center a rack in the oven and preheat the oven to 375 degrees F. Butter the shiny side of a piece of aluminum foil (or use nonstick foil) and fit the foil snugly into the crust. If the crust is frozen, you can bake it as is; if not, fill it with dried beans or rice (which you can reuse as weights but won't be able to cook after they've been used this way).

TO PARTIALLY BAKE THE CRUST: Bake for 25 minutes, then carefully remove the foil (and weights). If the crust has puffed, press it down gently with the back of a spoon. Transfer the crust to a cooling rack (keep it in its pan).

TO FULLY BAKE THE CRUST: Bake the crust for 25 minutes, then carefully remove the foil (and weights). If the crust has puffed, press it down gently with the back of a spoon. Bake the crust for another 7 to 10 minutes, or until it is firm. Transfer the crust to a cooling rack (keep it in its pan).

Galette Dough

STORING: The dough can be kept in the refrigerator for up to 2 days or wrapped airtight and stored in the freezer for up to 2 months. If you've frozen the dough, leave it on the counter to come to a workable texture and temperature.

Bonne Idée

SWEETER, FLAKIER GALETTE DOUGH: Increase the sugar to 3 tablespoons and the butter to 9 tablespoons (4½ ounces; 128 grams). I like the texture of this dough, but it's softer and stickier and not as easy to work with as the basic recipe.

I F THE FRENCH MADE PIES—and some of them do these days—I'd tell them to use this dough, which has the flakiness of the best all-American pie dough and the sweet butter flavor of the nicest French tart dough. It's quickly made in a food processor and it's both sturdy and supple.

1½ cups (204 grams) all-purpose flour	4 ounces; 113 grams) very cold unsalted butter, cut into 16 pieces (frozen butter is good here)
2 tablespoons sugar	
½ teaspoon fine sea salt	
1 stick (8 tablespoons;	¼ cup (60 ml) ice water

TO MAKE THE DOUGH: Put the flour, sugar and salt in a food processor and pulse a couple of times to blend. Scatter the pieces of butter over the dry ingredients and pulse until the butter is cut into the flour. At first you'll have a mixture that looks like coarse meal and then, as you pulse more, you'll get small flake-sized pieces and some larger pea-sized pieces too. Add a little of the ice water and pulse, add some more, pulse and continue until all of the water is incorporated. Now work in longer pulses—about 10 seconds each—stopping to scrape the sides and bottom of the bowl if needed, until you have a dough that forms nice bumpy curds that hold together when you pinch them. Just before you reach this clumpy stage, the sound of the machine working the dough will change—heads-up. Turn the dough out onto a work surface.

To incorporate the butter more evenly and to catch any dry ingredients that might have escaped mixing, separate small amounts of dough from the pile and use the heel of your hand to smear each piece a few inches across the counter. In French this is called *fraisage*, and it's the ideal way to finish blending a dough.

Gather the dough into a ball, flatten it into a disk and put it between two large pieces of parchment paper. (You can roll the dough between wax paper or plastic film, but if you use parchment, you'll be able to bake the galette directly on the bottom sheet of paper—no transferring needed.) Roll the dough, while it's still cool, into a circle about 12 inches in diameter. Don't worry about getting the exact size or about having the edges be perfect; when you construct the galette, the edges will be bunched up and pleated and they'll only look prettier if they're a bit ragged. The dough will be somewhat thick and that's fine—you want to have a little heft for a free-form pastry.

Slide the rolled-out dough, still between the papers, onto a baking sheet or cutting board and refrigerate it for at least 2 hours. (*Well wrapped, the dough can be refrigerated for up to 2 days or frozen for up to 2 months.*)

When you're ready to use the dough, leave it on the counter for a few minutes, just so that it's pliable enough to lift and fold without cracking.

Brioche
(In Loaf Pans or Coffee Cans)

Here's my tried-and-true, never-fail recipe for brioche, the buttery egg bread that's beloved not just by the French, but by anyone who's lucky enough to nab a slice. Although it's a breakfast bread, like challah or Greek egg bread, it has a bunch of other good uses: When it's stale, it makes fabulous French toast; it's exactly what you want for bread pudding or Bettelman (page 343); its crumbs can be used as a sopper-upper on the bottom of fruit tarts (see page 145); and it's surprisingly wonderful for ice cream sandwiches (page 388).

I've given you instructions for baking two loaves in regular loaf pans or coffee cans. I love making the loaves in coffee cans because they come out tall and perfectly round and make a beautiful base for cream and berries or Roasted Rhubarb with Bitters (page 335). Or use them, as I do, for ice cream sandwiches (page 388). When you bake in the cans, you get a topknot, which I consider the baker's prize: mine, all mine, to toast and slather with jam.

A WORD ON COFFEE CANS: Make certain that the cans you choose are all metal and that the interiors are uncoated. Cans that held about ½ pound of coffee are right for these loaves.

A WORD ON PLANNING AHEAD: The dough needs to rest overnight in the refrigerator.

Makes 2 loaves

STORING: After its refrigerator rest, you can cover the dough tightly with plastic film and keep it in the refrigerator for up to 3 days, or you can wrap it airtight and freeze it for up to 2 months. Allow the dough to thaw overnight in the refrigerator before using it. As for the baked loaves, they'll keep for 1 day at room temperature, during which time you can eat the brioche untoasted. After 1 day, and for up to 1 day more, the loaves will be delicious toasted. After that, think French toast, Bettelman (page 343) or crumbs.

¼ cup (60 ml) warm-to-the-touch whole milk	3 large eggs, lightly beaten, at room temperature
¼ cup (60 ml) warm-to-the-touch water	1½ sticks (12 tablespoons; 6 ounces; 170 grams) unsalted butter, at room temperature, cut into small chunks
3 tablespoons sugar	
4 teaspoons active dry yeast	
2¾ cups (374 grams) all-purpose flour	
1½ teaspoons fine sea salt	1 large egg

TO MAKE THE DOUGH: Pour the warm milk and water into the bowl of a stand mixer, add a pinch of the sugar and sprinkle over the yeast. Let the yeast rest for 3 minutes—it may or may not bubble—then stir with a wooden spoon or spatula until the mixture is creamy.

Fit the mixer with the dough hook, add the flour and salt and pulse the mixer on and off a few times to dampen the flour. Then mix at medium-low speed, scraping the sides and bottom of the bowl as needed, until you have a shaggy mass, 2 to 3 minutes.

Scrape down the bowl and, working on low speed, pour in the beaten eggs in 3 additions, beating until each is incorporated before adding the next. Beat in the remaining sugar, increase the mixer speed to medium and beat for about 3 minutes, until the dough starts to come together.

On low speed, add the butter in small chunks, beating until each piece is almost incorporated before adding the next. When all the butter is incorporated, you'll have a very soft, silky mixture that will look more like a batter than a dough.

Increase the mixer speed to medium-high and beat until the dough pulls away from the sides of the bowl and climbs up the hook, about 10 minutes. Don't wander too far away, because mixers doing a heavy job like this one have a tendency to creep to the edge of the counter. (That is the voice of experience you just heard.)

Lightly butter a large bowl, scrape the dough into it, cover with plastic film and let rise at room temperature until nearly doubled in size, an hour or so, depending upon the warmth of your room.

Deflate the dough by lifting it up around the edges and letting it fall back into the bowl with a slap. Cover the dough again and refrigerate it, slapping it down every 30 minutes until it stops rising, about 2 hours. Press the plastic against the surface of the dough and leave it in the refrigerator overnight.

The dough is ready to use after its overnight rest.

SHAPE THE DOUGH: Butter two 7½-×-3½-×-2-inch loaf pans or two coffee cans (see previous page).

Remove the dough from the refrigerator and turn it out onto a work surface. Divide the dough in half and press each half to flatten and push out some of the air. Shape each half into a ball, pressing out the air as you work.

FOR LOAF PANS: Divide one piece of dough into 6 even hunks. Shape each hunk into a tight ball by cupping your hand over it and pressing on it as you move it in small circles on the counter. Put the balls of dough in the loaf pan and repeat for the other loaf.

FOR COFFEE CANS: Place one ball seam side down in each can and press down on the dough until it flattens and touches the sides of the can.

THE RISE: The dough has to rise until it almost reaches the tops of the pans or cans. Put the loaves in a warm place, cover them with parchment or wax paper and let rise. Depending on the temperature of the room and the dough, the rise can take from 45 to 90 minutes; it may take longer in the coffee cans.

WHEN YOU'RE READY TO BAKE: Center a rack in the oven and preheat the oven to 400 degrees F.

When the loaves have risen properly, beat the egg with 1 teaspoon cold water and brush the tops with the egg wash, taking care not to dribble the egg down the sides of the pan (dribbles will keep the edges of the dough from rising evenly in the oven). Using just the tips of a pair of scissors, and holding the scissors perpendicular to the tops of the loaves, snip an X in the center of each ball of dough, if you're using loaf pans, or in the center of each loaf if using coffee cans. The snip should go ¼ inch to ½ inch deep.

Slide the pans into the oven and bake for 30 to 35 minutes, or until the loaves have risen and are golden brown. Transfer the pans to a rack and cool for 5 minutes before unmolding, then allow the breads to cool to room temperature on the rack.

Ladyfinger Batter

*Makes enough for
12 shortcake disks,
2 cake disks or about
24 ladyfingers*

STORING: You cannot
keep this batter; it must be
used as soon as it's made.

ALTHOUGH I'VE SEEN "ladyfingers" translated as *doigts de dames* (literally, "fingers of ladies"), the soft, oblong sponge cakes that we know as ladyfingers are more commonly known in France as *biscuits à la cuillère*, or "spoon cookies," and the batter is the basis of everything from bûche de Noël to tiramisu. It's very delicate—it depends on beaten egg whites and a light touch—and yet it's stood up through centuries. Like its younger cousin, the gâteau de Savoie (page 11), this batter was created for the royal House of Savoy, perhaps as early as the eleventh century, and, like the cake, it hasn't changed much, making me think that those early Savoyards weren't just talented, but wise as well.

You can use this batter to make traditional ladyfingers (page 217) to serve with tea or to use in tiramisu or a charlotte, a cake made of layers of cream and fruit surrounded by a band of ladyfingers and often including a few disks of ladyfinger cake in the interior. You can use it to make small circles of cake for shortcakes (page 338) and large ones, following the same guidelines to make freeform cakes. And stale ladyfingers, or even ladyfinger crumbs, can be a base layer of a galette (page 129), where they soak up excess fruit juices and add a touch of sweetness.

¼ cup (34 grams) all-purpose flour	3 large eggs, separated
2 tablespoons cornstarch	⅓ cup (67 grams) sugar

For instructions on oven temperature, how to prep the pan and what kind of piping bag and/or tip you'll need, refer to the recipe you're making that uses this batter. Have whatever the recipe requires ready before you start making the batter, which is delicate and should be piped immediately.

Sift the flour and cornstarch together onto a piece of parchment or wax paper—you'll be able to use the paper as a funnel to add the dry ingredients to the batter.

Working in the bowl of a stand mixer fitted with the whisk attachment, or in a large bowl with a hand mixer, beat the whites at medium-high speed until they turn opaque, begin to thicken and hold their shape. Very gradually beat in the sugar and, when it's fully incorporated, increase the mixer speed to high and beat for about 2 minutes more, or until the meringue is firm but still glossy.

Whisk the yolks in a small bowl just until smooth. Gently spoon about one quarter of the meringue over the yolks and whisk to blend. Scrape the yolks into the bowl with the meringue and, using a flexible spatula, fold the mixtures together lightly. Don't be too thorough now; this folding is only meant to get the process going. Add the dry ingredients to the bowl and start folding for real. Work quickly and lightly and don't be discouraged when the meringue deflates some; just blend the batter as completely as you can. You want to make certain that you don't have pockets of flour (check the bottom of the bowl, flour's favorite hiding spot), but don't be concerned if you have some specks of egg white here and there.

The batter is now ready to be piped and baked.

Cocoa Crumbs

SERVING: The crumbs
are a kind of fairy dust—
sprinkle them over anything
that needs a little magic.

STORING: The crumbs
can be kept in a sealed
container at room
temperature for up to
1 week. If you want to keep
them longer, store them
in the refrigerator, where
they'll keep for about
2 weeks, or pack them
airtight and freeze for up to
2 months. Run the crumbs
through your fingers to
declump before using.

I T ISN'T UNTIL YOU'VE MADE your first batch of cocoa crumbs that you realize you *need* to have them on hand at all times. Once you've sprinkled them over yogurt, ice cream, whipped cream, custards or puddings, or used them to top a tart, finish cupcakes or frosted cakes or cover chocolate truffles, you'll regret not having known about them sooner.

Essentially a baked streusel, the crumbs are small and sandy and snackable, but they're really only remarkable once you strew them over something—they need a mate.

I first had these in Paris at the restaurant Fish La Boissonnerie, where they added crunch and style to a bowl of roasted cherries and dark, dark chocolate *crémeux* (see page 376). My husband, Michael, and I loved the crumbs, and we were talking about them on the way home as we passed Le Comptoir, the always-crazy-busy bistro. We waved to Mao, the manager, and she motioned us in, saying, "Sit down; I want you to try a new dessert." Even after a full and good meal, hers was an invitation not to be refused, and so we sat and she brought out a *verrine* (a glass) filled, from the bottom up, with rhubarb gelée, chocolate mousse, roasted cherries and . . . ta-da: cocoa crumbs. Twice in one night! I took it as proof that crumbs were trending in Paris. I also took it as a sign that I should make some.

I've given you instructions for baked crumbs, but if you'd like, you can use the crumbs as a streusel: Press the unbaked crumbs over the top of a tart, pie, coffee cake or fruit and let them bake along with the dessert.

1 cup (136 grams) all-purpose flour	2 tablespoons sugar
⅓ cup (67 grams) packed light brown sugar	½ teaspoon fine sea salt
¼ cup (21 grams) unsweetened cocoa powder	5½ tablespoons (2¾ ounces; 78 grams) cold unsalted butter, cut into small cubes

Put all the dry ingredients in a medium bowl and, using your fingers, mix them together, making sure that there aren't any lumps in the brown sugar and cocoa powder. Drop in the butter bits and squeeze, rub or otherwise mash everything together until you have clumps and curds.

Cover the bowl and refrigerate for at least 2 hours (or for up to 3 days).

WHEN YOU'RE READY TO BAKE: Center a rack in the oven and preheat the oven to 300 degrees F. Line a baking sheet with parchment paper or a silicone baking mat.

Scatter the chilled mixture over the baking sheet and use your fingers to loosen the clumps. Bake for 15 to 18 minutes, or until the crumbs have separated into grains and small clusters. They'll look sandy and here and there you'll have some pebble-sized clumps. Transfer the baking sheet to a rack and let the crumbs cool to room temperature before using.

Caramelized Rice Krispies

*Makes about
8 servings*

STORING: "Cool" and "dry" are the bywords here—humidity will make the cereal very sticky. I've had success wrapping leftovers loosely in parchment and then in plastic and storing them in the refrigerator for 1 or 2 days.

IT'S HARD TO KEEP YOUR HANDS off this stuff. Everyday Rice Krispies are cooked in sugar until each piece of cereal is covered in caramel. The effect is a little like Rice Krispies brittle, and, like brittle, it's meant to be broken up and sprinkled with abandon over anything that needs some snap and crackle. I make it most often for Crispy-Topped Brown Sugar Bars (page 324) and then toss what's left over ice cream or puddings. Try it instead of cocoa crumbs with the Cold Chocolate Crémeux (page 376) or break off a shard and plant it in a cup of smooth and creamy panna cotta (I love it most with the Nutella-Banana Panna Cotta, page 374). The recipe makes more than you'll need, but if it didn't, you'd nibble away at it and be left with barely enough.

A WORD ON SERVING SIZE: How many this recipe serves is dependent on how you're using it. This batch will make enough to cover the Crispy-Topped Brown Sugar Bars and leave almost as much left over. And since there's certainly enough to add pizzazz to at least eight puddings, I've decided to say that that's how many servings you'll get.

½ cup (100 grams) sugar

3 tablespoons water

2 cups (53 grams) Rice Krispies

Line a baking sheet with parchment paper or a silicone baking mat. Have an offset spatula on the counter near you.

Sprinkle the sugar over the bottom of a saucepan or wide skillet that will give you enough room to stir comfortably—nonstick is always great when you're making caramel—and moisten it with the water. Turn the heat to medium/medium-high and bring the sugar to a boil, washing down any spatters on the sides of the pan with a silicone pastry brush dipped in cold water. When you see the first sign of the sugar turning color, remove the pan from the heat and immediately add the Rice Krispies.

Using a heatproof spatula or wooden spoon, stir until the syrup disappears and you see cakey white streaks on the bottom of the pan; the cereal will also look white and cakey.

Return the pan to medium heat and stir without stopping (and with caution) until each grain of cereal is coated with caramel, about 3 minutes or so, depending on your pan and the heat beneath it. The sugar may smoke, but that's fine—just keep going until you've got a nice, deep caramel color.

Scrape the Rice Krispies onto the lined baking sheet. Using the offset spatula, immediately spread the mixture out so that you've got a single layer. You have to do this quickly because the candy hardens almost instantly; it's inevitable that you'll have a few clumps and some pieces will break off, but try to spread the lion's share of the cereal out flat. Allow to cool.

To clean the pan, fill it with water and bring to a boil—the heat will resoften the caramel and make cleanup easier than you thought it was going to be.

Vanilla Pastry Cream

Makes about 2 cups

STORING: The pastry cream can be kept tightly covered in the refrigerator for up to 3 days. Whisk it well to loosen it before using.

THE CLASSIC FILLING for a fruit tart (page 151), profiteroles (page 238), cream puffs (page 226), éclairs (page 230) or anything else that needs something thick, soft, creamy and sweet.

1 moist, fragrant vanilla bean, or 1 tablespoon pure vanilla extract	⅓ cup (43 grams) cornstarch, sifted
2 cups (480 ml) whole milk	3½ tablespoons (1¾ ounces; 50 grams) unsalted butter, at room temperature, cut into 6 chunks
6 large egg yolks	
½ cup (100 grams) sugar	

If using a vanilla bean, cut it in half lengthwise and use the tip of the knife to scrape out the pulpy seeds. Bring the milk and vanilla bean pulp and pod to a boil in a medium saucepan. (If you're using extract, you'll add it later.) Cover the pan, turn off the heat and let infuse for at least 10 minutes, or for up to 1 hour.

Return the milk to a boil if you've used a vanilla bean; bring it to a boil if you're using extract.

Whisk the yolks, sugar and cornstarch together in a medium heatproof bowl until blended. Whisking constantly, drizzle in one quarter of the hot milk to temper, or warm, the yolks. Still whisking, add the remainder of the liquid in a steady stream. Remove the pod (if you have it), pour the mixture into the saucepan and, whisking vigorously and constantly, bring to a boil over medium heat. Keep at a boil—never stop whisking—for 1 to 2 minutes, then press the cream through a sieve into a clean bowl. Stir in the vanilla extract, if you're using it.

Leave the pastry cream on the counter for 10 minutes, then whisk in the butter until it is fully incorporated and the pastry cream is smooth and silky.

Either press a piece of plastic film against the surface of the cream and refrigerate it until it's thoroughly chilled, at least 2 hours, or fill a large bowl with ice cubes and cold water, set the bowl of pastry cream in it and leave the cream there, stirring occasionally, until it's cold. Use now, or cover and refrigerate until needed.

Chocolate Pastry Cream

ANY RECIPE THAT CALLS FOR PASTRY CREAM (page 430) can take this chocolate cream, so feel free to play around.

Makes about 2½ cups

STORING: The pastry cream can be kept tightly covered in the refrigerator for up to 3 days. Whisk it well to loosen it before using.

2 cups (480 ml) whole milk

4 large egg yolks

¼ cup plus 2 tablespoons (75 grams) sugar

3 tablespoons cornstarch, sifted

¼ teaspoon fine sea salt

7 ounces (198 grams) bittersweet chocolate, melted

2½ tablespoons (1¼ ounces; 35 grams) unsalted butter, at room temperature, cut into chunks

Bring the milk to a boil in a medium saucepan.

Whisk the yolks, sugar, cornstarch and salt together in a medium heatproof bowl until blended. Whisking constantly, drizzle in about ¼ cup of the hot milk to temper, or warm, the yolks. Still whisking, add the remainder of the milk in a steady stream. Pour the mixture into the saucepan and, whisking vigorously and constantly, bring to a boil over medium heat. Keep at a boil—never stop whisking—for 1 to 2 minutes, then press the cream through a sieve into a clean bowl.

Whisk in the melted chocolate. Leave the pan on the counter for 5 minutes, then whisk in the butter, stirring until it is fully incorporated and the pastry cream is smooth and silky.

Either press a piece of plastic film against the surface of the cream and refrigerate it until it's thoroughly chilled, at least 2 hours, or fill a large bowl with ice cubes and cold water, set the bowl of pastry cream in it and leave the cream there, stirring occasionally, until it is cold. Use now, or cover and refrigerate until needed.

Almond Cream

*C*RÈME ("CREAM") IS USED TO DESCRIBE so many different things in the French kitchen that it's hard to know if what you're getting will be creamy like heavy cream, like whipped cream, like lemon curd or, as in the case of almond cream, like none of these. Almond cream is a sweetened blend of butter, ground nuts, flour and egg that's always baked, most usually in tarts—it's the traditional base for baked fruit tarts (see Cherry Crumb Tart, page 148)—and often in fruit gratins. It's also used as a filling for croissants and raisin buns, pithiviers and Galette des Rois (page 102). Once you taste it, you'll know why pâtissiers depend on it for so many of their creations—you will too.

A WORD ON NUT CHOICES: While almond is the favored nut for this cream, hazelnuts come a close second and pistachios make a delicious cream with a pretty green color.

¾ stick (6 tablespoons; 3 ounces; 85 grams) unsalted butter, at room temperature	2 teaspoons all-purpose flour
	1 teaspoon cornstarch
	1 large egg
⅔ cup (132 grams) sugar	2 teaspoons dark rum or
¾ cup (75 grams) almond flour or an equal amount of ground skinned hazelnuts or pistachios	1 teaspoon pure vanilla extract

You can make the filling in a food processor, a bowl of a stand mixer fitted with the paddle attachment or a large bowl with a hand mixer. No matter what you're using, beat the butter until it is smooth and creamy, about 3 minutes. Add the sugar and beat for 1 or 2 minutes more. Add the almond flour or ground nuts, flour and cornstarch and beat until the mixture is smooth once again. Drop in the egg and beat for a minute or so, until it is thoroughly incorporated. Finally, beat in the rum or vanilla. The cream can be used now, but it's better if you press a piece of plastic film against the surface and refrigerate it for at least 1 hour or for up to 3 days.

Lemon Curd

Makes about 2 cups

STORING: Packed into an airtight container, the curd can be refrigerated for at least 3 weeks.

Thisᴴᴵˢ ʟᴇᴍᴏɴ ᴄᴜʀᴅ ɪs ᴍᴀᴅᴇ ᴡɪᴛʜ whole eggs rather than yolks alone, so it's lighter than the classic curd and a little less fussy to make. It has so many uses, from a tart or cream puff filling to a topping for cakes and cupcakes to a spread for toast, that you might want to keep a jar in your fridge as a just-in-case treat.

1¼ cups (250 grams) sugar
4 large eggs
1 tablespoon light corn syrup
About ¾ cup (180 ml) freshly squeezed lemon juice (from 4–5 lemons)

1 stick (8 tablespoons; 4 ounces; 113 grams) unsalted butter, cut into chunks

Working in a medium heavy-bottomed saucepan, whisk the sugar and eggs together until blended. Whisk in the corn syrup and lemon juice, then drop in the chunks of butter. Put the saucepan over medium heat and start whisking, taking care to work the whisk into the edges of the pan. If your whisk is too big to get into the corners, switch to a wooden spoon or a heatproof spatula. Cook, whisking nonstop, for 6 to 8 minutes, or until the curd thickens—it won't be very thick, but the change is easily perceptible. When you see a bubble or two burble to the surface and then pop, you're finished.

Immediately remove the pan from the heat and scrape the curd into a heatproof bowl or a canning jar or two. Press a piece of plastic film against the surface to create an airtight seal. Let the curd cool to room temperature before using or refrigerating.

Chocolate Ganache

Makes about 2 cups

STORING: Tightly covered, the ganache will keep in the refrigerator for up to 5 days or in the freezer for up to 2 months. Let it come to room temperature before using. You can also bring the ganache to temperature in a microwave oven—heat in very short spurts and don't forget to stir—or you can put the bowl over a saucepan of simmering water and stir until you get the consistency you want. However you warm the ganache, be gentle—too much heat, and it may separate.

GANACHE, an emulsion of chocolate, cream and, in this case, butter, has myriad uses in French baking. If you use it immediately, it makes a perfect glaze: Pour it over cakes or dip mini sweets into it. And if you chill the ganache, it's ideal for spreading between cake layers, for frosting or for making truffles. Poured into a tart shell and refrigerated, it firms just enough to hold its shape for slicing and then melts on your tongue.

8 ounces (227 grams) semisweet or bittersweet chocolate, finely chopped	½ stick (4 tablespoons; 2 ounces; 57 grams) unsalted butter, cut into 4 pieces, at room temperature
1 cup (240 ml) plus 2 tablespoons heavy cream	

Put the chopped chocolate in a medium heatproof bowl.

Bring the cream to a boil (you can do this in a microwave oven) and pour half of it over the chocolate. Wait for 30 seconds and then, using a whisk or a heatproof spatula, gently stir the chocolate and cream together in small circles, starting in the center of the bowl and working your way out in ever-widening concentric circles. Pour in the rest of the cream and repeat the circular mixing. When the ganache is smooth and shiny, drop in the butter pieces one by one, mixing until each piece is blended before adding the next. Be gentle—you don't want to beat the ganache, nor do you want to aerate it.

If you're using the ganache as a filling for a tart or glaze, use it immediately. If you're using it to fill and frost a cake, you'll have to wait for it to thicken. You can leave it on the counter, stirring occasionally (it thickens slowly), or you can set the bowl into a larger bowl filled with ice cubes and water, in which case, stir often and stay close—it thickens lightning-fast. Alternatively, you can put it in the refrigerator, checking on it and stirring frequently. If the ganache has firmed too much, you can always reheat it (see Storing).

White Chocolate Ganache

Makes about 1 cup

WHITE CHOCOLATE IS FUSSIER THAN DARK when it comes to making ganache: It has a very low tolerance for heat and an annoying tendency to separate if not cosseted. To get the best ganache, you must use a good white chocolate, not confectioners' chocolate. My preference is Valrhona Ivoire or white chocolate from Guittard.

10 ounces (283 grams) best-quality white chocolate, finely chopped	1½ tablespoons (¾ ounce; 21 grams) unsalted butter, at room temperature and cut into 3 pieces
⅔ cup (158 ml) heavy cream	

Put the chopped chocolate in a small heatproof bowl.

Bring the cream to a boil (you can do this in a microwave oven) and pour it over the chocolate. Let it sit for 30 seconds and then, using a whisk or heatproof spatula, gently stir the chocolate and cream together in small circles, starting in the center of the bowl and working your way out in ever-widening concentric circles. When the ganache is smooth, add the butter one piece at a time, stirring until it is incorporated.

If you're using the ganache as a filling for a tart or glaze, use it immediately. If you're using it to fill and frost a cake, you'll have to wait for it to thicken. You can leave it on the counter, stirring occasionally (it thickens slowly), or you can set the bowl into a larger bowl filled with ice cubes and water, in which case, stir often and stay close—it thickens quickly. Alternatively, you can put it in the refrigerator, checking on it and stirring frequently. If you miss the moment, you can always reheat the ganache (see Storing).

STORING: The ganache can be covered tightly and kept in the refrigerator for up to 5 days or frozen for up to 2 months. You'll have to bring it back to the consistency you need before using it, either by leaving it out at room temperature or warming it. Heat it in 5-second spurts in a microwave or put it in a bowl set over a pan of simmering water. With ganache (especially white chocolate ganache), the keys to success are very low heat and a very light touch.

Salted Caramel Filling

Makes about 1 cup

....

STORING: Covered tightly, the filling will keep in the refrigerator for up to 1 week.

STARTED MAKING THIS FILLING to sandwich between macarons (page 288), and I ended up using it to sandwich cookies and whoopie pies (page 200) and to tuck inside mini cakes, muffins, cupcakes and even *chaussons* (page 256). It spreads and pipes beautifully, sets firmly and melts just as it should—right on your tongue.

In France, part of the butter in the recipe would be a salted butter that is distinctly (rather than mildly) salted. Because the amount of salt in American butters is usually low by comparison and because the level varies, I use unsalted butter and then add as much salt as I want. I like fleur de sel in the caramel, but you'll find the salt you like and the amount you prefer.

Scant ⅔ cup (140 ml) heavy cream	unsalted butter, cut into 10 pieces, at room temperature
1 cup minus 2 tablespoons (175 grams) sugar	½ teaspoon fleur de sel or ¼ teaspoon fine sea salt, or more to taste
1¼ sticks (10 tablespoons; 5 ounces; 142 grams)	

Bring the cream to a boil in a small saucepan on the stovetop or in a microwave oven. Remove from the heat.

Pour the sugar evenly over the bottom of a wide high-sided skillet—nonstick is great here. Put the skillet over medium-high heat and stay close, with a heatproof or wooden spatula in hand. When you see the sugar melting around the edges of the pan, start stirring, making small circular motions all around the edges and then, as more sugar melts, widening the circle. Cook and stir until the sugar turns a light blonde color—think ale. Turn off the heat, stand back and add 4 pats of the butter. Swirl the pan or stir as the mixture sputters and then, still standing back, add the cream a little at a time. Return the caramel to medium-high heat and cook and stir until smooth, 1 minute or so. Stir in the salt.

Carefully pour the caramel into a heatproof container (I use a 1-quart Pyrex measuring cup) and cool for about 20 minutes, stirring frequently. Ideally, you want the caramel's temperature to go down to 140 degrees F before proceeding.

When the caramel has cooled, put the remainder of the butter in a small bowl and, using a flexible spatula, mix it until it has the consistency of mayonnaise. You can incorporate the butter with an immersion blender (my choice—it's why I pour the caramel into the measuring cup), blender, mini processor or spatula. Bit by bit, blend, process or beat in the butter, beating for at least 1 minute after each bit goes in and for another minute after all of the butter is incorporated. If you used a blender or processor, stir the caramel a couple of times to deflate some of the bubbles. Scrape the mixture into a container, press a piece of plastic film against the surface and refrigerate until chilled.

Give the cold filling a couple of turns with a spatula before piping or spreading it.

Whipped Cream

WHEN YOU SEE THE WORD "*CHANTILLY*" on a French menu, you know the dish will have whipped cream. To get cream to whip—a magical transformation—it must be very cold. If your kitchen is warm, consider putting the mixing bowl and whisk in the freezer. Of course the cream itself should come straight from the refrigerator too.

Cream whips to about twice its volume. If you want to fill and cover a layer cake, you'll need to double this recipe.

Makes about 1½ cups

1 cup (240 ml) very cold
   heavy cream
1–4 tablespoons confectioners'
   sugar, sifted

1 teaspoon pure vanilla extract
   (optional)

Working in the bowl of a stand mixer fitted with the whisk attachment, or in a large bowl with a hand mixer or a balloon whip, beat the cream and 1 to 2 tablespoons sugar together just until the cream starts to thicken. Taste and add more sugar, if you'd like, then continue to beat until you get the thickness you want. I use my stand mixer and start off slow, then increase the speed and when the cream is almost whipped the way I want it, I finish it by hand with a whisk. Hand finishing reduces the risk of overbeating and turning your cream into sweetened butter. When the cream is just right, stir in the vanilla extract, if you're using it.

STORING: Whipped cream is best served soon after it's made, but it will keep, covered, in the refrigerator for a few hours. Give it a go-round with a whisk just before serving. To keep the cream longer— or to get a thicker cream— line a strainer with a piece of moistened cheesecloth, place the strainer over a bowl and put the cream in the strainer. Wrap the whole setup in plastic film and refrigerate it for up to 24 hours.

Made-at-Home Crème Fraîche

Makes 1 cup

STORING: Crème fraîche will keep in the refrigerator for about 2 weeks. The longer you keep it, the tangier it will get.

CRÈME FRAÎCHE IS LIKE OUR SOUR CREAM in texture and tang, but it's denser and, unlike sour cream, it can be cooked without curdling. It can also be whipped—a treat.

You can find crème fraîche in specialty and cheese markets and in some supermarkets, but you can also make a tasty version at home—just remember to start a couple of days in advance.

- 1 cup (240 ml) heavy cream
- 1 tablespoon plain yogurt or buttermilk

Put the cream and yogurt or buttermilk in a clean jar with a tight-fitting lid and shake for 1 to 2 minutes.

Put the jar on the counter and leave it for 12 to 24 hours, or until the cream thickens slightly. The amount of time it will take for the cream to set will depend on the temperature of your room—the warmer the room, the quicker the set.

When the cream is thick, refrigerate for at least 1 day before using.

Crème Anglaise

SOMETIMES CALLED pouring custard or English custard, crème anglaise is a rich custard that's only slightly thickened. It's served as a sauce over or around cakes or chocolate desserts, and it's also very good with berries.

While you can certainly use the crème as soon as it cools, it's much better if you wait for 24 hours. Giving the custard a day in the refrigerator thickens the texture and deepens the flavor.

Makes about 2½ cups

STORING: Covered well, the crème anglaise will keep in the refrigerator for up to 3 days.

2　moist, fragrant vanilla beans or 2 tablespoons pure vanilla extract
1　cup (240 ml) whole milk
1　cup (240 ml) heavy cream
6　large egg yolks
½　cup (100 grams) sugar

Have a heatproof bowl with a strainer set over it at the ready for when the custard is cooked, and have a larger bowl ready to use for cooling the sauce.

If you're using vanilla beans, cut them in half lengthwise and use the tip of the knife to scrape out the pulpy seeds. Bring the milk and cream to a boil in a medium heavy-bottomed saucepan. Toss the vanilla pulp and pods into the pan, remove from the heat, cover and allow the mixture to infuse for 30 minutes. Bring the milk and cream back to a boil; remove the vanilla pods. (If you're using extract, bring the milk and cream to a boil; you'll add the vanilla later.)

Working in a large bowl, whisk the yolks and sugar together until they are blended and just slightly thickened. Whisking nonstop, slowly drizzle in about one quarter of the hot liquid to temper the eggs and keep them from cooking. Once the eggs are acclimatized to the heat, you can whisk in the remaining liquid a little more quickly. Pour the mixture back into the saucepan.

Cook the custard over medium heat, stirring constantly with a wooden spoon or heatproof spatula and making sure to get into the edges of the pan, until the custard thickens slightly and coats the back of a spoon; if you run your finger down the back of the spoon, the custard shouldn't run into the track. The custard should reach at least 170 degrees F (but not more than 180 degrees F), as measured on an instant-read thermometer. Immediately remove from the heat and pour the custard through the strainer into the bowl; discard whatever remains in the strainer. Stir in the vanilla extract, if you're using it.

Fill the larger bowl with ice cubes and cold water, set the bowl of crème anglaise in the water bath and allow it to cool, stirring frequently. When the sauce is chilled, either press a piece of plastic film against its surface or pour it into a jar and cover. Refrigerate for at least 4 hours before using; 24 hours is preferable.

Bittersweet Chocolate Sauce

Makes about 1½ cups

STORING: The sauce can be packed into an airtight container and kept in the refrigerator for up to 3 weeks. When you want to use it, heat it gently in a microwave oven or in a saucepan over very low heat.

Y OU CAN USE THIS SAUCE over or around tarts, cakes, puddings and custards, but you *must* use it over profiteroles (page 238).

For the sauce to be at its most voluptuous, it should be warm. Reheat it gently before serving.

½ cup (120 ml) heavy cream	4 ounces (113 grams)
½ cup (120 ml) whole milk	bittersweet chocolate, finely
½ cup (120 ml) water	chopped
6 tablespoons (75 grams) sugar	

Put all the ingredients in a medium heavy-bottomed saucepan, over medium-low heat and bring the mixture to a boil, stirring occasionally to blend. When it reaches a boil, lower the heat and let the sauce simmer for 10 to 15 minutes—don't leave the kitchen; this is a bubble-up brew—or until the sauce is thick enough to fully coat a metal spoon. If you run your finger down the back of the spoon, the sauce shouldn't run into the track you've created.

Let the sauce cool for about 10 minutes before serving.

Hot Fudge Sauce

Makes about 1¼ cups

STORING: Packed into a tightly covered jar, the sauce will keep in the refrigerator for up to 3 weeks. When you want to use it, warm it gently either in a microwave oven or in a saucepan over low heat until it is pourable.

THERE'S NOTHING FRENCH ABOUT THIS SAUCE, but serve it hot and shiny over ice cream, brownies (page 322) or cake and issues of origin will never come up.

½ stick (4 tablespoons; 2 ounces; 57 grams) unsalted butter, cut into 8 pieces

6 ounces (170 grams) bittersweet or semisweet chocolate, finely chopped

¾ cup (180 ml) heavy cream

3 tablespoons light corn syrup

2 tablespoons sugar

¼ teaspoon fine sea salt

Set a heatproof bowl over a saucepan of simmering water, put the butter in the bowl and top with the chocolate. Heat, stirring once or twice, until the butter and chocolate are melted and smooth. Keep the heat very low—you don't want the mixture to get so hot that the butter and chocolate separate. Transfer the bowl to the counter.

Working in a small heavy-bottomed saucepan, stir together the cream, corn syrup, sugar and salt and bring to a boil. Boil for 1 minute, then remove from the heat.

Pour about one quarter of the hot cream over the chocolate and, working with a heatproof spatula and starting in the center of the bowl, stir in ever-widening concentric circles. When the mixture is smooth, pour over the remainder of the cream in 2 additions, stirring in the same pattern until the sauce is shiny and smooth.

Allow the sauce to cool for about 10 minutes before using.

Hard-Crack Chocolate Sauce and Coating

IF DAIRY QUEEN EVER OPENS IN FRANCE, I bet this would become a favorite—the coating is very like the one called Magic Shell. It's a chocolate sauce that hardens as soon as it hits something very cold, like the elegant Marquise au Chocolat (page 357) or Esquimaux Pops for Grown-Ups (page 386).

The recipe is simpler than simple: chocolate and coconut oil (the ingredient currently being hailed as a miracle food here and in France). I found the proportions on the web, where homemade Magic Shell was making the rounds with a speed that bordered on supersonic. Most of the people who made the recipe used chocolate chips, but you can use regular chocolate. However, because coconut oil has a strong flavor, you might not want to use your most expensive chocolate.

You can find coconut oil in natural food markets and most major supermarkets. It comes in jars, is softly solid and is meant to be kept at room temperature. The easiest way to measure it is to scoop it out of the jar and press it into the measuring spoon.

7 ounces (198 grams) semisweet or bittersweet chocolate, coarsely chopped	2 tablespoons coconut oil, at room temperature

Stir the chocolate and coconut oil together in a heatproof bowl. Put the bowl over a saucepan of simmering water and heat, stirring often, until the chocolate melts and you have a smooth mixture. Stay close; you don't want the sauce to get too hot.

You can use the sauce now or pour it into a heatproof jar and cover when it reaches room temperature.

Makes about ½ cup

SERVING: Either drizzle the warm sauce from the tip of a spoon over your very cold dessert or, if you've got something like an ice-cream pop, dip your cold, cold sweet into the sauce.

STORING: Kept in a tightly sealed jar at room temperature, the coating will hold for about 2 weeks; kept in the refrigerator, it will be fine for about 1 month. Warm it for about 30 seconds in a microwave oven (or over a pan of hot water) before using.

Hot or Cold
Salted Caramel Sauce

T HERE ARE SOME FLAVORS I always associate with France despite the fact that they are not only available in the United States, but popular here too. Hazelnut is one, and caramel is another. No sooner do I pour caramel sauce over a pudding than I feel it's French.

This caramel sauce can be served hot or cold: Hot, it's thick; cold, it's less thick. If you'd like, you can have both hot and cold sauce from this recipe—just divide the sauce in half when it's cooked and thin only half of it with extra cream.

In addition to using the warm version as a sauce—it's great for sundaes—I like to offer it as a dip with freshly fried Nun's Beignets (page 240) and Merveilles (page 246). The cold sauce can go over ice cream too, but I love it with Le Cheesecake Round Trip (page 96), Rice Pudding (page 380), Coconut Tapioca (page 382) and even Hot Chocolate Panna Cotta (page 373).

Makes 1½ to 2 cups

STORING: Hot or cold, the sauce should be packed into a jar—press a piece of plastic film against the surface—and kept in the refrigerator, where it will be fine for up to 1 month. The hot sauce should be heated gently (I do this in a microwave oven) before serving. After being refrigerated, the cold sauce might also need a little heat to get pourable.

1 cup (200 grams) sugar
3 tablespoons water
1 tablespoon light corn syrup
¾–1¼ cups (180–300 ml) heavy cream (depending on the temperature of the sauce), or as needed, warm or at room temperature

½ teaspoon sea salt, preferably fleur de sel
2 tablespoons (1 ounce; 28 grams) unsalted butter, at room temperature
1½ teaspoons pure vanilla extract

Pour the sugar, water and corn syrup into a 2-quart heavy-bottomed saucepan. Put the pan over medium-high heat and cook—don't stir the ingredients, but once they melt and start coloring, swirl the pan—until the caramel, which will boil and may even smoke, turns a medium amber color. You can check the color by dropping some on a white plate. As the caramel cooks, it will spatter onto the sides of the pan; wash down the sugar with a silicone pastry brush dipped in cold water.

Turn off the heat and, standing back, add ¾ cup cream, the salt and butter. The mixture will sputter furiously, but the sauce will calm down and when it does, stir with a heatproof spatula or wooden spoon until it is smooth and creamy. Stir in the vanilla extract.

If you'll be serving the sauce hot, you have nothing more to do now than to serve it, or to serve later, pour it into a heatproof jar.

If you want to serve the sauce at room temperature or cold, you have to thin it—this is where the extra ½ cup cream comes in. If you want to serve the sauce both hot and cold, divide it in half and stir ¼ cup cream into half the sauce. Or, for the full recipe, stir in ½ cup. The cold sauce will still be thick but it will remain pourable. If you want it even thinner, experiment by adding just a little more cream.

Raspberry Coulis

Makes about 1 cup

THERE WAS A MOMENT when I thought raspberry coulis (coo-*lee*)—crushed raspberry sauce—was as overused as the ubiquitous mint leaf tossed onto a dessert for color. But just because something is used unthinkingly doesn't mean that it's not wonderful, and raspberry coulis is wonderful over anything chocolate or vanilla, and it's naturally good with other berries.

You can make the sauce with fresh or frozen berries. If you use frozen, choose berries that are individually frozen with no sweeteners and allow them to thaw enough to blend or process.

1 pint (about 250 grams) fresh or partially defrosted frozen raspberries	3 tablespoons sugar, or more to taste

Put the berries and sugar in a blender or food processor and whir until pureed. Taste and add more sugar if you think the sauce needs it.

Press the coulis through a strainer to eliminate the seeds—or don't.

STORING: The coulis is not meant to be kept. You can make it a few hours ahead and keep it covered in the refrigerator, but its flavor and color are most vibrant if you use it when freshly made.

Bonne Idée

You can use the same technique—adjusting the amount of sugar and adding lemon or lime juice, if you'd like—to make coulis with blueberries, strawberries, blackberries, passion fruit, mango or pineapple.

Spiced Hibiscus Syrup

Makes about 1 cup

STORING: The syrup will keep for about 2 weeks in a covered jar in the refrigerator.

I ORIGINALLY CREATED THIS JEWEL-RED SYRUP to go with rice pudding (page 380) topped with fresh strawberries, but once I made it I found many other uses for it, including drizzling it over ice cream or thick Greek yogurt. A spoonful in a glass of sparkling water makes a great cooler; a spoonful in a glass of sparkling wine makes an even greater cooler.

I prepare the syrup with dried hibiscus flowers, available in natural food and Middle Eastern markets, but you can use hibiscus-flavored tea in its place. If hibiscus is the first ingredient listed, as it is for Celestial Seasonings' Red Zinger tea, for example, it will make a fine syrup.

½ moist, fragrant vanilla bean, split	Strip of fresh orange peel
1 cup (240 ml) water	2 tablespoons dried hibiscus flowers (or 3 hibiscus tea bags)
1 cup (200 grams) sugar	
10 black peppercorns, bruised	1 lemon, halved
5 cardamom pods, crushed	

Scrape the pulp from the vanilla bean and toss it and the pod into a 2-quart saucepan. Add the water, sugar, peppercorns, cardamom and orange peel and bring to a boil, stirring to dissolve the sugar. Lower the heat slightly and boil the syrup for 5 minutes. Add the hibiscus flowers (or tea bags) and simmer for 2 minutes more. Remove the pan from the heat and allow the syrup to steep for 20 minutes.

Strain the syrup, discarding the solids, and refrigerate until cold. Before using the syrup, squeeze in as much lemon juice as you'd like.

Candied Petals, Flowers, Leaves or Herbs

FINISHING A DESSERT with a sugared flower, herb, petal or leaf is beautiful and easy. The hardest part of the process is finding the right flower or herb to candy: It must be edible, and it must never have been sprayed or treated in any way. I'm most likely to candy rose petals, in part because—like just about everyone else in Paris—I've got rose fever: The color, shape and fragrance of the flower are high on my list of great pleasures. But violets and nasturtiums can also be candied, as can herbs (think mint, cilantro, lemon balm, basil or even rosemary, although candied rosemary is only for decoration, not for eating) and the leaves from scented geraniums.

A WORD ON PLANNING AHEAD: Whatever you candy will need to rest overnight in a dry, dry place.

STORING: You can hold the candied decorations for up to 1 day, provided you keep them in a cool, dry place. It's best to leave them uncovered.

Edible fresh petals, flowers, leaves or herbs

Very fresh egg white(s), preferably organic

Sugar

Rinse whatever you're candying under cold water, shake off the excess water and dry completely between layers of paper towels.

Working in a small bowl, whisk the egg white(s) until foamy. Put some sugar in another small bowl and have a sheet of parchment or wax paper or a silicone baking mat nearby.

One by one, dip a petal or leaf into the beaten egg white. Coat with the white, lift up and let the excess drip back into the bowl, then run both sides of the petal or leaf through the sugar—you're looking for a light coating. Place the candied decoration on the paper or mat and carry on.

Let the petals or leaves dry overnight.

French Vanilla Ice Cream

I N ORDER TO MAKE a great vanilla ice cream, you need two things: great vanilla and a flawless crème anglaise.

For the vanilla, choose soft, pliable, plump and fragrant vanilla beans or your favorite pure vanilla extract. For the crème anglaise, the secret is to cook the custard until it is thick enough for you to run your finger down the back of the spoon and have the track stay. Take the custard's temperature, and it should be at least 170 degrees F and not more than 180 degrees F.

Makes a generous 1 quart

STORING: Packed tightly in a covered container, the ice cream will keep in the freezer for about 2 weeks.

2 moist, fragrant vanilla beans, or 2–2½ tablespoons pure vanilla extract (to taste)	2 cups (480 ml) heavy cream
2 cups (480 ml) whole milk	6 large egg yolks
	¾ cup (150 grams) sugar

Have a heatproof bowl with a strainer set over it at the ready for the cooked custard.

If you're using vanilla beans, cut them in half lengthwise and use the tip of the knife to scrape out the pulpy seeds. Bring the milk and cream to a boil in a medium heavy-bottomed saucepan. Toss the vanilla pulp and pods into the pan, remove the pan from the heat, cover and allow the mixture to steep for 30 minutes. Bring the milk and cream back to a boil; remove the vanilla pods. (If you're using extract, bring the milk and cream to a boil; you'll add the extract later.)

Working in a large bowl, whisk the yolks and sugar together until they are blended and just slightly thickened. Whisking nonstop, drizzle in about one third of the hot liquid to temper the eggs and keep them from cooking. Once the eggs are acclimatized to the heat, you can whisk in the remaining liquid a little more quickly. Pour the mixture back into the pan.

Cook the custard over medium heat, stirring constantly with a wooden spoon or heatproof spatula and making sure to get into the edges of the pan, until the custard thickens slightly and coats the back of a spoon; if you run your finger down the back of the spoon, the custard should not run into the track. The custard should reach at least 170 degrees F (but not more than 180 degrees F), as measured on an instant-read thermometer. Immediately remove the pan from the heat and pour the custard through the strainer into the bowl; discard whatever remains in the strainer. Stir in the vanilla extract, if you're using it.

The custard needs to cool before you churn it and, while you can put it directly into the fridge, the quickest and easiest way to bring down the temperature is to set the bowl into a larger bowl filled with ice cubes and cold water. Stir the custard from time to time as it cools. It's ready to use when it reaches room temperature.

Scrape the cooled custard into the bowl of an ice cream maker and churn according to the manufacturer's instructions. Pack the ice cream into a container and freeze it for at least 2 hours, until it is firm enough to scoop. If the ice cream is very firm, allow it to sit on the counter for a few minutes before scooping.

Chocolate Ice Cream

THINK OF THIS AS double-whammy chocolate ice cream because it starts with a ganache that becomes a crème anglaise and is then churned. It's rich and dark and smooth and delicious. Because you are going to mix the chocolate with cream and eggs, choose a bold chocolate that can hold its own.

Makes about 1 quart

STORING: Packed tightly in a covered container, the ice cream will keep in the freezer for about 2 weeks.

6 ounces (170 grams) semisweet or bittersweet chocolate, finely chopped	1 cup (240 ml) whole milk
	4 large egg yolks
	⅓ cup (67 grams) sugar
1½ cups (360 ml) heavy cream	Pinch of fine sea salt

Put the chocolate in a large heatproof bowl. Bring ¾ cup of the cream to a boil. Pour the cream over the chocolate and let sit for a minute, then, using a heatproof spatula and starting in the center of the mixture, slowly stir the cream into the chocolate in ever-widening concentric circles. Set aside.

Have a heatproof bowl with a strainer set over it at the ready for the cooked custard.

Bring the milk and the remaining ¾ cup cream to a boil in a medium heavy-bottomed saucepan.

Meanwhile, working in a medium bowl, whisk the yolks and sugar together until blended and just slightly thickened. Whisking nonstop, drizzle in about one third of the hot liquid to temper the eggs and keep them from cooking. Once the eggs are acclimatized to the heat, you can whisk in the remaining liquid a little more quickly. Add the salt and pour the custard back into the pan.

Cook the custard over medium heat, stirring constantly with a wooden spoon or heatproof spatula and making sure to get into the edges of the pan, until the custard thickens slightly and coats the back of a spoon; if you run your finger down the back of the spoon, the custard should not run into the track. The custard should reach at least 170 degrees F (but not more than 180 degrees F), as measured on an instant-read thermometer. Immediately remove the pan from the heat and pour the custard through the strainer into the bowl; discard whatever remains in the strainer.

Slowly and gently stir the custard into the ganache.

The custard needs to cool before you churn it and, while you can put it directly into the fridge, the quickest and easiest way to bring down the temperature is to set the bowl into a larger bowl filled with ice cubes and cold water. Stir the custard from time to time as it cools. It's ready to use when it reaches room temperature.

Scrape the cooled custard into the bowl of an ice cream maker and churn according to the manufacturer's instructions. Pack the ice cream into a container and freeze it for at least 2 hours, until it is firm enough to scoop. If the ice cream is very firm—and ice cream made with good chocolate can be pretty firm—allow it to sit on the counter for a few minutes before scooping.

Dark Chocolate Sorbet

THIS IS MY FAVORITE SORBET—so dark and delicious that it's the only one I know that can almost replace its ice cream cousin. Unlike ice cream, this sorbet contains milk, not cream, and has no eggs; what it's got is flavor—a lot of it.

A WORD ON NOMENCLATURE: Because of the milk, this should actually be called a sherbet, but every French chef I know who makes it refers to it as sorbet.

Makes about 3 cups

STORING: Packed tightly in a covered container, the sorbet will keep in the freezer for up to 2 weeks.

1 cup (240 ml) water	7 ounces (198 grams)
1 cup (240 ml) whole milk	bittersweet chocolate,
¾ cup (150 grams) sugar	coarsely chopped

Stir all the ingredients together in a 3- to 4-quart heavy-bottomed saucepan, put the pan over medium heat and, stirring frequently, bring to a boil. (It seems odd to boil chocolate, I know, but here you can and must.) Lower the heat and boil gently for 5 minutes, stirring occasionally and keeping a close eye on the pan, because the potential for boil over is high.

Pour the mixture into a heatproof bowl or measuring cup and refrigerate until chilled. You can quick-chill the mixture by putting the bowl into a larger bowl filled with ice cubes and cold water.

Scrape the sorbet mixture into the bowl of an ice cream maker and churn according to the manufacturer's instructions. Pack the sorbet into a container and freeze for at least 2 hours, until it is firm enough to scoop.

Roasted Strawberries

*Makes about
10 servings*

SERVING: Roasted
strawberries are perfect in
the strawberry shortcakes
(page 338) and delicious
with yogurt and Crunchy
Granola (page 408), but
you can use them any way
you'd use a fruit sauce.

STORING: Packed into a
covered jar, the berries will
keep in the refrigerator for
up to 1 week.

THINK OF ROASTED STRAWBERRIES as the sweet equivalent of a condiment, something extra to perk up a dish, add depth to it or up the game of other ingredients. Eaten by the spoonful, the strawberries are delicious—they're soft, not too sweet and subtly flavored with olive oil, lemon juice and, if you'd like, sweet vinegar—but they really come into their own when they're added to a dish. They're wonderful over rice pudding (page 380), ice cream, gâteau de Savoie (page 11) or toast, and perhaps at their best hidden between the cream and the cake of a strawberry shortcake (page 338).

1 pound (about 4 cups; 454 grams) strawberries, hulled and halved, or quartered if large

1 tablespoon sugar
Small pinch of ground cloves (optional)

1 tablespoon extra-virgin olive oil

1 teaspoon saba (a grape-must reduction) or thick balsamic vinegar (optional)
Freshly squeezed lemon juice, to taste
Crushed pink peppercorns or freshly ground black pepper (optional)

Stir the berries, sugar and cloves, if you're using them, together in a bowl. Set aside for 15 minutes, stirring occasionally, while you preheat the oven.

Center a rack in the oven and preheat the oven to 375 degrees F. Line a baking sheet with parchment paper or a silicone baking mat.

Give the berries a last stir, then turn them and the juice that has accumulated out onto the lined baking sheet. (I arrange the berries cut side down, but I'm not sure that it's important; it's a habit.)

Bake for 30 to 35 minutes, or until the berries are soft to the touch—they should have some give, but they shouldn't collapse when pressed—and the juices are bubbling but not burned. Using a pancake turner, scrape the berries and juices into a bowl. Stir in the olive oil and saba or vinegar, if you're using it. Allow the berries to cool, then taste and decide if you'd like to add a squirt of lemon juice and/or some pepper.

Candied Orange Peel

ANDIED PEEL is an incontrovertible French classic. Served with some of its syrup, it can turn a scoop of vanilla ice cream into a sundae or both soak and dress up a slice of plain cake. It can also be added to batters, doughs and candies (I use it all the time in my Chunky Chocolate Fruit-and-Nut Bars, page 394, and often in my Honey-Nut Nougat, page 399, and Chocolate Truffles, page 397). Removed from the syrup, it's an ingredient for fruitcakes (I use it in the Alsatian Christmas Bread, page 57). And dried and tossed in sugar (see Bonne Idée), it's a snack and a favorite at Christmastime, when the fanciest fruit vendors offer it as a nibble.

It takes some time and a candy thermometer to make the peel, but it's worth every second for the pint that will keep for weeks in your refrigerator.

Of course you can also use this recipe to candy grapefruit, lemon or lime peel.

A WORD ON THE CORN SYRUP: In France, a recipe for candied peel would include glucose and the suggestion that you go to your local pharmacist to purchase it. I've substituted a few spoonfuls of corn syrup here. The glucose and corn syrup serve the same purpose: They keep the syrup from crystallizing.

Makes 1 pint

STORING: Packed in their syrup and stored in the refrigerator, the peels will keep for about 2 months.

3 navel oranges (you want oranges with thick skin)
3 cups (710 ml) water
2 cups (400 grams) sugar

2 tablespoons light corn syrup
Squirt of freshly squeezed lemon juice

Have a heatproof pint-sized jar with a lid on hand.

Using a paring knife, cut a slice from the top and bottom of each orange. Standing each orange on a board and, cutting from top to bottom, slice off bands of peel, pith and a very thin layer of fruit; each band should be about 1 inch across. It's important that you get a sliver of fruit with every band, but only a sliver—this is really about the peel. Reserve the peeled oranges for another use.

Bring a 3- to 4-quart saucepan of water to a boil. Drop in all the strips of peel and boil for 1 minute, then drain in a sieve and run under cold water. Refill the pan and repeat the process twice—this preliminary boiling will rid the peel and pith of bitterness.

Rinse out the pan, and pour in the water, sugar, corn syrup and lemon juice. Stir to combine, then drop in the peels and, if you have one, attach a candy thermometer to the pan. Bring to a boil, then lower the heat to medium and cook at a lively simmer—keeping an eye on the pan, since sugar has a tendency to bubble up exuberantly—until the thermometer reaches just

Bonne Idée

SUGARED CANDIED PEEL:
While the peel and syrup
are bubbling away, spread
a thick layer of sugar on a
plate or baking sheet. When
the peels are candied, use
tongs to lift each piece
out of the syrup, letting
the excess syrup drip back
into the pan, and place on
the sugar. Toss the peels
with the sugar to coat each
piece, transfer to a rack
and let the peels dry for an
hour or so. Store the peels
in a covered container so
that they don't become
brittle. Reserve the syrup
for drizzling over cakes, ice
cream or custards.

about 230 degrees, 35 to 45 minutes. The syrup will be very thick and greatly reduced and the peels will be tender and translucent—your cues if you're working without a thermometer.

Carefully—sticky sugar syrup is dangerous—spoon the peels and syrup into the jar. Close the lid and cool to room temperature, then refrigerate until ready to use.

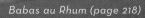
Babas au Rhum (page 218)

Palets de Dames, Lille Style (page 272)

INDEX

Page references in *italic* refer
to illustrations.

A

Adam, Christophe, 230
almond(s):
cake, plain and simple, 8–9
chocolate-covered toffee
breakups, 402–4, *403*
cocoa crunch meringue
sandwiches, 293–95,
294
cream, 432
cream, in galette des rois
(kings' cake), 102
cream, in pithiviers, 99–102,
100
cream–apricot tart, 146
croquets, 310–11, *311*
crunchy granola, 408–9
desert roses, 391–93, *392*
financiers, traditional, 205
fruit and nut croquants,
307–9, *308*
granola energy bars,
328–29, *329*
honey-nut nougat, 398–401,
400
lemon cream, 138–40
lemon squares, French style,
326–27
topping, crunchy, pear tart
with, *126*, 127–28
almond flour, 288, 297
almond stripes, 296
Alsatian Christmas bread
(baerewecke), 57–60, *58*
Basque macarons (muxuak),
284–85
cherry crumb tart, 148–50,
149

chocolate chip cookies,
Edouard's, 298–300,
299
classic Linzer cookies, 306
cocoa Linzer cookies, 304–6
double-butter double-baked
petit beurre cookies,
270–71
lemon squares, French style,
326–27
Parisian macarons, *286–87*,
288–91
sweet tart dough with nuts,
415
tiger cakes, 197–99, *198*
Alsatian:
apple tarte flambée, 118–20,
121
bettelman, 343–44
cheesecake, 31–32, *33*
Christmas bread
(baerewecke), 57–60, *58*
cocoa Linzer cookies, 304–6
streusel-topped rhubarb
lime tart, 160–61
amaretto-apricot truffles, 397
anise (seeds):
-flavored liqueur, in
canistrelli, 317–19, *318*
olive oil and wine cookies
with, 316
Aoki, Sadaharu, 292
apple(s):
bettelman, 343–44
chaussons, 257
croustades, petite, *252*,
253–55
gâteau Basque fantasie,
110–13, *112*
kuchen: a tall apple-custard
tourte, 16–19, *17*
and lemon tart, Martine's,
116–17

matafan, 341–42
pielettes, *122*, 123–24
rings, dried, in Alsatian
Christmas bread
(baerewecke), 57–60, *58*
roll-up tart à la Mme
Bouchet, 134
speculoos crumble, 336–37
squares, custardy, 20–21, *21*
tarte flambée, 118–20, *121*
weekend cake, 14–15
apricot(s):
almond cream tart, 146
dried, amaretto truffles, 397
dried, in Alsatian Christmas
bread (baerewecke),
57–60, *58*
dried, in desert roses,
391–93, *392*
raspberry tart, 145–46
summer fruit gratins, 346
summer-market galette,
154–55

B

babas au rhum, 218–21, 220, *461*
baby cakes, 186–224
babas au rhum, 218–21, *220*
black-and-white marbled
madeleines, 215–16
cannelés, 222–24, *223*
ladyfingers (biscuits à la
cuillère), 217
lemon madeleines, 212–14,
213
limoncello cupcakes,
194–96, *195*
matcha tiger cakes, 208
molten surprise cakes, 193
Nutella buttons, 188–90, *189*
soft-centered chocolate tea-
cup cakes, 191–93, *192*